The Bullets, the Wizards, and Washington, DC, Basketball

Brett L. Abrams
Raphael Mazzone

THE SCARECROW PRESS, INC.
Lanham • Toronto • Plymouth, UK
2013

Published by Scarecrow Press, Inc.
A wholly owned subsidiary of The Rowman & Littlefield Publishing Group, Inc.
4501 Forbes Boulevard, Suite 200, Lanham, Maryland 20706
www.rowman.com

10 Thornbury Road, Plymouth PL6 7PP, United Kingdom

British Library Cataloguing in Publication Information Available

Library of Congress Cataloging-in-Publication Data

Abrams, Brett L., 1960-
The Bullets, the Wizards, and Washington, DC basketball / Brett L. Abrams, Raphael Mazzone.
p. cm.
Includes bibliographical references and index.
ISBN 978-0-8108-8554-7 (cloth : alk. paper) — ISBN 978-0-8108-8555-4 (ebook) 1. Basketball—Washington (D.C.)—History. 2. Washington Bullets (Basketball team)—History. 3. Washington Wizards (Basketball team)—History. I. Mazzone, Raphael. II. Title.
GV885.73.W18A37 2013
796.323'6409—dc23

2012024449

∞™ The paper used in this publication meets the minimum requirements of American National Standard for Information Sciences—Permanence of Paper for Printed Library Materials, ANSI/NISO Z39.48-1992.

Printed in the United States of America

Contents

Introduction: An Understudied Subject

Several years ago, I looked out the windows while riding along the Red Line on the Metro train toward the Union Station stop and saw a cylindrical building. I wondered what it was. Maybe it was an armory or a warehouse of some sort? I asked around and received a variety of responses. One longtime resident told me that the building was the Washington Coliseum. He said he went ice skating there when he was a child.

After that, I met Dave McKenna, the sports columnist for the weekly newspaper, to discuss my book on built and proposed stadiums in Washington, D.C., and the metropolitan area. "Have you ever been to Uline Arena?" he asked. I said no, so we drove over to the cylindrical building on M Street and Third Street, NE.

We walked inside. It now serves as a parking lot for local businesses. Around the outside walls are decaying rows of bleacher seating. Dave told me that they used to play minor league hockey here and basketball too. As we made our way back outside, he stood in front and pointed to a spot on the sidewalk. "I saw the Beatles play here. It was their first concert in the United States."

While I realized that the claim about the Beatles would interest most people, I focused on the basketball. My searches through the public library stacks resulted in me finding one book on the beginnings of the National Basketball Association (NBA), which offered a little information about the arena and its resident, the Washington Capitols. The limited material confirmed my long-held perception: The teams in professional sports in Washington, D.C., history have received little in-depth coverage.

Since so few books contain information on any professional teams from the area, I began looking at the old newspapers in the Washington, D.C., Public Library's Washingtoniana Collection. The city indeed has a long professional basketball tradition. Washington had a team in the first "national" professional league back in the 1920s. Nearly two decades later, the city had a team in another new league, one that eventually became the NBA. Washington and the regional area also played roles in the other attempts to forge professional basketball leagues during the 1960s and 1970s.

Several big names from the sporting worlds appeared linked to the ownership and management of the city's teams. The National Football League's Redskins founder, George Preston Marshall, owned Washington's first pro team. Arnold "Red" Auerbach, the renowned coach and general manager, started his NBA career with the Washington Capitols. One of the forerunners of U.S. soccer, Earl Foreman, owned two D.C. teams. He provided inspiration to his fellow owners to keep fighting for the American Basketball Association (ABA) merger with the NBA. Bullets and Wizards owner Abe Pollin served on a variety of committees that shaped NBA decisions and policies on expansion and contracts, amongst other things.

The Washington teams also featured notable players from each era. The Palace Laundry team included Rusty Saunders, Elmer Ripley, and George "Horse" Haggerty. The Washington Capitols, the city's early NBA squad, featured forward Horace "Bones" McKinney and guard Bob Ferrick and, in its last years, Bill Sharman and Earl Lloyd. The short-lived American Basketball League (ABL) Washington Tapers had two-sport star Gene Conley. The ABA team the Washington Capitols/Virginia Squires included well-known stars Rick Barry and Larry Brown, and, later on, Dr. J. (Julius Erving) and George Gervin. The Baltimore Bullets, Capitol Bullets, Washington Bullets, and Washington Wizards have also had a number of great players, particularly guard Earl "The Pearl" Monroe, center Wes Unseld, forwards Elvin Hayes and Bernard King, and center Moses Malone.

A number of books that document the histories of professional sporting teams fill the shelves. The most comprehensive coverage centers on Major League Baseball, and these books have extensive "biographies." The biographies of basketball teams feature the best-known franchises, including the Boston Celtics, Los Angeles Lakers, New York Knicks, and Chicago Bulls. The Portland Trail Blazers fall into a special category, as they have two in-depth, single-season coverage works devoted to their franchise (David Halberstam's *Breaks of the Game* and Kerry Eggers's, *Against the World*). These books are a joy to read, and I wanted to produce a biography for the rich tradition of Washington, D.C.'s, professional basketball teams.

The stories of each of these team's players, how and where they played the game, and the relationships among them, appeared to be the most fascinating parts to feature in the team biographies. How had other books covered these aspects of professional basketball in the United States? The information about this aspect of the game during the first "national" professional basketball league was the most limited. Murry Nelson, in his article "Old Celtics," and Robert Peterson, in his book *Cages to Set Shots*, provide the most details. Todd Gould and Gus Alfieri, in their respective books, *Pioneers of the Hardwood* and *Lapchick*, offer more information about some of the early players in Indiana and New York. These authors and a few others provide some additional material on the executives and operations of the league.

More extensive coverage exists on the origins of the NBA. Leonard Koppett's *24 Seconds to Shoot* lays the groundwork. It points out the possibilities of an extensive study of the inner workings of the sport. Neil Isaac's *Vintage NBA*, with its extensive interviews with the people involved in playing and other aspects of the sport, shows the benefits of such an approach, documenting the daily experiences of living in the sport. Charley Rosen's *The First Tip-Off* illustrates the advantages of looking at individual teams to better understand the players and the unit that they forged.

Few stories have emerged about the two leagues that competed against the NBA. The operation of the ABL in the early 1960s has been described briefly in general accounts of the post–World War II sports era. Some basketball historians have done well in documenting who played in the ABL and, to a lesser extent, the style of game. Terry Pluto's *Loose Balls* provides descriptions of the operation of the ABA for a decade beginning in the late 1960s. The book offers glimpses of the various teams and insights into the players and league play through interviews with participants.

The Bullets, the Wizards, and Washington, D.C., Basketball aims to provide biographies of the Washington teams. It features issues related to the operation, players, living experiences, and games in these professional leagues through the prism of the Washington, D.C., teams. The size and scope of this book required that I find a partner to write it with. My coauthor, Raphael Mazzone, brought college sports experience, photographic archives, and editing background to the project. We examined a few archives, local and national newspapers, and back issues of both general interest and sporting magazines to uncover the story of the five franchises. We verified and fleshed out this information and asked questions to a number of former players, coaches, and assistants regarding the specifics of playing in the professional leagues.

Our correspondents relished their time playing professional basketball. Several characterized the experience as the most exciting of their lives. The game offered great joy and connections with friends, which most of the men have maintained over the years. For these men, the NBA represented the epitome of the professional game, and all respect the league. Most viewed being in the league as a profession and realized several important things that enabled them to remain in the league as long as they did. Their bodies were the instruments, and the better condition they were in, the better their chance for success. The game deserved respect. Everyone came with amazing physical and athletic abilities. The successful player became a student of the game. They learned from those who tried to teach them; they reviewed video to see their own possibilities for improvement; and they continually practiced the game to make improvement possible. They ask that those who play now and those who will play in the future appreciate the league and those who paved the way before them.

This study could not have happened without a number of people, who offered a great deal of support. The Naismith Memorial Basketball Hall of Fame Library in Springfield, Massachusetts, has a number of important scrapbooks and official documents. I greatly appreciate the efforts of their historian and archivist, Matt Zeysing, who helped considerably despite being understaffed. The National Archives and Records Administration textual reference department houses important District of Columbia records. And the Library of Congress is a treasure trove, and the librarians in all the departments were extremely supportive.

Most important were the former players and coaches of all the Washington-area teams. These men and, in certain instances, their wives and children reacted graciously to an inquiry from a stranger. They gave generously of their time and responded with kindness to a long series of questions. I thank the following for their time and consideration in giving me an interview: Al Bianchi, Bernie Bickerstaff, Charles Davis, Bob Ferry, Tom Hammonds, Charlie Hardnett, Ira Harge, Bailey Howell, Warren Jabali, Roger Kaiser, Tom Kropp, Mitch Kupchak, Bob "Slick" Leonard, Don MacLean, Tracy Murray, Don Ohl, Roger Phegley, Brent Price, Gene Shue, and Roland "Fatty" Taylor. Special thanks go to Frank Jr. and Steve Katkaveck, the family of the late Leo Katkaveck, first for saving historical documents and, second, for taking the time to find them and provide me with copies.

CHAPTER ONE

George Preston Marshall and the Palace Five

Churches, youth groups, YMCAs and YMHAs, and business and corporations all had basketball teams during the 1900s and 1910s. The game began to thrive in colleges, and the National Collegiate Athletic Association (NCAA), along with the Colored Intercollegiate Athletic Association (CIAA), moved to standardize the rules and create league competition.[1]

In the segregated city of Washington, D.C., basketball flourished among both blacks and whites. Howard University won the intercity black basketball championship in 1913.[2] Public school leagues popularized the sport among boys and girls. Throngs of fans attended the amateur-league games, despite the Congress Heights Yankees winning the first four championships before Aloysius wrested the title in 1923.[3]

The Yankee winning tradition would become the sole province of New York City's baseball team. The amateur neighborhood team grabbed the attention of a wealthy businessman who wanted to be associated with these successful sportsmen. George Preston Marshall arranged to switch the Yankees from a neighborhood team to an industrial squad. The Yankees became the Laundrymen, and the players took jobs with the Palace Laundry Dry Cleaning Company.

The owner cut a figure out of *The Great Gatsby*. Not yet 30, George Preston Marshall (figures 1.1 and 1.2) built the laundromat his father started into a chain serving the Washington area. The nattily dressed West Virginian prompted sportswriters to call him "Gorgeous George," or the last surviving man-about-town on the banks of the Potomac. Marshall shaped the team's personnel over the next few years.

Figure 1.1. George Preston Marshall with football.
Courtesy Library of Congress.

The Palace Laundry Five played again in the district's amateur league. They also played against professional teams that traveled around picking up games against the best amateurs in cities and small towns across the country. Traveling to play exhibition games was part of the popular tradition of barn-

Figure 1.2. The Palace Laundry store.
Courtesy Library of Congress.

storming, which provided entertainment to less populated areas and brought stars and featured acts into a town for the inhabitants to see. While professional teams from all along the East Coast barnstormed, the most popular and successful team was the New York Celtics.

The Celtics were masters of professional basketball 1920s style. A center tap-off occurred after each score, so a strong, tall center enabled a team to control the ball off the start. Shots were infrequent and often came from as close a range to the net as possible, so the game required ball movement. Teams had key ball handlers who could dribble with two hands and stop and start at will. Defenses played rough-and-tumble, committing fouls that sent opponents to the foul line for a single shot. Most teams played a strategy to make teams beat them at the foul line rather than give up high-percentage shots.[4]

In early 1924, about 2,000 spectators paid to watch the Celtics outclass the Palace Laundry. The outcome was never in doubt, as the Celtics won 45–23 and could have scored more. The tall center Joe Lapchick tossed in five field goals, and Nat Holman exhibited the bulletlike passing and cleverness in team play that spectators came to see.

Marshall continued to improve his team. He brought in more polished players. The Palace Five won the District Basketball League and then moved into the professional ranks. Washington picked up a former Celtic big man, George "Horse" Haggerty. With the importance of the tip-off, Marshall thought he had acquired an important player to win possession of the ball. Among their earliest victories was the first basketball game played in Alexandria, Virginia, at the armory court. Under Marshall's management, the team attracted crowds in ungodly numbers to see games on Sunday nights at the Arcade.

In the days before arenas, basketball teams played on dirt or heavily polished floors with boisterous crowds throwing things at the opposing players. Caging around the game tried to minimize the crowd's interference and limited the number of times the ball went out of bounds. But the "cagers," as players became called, found that the encasement enhanced the brutality of the game. Initially, there was no "caging" around the dance floor on which the Palace Laundry played.[5]

Originally a car barn for the trolley, investors revamped the building where the Palace Laundry played into an entertainment center sitting on top of one of the city's largest food markets. The Arcadia sat in the wealthy neighborhood of Columbia Heights. Upon entering the upper lobby, a patron saw a luxuriously furnished and decorated lounge on the right. A men's smoking room and ladies lounges were nearby. To the left of the lobby was the pool and billiard room, with bowling alleys in the rear. The auditorium covered the greater part of the second floor, with large reflectors hanging in the center to produce a brilliant intensity of illumination for dancing or the professional basketball games played there.[6]

The first decades of the twentieth century enshrined the consumer culture in which we swim in these days. The city, like the rest of the country, had more people with both disposable income and the leisure time to enjoy entertainment. Large corporations emerged to promote and commercialize these fun-time activities, including movies, radio, and sports. The 1920s became known as the "golden age" of sports. With boxing, baseball, and college football already highly popular and pulling in big money, entrepreneurs could see the same possibility for basketball.

The Palace Five played the Celtics in the winter of 1925 at their new home. More than 2,500 fans came to see the Sunday night battle. With Haggerty playing a stellar role of keeping the champions at bay, the game remained a close, low-scoring affair. The Celtics held a 19–14 lead, and then

Haggerty and another new addition to the Palace Five, forward John "Red" Conaty, scored a half dozen points to give the Laundrymen a one-point lead. The Palace went into a game of freezing the ball, holding on to it and throwing simple passes to one another to use up the remaining two minutes of the contest. Holman stepped in between a pass and moved down the court to score the winning field goal.

The American Basketball League Begins

The Sunday evening game turnout at the Arcadia sparked talk of a possible East Coast professional basketball league. Whether Gorgeous George's idea, or the outgrowth of talks between George Halas and Joe Carr of the then fledging National Football League, the American Basketball League (ABL) aimed higher than the previous regional professional leagues. Like Marshall, other team owners had previous business experience as proprietors of cigar stores, an arena, or a department store. They noted the upsurge of spectator interest in sporting events among the public and thought that basketball could have consumer appeal, and/or they had experienced the sporting appeal themselves and wanted to participate in that world.

With franchises in Boston, Brooklyn, Buffalo, Chicago, Cleveland, Detroit, Fort Wayne, Rochester, and Washington, the ABL comprised what was then considered a national market, much like Major League Baseball's (MLB) loop. The owners adopted a constitution similar to the one used in professional baseball and devised a schedule and playoff system. The teams played two seasons, consisting of 14 games in the first and 16 in the second, with the winning team of the first season pairing off with the winning team of the second season for the league championship.

The New York Celtics declined to join the new league. As the most famous professional basketball team, they thought that it would be more financially lucrative to remain independent. The Celtics continued making money from barnstorming, as the Washington Palace Five played the team for two games after they had started play in the new ABL. Holman's photograph appeared in the Washington newspapers as a promotion for the Celtics coming to town. They played and bested the Palace squad. The next week, Washington played the Celtics in the inaugural game at Madison Square Garden and lost 35–31 in an unrestrained scrap before 15,000 fans.

While the core of the Celtics remained consistent since the early 1920s, others played with the team then left for pursuits outside of sports. Still other former Celtics appeared on the rosters of the new ABL teams. They were often some of the best players and biggest names in the game. While the new

Rochester teams picked up a former Celtic guard, the Washington team had Horse Haggerty. Washington's former Celtic represented a mixed bag. Critics observed that Haggerty's almost total focus on defense limited his usefulness; however, he occasionally contributed on offense in the team's biggest games, using his size and strength to score easy baskets around the rim.

The Palace Five owner decided to search in other areas of the basketball world for talent. That search led him to the college ranks and the hiring of Dr. Lou Sugarman, former coach of the Princeton University Tigers basketball team. In addition to head coaching responsibilities, Dr. Sugarman also served as the team's general manager. The preparations of the arena anticipated success on the court and in the stands. The Arcadia had reserved seating for 2,000, and the management made arrangements for another 2,000 people to be able to sit in unreserved seating.

The basketball team and Arcadia management viewed the professional game as one part of an evening's entertainment. Spectators settled in for a preliminary game of amateur basketball starting at 7:30 p.m. These games featured local preparatory and public schools, independent teams, and recreational organizations. The participants often featured rivalries, like the one between Washington, D.C., and New York City Catholic school teams, two local schools, or between different ethnic groups, such as the Jewish Community Center against St. Mary's Celtics of Alexandria, Virginia. The latter kind of ethnic rivalry in sports was common in the 1920s, as tensions existed between different newer and older immigrant groups. Anti-immigrant attitudes pervaded the culture and society so broadly and powerfully that Congress passed new anti-immigration laws, restricting the number of newer immigrant groups that could enter the United States.

After the amateur preliminary game, the professional game followed. Halftime events ranged from honoring a player from a local university to a dance program of Irish music and vocal selections. After the game, the spectators made their way onto the floor for dancing until 1 a.m. As one columnist noted after the first game in Brooklyn, there was more involved in the ABL than the winner of the series of games. The social prestige of the capital was on trial, as Washington residents attending the game wore their other suits, while the flower of Brooklyn society came with silk-faced lapels cut low, their shirt fronts as white as snow.

The Washington Palace Five squad won their opening contest and played their first Washington, D.C., game the next Sunday evening. The spectators came from the same class as in Brooklyn and also excluded African Americans due to the city's de facto segregation. Despite Washington's victory, the reporter stated that the game offered the crowd little to get excited about.

The game lacked spectacular shots, and the frequent personal fouls slowed the game considerably. The style showed in the 18–17 final score. The next league game against Rochester did not fare as well. Washington lost to a team that exhibited better ball movement and a scoring touch.

While such low-scoring games were not unusual in the league, most tilts resulted in at least one team scoring 30 points. Teams either scored close to the basket, with a tall player who towered over others, like Philadelphia's 6-foot, 7-inch center, Francis "Stretch" Meehan, or played with greater speed, which helped them get in close before the defensive team clamped down around the lane. Observers described defense as involving "more holding and shoving than ordinarily is seen in a wrestling bout,"[7] and "getting away with nearly all the fouls in the basketball repertoire short of murder."[8]

Even with these rough game conditions, the Palace Five had a winning record; however, Marshall decided that the team needed more offensive punch. He arranged for a swap of forwards with the Brooklyn Arcadians. Washington traded starting forwards Red Conaty and Rody Cooney, a pair of speedy players, for shooters George Glasco and Russell Collier "Rusty" Saunders.

Certainly, the Washington leadership thought the team needed the change and knew of these players' abilities. According to Glasco, the pool of players qualified to play professional basketball numbered no more than 100 or so. The 20-year-old Saunders, himself a native of Trenton, New Jersey, was like many ABL players in that they hailed from the urban northeastern United States. Players came from the ethnic groups that settled in that part of the country. Many, like the two men Washington traded (Conaty and Cooney), came from Irish backgrounds. Glasco came from an English-Welsh background and Saunders from older stock, of English and Scottish.

The Washington team management sought a star presence for their team. At the age of 20, Saunders had youth appeal. As one newspaper described him, the 6-foot, 2-inch, 200-pound forward with the big number 7 arched across his back was the object of all eyes in local games, with a keen shooter's eye and presence in the thick of the fight at all times. Sporting teams required stars to win games and bring in fans. Even the team from the smallest city in the league, Fort Wayne, had one star, Homer Stonebraker. One team in the league led this trend, as the Cleveland Rosenblums, owned by department store magnet Max Rosenblum, had Nat Hickey, John "Honey" Russell, and Max "Marty" Friedman.

While the concept of star power was admirable, the timing of the trade made little sense. After spending all of the off-season training and gaining chemistry, the trade interrupted the team and it took most of the first half of the season to recover. The experts argued that both teams would benefit from the switch, but, in actuality, Conaty's scoring average improved and Saunders's dropped. With one game left in the first half of the season, Washington needed to win against a tough Cleveland team, while also needing Brooklyn to lose its game to tie for the top spot. Washington won a rough battle in which the two teams combined for 53 foul shot attempts; however, Brooklyn defeated Fort Wayne, 28–26, and Brooklyn edged out Washington for first place for the first half of the season by one game.

The second season began well for the Washington squad. Midway through, Marshall made another switch and fired Sugarman as the team's coach. Guard Ray Kennedy, the team's field captain, became the team's new coach. At 29 years of age, Kennedy had the reputation for analyzing an opponent's weakness and acting quickly to take advantage of what he saw on the floor. Many considered him the brainiest player in the game. Under Kennedy's leadership, the team faced off against Cleveland in a battle for first place. In front of a capacity crowd of 11,000 fans in Cleveland, Washington took a 16–14 halftime lead behind Glasco's and Saunders's shooting accuracy at the foul line. Cleveland took the lead in the second half behind Hickey's scoring and the team's accurate foul shooting. As Washington tried to mount a comeback, mirroring Washington's advantage in the first half, Cleveland passed the ball, making no effort to score during the last five minutes of the game, and sealed the victory. The Palace Five ended the second half of the season in second place and out of the playoffs.

After the regular season ended, the ABL held its first championship. The Brooklyn and Cleveland series was dubbed a "World Series." Washington fans read about the contest in Kennedy's special articles, which appeared in the *Washington Post*. Kennedy predicated that Brooklyn would win because of having Walter "Tillie" Voss at center.[9] The manager-captain of the Palace club rated the two teams even at both the guard and forward positions. He looked accurate when the Arcadians won the first game. Cleveland got all-around scoring to win the next two games in front of the Cleveland crowd of 10,000 per game. Brooklyn guard Cooney started game four off well back at the home court of the Seventy-First Regiment Armory in New York. He scored from the foul line, and teammate Conaty followed with another. But Cleveland's Dave Kerr and Carl Husta tied things up. "From then on the going was fast and furious. Red Conaty tried two long ones [that] just missed. Garry Schmeelk threw one from far past the center [that] hit the rim and fell out. Elmer Ripley put Brooklyn in the lead again with two in succession."[10] Husta scored again to put them up, 18–16. Cleveland then aroused the ire of the crowd by holding the ball under its own basket, making no attempt to take the offensive. Finally, Brooklyn's Conaty got the ball and scored, but Husta scored twice, enough for Cleveland to grab a 23–22 victory and the championship title.

Despite not making the playoffs, entrepreneurs in Washington, D.C., identified an opportunity that emerged from the ABL. The new owners of the Arcade building envisioned an arena built on its adjoining property. Promoter John S. Blick dubbed his project the Madison Square Garden of Washington. Meanwhile, music magnet Meyer Davis and Palace Five team owner George Preston Marshall drew up similar plans. The pair envisioned an arena named Capital Square Garden, which would be located downtown on First and B Streets (now Constitution Avenue), NW. The Laundrymen's owner planned to construct accommodations for 7,000 spectators, which the article claimed basketball could draw in Washington, as it had assumed gratifying proportions in the city. Marshall appeared to be moving toward vertical integration, owning the building where his basketball team played.

The ABL leadership made several changes before the start of the second season in 1926–1927. The Boston franchise did not make it through the inaugural season, so the owners invited a squad from Baltimore to replace them. Several prominent Baltimore men created the Baltimore Basketball Exhibition Company, Inc. and funded this team and organization. The league increased the number of games by nearly 33%, from 16 to 21, and teams would continue to play barnstorming games outside of the league. The Washington franchise (figure 1.3) was scheduled to play home games on Sunday and Monday evenings. They were to play most of their road games on Tuesdays, Wednesdays, and Saturdays.

The leadership of the Palace Five decided to make a trade in the hopes of strengthening their team. The newcomer was guard Elmer Ripley, while guard Bob Grody left for Brooklyn. The newspapers saw this as sacrificing bulk for speed. Laundryman Rusty Saunders penned an article for the local newspaper, informing the fans that, "We've got one of the fastest and most accurate clubs in the league this year and expect to win the chance to play for the title by leading the other teams in at least one of the two halves scheduled."[11] The team lacked a true center, and, of the three men under consideration, Saunders noted that each was taller than six feet and had lots of fight. The arena now seated 2,800 comfortably and also featured new glass backboards. Before the season started, the team paid its respects to President Calvin Coolidge.

Figure 1.3. Bob Grody and Ray Kennedy of the Palace Laundry team.
Courtesy Library of Congress.

ABL Season Two

In its second season, the ABL had more stars. This was the era of Babe Ruth, Jack Dempsey, and Red Grange, the era of the larger-than-life sports star who embodied the Horatio Alger myth of climbing from the bottom of the ladder through talent and perseverance. The Chicago Bruins now had John "Honey" Russell, and the newly formed Philadelphia Warriors' roster contained Chick Passon and fan favorite "Stretch" Meehan. Cleveland retained two of its stars, and Washington kept Rusty Saunders and Ray Kennedy. When the Celtics joined the league, taking over for Brooklyn's squad, they brought their noted players, Nat Holman and Joe Lapchick. Could the ABL use these big names to make itself into a league as big as MLB? Unfortunately for the ABL, it lacked the outlets to magazines and other pre-established baseball friendly national media, like the *Sporting News* and other publications. Without large media markets, creating a big-name star proved to be a difficult task.

While the league's top players made $10,000 salaries for the season, including Nat Holman and Cleveland player-coach Marty Friedman, others played on contracts averaging $800 a month. Despite the good pay, the team owners retained specific advantages in the relationship. The contracts for players were based on those used in MLB. Those contracts enabled owners to treat players like chattel. They could release them at any time. Most important, the team controlled the players' services in the league through a reserve clause that beholden the players to the team with which they originally signed; therefore, players could not negotiate with other teams in the league unless the original team allowed them to do so.

The first half of the season went similarly to the previous year's effort. The team found itself battling with Cleveland for the top spot. The league saw several subtractions in the first half, with both Detroit and Brooklyn dropping out of the league. Baltimore decided to remain in the league, even though the team's poor record created abysmal attendance figures. The New York Celtics opted to take Brooklyn's spot in the league. When the Celtics came to play in Washington the day after Christmas, the largest basketball crowd in Washington history watched the home team lose in overtime by a score of 39–32. With the tough loss, the Palace Five trailed Cleveland by one game as the first half of the season wound down. Needing to win their last game and awaiting the Cleveland result, the Palace Five played poorly in the first half against Philadelphia, prompting the crowd to chant "Give us Baltimore." Philadelphia fans always seemed to have been raucous and tough, as their chant implied that they would rather have seen the worst team in the league than the Palace Five's floor efforts. Losing to Philadelphia, Washington finished behind Cleveland again.

All reports indicate that the teams did well with attendance and finances. The highest-grossing regular-season game occurred when 9,000 fans attended a game in Philadelphia. Washington regularly drew 1,500 to 2,000 fans per game, a slight drop off from the prior year, but, with more games being played, a slight decline was understandable.[12] Marshall trumpeted the league's success to members of the press. He assured famous columnist Damon Runyon that all the big-city teams drew well. With the split of the gate going 2/3 to the home team and 1/3 to the visiting squad, Marshall promised Runyon that all teams were making money.[13]

The second half of the ABL season began with high expectations for most of the teams in the league. The Brooklyn Celtics started exceptionally well, while Cleveland and Philadelphia struggled. With Kennedy and Saunders among the top five scorers in the league, the Palace Five started out with a 7–1 record. The team faced a big road trip out "west" to Fort Wayne, Indiana.

The Laundrymen could not win them all and eventually fell to third place behind both the Brooklyn Celtics and Fort Wayne Hoosiers. The Celtics capped off their season with a win over the Cleveland Rosenblums for the ABL championship.

The Palace Laundry Five did not make the playoffs for the second year in a row; however, the Washington squad proved to be the best barnstorming team in the ABL. The Laundrymen set a record for the amount of travel accomplished by a team on barnstorming exhibitions. The Palace team traveled 16,000 miles for 87 games over a 129-day span, averaging roughly five games of basketball per week. The previous record holders, the Celtics, played more than 100 games, but most of their contests were relatively close to New York City. The Palace Five quintet played in 45 cities covering 13 states for both ABL and barnstorming games. Locations ranged from those near Washington, for example, Alexandria, Virginia, and south to Charlotte, North Carolina, and west to places like Milwaukee, Wisconsin, and Flint, Michigan. Although Marshall did not get a championship, he certainly got his salaries' worth out of his basketball players.[14]

The Washington team provided Marshall with an additional benefit from their games. As a team playing under a company banner, all Palace Five games promoted Marshall's laundry and dry cleaning business. The barnstorming spread his company name throughout the East and Midwest, as the team played in small towns and cities. They received media coverage that included photographs and drawings of the big-name players, for instance, Ray Kennedy and Rusty Saunders, as well as descriptions of the upcoming game against a local team. The only other team in the ABL with a similar situation was the Cleveland Rosenblums, who promoted the department store of the same name.

The league leadership met at the season's end to examine the shape of the game and make changes. The Baltimore franchise left the league. The Celtics spent the last season alternating home games between Brooklyn and Manhattan. Once sports promoter Tex Rickard purchased the Celtics, he officially moved the team to Manhattan so they could play all their home games in Madison Square Garden. Brooklyn, which had a baseball team that fiercely competed with the ball team based in Manhattan, was now without a basketball team. Another owner tried again in Detroit. The league's board turned down the remainder of the applications to get a team into the ABL. Once again the league added games, bringing the total season to 56 games.

The leaders also decided to alter the playoff system by discarding the first and second halves structure. Instead, the eight teams were divided into a four-team Eastern Division and a same-sized Western Division. Washington was grouped with the champion Celtics. The first- and second-place teams in the two divisions would have a playoff, with the winner meeting the winner from the other division in the league championship.

The biggest headache for the league management involved controlling the amount of fouling. Fouls slowed the game and emphasized ruggedness over grace and speed. An attempt to limit personal fouls on a player to four resulted in too much resistance and people fouling out of games, yet some argued for a return to that limit. President Carr proposed the idea of having the fouling player sit out for a limited amount of time so his team plays one man down, as is the practice when a foul is committed in hockey. The leaders decided to limit personal fouls to five per player and to limit free throws only to players fouled while in possession of the ball. Only a player fouled while shooting would receive two free throws.

The ABL owners also considered a rule proposed by the Joint Rules Committee on basketball. The rule limited the dribble to one bounce. Afterward, a player would have to shoot or pass the ball in the air. Before the pro owners met to deliberate on this change, Marshall declared the rule stupid, stating, "The dribble is one of the most spectacular plays of basketball, and when you take it away the games are going to be drab affairs devoid of the excitement and speed for which basketball has gained an enviable reputation in the athletic world."[15] Marshall assured the press that the pros would not adopt the rule, and they did not, but he did not win other attempts to change the operation of the ABL. Marshall could not convince the other owners to support his effort to extend the number of games to 70. In addition, his attempt to pattern the schedule after baseball, creating longer home and away stretches of games, did not succeed.

Back in Washington, while Marshall and his partner hired noted architect Jules Henri de Sibour, they did not follow through on their arena plans. Meanwhile, the Arcadia Market and Amusement Company did. With plans to invest $1.5 million for improvements, the company envisioned a 10,000-seat arena that could host basketball games, college track meets, boxing and wrestling matches, bicycle races, hockey matches, and ice skating. They planned to rearrange the bowling and billiard facilities and combine the new with unused space to create dressing rooms, clubrooms, showers, and exercise rooms. In the spring of 1927, the Arcade Company issued bonds for $1.4 million with expectations that all the alterations would be completed by November 1 of that year.

The Palace Five owner again engaged in his usual wheeling and dealing. He traded with the Philadelphia Warriors, giving them Ted Kearns, George Glasco, and Tillie Voss. In exchange for a backup guard, a forward who averaged 5 points a game, and his team's center (who averaged 4.2 points a game), the Laundrymen received lanky center Francis "Stretch" Meehan, Herman "Chick" Passon, who averaged 9 points a game, and part-time player Harry Riconda. While the deal looked excellent on paper, the owner faced three large problems: none of the three men signed a contract for the upcoming season. They all demanded more money and met a determined resistance. "Meehan was paid, in my opinion, a ridiculous salary by the Philadelphia club last year and will never draw any such amount with my team," said Marshall. "I am not even figuring on him if you want to know the truth."[16]

ABL Season Three

As the season neared, the Palace Five needed to put together a team roster. Coach Ray Kennedy went to visit each of the holdout players to convince them to return. Meanwhile, Marshall threatened the players with suspension and a $100 fine if they did not return signed contracts. Elmer Ripley signed but was also the basketball coach at Georgetown University. His contract required that he only play in league games, enabling him to have the time to serve as the university's coach. Harry Riconda stated that he would not return to Washington, claiming that he was a free agent. Stretch Meehan and Chick Passon spurned the contracts offered to them. Even some of the players who lost their spots when the Celtics took over the Brooklyn team, including such Laundrymen from previous years as guard Bob Grody and forwards Rody Cooney and Red Conaty, declined to sign. These contract disputes illustrated that players perceived that they had alternatives inside and outside of the ABL. Passon and Conaty eventually signed and moved with the team to Brooklyn. Riconda and Meehan waited out the year and played for Paterson and Trenton, respectively, during the 1928–1929 season. The problems raised questions about playing for Washington under owner Marshall. Why would so many players balk?

The smaller, undermanned Palace Five opened the season poorly. Before a crowd of 2,000 on opening night, the team was humbled. The following evening, with a crowd of less than 1,200 for ladies night, Rochester totally outplayed Washington. The team struggled to a 1–10 beginning, as their lack of a center to contest tip-offs, which Meehan would have done, and injuries, hampered the squad. Despite the poor league play, Marshall's squad continued to perform in barnstorming games in the nearby states of Ohio and Pennsylvania.

The Palace Laundry Five played exhibition games over the Christmas and New Year's holiday season. At the beginning of 1928, Marshall announced the sale of the Palace basketball team to investors in Brooklyn. The Brooklyn team assumed the spot of Washington in the ABL. There were several reasons offered for why the Palace Five left the ABL. Some realized that this new big-money sport faced a crisis. The Detroit franchise had been disbanded, and Washington shifted to Brooklyn because of poor attendance. They understood that Marshall said the team was a bad investment because of low attendance; however, Marshall's statement explained that the team grew from a small scale to a large enterprise that required more of his personal attention than he could give without neglecting his other interests. He became involved with the construction and running of the team rather than relying on his team's coach or another basketball expert. Thus, Marshall had to make a choice about managing his time and chose to devote most of it to his primary business rather than the secondary sporting business. Many other owners relied on basketball people to make many decisions. Celtics' owner Tex Rickard ran Madison Square Garden; Philadelphia's Jules Aronson managed his arena and sporting promotions; Clarence Alter the turned job of team management over to Bernhard "Benny" Borgmann, one time member of the Original Celtics; and George Halas ran his Chicago Bears football team.

All points seem valid. The team drew fewer fans than in previous years, but the squad did not play as well either. Running the team in the ABL and its exhibitions required resources and time, which certainly took time away from Marshall's laundry empire; however, Marshall had rejected an offer of a ridiculously low $15,000 for the team the previous year. The Brooklyn team wanted a squad of its own after the Celtics moved to Manhattan, so the sale seemed to be an opportunity for Marshall to sell the team for a gain.[17]

The loss of the ABL franchise in Washington hampered basketball in the city. The Washington Independent Basketball League also had to abandon its schedule because of the lack of playing facilities. While noting the keenest appreciation for Marshall's efforts, a columnist for a local newspaper noted that losing the professional basketball team was a distinct loss to Washington sportsdom. The moving of the Palace Five franchise from Washington set a precedent that other teams would follow in the future.

The New York Celtics won the championship again. The league officials feared for the continuation of the league. Attendance fell throughout the league, even in previously successful cities like Cleveland. They decided to divide many of the Celtics' key players among other teams. The ABL returned to its earlier format of first-half and second-half winners and a single playoff between the first-place teams from each half. Despite the efforts, the league struggled. Three of the top Celtics players sold themselves as a group to Cleveland, which went on to win two consecutive titles and then dropped out of the league midway through its final season. At the close of the 1931 season, in the midst of the Great Depression, the teams ceased operations.[18]

Regional ABL Begins

After a two-year hiatus, an American Basketball League returned. This time, the teams came from up and down the Eastern Seaboard, ranging from Boston, Massachusetts, and New Haven, Connecticut, to Wilmington, Delaware, and Baltimore, Maryland. Mascots included a sand sniper, jewels, a moose, and a red devil. Teams lasted a season and merged. Or they made it through two seasons and then a new franchise emerged in the city and took on a new team name.

The players did not have yearly salaries as in the ABL but rather worked for a per-game pay rate. This enabled owners to make personnel changes without incurring financial obligations. While some players remained with a single team for a few years, many, particularly those unlucky enough to be with a franchise that failed, moved from team to team per season. These factors limited the consistency of player and team association, which fosters league history and fan appreciation

Washington's experience in the circuit was unique. For the first few years that the revamped ABL existed, teams came to Washington to play exhibition games against the Heurich Brewery basketball team. Located on D and 26th Streets, NW, along the Potomac River, the Brewery was one of the city's largest private employers. Its team of professionals played some of the best competition from the ABL, at first in George Washington University's gymnasium, but, within a year, at the Heurich gym near the plant.

By the summer of 1938, the U.S. economy had partially recovered from the worst effects of the Great Depression. The six present members of the ABL annual organization meeting received applications for franchises from cities as far away as Montreal, Boston, Washington, and the Midwest. While Chris Heurich Jr. denied that he submitted an application, the building of a new indoor stadium certainly fueled rumors. Heurich eventually got a franchise and made plans to create an environment for the games. This included a public address system and announcer, as well as pregame and halftime features and musical interludes that were every bit as colorful as those employed by George Preston Marshall and his Palace Laundry.

The team played a 36-game schedule. Within a few games, the Washington Heurichs realized that many of the players needed to improve their performance had been replaced on the squad. The team's general manager, Bob

McDonald, and sponsor Heurich soon lost their team captain to a career-ending knee injury. All changes fell short, as the team ended their inaugural season with a 7–22 record. Players sometimes wondered whether basketball served as the main draw. "At halftime of a game, fans would go down to the bar and have a drink," said Morris "Moe" Spahn, an ABL player with Jersey. "After the game the crowd would have a dance to canned music or a band. I think the dance was the real reason they came to the game."[19]

The team improved its personnel and changed its name for the next season. While continuing to promote the family name and business as the Heurich Brewers, the team played well during the season, which was reduced to 32 games. Led by two of the league's top 10 scorers, Phil Rabin and Morris "Moe" Dubilier, the Brewers finished in second place. The team qualified for the playoffs, which followed a different format, a round-robin. The new style did not suit the Brewers, who won only one of the six games that they played against the other four qualifying teams.

After not having an arena in the city, two competing groups emerged to build a basketball and hockey arena. The man running the district's four public golf courses, Severine G. Leoffler, joined with a partner to construct Riverside Stadium. Located on the Potomac down by Heurich's Brewery, the stadium seated 6,500, and the owners planned to host boxing, wrestling, ice skating, hockey, and traveling events. Although a typical arena in terms of size for the ABL venues, Washington had one of the newest and nicest places to play. Most teams competed in dingy, cramped auditoriums.

On the opposite edge of the city, on Capitol Hill behind the Union Railroad station, an ice manufacturer planned to open a skating rink. Several members of the Washington Board of Trade created the Capitol Garden Co., Inc., for stock outlay that consisted of 6,000 shares preferred at par value of $50 and 12,000 shares of common. The funds paid for the erection of a sports center, with seating capacities ranging from 7,000 for ice hockey to 11,000 for boxing and trade shows. At the end of summer in 1940, the District of Columbia issued a permit to M. J. Uline for a one-story brick and concrete block ice skating rink at 1140 Third Street, NW, for $240,000.

The ABL returned to the first-half and second-half format that they used in the first few years. In Washington, owner Leoffler provided Riverside Stadium with the facilities to host basketball. Leoffler convinced George Washington University, as well as Heurich, to play their home games at the location. Now simply the Brewers, the team received another strong scoring year from Rabin and Dubilier. The results were not the same, however, as the team finished each half in third place and did not qualify for the playoffs.

One month before the United States entered World War II after the attack on Pearl Harbor, Chris Heurich Jr. stated that he wanted out of the basketball world. Similar to George Preston Marshall, Heurich faced more responsibilities at the brewery. Heurich said the following:

> I feel that professional basketball definitely is a part of Washington's budding sports program. . . . Therefore, in view of the faithfulness and loyalty during the time they have been employed at the brewery, I am happy to turn over the Heurich team to player-coach Max Posnack and Harold "Whitey" Wilson.[20]

The players opted to play the home games at Turner's Arena on 14th and W Streets, NW, rather than Riverside Stadium. The league played only 25 games that season, and Washington finished below .500 each half in their last season in the ABL.

As noted New York sports columnist Dick Young argued, the second incarnation of the ABL failed to capture the hoop public. The league operated with limited money, playing their games with minimal investment. Thus, they hired players without benefit of a yearly contract and played the games inside dingy, cramped auditoriums. With U.S. entry into World War II, the ABL scaled back significantly. The Washington Brewers dropped out, and the remaining five teams played less than 15 games. The team continued to play during the winter of 1942–1943, but it relocated to the Heurich gym. Several of the same men, including Wilson and Posnack, continued with the team, joined by such new players as Arnold "Red" Auerbach. The Brewers devoted their games to the war effort. They played teams from the local military bases and charged a nominal admission, which they donated to the USO.

The league remained at five teams until a new Washington squad joined during the fall of 1944. Dubbed the Washington Capitols, the owners, Mike Conte and Tom Andre, hired one of the original New York Celtics as the coach. John Pete Barry supervised a tryout at the local high school gymnasium for local players with basketball experience. Several players already signed to contracts were also on hand to participate in the scrimmages. Within a few weeks, Barry assembled a team ready to begin the season at the arena originally built in competition with Riverside Stadium, the Uline Arena.

The Capitols featured a mixture of league veterans and younger players. Among this crew was a veteran from Marshall's Palace Laundry, Red Conaty. After playing professional basketball with teams in New York and Baltimore through the 1930s and early 1940s, the guard returned to Washington. The team played only half of the season in Washington. The lack of attendance caused the owners to move the Capitols to Paterson, New Jersey. They switched their nickname from the Capitols to the Crescents. The team still finished in last place, with a record of 3 wins and 23 losses.

Like the team that Marshall sold nearly two decades earlier, the Paterson squad continued as a franchise after leaving Washington. Many of the players went with the team or continued with Paterson, including one of the old Brewers, Phil Rabin. One of the men who did not, Red Auerbach, stayed in Washington and played a large part in the repurposing of the Capitol brand in D.C. basketball.[21]

Notes

1. Bob Kurda, *How Washington and New York Gave Birth to Black Basketball and Changed America's Game Forever* (Charlottesville: University of Virginia Press, 2006): 3–5, 11–45.
2. "Yankees Triumph Over Dominic Quint, 32–25," *Washington Post*, February 27, 1923, 19.
3. "In the Press Box with Baxter," *Washington Post*, January 25, 1924, S3.
4. Murray Nelson, "The Original Celtics and the 1926–27 American Basketball League," *Journal of Popular Culture*, vol. 30 (Fall 1996), 87–88.
5. Robert W. Peterson, *Cages to Jump Shots: Pro Basketball's Early Years* (New York: Oxford University Press, 1990), 76–88.
6. *Washington Post*, January 8, 1927, 16.
7. "In the Press Box with Baxter," *Washington Post*, January 20, 1926, 17.
8. "Chicago Five Will Test Palace," *Washington Post*, January 23, 1926, 16.
9. Ray Kennedy, "Kennedy Picks Brooklyn to Win," *Washington Post*, April 7, 1926, 15.
10. Ray Kennedy, "Clevelanders Win Cage Title," *Washington Post*, April 10, 1926, 15.
11. Rusty Saunders, "Palace Pros Better Fortified for League Season, Says Star," *Washington Star*, November 16, 1926, 13.
12. Jesse A. Linthicum, "Commenting On Sports," *Baltimore Sun*, January 23, 1927, S3.
13. "Sports as Viewed by Damon Runyon," *Chester Times*, January 14, 1927.
14. *Kingsport Times*, February 1, 1927, 6; "Noted Cager to Play at Shelby Thursday Night," *Mansfield News*, February 6, 1927, 12; "Foul Rulings Occupy League," *Washington Post*, March 6, 1927, 22.
15. "Dribble Rule Spurned by Pros," *Washington Post*, April 17, 1927, 18.
16. Special to the *Washington Post*, "Meehan May Hold out on Washington Pros," *Washington Post*, September 8, 1927, M17.
17. Frank H. Young, "Losing Streak Broken by Palace," *Washington Post*, December 5, 1927, 17; "No Pro Team for Capital," *Daily Mail*, January 4, 1928, 16.

18. Leonard Koppett, Bob Bellotti, Bob Ryan, Ken Shouler, and Stan Smith, *Total Basketball: The Ultimate Basketball Encyclopedia* (New York: Sportclassic Books, 2003), 50–51.

19. Jan Hubbard, ed. *The Official NBA Encyclopedia* (New York: Doubleday, 2000), 45–46.

20. "'New' Brewer Five Preps for Inaugural," *Washington Post*, December 30, 1942, 16.

21. Robert Bradley, John Hogrogian, John Grasso, and Steve Brainerd, "American Basketball League," Association for Professional Basketball Research, www.apbr.org/abl2552.html (retrieved September 11, 2009).

CHAPTER TWO

Red Auerbach and the Washington Capitols

Known for his fiery temperament and flaming red hair, Arnold "Red" Auerbach attended George Washington University on a basketball scholarship. Upon graduation with a master of arts degree, he found himself a member of the Washington Brewers serving the U.S. effort in World War II. Shortly thereafter, he joined the U.S. Navy and served at Norfolk, Virginia, as a basketball coach for the services' team.

With the end of the war, Auerbach returned to Washington, D.C. He coached George Preston Marshall's Redskins basketball team, which played against a team sponsored by the New York Giants and Philadelphia Eagles along the East Coast. They played their home games at Uline Arena, catching the attention of the arena owner, Migiel "Mike" Uline. After the Capitols of the American Basketball League (ABL) moved to Paterson, New Jersey, no professional basketball team played at Uline. Auerbach tried to convince Uline to field a team in the new league that other arena owners wanted to start. The fellow owners of the arenas in the bigger cities across the country were also looking for more activities to stage in their spaces. Despite having National Hockey League (NHL) teams as tenants, the arena owners had many dark evenings when no Ice Capades or circuses were in town. They could see from the limited success of the ABL and the Midwestern-based National Basketball League (NBL) that the indoor sport could be the solution they sought.

Born in the Netherlands, Uline worked in a Cleveland ice plant as a teenager. During a visit to Washington in the mid-1930s, he discovered that the city offered a business opportunity for an ice manufacturer. An inventor with more than 60 patents, the tall and soft-spoken man also had a strong stubborn streak. While cultivating a reputation as a straight dealer, the Federal Trade Commission brought charges against Uline and four other ice companies for entering price-fixing agreements.

Uline competed with Riverside Stadium and Turners Arena in the promotion of sports in Washington, D.C. He hired the general manager away from Riverside to take over the duties of managing the arena. He sponsored an American Hockey League team that helped force the team at Riverside out of business and then dropped sponsorship of his own team. He battled to get the best boxing promoters to use his arena, which could seat 8,000, as opposed to Turner's 3,000 seats. The arena achieved attention as a notable form of its era, appearing in *Architectural Record* the year of its construction (fig. 2.1).

On the second anniversary of the D-Day invasion, Uline joined the other big-city arena owners at the Commodore Hotel in New York. The men believed that the probable boon economy with consumer spending in the post–World War II United States warranted an investment in a "national" basketball league. Their thinking seemed valid as they watched Major League Baseball (MLB) have its highest-selling ticket year since the mid-1920s.[1]

The United States experienced a rash of strikes and fits and starts as a result of the economy changing from a war footing. Even with that economic turmoil, the economy grew overall. The pent-up consumer demand from years of World War II's rationing, the housing boom in suburbia, the birth

Figure 2.1. Sketch of Uline Arena.
Courtesy of the D.C. Public Library, Washingtoniana Division.

of the baby boom, and the strong labor unions in manufacturing all spelled increased consumer spending and a larger economy. In the United States, the gross national product increased from $200 million to $500 million in 15 years. Steady, long-term employment in both blue- and white-collar occupations increased disposable income, which allowed more people to enjoy more leisure time.[2]

Uline could see the growth around him in Washington. The city grew in population and wealth as a result of the expansion of the Federal Government during the New Deal and World War II. With a population of more than 800,000, a ripe market existed for the entertainment dollar. Uline Arena sat on the edge of a warehouse district in the city's northeast quadrant, near the main train line and Union Station. The arena received good public transit on its northern and southern borders but offered little parking for those who drove. Northeast was the second most populated section in the city, with more than 187,000 people, and the area around the arena contained working and lower-middle-class enclaves of predominantly white families. A small number of black families lived in the area as well. The white citizens association had one of the largest memberships, and after getting local schools and parks during the previous 20 years, their main concern in the 1940s was maintaining property values. By 1950, blighted blocks appeared throughout the eastern and southern portions of the neighborhood. Yet, the area around Uline Arena did not appear at the top of the list for reported crimes in Washington, D.C.[3]

The Basketball Association of America's Beginnings

The group of arena owners shared a similar perspective before the meeting occurred. They soon debated territorial rights and then faced the biggest sticking point: What percentage of receipts from gates ought to go to the league and to the home team? The owners decided that visiting teams would not earn a share of the gate receipts. They structured the league like professional hockey, using a similar playoff structure and even appointed the president of the American Hockey League, Maurice Podoloff, as leader of the newly christened Basketball Association of America (BAA). The top team in the NHL, Montreal, did not get a franchise, while Uline, who did not own one, did get the franchise, the Washington Capitols. By the fall, 11 teams opened training camps.

The BAA divided itself up into Eastern and Western divisions rather than play the two half seasons, like the ABL. Washington, Philadelphia, New York, Providence, Boston, and Toronto comprised the East. The West consisted of Chicago, St. Louis, Cleveland, Detroit, and Pittsburgh. The inaugural season featured 60 games, starting in November and ending with the playoffs in April. The BAA opted for an odd playoff system, as the second-place teams from each division and the two third-place teams squared off against one another.[4]

Like the first ABL, the BAA used contracts similar to professional baseball. The league limited the number of players allowed on a team to 12 and capped total salaries at $55,000. Most player salaries averaged $6,000, with $4,500 at the low end. Like Chicago, Philadelphia, and New York, Washington paid for a big star, as guard Bob Feerick earned more than $9,000. As with the ABL, all the players were Caucasian, and many came from urban ethnic groups—Irish, Jewish and Italian. Unlike the ABL, the players were taller. Each of the franchises had two or three men who stood at least 6 feet, 5 inches tall. Also different from the earlier league, there were more southerners and westerners, and many of the players were college graduates who could have worked in other professions. The players in this league often worked at jobs during the off-season, and some found little financial incentive to stay in the BAA or, later, the National Basketball Association (NBA). One player noted that he made more money in three years working for a distilling company than he did playing for the Minneapolis Lakers. The players also accumulated no retirement benefits during their playing days.

Uline, whom Auerbach met while playing barnstorming basketball games, gave Auerbach the responsibility of assembling the basketball team. Auerbach turned to some of the men he knew from the Navy league. While watching such fellow sailors as Bob Feerick, Johnny Norlander, and Bones McKinney play, "he had thought that these players formed the nucleus of a great pro club." Auerbach started by summoning Bob Feerick from Santa Clara, California, and he then called on Johnny Norlander and former Georgetown Hoya Johnny Mahnken. Feerick brought with him fellow guard Freddie Scolari and then convinced Bones McKinney to sign with the Capitols rather than follow through with his plans to play for the Chicago Stags.[5]

Washington started their first month with a 2–3 record before running off a streak of 17 consecutive wins. The city's newspapers gave the team solid coverage, not only covering the games, but mentioning when the team offered basketball clinics to local children. They also provided occasional profiles of Auerbach and the occasional player, particularly McKinney. The lanky North Carolinian played forward and occasional center for the squad. McKinney became a fan favorite with his antics on the floor. The emotional and demonstrative Bones would talk all the time during the game, banter with referees, and play act, and he once shot a free throw backward. Scolari, nicknamed "Fat Freddie" for his roundish shape, had great shooting range and was a favorite of the women. Feerick was the team's best shooter and player, and he and McKinney felt they knew more about coaching than Auerbach. They initially did, but the coach learned quickly.

The Washington team epitomized team play. The sports columnist for the *Toronto Globe and Mail* called the Caps the classiest team in the pro loop, who displayed a diversified attack. The Toronto Huskies offense did little but give the ball to their player-coach Ed Sadowski, the 6–foot, 5-inch center who missed more often than he scored, and the team played woeful defense. Most teams ran a vintage pro offense, filled with set shots and give-and-go plays, which was plodding and predictable and led to rough, tightly contested defensive play. Successful teams, like the Rochester Royals of the NBL, which later became part of the NBA, emphasized a defensive style that smothered opponents.[6]

Many of the players enjoyed this style of play. They observed that scoring in double figures was difficult. Great plays emerged when a skillful player with smarts would freeze the ball and make the defense have to take a gamble, and then he passed the ball to the newly created space. As Hall of Famer Bobby Wanzer argues, the game put a premium on working hard for a good shot and the virtues of ball control. Another rule prohibited zone defense, which forced man-to-man coverage. Besides rules, players enforced a style that made the game more about ball movement than playing individually and vertically. The players did not consider the dunk shot sportsmanlike. As John Ezersky recalls, "As far as playing above the rim is concerned, you'd never dream of doing that. You'd do it once, dunk over someone, and if you tried to do it again they'd let you have it."[7]

The Capitols' playing conditions were not ideal. The arena had loose floorboards, poorly hung baskets, and condensation caused by heat. Sometimes, the temperatures dropped so low that the players wore overcoats as they sat on the bench. Washington shared this misfortune with other teams in the league, like St. Louis and Baltimore, who did not have legitimate arenas. Games took place in an old roller-skating rink in Baltimore and a fairgrounds building in St. Louis. In each place, the playing surface was affected by a leaky roof, a warped floor, and little heat.

Traveling in the league sometimes became adventurous. Teams provided players with $6 per day for food when they traveled, which allowed $0.75 for breakfast, $1.25 for lunch, and $3 for dinner and beers. The teams spent an average of $8,000 during a single year to get the team to road games, generally via train. On many occasions, the players piled into rented cars, their long legs cramped in the back as they journeyed between cities to get to that night's game.

The Capitols continued to play well. The team faced the rival New York Knicks on the road, and the Knicks broke out to a flying start. Ahead 12–7 midway through the first quarter, everything turned black for the Knicks within two minutes, as the stylish Capitols scored 12 consecutive points. The Knicks trailed by 16 at halftime, and then the defense and offense crumbled, when Bob Feerick, Johnny Norlander, and Bones McKinney found the range from everywhere on the floor. By game's end, Feerick won the fancy of the spectators with his feinting.

By the end of March 1947, as the finish of the regular season approached, the Capitols topped the Eastern Division with a record of 49 wins and 11 loses. Chicago led the Western Division. Feerick finished with an average of 16.8 points per game, trailing only the Philadelphia Warriors' "Jumping Joe" Fulks.[8]

The odd playoff system came into effect as the schedule was released. The second-place teams in the Eastern and Western divisions played one another, as well as the third-place teams, and the two Eastern teams, Philadelphia and the New York Knickerbockers, emerged victorious. Then Philadelphia and New York played one semifinal, while the two first-place teams played the other. Washington lost to Chicago four games to two. Years later, at least a few of the Capitols believe that they were robbed by poor officiating. Philadelphia seized the league's first title, defeating the Chicago Stags handily, four games to one.[9]

The Capitols proved to be representative of the league's financial situation. They placed in the middle of the pack in attendance and net receipts and lost money, like most teams. They drew more than 65,000 paid fans and netted nearly $100,000, the fifth-largest amount in the league. The BAA teams that did not fare as well, including Cleveland, Detroit, Pittsburgh, and Toronto, all folded after the first season. Of the lower-earning group, only the Boston Celtics stayed in the league. Uline declared himself satisfied with the team's playing and coaching. Despite their early exit, the players split $12,000 from the playoffs into 10 shares, which was a nice bonus when the average salary was $4,000 a year.

Uline joined with the BAA owners to make changes to increase the team's financial stability. The Board of Governors reduced the schedule from 60 to 48 games and opted to end the playoffs by March so as to not conflict with the beginning of the baseball season. They were unsuccessful in implementing this change in the timing of the playoffs. Team size dropped from 12 to 10 players to help reduce total salary costs. The owners also bemoaned the meager gate receipts and talked about making such changes as tinkering with the length of the game and scheduling doubleheaders to increase attendance.[10]

BAA Season Two: Retrenchment

The owners remained committed to making the BAA a success. The league added a team based in Baltimore to round out to eight teams. The Bullets came over from the ABL, where they had won the championship the two preceding years. Still, the BAA represented the second-best professional league. General Electric, Firestone, and Goodyear started the NBL in 1937. The Midwestern-based industrial league had some of the best basketball players. They also received strong support from their fan bases in the small towns the teams called home.

The second year generated plenty of drama on and off the court for the Capitols. Now placed in the Western Division with holdovers St. Louis and Chicago and the new Baltimore team, the Capitols started slowly, only reaching the .500 mark by the middle of December. Articles in the local newspapers asked what was wrong with the team. One observer noted that the entire league had improved. The team continued to flirt with being average for the next few months.

Off the court, the owner made big headlines. African Americans in Washington protested Uline's segregation policies for five years. Uline allowed blacks to attend boxing matches but not basketball and hockey games. He addressed his critics, saying, "Why pick on me, I'm no pioneer, I'm a businessman. Why should I be the first?"[11] His building cost money, he argued, so he had to cater to the majority of people from whom he received the most money. By early 1948, Uline changed his policy, stating that his decision was prompted by the "trend of the times." While racial hatred and intolerance did not end with entry into Uline Arena, the change in policy offered spectators and athletes more opportunities in the nation's capital.[12]

Uline garnered more headlines with statements he issued in frustration with his business situation. He used to rent to college and high school basketball teams for $1,300 an evening. The cost was so high that the building of the much smaller National Guard Armory prompted the schools to leave Uline en masse. The armory charged 15% of the gate or $250 per game, whichever was higher. Uline made an offer of a reduced rate that sparked little interest. He complained about the unfairness of competing against the government-run armory and blamed it for his arena being dark three nights a week. He concluded with a threat to sell off or destroy his arena.

The Capitols generated income for the arena, even though Washington again placed fifth in net receipts, but this time out of only eight teams. The 24 home games generated more than $78,000 in income for the team, nearly 25% more than the inaugural season. This compared moderately well with New York and Philadelphia, which each averaged more than 4,000 fans per home game. As a visiting team, Washington drew well in every city. As the coach of the New York Knicks said, the Caps have a flashy style of play that crowds enjoy. Since revenues were based on home gate receipts and visiting teams did not share in the profits, the BAA's revenue system hurt Uline and the Capitols.[13]

During the middle of the season, Auerbach strengthened the team by picking up forward Sidney "Sonny" Hertzberg from the Knickerbockers for the $100 waiver price. The Capitols engaged in a three-way battle for the second- and third-place positions in the division. In late February, the Caps hosted Chicago before more than 3,000 fans. Playing without big gun Bones McKinney, the Capitols fell behind early. With their shooting off and many passes being intercepted by the tall visiting players, the Caps could not catch up, and the loss dropped them into third place, behind first-place St. Louis and Chicago.

Weeks later, a crowd of 2,800 Washingtonians watched one of the worst performances of the year from the home team. Poor officiating made things worse, with both McKinney and Scolari fouling out. Irate customers threw programs at the officials and booed vociferously, causing the game to be held up twice. Less than 30 minutes after the scoreboard carried the news of the 71–54 loss, the board ripped loose from its ceiling moorings and plaster and pulleys came tumbling down, making two massive holes in the court.

The Capitols finished tied with Chicago and Baltimore for second place in the division. Each team won 28 games and lost 20. They flipped a coin, and Washington drew Chicago, who defeated them in a one-game playoff. When Baltimore defeated Chicago in their one-game playoff, the Capitols finished in last place and did not qualify for the playoffs (figure 2.2). While disappointed, the newspaper reporters covering the team defined the year as successful and informed fans that Auerbach would begin traveling to watch collegiate all-star games to be ready for the upcoming draft.[14]

While the Baltimore Bullets went on to win the BAA title, leaking news about the Capitols had fans concerned. McKinney, Feerick, and Scolari all planned to quit the team, as Uline continued to discuss giving up on the arena business. By early spring, the 70-year-old owner announced that the Capitols would be back in the fall for the third season. Word leaked that Uline offered the position of Capitols coach to Naval Academy basketball

Figure 2.2. Chick Halbert, Charles Gilmur, Fred Scolari, John Mandic, and Jack Nichols of the 1949–1950 Washington Captiols.
Reprinted with permission of the D.C. Public Library, Star Collection, © *Washington Post.*

team coach Ben Carnevale. The owner immediately denied taking the action and stated that, "We don't plan a change, at this time, but Carnevale is a mighty fine coach."[15] Auerbach expressed great surprise at the news. One month later, Uline announced that Auerbach would be reemployed, again on a one-year contract. The pair then went to the BAA meeting in Chicago, where they drafted guard Leo Katkaveck (figures 2.3 and 2.4) and center Jack Nichols. The latter, at six feet, seven inches, complemented Clarence "Kleggie" Hermsen, who stood six feet, nine inches and came over in a trade from the champion Baltimore Bullets.[16]

BAA Season Three: Franchise Raid

The BAA shared a peaceful coexistence with the NBL during the first two years; however, before the start of the 1948–1949 season, BAA president Maurice Podoloff pushed for a merger of the two leagues. After failing, he convinced four of the NBL's strongest teams to join the BAA. The league

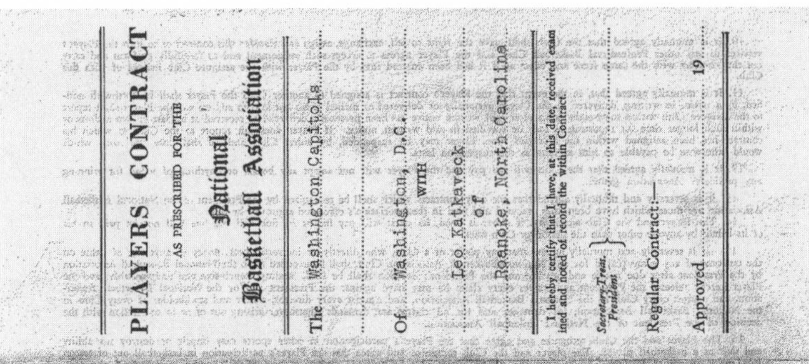
PLAYERS CONTRACT
AS PRESCRIBED FOR THE
National
Basketball Association
The Washington Capitols
Of Washington, D.C.
WITH
Leo Katkaveck
of
Roanoke, North Carolina
I hereby certify that I have, at this date, received examined and noted of record the within Contract.
Secretary-Treas.
President.
Regular Contract:—
Approved 19

IMPORTANT NOTICE TO PLAYERS AND CLUB PRESIDENTS

Every player before signing a contract should carefully scrutinize the same to ascertain whether all of the conditions agreed upon between the Player and Club President have been incorporated therein, and if any have been omitted the player should insist upon having all the terms, conditions, promises and agreements inserted in the contract before he signs the same.

NATIONAL BASKETBALL ASSOCIATION

UNIFORM PLAYER CONTRACT

THIS AGREEMENT made this 19th day of August by and between Washington Capitols (hereinafter called the Club), a member of the National Basketball Association, and Leo Katkaveck of the City, Town of Roanoke, N. C. (hereinafter called the Player).

WITNESSETH:—

In consideration of the several and/or mutual promises and/or agreements hereinafter contained, the parties hereto promise and agree as follows:

1. The Club hereby employs the Player as a skilled Basketball Player for the season 1950-1951 which includes the Club's training season, all regular Association games, all exhibition games scheduled during such season and includes the playoffs at the close of the schedule season for which additional compensation is to be received by the player as may be provided by the Association.

2. The club agrees to pay the Player for rendering services described herein the sum of $ 4,500.00 in twelve equal semi-monthly payments beginning with the first of said payments on November 15th of the season above described and continuing with such payments on the first and fifteenth of each month until said sum is paid in full. Provided however if the Club does not qualify for the playoffs the payments due subsequent to the conclusion of the schedule season shall become due and payable immediately after the conclusion of the schedule season.

3. The Club promises and agrees to pay the reasonable board and lodging expenses of the Player while playing for the Club in other than the Club's home city and will pay all proper and necessary expenses of the Player and his meals enroute.

4. The club may from time to time during the continuance of this contract establish reasonable rules for the government of its players "at home" and "abroad," and such rules shall be a part of this contract as fully as if herein written and shall be binding upon the player, and for violation of such rules or for any conduct impairing the faithful and thorough discharge of the duties incumbent upon the player, the club may impose reasonable fines upon the player and deduct the amount thereof from any money due or to become due to the player. The club may also suspend the player for violation of any rules so established, and during such suspension the player shall not be entitled to any compensation under this contract. When the player is fined or suspended, he shall be given notice in writing, stating the amount of the fine or the duration of the suspension and the reason therefor.

5. The Player promises and agrees (a) to report at the time and place fixed by the Club in good physical condition; and (b) to keep himself throughout the entire season in good physical condition; and (c) to give his best services, as well as his loyalty, to the Club, and to play basketball only for the Club unless released, sold or exchanged by the Club; and (d) to be neatly and fully attired in public and always to conduct himself on and off the court according to the highest standards of honesty, morality, fair play and sportsmanship; and (e) not to do anything which is detrimental to the best interests of the Club or of the National Basketball Association or of professional sports.

5a. In addition to his services in connection with the actual playing of basketball, the Player agrees to cooperate with the Club and participate in any and all promotional activities of the Club and its Association, which, in the opinion of the Club, will promote the welfare of the Club or professional basketball, and to observe and comply with all requirements of the Club respecting conduct and service of its teams and its players, at all times whether on or off the playing floor.

6. If the Player, in the sole judgment of the Club's physician, is not in good physical condition at the date of his first scheduled game for the Club, or if, during the season, he fails to remain in good physical condition, unless such condition results directly from playing basketball for the Club, so as to render him, in the sole judgment of the Club's physician unfit to play skilled basketball, it is mutually agreed that the Club shall have the right to suspend such Player until such time as, in the sole judgment of the Club's physician, the Player is in sufficiently good physical condition to play skilled basketball, and in the event of such suspension, the annual sum payable to the Player shall be proportionately reduced as the length of the period of disability, during which, in the sole judgment of the Club's physician, the Player is unfitted to play skilled basketball, bears to the season. If the Player is injured as a direct result of participating in any basketball practice or game played for the Club, the Club will pay the Player's reasonable hospitalization until he is discharged from the hospital and his reasonable medical expenses and doctor's bills, provided the hospital and the doctor are selected by the Club, and provided further, that the Club's obligation to pay said medical expenses and said doctor's bills shall terminate at a period not exceeding eight weeks (8) after the injury. It is also agreed that if the Player's said injury or injuries resulting directly from playing for the Club render him, in the sole judgment of the Club's physician, unfit to play skilled basketball for the balance of the season or any part thereof, then during such time as the Player is unfit to play skilled basketball, but in no event beyond the season described in paragraph 1, the Club shall pay the Player the compensation hereinbefore provided for and the Player releases the Club from any and every additional obligation or liability, claim and demand whatsoever.

7. The Player agrees to give to the Club's coach or the Club's physician (a) written or verbal notice of any minor injury suffered by him as soon as possible, but in any event, within forty-eight (48) hours thereafter; and (b) written notice of any major injury sustained by the Player as soon as possible, but in any event within four (4) days after the sustaining of such injury, each such notice to state the time, place, cause and nature of said injury.

8. Should the player become disabled as provided in the preceding section, he will submit himself to a medical examination and treatment by a regular physician, in good standing, to be selected by the Club. Such examination when made at the request of the Club shall be at its expense, unless made necessary by some act or conduct of the player contrary to the terms of this agreement or rules and regulations made under it.

9. The Player represents and agrees that he has exceptional and unique skill and ability as a basketball player; that his services to be rendered hereunder are of a special, unusual and extraordinary character which gives them peculiar value which cannot be reasonably or adequately compensated for in damages at law, and that the Player's breach of this contract will cause the Club great and irreparable injury and damage. The Player agrees that, in addition to other remedies, the Club shall be entitled to injunctive and other equitable relief to prevent a breach of this contract by the Player, including, among others, the right to enjoin the Player from playing basketball for any other person or organization during the term of this contract.

Figure 2.3. Leo Katkaveck's Contract (front).
Courtesy of the Katkaveck Family.

10. It is mutually agreed that the Club shall have the right to sell, exchange, assign and transfer this contract or to loan the Player's services to any other Professional Basketball Club and the Player agrees to accept such assignment and to faithfully perform and carry out this contract with the same force and effect as if it had been entered into by the Player with the assignee Club instead of with this Club.

11. It is mutually agreed that, in the event that the Player's contract is assigned to another Club the Player shall be forthwith notified, by a notice in writing, delivered to the Player personally or delivered or mailed to his last known address and the Player shall report to the assignee Club within forty-eight hours after said written notice has been personally delivered or received at his last known address or within such longer time for reporting as may be specified in said written notice. If Player does not report to the Club to which his contract has been assigned within the aforesaid time, Player may be suspended, by either Club and he shall lose the sums which would otherwise be payable to him as long as the suspension lasts.

12. It is mutually agreed that the Club will not pay and the Player will not accept any bonus or anything of value for winning any particular Association game.

13. It is severally and mutually agreed that the only contracts which shall be recognized by the President of the National Basketball Association are those which have been duly executed and filed in theAssociation's office and approved by him.

14. The Player and the Club agree that if either is fined, he or it will pay his or its fine and the fine will not be paid in his or its behalf by anyone other than the person or Club fined.

15. It is severally and mutually agreed that any player of a Club, who directly or indirectly bets money or anything of value on the outcome of any game played for any National Basketball Association Club, shall be expelled from the National Basketball Association by the President after due notice and hearing and the President's decision shall be final, binding, conclusive and unappealable; and the Player hereby releases the President and waives every claim he may have against the President and/or the National Basketball Association, and against every Club in the National Basketball Association, and against every director, officer and stockholder of every Club in the National Basketball Association, for damages and for all claims and demands whatsoever arising out of or in connection with the decision of the President of the National Basketball Association.

16. The Player and the Club recognize and agree that the Player's participation in other sports may impair or destroy his ability and skill as a basketball player. The player and the Club recognize and agree that the Player's participation in basketball out of season may result in injury to him. Accordingly the Player agrees that he will not engage in professional boxing or wrestling; and that, except with the written consent of the Club, he will not engage in any game or exhibition of basketball, football, baseball, hockey, lacrosse, or other athletic sport.

17. The Player agrees that his picture may be taken for still photographs, motion pictures or television at such times as the Club may designate and agrees that all rights in such pictures shall belong to the Club and may be used by the Club in any manner it desires. The player further agrees that during the playing season he will not make public appearances, participate in radio or television programs or permit his picture to be taken or write or sponsor newspaper or magazine articles or sponsor commercial products without the written consent of the Club, which shall not be withheld except in the reasonable interests of the Club or professional basketball.

18. The player agrees and covenants that during the life of this contract he will not tamper with or enter into negotiations with any other player under contract or reservation to any Club, which is a member of this Association, for, or regarding, his future or present services without written consent of the Club of which the Player negotiated with is a member, under penalty of a fine.

19. (a) The Player may terminate this contract, upon written notice to the Club, if the Club shall default in the payments to the Player provided for in paragraph 2 hereof or shall fail to perform any other obligation agreed to be performed by the Club hereunder and if the Club shall fail to remedy such default within ten (10) days after the receipt by the Club of written notice of such default. The Player may also terminate this contract as provided in sub-paragraph (f) (4) of this paragraph 19.

(b) The Club may terminate this contract upon written notice to the Player (but only after requesting and obtaining waivers of this contract from all other Clubs) if the Player shall at any time:

(1) fail, refuse or neglect to conform his personal conduct to the standards of good citizenship and good sportsmanship or to keep himself in first class physical condition or to obey the Club's training rules; or

(2) fail, in the opinion of the Club's management, to exhibit sufficient skill or competitive ability or qualify or continue as a member of the Club's team; or

(3) fail, refuse or neglect to render his services hereunder or in any other manner materially breach this contract.

(c) If this contract is terminated by the Club by reason of the Player's failure to render his services hereunder due to disability resulting directly from injury sustained in the course and within the scope of his employment hereunder and written notice of such injury is given by the Player as provided herein, the Player shall be entitled to receive his full salary for the season in which the injury was sustained, less all workmen's compensation payments paid or payable by reason of said injury.

(d) If this contract is terminated by the Club during the training season, payment by the Club of the Player's board, lodging and expense allowance during the training season to the date of termination and of the reasonable traveling expenses of the Player to his home city and the expert training and coaching provided by the Club to the Player during the training season shall be full payment to the Player.

(e) If this contract is terminated by the Club during the playing season, then, except in the case provided for in sub-paragraph (c) of this paragraph 19, the Player shall be entitled to receive as full payment hereunder such portion of the semi-monthly payment stipulated in paragraph 2 hereof as the number of days of his actual employment during the semi-monthly period during which termination of this contract takes place bears to fifteen the number of days in said semi-monthly period provided, however, that if this contract is terminated under sub-paragraph (b) (2) of this paragraph 19 for failure to exhibit sufficient skill or competitive ability, the Player shall be entitled to an additional amount equal to payment for three days ascertained as provided in this paragraph plus the reasonable traveling expenses of the Player to his home.

(f) If the Club proposes to terminate this contract in accordance with sub-paragraph (b) of this paragraph 19, the procedure shall be as follows:

(1) The Club shall request waivers from all other clubs. Such waiver request must state that it is for the purpose of terminating this contract and it may not be withdrawn.

(2) Upon receipt of the waiver request, any other club may claim assignment of this contract at a waiver price of $1.00, the priority of claims to be determined in accordance with the Association Rules.

(3) If this contract is so claimed, the Club shall, promptly and before any assignment, notify the Player that it had requested waivers for the purpose of terminating this contract and that the contract had been claimed.

(4) Within 3 days after receipt of notice of such claim, the Player shall be entitled, by written notice to the Club, to terminate this contract on the date of his notice of termination. If the Player fails so to notify the Club, this contract shall be assigned to the claiming club.

(5) If the contract is not claimed, the Club shall promptly deliver written notice of termination to the Player at the expiration of the waiver period.

(g) Upon any termination of this contract by the Player, all obligations of both parties hereunder shall cease on the date of termination, except the obligation of the Club to pay the Player's compensation to said date.

20. In case of dispute between the Player and the Club, the same shall be referred to the President of the Association as an arbitrator, and his decision shall be accepted by all parties as final; and the Club and the Player agree that any such dispute, or any claim or complaint by either party against the other, shall be presented to the President within one year from the date it arose.

21. The Club and the Player severally and mutually promise and agree to be legally bound by the Constitution and By-Laws of the National Basketball Association and by all the terms and provisions thereof, a copy of which is and shall remain open and available for inspection by the Club, its directors, officers and stockholders and by the Player at the main office of the Association and at the main office of the Club.

22. (a) On or before October 1st (or if a Sunday, then the next preceding business day) next following the last playing season covered by this contract, the Club may tender to the Player a contract for the term of that season by mailing the same to the Player at his address following his signature hereto, or if none be given, then at his last address of record with the Club. If prior to the November 1 next succeeding said October 1, the Player and the Club have not agreed upon the terms of such contract, then on or before 10 days after said November 1, the Club shall have the right by written notice to the Player at said address to renew this contract for the period of one year on the same terms, except that the amount payable to the Player shall be such as the Club shall fix in said notice; provided, however, that said amount shall be an amount payable at a rate not less than 75% of the rate stipulated for the preceding year.

(b) The Club's right to renew this contract, as provided in subparagraph (a) of this paragraph 22, and the promise of the Player not to play otherwise than with the Club have been taken into consideration in determining the amount payable under paragraph 2 hereof.

23. This agreement shall be construed to have been made under and shall be governed by the Laws of the State of D.C.

24. This Agreement contains the entire agreement between the Parties and there are no oral or written inducements, promises or agreements except as contained herein.

IN WITNESS WHEREOF the Player has hereunto set his hand and seal and the Club has caused this contract to be executed by its duly authorized officer.

Washington Capitols

WITNESSES:

By ________ V- President.

____

________ Player.

____

Player's Address Roanoke, N.C.

Figure 2.4. Leo Katkaveck's Contract (back).
Courtesy of the Katkaveck Family.

expanded to 12 teams. With the entrance of the Fort Wayne Pistons, Indianapolis Jets, Rochester Royals, and Minneapolis Lakers, each team played a 60-game schedule.

The BAA officials again reorganized the league and playoff structure. They placed all four former NBL teams in the Western Division, with Chicago and St. Louis. Both Baltimore and Washington moved into the Eastern Division, joining Boston, New York, Philadelphia, and Providence. They created a divisional semifinal round in which the first and fourth place teams and the second and third place teams would play each other. The winners of those contests would move forward to the play in the division finals, with the winners headed to the championship game.

The BAA teams had their games aired on radio and raised some income through the contract. The Washington Capitols were similar to the Chicago Stags and New York Knickerbockers in appearing on the new medium of television. Washington was one of the first cities in the nation with four television stations by the late 1940s. The DuMont network started carrying games from the Uline Arena in late December of the first season. Television networks needed programming for the few hours of early evening broadcasting that they carried, and sporting events were inexpensive and available. The team continued to appear on WTTG, which paid Uline approximately $300 for the video rights to each of their 30 home games, or close to $10,000. The media coverage helped a team and game that were both in their infancy.

The new season found six of the Capitols returning, including the coach. Washington reporters dubbed the coach the "Young Fox" of basketball, after his shrewd off-season acquisitions. Auerbach built a team he described as versatile, saying, "The Caps are four teams, and I classify them as rough, smooth, fast, and big." Capitol players saw other virtues in the team. Scolari called the Capitols the "damnedest team I've ever played on. This club is completely relaxed and doesn't worry about a thing. The boys think it's the natural thing to come from behind." McKinney said, "Nobody's selfish, and we're all out to win. I say we have the old college spirit."[17]

National newspapers sang the team's praises as the 1948–1949 season began. The Capitols started the season zipping off 15 wins, including some of the come-from-behind variety. The team trailed the lowly Providence Steamrollers by 52–48 in the fourth quarter, when power forwards Kleggie Hermsen and Dick O'Keefe took over. Their series of buckets in a quick four-minute span put Washington ahead, 54–53. The Capitols guards, Feerick and Scolari, then assumed control, and, four minutes later, the Capitols led by eight and the team never looked back.

The Capitols lost their first game in early December and did not lose more than two games in a row until the 40th game of the season, when they had a record of 30 wins and 10 losses. The team skidded a little bit during the months of February and March, ending up with a 38–22 record, but it was still good enough to be atop the Eastern Division. Led by the Baltimore Bullets and their coach and captain, Harry "Buddy" Jeannette, teams found a league rule that they could use to their advantage against the sharpshooting Capitols. The teams would intentionally foul a Capitol, permitting them to shoot only one foul shot. The opposing team would then get the ball, thus reducing the Capitols potential point tally from two points to a single point each time they had the ball. The number of fouls allowed per player had increased the previous season from five to six, thus the strategy could be employed more often. The league's rule committee changed the rules for the 1950–1951 and 1953–1954 seasons in an attempt to eliminate this intentional fouling approach. The strategy turned the game into brief staccato spurts of action broken up by endless parades to one end of the court or the other for free throws. This was certainly not the best way for the struggling league to market its product.[18]

Since their inception in the league, the Capitols played a team game, with strength on offense and defense. In the 1948–1949 season, they concentrated on producing more offense. The team scored almost 82 points a game, eight points more than they averaged the previous season. They finished sixth in the league of 12 teams. They finished fifth in the league in defense, allowing their opponents 79 points a game.

Guard Bob Feerick again led the team in points, but Bones McKinney and Kleggie Hermsen also topped the 700 point total, with an average of 12 points per game. The big men also did battle under the boards, as part of the game in these days included the ability to suffer some physical abuse. One opponent admired McKinney's toughness, as well as the constant chatter he kept going during a game.

The Capitols played a balanced team game. Feerick's point total placed him 14th amongst the league's leaders. "Jumping Joe" Fulks remained one of the league's highest scorers, with double Feerick's output. But even "Jumping Joe" now had to take second place to the league's newcomer, the Minneapolis Lakers' star George Mikan. A two-time points leader in the NBL, "Mr. Basketball" brought his dominant post game to the BAA and led all scorers, with 1,698 points, for an average of more than 28 points a game.

While the four NBL teams joined the BAA, they maintained a pride in their origins. During the Lakers' last visit to Uline Arena, Mikan informed the Washington media that the Capitols might be good enough to come out of the Eastern Division in the playoffs. He asserted that the Capitols would not beat the Western Division champion if it was the Lakers or Royals. The two NBL teams would be facing the Chicago Stags and St. Louis Bombers as their first-round opponents. Washington, as the top seed in the Eastern Division, faced fourth-place Philadelphia. The reigning champion Bullets took on the New York Knicks.[19]

Two major injuries occurred as the Capitols season wound down. Feerick suffered a torn knee cartilage, and Scolari broke a finger. Without the two regulars, the newspaper sports pundits thought it would take a miracle for the Capitols to win in the postseason. The Capitols opened the series in Philadelphia, and a sizable delegation of Washingtonians took the train up and bought a ticket, arranged by the team.

In the first half, the lead seesawed between the two teams. Then the Capitols front court of Bones McKinney, Kleggie Hermsen, Dick Schulz, and rookie Jack Nichols took over by scoring with regularity. The big men also made a habit of controlling the backboards. The Washingtonians who went by train came home happy, as the Capitols beat the Warriors, 92–70. Back at home, for the next game, the Capitols led by 19 points midway through the third quarter. Then they watched as the Warriors nearly overhauled them late in the fourth quarter. Free throws by guard Sonny Hertzberg iced the win, and the Capitols joined Minneapolis and Rochester in eliminating their opponent in two games.

In the newspapers, the fans read about some of the players' game-day habits. McKinney ate pork chops or scrambled eggs on game day and wore an old shirt that he had on for the Philadelphia series. Hertzberg went to the movies every game day "to get my mind off it" and dined early. "I like to go to a game hungry," he said.[20]

Regardless of these superstitions, the Capitols faced a tough opponent in New York. The Knicks defeated Baltimore in the semifinals and came in confident that they could win this best-of-three series. Coached by legendary original Celtic Joe Lapchick, New York beat the Capitols in the team's last three meetings during the regular season behind forwards Carl Braun, John "Bud" Palmer, and Ray Lumpp.

Ironically, the next home game in Washington would need to be played at the National Guard Armory. Uline scheduled the Shrine Circus at his own arena for the last week of March. The new location was more spacious than Uline but dimly lit for the 4,000 fans and players. The Capitols took advantage of New York mistakes to take a three-point lead in a low-scoring 38–35 affair at halftime. The big men took over in the second half, with Nichols,

Norlander, and Hermsen making their shots and Hertzberg scoring baskets at crucial stages. Washington won comfortably, 77–71.

Two days later, for game two, the teams played before 10,000 fans at Madison Square Garden. Braun and Palmer staged a great two-man act to stake the Knicks to a 22–20 first-quarter lead. The Knicks pressed their advantage until Scolari came off the Capitols bench and fired up a rally. With Hertzberg covering Braun like a blanket, and McKinney and Scolari hitting shots, the Capitols took the lead. New York fought back, but McKinney kept getting hotter as the crowd razzed him for his showboating tactics. The Knicks held a two-point lead going into the fourth quarter, but the teams ended up going into overtime. The Knicks won by two points, 86–84, sending the season down to a single-game showdown in Washington.

Indicative of the series, the two teams traded the lead six times in the first quarter. In the final seconds, Matt Zunic of Washington and New York's Johnny Palmer dove to the ground for a loose ball and came up scuffling. Spectators rushed on the floor, but officials broke up the melee and allowed both players to stay in the game. Hertzberg took control in the second quarter, and, at halftime, Scolari's long-range set shot gave Washington a 10-point bulge. The Knicks sent in their fast squad, and their full-court press slowed the Capitols' offense. The Knicks cut the lead to 63–62. Dick Schulz steadied the Caps, making two unanswered baskets, and the team coasted the rest of the way to an 84–76 victory, winning the Eastern Division.

The Capitols went on to play the Lakers for the 1948–1949 league championship, when the team had the chance to make Mikan eat his words. The Capitols went up against the best basketball player in the country without their own best guard, Feerick. Feerick hobbled ineffectively during the final game against the Knicks, his left leg in a protective brace that extended from calf to thigh.

The best-of-seven series opened in Minneapolis and drew more than 10,000 spectators. The first game was a tight affair. The Capitols were nine-point underdogs, which seemed accurate as the Lakers jumped out to an early lead and held a 23–13 lead after one quarter. Scolari, Nichols, and Hertzberg poured in buckets in the middle of the second quarter to help the Capitols close to within six. Mikan answered, and the Lakers took the lead into the half. They maintained the advantage throughout the second half, despite fine shooting by the Capitols' big men. The Lakers won the first game, 88–84. The next night, even more fans came out to support the home team, and the Lakers did not disappoint when they won the second game, going away by a score of 76–62.

The series shifted to Uline Arena for games three through five. Washington fans did not turn out in the same numbers, with all three games drawing less than 5,000 spectators. The Lakers seized control of the third game behind Mikan's strong play, just as they had in the earlier games. The center collected 35 points, and the Lakers held a 43–29 lead at halftime and won the game easily by a score of 94–74. On the verge of being swept, the Capitols' fortunes looked bleak, as Mikan contributed 10 quick points, and the Lakers led by 11. The Washingtonians rallied and tied the score at 22, behind 11 points from Hermsen and Nichols, and led at halftime, 45–35. Nichols went on to score 27 points, and the Capitols took their first victory of the series, 83–71.

The next game started like the others. Even with an injured right wrist, Mikan scored 18 points, and the Lakers led 40–24 at halftime. The Capitols got their balanced attack in gear in the second half. Nichols and Hermsen led the way with 13 points each, McKinney and Scolari chipped in 11, and Hertzberg's 10 points reversed fortunes and enabled the Capitols to overtake the Lakers, 74–65.

The teams returned to Minnesota and played the sixth game in St. Paul. Mikan poured in 29 points, and the Capitols could not hit their long-range set shots to counterbalance the big man. The Lakers won by the biggest margin of victory in the series, 77–56, and took the title. Although the series went six games and involved traveling three times between the cities, it took only 10 days to be completed, unlike the marathons of today's game. Two years later, Mikan's dominance in the game led to the adoption of a rule that widened the paint area from 6 to 12 feet to allow for more maneuvering by the teams opposing the intimidating big man. Wilt Chamberlain would prompt the shift from 12 to 16 feet in another 15 years.[21]

The National Basketball Association: Uline's Mistake

The team spent no time recognizing its achievements or licking its wounds. Instead, the Capitols imploded in the executive offices. Auerbach requested that Uline give him a three-year contract to coach the team. "I think my record entitles me to a longer contract," he told the reporters.[22] Local newspapers observed that Auerbach had done much for Washington basketball as both a coach and general manager who had made shrewd acquisitions that enabled the Capitols to make the finals. Uline chose not to make the coach the offer. Feerick had been angling for the coaching job and when Auerbach resigned, Uline appointed him the player-coach. Auerbach's resignation made national news but appeared to generate few second thoughts from team executives.[23]

Changing coaches has always been part of sports. Only Baltimore, Chicago, and Philadelphia had retained their coaches for as long as the Capitols during the league's first three years. Those three teams, like the Capitols, had made it to the league finals. Other teams that regularly made the playoffs maintained their coaches, including Joe Lapchick in New York, John Kundla in Minneapolis, and Al Cervi with the Syracuse Nationals. The continuity in coaching style and team structure benefited these teams, and its loss certainly hampered the Capitols. Uline wanted a championship, but, according to Auerbach, he did not understand the effort it took to win in the sport: "He was never a basketball guy. He didn't really understand basketball."[24]

Coaches enjoy taking control of a team. Bob Feerick began making his imprint on the Capitols. He traded Sonny Hertzberg for Charles "Chick" Halbert of the Boston Celtics and shipped off Kleggie Hermsen to Chicago for Chuck Gilmur. Finally, he signed 35-year-old Joseph "Chick" Reiser to a one-year contract. The swapping of these players hurt the Capitols, as they lost the cohesion and team spirit achieved on their way to reaching the finals. The degree of change that swept through the team was unprecedented.

The owner continued his activities during the off-season. During negotiations for broadcast rights to the 1949–1950 season, Uline demanded $75,000 for the rights to televise the 35 Capitols home games. The DuMont Station and its sponsor reportedly offered $800 per game, which the team ownership rejected. By the time he found a commercial sponsor willing to underwrite the airing of the games, DuMont informed Uline that they had already put together a fall television schedule and had no slots available on the nights that the games were to be played.

Uline also held on to a losing position at the BAA Board meetings. The Capitols owner voted against a merger between the NBL and BAA; however, the majority supported bringing the six NBL franchises into a new league for the 1949–1950 season, to be known as the National Basketball Association (NBA). The board placed Syracuse in the Eastern Division with New York, Baltimore, Boston, Philadelphia, and Washington. A Central Division included Chicago, Minneapolis, Fort Wayne, Rochester, and St. Louis. The new Western Division included Anderson, Sheboygan, Indianapolis, Tri-City, Waterloo, and Denver. The Providence Steam Rollers, one of the original BAA teams, dropped out of the new league.

The newfound league did not spark positive responses from the Capitols leadership. Feerick succinctly said, "There are too many teams."[25] The number of games climbed to 68, as Washington played each of the old BAA teams six times and each of the former NBL teams four times. Uline focused on the merger, prompting additional expenses. He noted that sending 11 players to Denver would cost $2,200. Two decades earlier, the owners of the ABL team, particularly George Preston Marshall, had the team barnstorm to earn their travel. This was not the norm in the BAA and NBA, although some teams, like the Lakers, did postseason tours, which included 32 games in 30 days.

The new season began rather inauspiciously for the Capitols. A quarter of the way through the season, their record stood at eight wins and eight losses. The *Christian Science Monitor*, one of the national newspapers covering the professional game, noted that the Washington Capitols, usually a power, were now the once-mighty Capitols. The offense was not as explosive as it was the year before, dropping from an average of 82 points a game to 76 points a game. By midseason, the team had won five and lost 15 games to the league's winning teams, while beating up on the squads with losing records. In early December, at Chicago, the Capitols were only in the game for the first half, trailed at intermission by 11, and only tallied four field goals during the second half.[26] Later that month, a win against a strong Syracuse team prompted an Associated Press story writer to note that, the "Washington Capitols flashed their former brilliance."[27]

The balanced scoring and team approach continued under Feerick. The player-coach led the scorers one game, and Freddie Scolari and Johnny Norlander led the next one. In January, while the Ice Capades skated at Uline Arena, the team embarked on their longest road trip of the year, of seven league games and an exhibition in 12 nights. The Capitols romped over the weak St. Louis Bombers and then geared up for the big game against the Red Auerbach-coached Tri-City Blackhawks. The Capitols hung tight and beat the Blackhawks, 65–62.

The team returned home hovering around the .500 mark. Rumors began to circulate about trading away particular team members, especially Jack Nichols. One story had the team giving up their center, who was averaging 13 points a game, for two players and $5,000 in cash. Instead, Red Auerbach and the Tri-City Blackhawks swooped in, trading Don Otten for Nichols. "Big Don" went on to average a point a game more than Nichols for the Capitols, and he was then sold outright to the Baltimore Bullets after 16 games of the next season.

By mid-February, the Capitols had endured a season-high five-game losing streak. They snapped it against a solid Anderson Packers team and faced off at home against Red Auerbach's squad. The Washington newspapers featured articles about the Capitols' upcoming opponents. They extended that coverage for the Tri-City team and highlighted the return of Auerbach and referred to the game as a grudge match. The officials dominated the first half with incessant whistles, turning the game into a foul-shooting contest. The Blackhawks took a ten-point lead in the third period, before Freddie Scolari and Chick Reiser made key shots to close the gap. But the Blackhawks, behind Gene Vance's key shooting, won, 85–81. Vance was able to contribute in the game, even though his plane was delayed and arrived in Washington late, because Auerbach stalled and pushed the start of the game back half an hour. The change in time proved to be the difference in the game, as Vance was a pivotal piece in the closing minutes.

While the loss stung, the Capitols rebounded with a big win against Indianapolis in their next game; however, a four-game skid followed, dropping the team to a record of 25 wins and 32 losses. Fortunately, Baltimore, Boston, and Philadelphia were also in the same division. None went on to win more than 26 games, so the Capitols' 32–36 record placed them in third in the Eastern Division.

The team could save the season with a strong showing in the playoffs. The Capitols faced the second-place team in the Eastern Division, the New York Knicks. The top team, the Syracuse Nationals, played the fourth-place Philadelphia Warriors. Each of the other divisions divided on a similar basis. Auerbach's Tri-City team lost their series to the Anderson Packers two games to one.

The Capitols started their playoff series at the Uline Arena against their major rivals from New York in a best-of-three series. Washington was again bitten by the injury bug at playoff time, with Johnny Norlander and Chuck Gilmur sidelined. The team needed to win the home game, because the following two games would be played at Madison Square Garden. The small crowd of 1,800 fans had much to cheer about, as Freddie Scolari hit from the field and Don Otten piled up points from the free throw line to give the home team a 45–42 lead at halftime. Joined by Chick Halbert, the Washington team continued making big shots to take an 80–71 lead halfway through the final quarter. Then Carl Braun and Vince Boryla led the Knicks with a hard driving comeback. In the final minutes, the Knicks doubled Washington's point total and took the first game, 90–87.

The two teams went to New York to play game two the next evening. The undermanned Capitols trailed the Knicks by nine points at the half. Otten and Scolari kept the Capitols in the game until the first minutes of the third quarter. The injury bug stung again, as Scolari tripped over a sideline chair and sprained his ankle. Down to eight players, the veteran Capitols could not keep up with the younger and faster Knicks, who outran the Washington squad to a 103–83 victory.

The attendance for the season dipped slightly compared with previous years. The team averaged about 2,200 fans per home game. This provided a net gate to the team of approximately $3,700. The addition of the new NBL teams again seemed unfavorable to Capitols' management. General manager Robert U. Foster, grandson of Mike Uline, informed the media that the games with teams from smaller cities, like Sheboygan, Anderson, and Waterloo, didn't have great appeal in Washington, D.C. While what Foster stated might have been true, the Capitols drew only 3,700 to a home game against the reigning champion Lakers, the team who defeated the Capitols for the title the previous season. According to the team's executives, with team salaries running to $77,000 and the addition of travel costs, Uline was fortunate to break even on the operation of the Capitols for the season.[28]

Most of the team owners of the old BAA teams also owned the arenas where the teams played. A few, like Uline, did not make money with their teams. One, Boston's Walter Brown, accepted the team's financial losses because of the income made by the use of the arena. Uline could have looked at the situation similarly, because he was already complaining about having several unused evenings in the arena schedule.[29]

Uline and his team shared certain factors with the former NBL teams that were now members of the NBA. All of these teams felt a monetary squeeze, and several played in places that offered the similar smallish seating capacity of Uline Arena. Syracuse played in the Syracuse Coliseum, which had seating for 7,500. The Waterloo Auditorium Hippodrome was the same size. Sheboygan played their games in the 3,500-seat Municipal Auditorium and Armory. Tri-City's gym seated about 4,500. The Fort Wayne Pistons' home location was the North Side High School Gym, which visiting players nicknamed the "Tub of Blood" because the stands came right down over the floor. Fans would lean down and sometimes touch or hit the visiting or opposing players. In Syracuse, fans threw cups full of Coke, programs, and even batteries at opposing players. As with Uline's Capitols, both the Royals and Pistons were subsidized by the owner's other business. Fred Zollner subsidized the Fort Wayne Piston team with the family's Zollner Machine Works, which produced finished pistons for truck and airplane engines. Les Harrison's Rochester Royals received backing through Eber Brothers, a fruit, vegetable, and liquor wholesaler.

The NBA underwent another round of significant change in the off-season. After one year in the league, the Anderson Packers, Denver Nuggets, Sheboygan Red Skins, and Waterloo Hawks all dropped out of the NBA. Two more of the original members of the BAA also folded, the Chicago Stags and the St. Louis Bombers. The 11 teams returned to a two-division format. The Capitols remained in the Eastern Division, with Baltimore, Boston, New York, Philadelphia, and Syracuse. The top four teams in each division would make the playoffs.

The collapse of these teams left many players seeking new places to play. As in the past, the league held a dispersal draft for the remaining teams to claim from this pool of players. A sizable number of each team's players were not selected. The top players for both St. Louis and Chicago became earmarked for certain franchises, with St. Louis's forward, Ed Macauley, going to the Boston Celtics and Chicago's forward, Max Zaslofsky, going to the New York Knicks. Philadelphia picked up Chicago's leading guard, who became an All-Star for the next few seasons, and Tri-City selected St. Louis's best guard, John Logan. Washington chose guard Frank Kudelka, who was Chicago's seventh leading scorer, and Ariel Maughan, St. Louis's 6–foot, 4-inch forward who ranked seventh on the team in shooting percentage.

The Capitols' Demise

The Capitols team experienced major change as well. The team's coach, Bob Feerick, left to take a job as a basketball coach at his alma mater, Santa Clara University. The Capitols leadership named Bones McKinney as the team's new coach. McKinney made plans for the college basketball draft, asking Johnny Norlander and Dick O'Keefe to work out with a few of the college players that the team had interest in drafting. The team selected Bill Sharman, a guard from UCLA, who later catapulted to fame with the Boston Celtics in the 1950s. They also chose Dick Schnittker, who received a bonus of $11,500 from owner Mike Uline. The team then drafted two of the players that Norlander and O'Keefe worked out with, guard Harold Hunter and forward Earl Lloyd. Both men were African American and, along with the draft choice of Boston, Chuck Cooper, and Nat "Sweetwater" Clifton, signed by the New York Knicks, would be ready to integrate the NBA.

World events also influenced the Capitols. The North Korean army invaded the Republic of Korea (South Korea) in June 1950. After a decision by the United Nations' Security Council, member states could provide military assistance. The United States sent air, navy, and army forces to assist South Korea. The U.S. government drafted able-bodied men to serve in the armed forces. Sports teams had a wealth of those men, and the Capitols faced having two of their newest players, Schnittker and Lloyd, shipped off to the armed forces. Following the passage of the Selective Service Act of 1948, males between the ages of 18 and 26 remained eligible to be called up for as long as 21 months of the time spent in the armed services.[30]

Capitols' management, in particular Robert Foster, worked to improve the team and its circumstances. The Capitols arranged for the Gunther Brewing Company of Baltimore to sponsor the team's radio and television coverage. They signed Don Otten, the team's 7-foot center, to a contract, after initially losing him to a rival league. The squad had 13 players signed, fully aware that league rules limited a team to 11 players in uniform for any game. The pundits in the local newspapers projected that the team lacked height, besides the 6-foot, 9-inch Chick Halbert, and also that they had limited playmakers among the guards.

With a blending of these newcomers and veterans Chick Halbert, Freddie Scolari, and Johnny Norlander, the Capitols lost their first road game against Rochester, 78–70. They opened their home season with a game against the Indianapolis Olympians on the first day of November. The Capitols ran up an 18-point lead in the first half behind rookies Earl Lloyd, Dick Schnittker, Bill Sharman, and Alan Sawyer on the way to a 100–84 romp. The crowd witnessing the game numbered less than 1,700, an unfortunate omen for the future.

Despite this array of new and longtime talent, the team won six games and lost 12 by the close of the first month of the season. Beside Freddie Scolari and Frank Kudelka, no individuals were playing up to their expectations. As a team, what coach Bones McKinney envisioned as a squad that would win with a combination of speed and accurate shooting never materialized.

The biggest achievement of the early portion of the season was the presence of Earl Lloyd on the Uline Arena floor on opening night, October 31. On Halloween, Lloyd became the first African American to play in the NBA. Soon he would don Uncle Sam's uniform. Already limited, the Capitols now played without his offense and defense. By the end of December, their record moved to 9 wins and 21 losses.

Rumblings occurred in Washington and a few other NBA cities. The owner of the Tri-City Blackhawks made an offer to the Capitols ownership in the middle of December. He said, "Tri-City has lost two of its best men to the armed services. . . . The only way to solve our problem . . . is to buy out Washington and merge it with Tri-City."[31] Foster refused to comment on the team's financial status but did state that, "We do not intend to sell the Caps."[32] The next day, Foster admitted that the team had already lost $30,000 for the season (actually over the last one and a half seasons), with attendance averaging in the low 1,000s and the average gate about $700 less than the previous year. He added that Baltimore, Tri-City, and Rochester were also below their averages from last season.

The Capitols management tried to generate fan support and interest. They tried a night to honor McKinney. They tried typical promotions, including local teams playing in the preliminary game, plus all-women teams. They also tried other promotions, such as having a musical performance between halves. One featured a local "hillbilly" singer, a style of music that was a precursor to rock and roll. These activities generally did not work well.

While the Capitols owners refused to sell to another owner in the league, they started discussions with the Heurich Brewing Company in early January. The former owners of a basketball team in the ABL turned down the chance to purchase the team. General manager Robert Foster and coach Bones McKinney visited Christian Heurich Jr. and discussed the ways the team could be promoted under new management. Heurich took the proposal to the board of directors, who rejected it as risky because of the international situation. Perhaps the international situation meant too much risk, but the domestic beer market proved fiercer. Local and regional breweries faced increasing competition with emerging national brands, and this battle ended the Heurich Brewing Company's existence in 1956.

Other groups, including the Touchdown Club, with its local sportsmen, attempted to purchase the team before Uline officially folded. The members formed a four-man subcommittee empowered to meet with NBA president Maurice Podoloff. The club determined that the Capitols needed $51,000 to continue operation for the remainder of the year. This included $36,000 in salaries, $4,500 in transportation, $1,700 in player travel expenses, and $9,000 to rent Uline Arena. If the club received $4,300 from the television receipts and managed to average a net of $2,000 per home game, then the most that they could lose would be $17,000. The subcommittee members suggested that other teams might sacrifice a player or two to keep the Capitols in business. Podoloff disagreed, suggesting that he could not ask teams fighting for a playoff berth to give up good players.

The NBA officials accepted the folding of the Washington Capitols. Podoloff rearranged the remaining schedule to eliminate the team. They quickly arranged to liquidate the Capitols' assets, as players went to new teams throughout the league. Syracuse, Rochester, and Minneapolis received the first pick of players, and the remaining clubs got selection rights based on reverse order of the standings. When approached by a group of Washington businessmen who raised money on the condition of returning the team to its former status, Podoloff eventually told them that their offer appeared too late.

Participants and sports reporters who observed the team offered several reasons for the collapse of the Capitols. Too many potential customers viewed the pleasure of seeing the team play as not worth the struggle of getting to the out-of-the-way arena. The so-called popular prices were too high to be anything but unpopular. Fans spent $5 to take a date to the game and were out of the arena by 10:30 p.m., too early in the evening. The Capitols were a top attraction on the road but got no share of that income. They never approached the same dominant team they were during years under Auerbach. Finally, the Capitols were a whopping television show and made fans and customers. When sponsors could no longer buy television time, interest in the Caps declined.[33]

The Capitols were representative in their departure from the NBA during the 1950s. The Indianapolis Olympians dropped out in 1953. The Baltimore Bullets followed the next season. Others left for bigger cities. The Hawks moved from Tri-City to Milwaukee to St. Louis; the Pistons moved from Fort Wayne to Detroit; and the Rochester Royals moved to Cincinnati. By the late 1950s, when the Boston Celtics, under the stewardship of Red Auerbach, began their domination of the league, the NBA had eight teams. They included the big cities along the East Coast; Syracuse; and a few of the Midwest's largest cities, including Detroit, Minneapolis, St. Louis, and Cincinnati. Washington, D.C., and Chicago were conspicuous in their absence.

Uline claimed to have lost $150,000 during his tenure as team owner in the BAA and NBA; however, he and his grandson, Robert Foster, started a Washington Capitols team in the American Professional Basketball League for the 1951–1952 season. The ABL remained the operation that it had been prior to the BAA. With teams based in the smaller cities of Pennsylvania, New York, New Jersey, and Connecticut, the league often started a season with eight teams and, before the close of a 40-game schedule, ended with five or six.

The 1951–1952 ABL began this season with eight teams. They included Washington, D.C., and the cities and towns of Scranton, Wilkes Barre, and Carbondale, Pennsylvania, as well as Saratoga and Elmira, New York, and also Manchester and Bridgeport, Connecticut. The Capitols team included several familiar names. The 37-year-old coach, Chick Reiser, played with the Capitols for his last season in the NBA. Old favorite Sonny Hertzberg returned after being let go by coach and general manager Red Auerbach of the Boston Celtics. Three of the NBA Capitols' draft selections from the previous year played with the team as well. Two, Tommy O'Keefe and Dick Schnittker, came over from the NBA version of the Capitols. The third, African American guard Harold Hunter, did not make the NBA team. The Capitols started well at the mid-November opening game and compiled a record of 12 wins and 10 losses.

However, the team did not draw supporters. The average crowd for a game numbered around 700, and the team needed to draw 1,100 fans to break even. Mike Uline announced a plan to run the team as a cooperative, with players sharing profits. Even with ushers and doorkeepers donating their services, the team realized a gate of $1,200 from a Saturday night game. The team owed $300 to the visiting team, $240 in taxes, $125 to run the arena, and another $100 to league officials, leaving them with less than $500. Uline disbanded the team. Eight of the players went to other ABL teams, and many went on to play until the league ceased operation after the 1952–1953 season. Schnittker went to Bridgeport but returned to the NBA the following season and won a championship with the Minneapolis Lakers.

The major professional sports had a limited number of active franchises and represented a small section of the geographical United States. For some owners, these factors sparked thoughts of franchise relocation and expansion. With more people living throughout the entire country, air travel making transportation shorter and more reasonable, and television providing millions of dollars, markets existed in most of the states in the union. The South and West lacked ball teams. Brooklyn Dodgers owner Walter O'Malley and New York Giants owner Horace Stoneham took the opportunity and moved their teams across the country to Los Angeles and San Francisco, respectively, for the 1958 MLB season. While one or two NBA owners also considered relocating, the league's Board of Governors considered adding a few teams through expansion.

Some men outside the ranks of the existing major league team owners saw the lucrative aspects of sports. In the mid-1950s, a group operated the Pacific Coast League as an "open" league that limited the MLB teams from drafting their best players, a move viewed as an effort to develop a competing baseball league. When the two New York National League teams left, lawyer William Shea worked with the group to create the Continental Baseball League. Their struggle would come in Congress as a battle over MLB's antitrust status.

Other professional sports leagues lacked the protection that baseball antitrust status afforded the sport. After getting turned down for a franchise, Lamar Hunt, the son and heir of Texas oil millionaire H. L. Hunt, led a group that started the American Football League. Like Hunt, Harlem Globetrotters' owner Abe Saperstein did not receive a franchise when the NBA chose to expand. Saperstein opted to start a new league, called the American Basketball League.

Notes

1. Red Auerbach and John Feinstein, *Let Me Tell You a Story: A Lifetime in the Game* (Boston: Little, Brown and Company, 2004), 34–46.

2. Richard O. Davies, *America's Obsession: Sports and Society since 1945* (Fort Worth, TX: Harcourt Brace College Publishers, 1994), 4–12.

3. U.S. Census Bureau, *U.S. Decennial Census, 1950 Census of Population: Volume II: Characteristics of the People, Part 9: Washington, D.C.* (Washington, D.C.: U.S. Government Printing Office, 1950); District of Columbia Board of Commissioners, *Report of the Government of the District of Columbia* (U.S. Government Printing Office, 1945), 227; Boyd and Ball Consulting, "A Historical Study of Near Northeast Washington, D.C.," H Street Community Development Corporation, July 15, 2001, section V.

4. Basketball Association of America, "League Minutes 1946," www.apbr.org/baaminutes.html (retrieved February 4, 2010).

5. Leonard Koppett, *24 Seconds to Shoot: The Birth and Improbable Rise of the NBA* (New York: Total Sports, 1999), 2–22.

6. Scrapbooks: BAA November 1946–March 1947, at Naismith Basketball Hall of Fame Library. Newspaper clippings collected by the League President's Office.

7. Neil D. Isaacs, *Vintage NBA: The Pioneer Era, 1946–1956* (Indianapolis, IN: Masters Press, 1996), 29.

8. Koppett, *24 Seconds to Shoot*, 25–30; Charley Rosen, *The First Tip-Off: The Incredible Story of the Birth of the NBA* (New York: McGraw-Hill, 2008), 211–15.

9. "NBA Rules History," NBA.com, www.nba.com/analysis/rules_history.html (retrieved February 2, 2010).

10. "BAA Finances," Naismith Basketball Hall of Fame Library; Bulletins (July 1946–December 1946); "BAA Bulletins" (January–May 1947). Published by the League President's Office.

11. "Uline Tells Armstrong Off On DC Arena Bias," *New York Amsterdam News*, February 8, 1947, 11.

12. "No Tears at This Farewell," *Baltimore Afro-American*, December 13, 1947, 15; Fred Leigh, "Capital Sportlight," *Baltimore Afro-American*, February 7, 1948, 17.

13. Basketball Association of America, "League Minutes 1947," www.apbr.org/baaminutes.html (retrieved February 4, 2010).

14. "Caps Try to Replace Auerbach; Carnevale Turns Down Offer," *Washington Post*, March 11, 1948, B5; Morris Siegel, "Mahnken May Go as Player Deals Are Hinted," *Washington Post*, March 27, 1948, 10.

15. "Caps Try to Replace Auerbach; Carnevale Turns Down Offer," *Washington Post*, April 22, 1948, 20.

16. "Caps Sign Auerbach Again; Riley Leads Lions Once More," *Washington Post*, May 16, 1948, C4.

17. Jack Walsh, "Red Says Secret of Caps' Success No Secret; It's 4 Teams–'Rough, Smooth, Fast, Big,'" *Washington Post*, November 27, 1948, 14. For televi-

sion, see Jeff Neal-Lunsford, "Sport in the Land of Television: The Use of Sport in Network Prime-Time Schedules, 1946–1950," *Journal of Sport History*, vol. 19, no. 1 (Spring 1992), 65–76, and David Weinstein, *Live from the Nation's Capital: A History of Television in Washington, D.C., 1946–1958* (Ann Arbor, MI: UMI, 1997).

18. "NBA Rules History," www.nba.com/analysis/rules_history.html; Ev Gardner, "Foul 'Em and Beat 'Em Is the Anti-Caps Formula," *Washington Daily News*, January 29, 1949, 15.

19. Basketball Association of America, "League Minutes 1948," www.apbr.org/baaminutes.html.

20. Bill Bains, "Caps' Superstitions," *Washington Star*, March 27, 1949, B-2.

21. Charles Salzberg, *From Set Shot to Slam Dunk: The Glory Days of Basketball in the Words of Those Who Played It* (New York: E. P. Dutton, 1987), 15–28.

22. Morris Siegel, "Auerbach May Quit As Caps' Coach," *Washington Post*, April 24, 1949, C1.

23. AP, Stags Swap Gilmur For Caps' Hermsen," *Christian Science Monitor*, October 5, 1949, 18.

24. Auerbach and Feinstein, *Let Me Tell You a Story*, 53.

25. Jack Walsh, "Basketball Loop Merge, Caps Stay in: Pro Basketball Merges into 18-Team Loop," *Washington Post*, August 4, 1949, 15.

26. "Capitols Only .500 Club," *Christian Science Monitor*, December 7, 1949, 18.

27. "Washington Subdues Syracuse Five, 87–85," *Baltimore Sun*, December 29, 1949, 15.

28. Jack Walsh, "Club Won't Fold Despite Being In Red, Foster Says," *Washington Post*, February 14, 1950, 12.

29. Shirley Povich, "This Morning," *Washington Post*, April 30, 1950, C1; "McKinney to Coach Washington Capitols," *Baltimore Sun*, March 10, 1950, 19; "Caps Draft Two Sepia Cage Stars into NBA," *Pittsburgh Courier*, April 29, 1950, 23.

30. William Chafe, *The Unfinished Journey: America since World War II* (New York: Oxford University Press, 2010), 108, 186; Commerce Clearing House, *Selective Service Act of 1948*, Public Law 80-759, 62 (1948).

31. "Caps Reject Tri-City's Bid to Buy Team and Merge It," *Washington Post*, December 14, 1950, B8.

32. Herb Heft,"Foster Says Four Others Also in Red," *Washington Post*, December 15, 1950, B9.

33. "Two Problems Face NBA Pro Court League,"*Christian Science Monitor*, January 9, 1951, 10; Earl Lloyd and Sean Kirst, *Moonfixer: The Basketball Journey of Earl Lloyd* (Syracuse, NY: Syracuse University Press, 2010), xvii.

CHAPTER THREE

Abe Saperstein, Harry Lynn, and the Washington Tapers

With the dawn of the new decade, several businessmen decided to gamble that the country had markets that would support new sports' leagues. The professional football upstart American Football League (AFL) completed its planning in 1959. The inaugural season started in 1960, with teams in Boston, Buffalo, Dallas, Denver, Houston, Los Angeles, New York City, and Oakland. The league would differentiate its product from the National Football League (NFL) with a more offensively focused game.

The AFL had an exclusive television contract with ABC. The first three years of the league were filled with changes: a stable ownership in New York, a Los Angeles relocation to San Diego, and a Dallas relocation to Kansas City. Despite these changes, in addition to others, the league obtained a more lucrative television contract NBC, which enabled it to compete with the established NFL for the top players.

While professional football was making inroads to new markets, both geographically and on television, ownership in the National Basketball Association (NBA) was a desirable product. Interested parties placed applications in front of the NBA's Board of Governors, and these included such figures as an entertainment magnet in Pittsburgh, a promoter in Los Angeles, and the owner of the Harlem Globetrotters basketball team and entertainment spectacle. Just as the NFL owners had with several of the men who bought teams in the new AFL, the current eight team owners in the NBA rejected these applications.[1]

The distinctions between the professional football and basketball leagues were as significant as between the two sports themselves. The NFL had been on broadcast television throughout the 1950s, and the television ratings for the 1958 title game, labeled the "Greatest Game Ever Played," amounted to 11 million households and 45 million people. For comparison's sake, the popular television program *Gunsmoke* topped the ratings for programs, with 17 million households. That title game increased the popularity of professional football. By 1961, CBS paid millions to broadcast every game across the country through a regional network system. The NFL franchises secured financial stability for all their members, which would allow for the expansion of the number of franchises.

Professional basketball lacked the type of national and regional scope of football and failed to generate anywhere close to the same degree of interest. Like professional football, professional basketball's weekly network game aired on DuMont, which as the smallest, or fourth, network, limited the potential audience. The broadcast games drew poor ratings, even after the inclusion of the 24-second shot clock to speed up offenses in the mid-1950s.

However, the league had growth potential. Its teams moved into larger television markets, and the contract switched to airing on one of the two largest networks during the era, NBC. But by the close of the decade, ratings remained stagnant. Whereas football generated a rating of 10.4, or 15 million households, basketball averaged a 5 rating, or 9 million viewers. The networks failed to make the game appealing on the small set, and the basketball hierarchy showed some limitations as well. Most importantly, the NBA had limited appeal in the country's largest markets, as New York, hailed as a basketball mecca, fielded a poor team. The other larger markets, Chicago and Los Angeles, lacked teams. The next network to broadcast the sport, ABC, paid less than $1 million annually. The fee could not guarantee NBA franchises financial stability.[2]

False Start

Several of the individuals who were turned down for NBA franchises started a new professional league, the American Basketball League (ABL). The league officials and team owners issued statements in early 1960 that claimed that the ABL was not in competition with the NBA. The ABL's initial six franchises, in Chicago, Los Angeles, San Francisco, Kansas City, Cleveland, and Washington, D.C., were not located in any NBA cities. "We're not taking any slaps at the NBA. We're in six cities where the established league doesn't have any teams," said Harry Lynn, the lead owner among 18 investors in the new Washington team.[3]

Lynn's statement would ultimately prove to be short-lived. The Coliseum Commission in Los Angeles met during the spring to decide what professional basketball team would play in the city for upcoming 1960–1961 season: the Los Angeles Jets of the ABL or a transplanted Minneapolis Lakers team from the NBA. The Jets were a new team with undetermined personnel but a notable player-coach, former Boston Celtic great Bill Sharman. The Minneapolis Lakers finished with a 25–50 record but made it to the Western Division finals. They finished seventh in an eight-team league in attendance. A sports columnist for the *Los Angeles Times* expressed no surprise when the Coliseum Commission selected the Lakers over the Jets. It was only logical that they chose a team loaded with stars over a team of undetermined potential. Most intriguingly, he claimed that this decision was the death knell of the ABL. The commission's decision meant that the ABL team would be competing against an established NBA franchise in the largest market in which it had a team.[4]

The setback did not stop the league's main visionary, Abraham M. "Abe" Saperstein. Born in London England, Saperstein moved with his family to Chicago, Illinois, as a young boy, where he played basketball in high school. After playing semiprofessional basketball for a few years, Saperstein took over an all-African American team, the Savoy Big Five, in Chicago, during the mid-1920s. They won an amazing number of games and quickly found teams reluctant to play against them. Saperstein modified the team's play to include basketball wizardry and razzle-dazzle, and he renamed the squad the Harlem Globetrotters. The Globetrotters eventually became a worldwide phenomenon, and Saperstein earned a significant amount of money from the team.

Now 58 years old and unable to fulfill his desire of owning a NBA franchise, Saperstein continued pursuing activities to build the ABL. His efforts included developing a league office, trying to garner a television deal, and adding more franchises. Each team was required to put in $10,000 for establishment of a league office and demonstrate that they had a minimum of $200,000 in invested capital. Saperstein took the reins of the Chicago franchise, and, as a sports promoter and basketball insider, he shared a professional background with a few of the other ABL owners. Vito Guarino and his stepson, Len Corbosiero, in Los Angeles, were basketball promoters. Phil Fox, one of the backers of the Kansas City Steers, was a former NBA referee. Leonard "Lenny" Litman, who also went on to be the franchise owner in

Pittsburgh, was a journalist and nightclub owner. However, other league owners had different professional experiences than Saperstein. The owner in San Francisco, George McKeon, was a construction company magnate. Harry Lynn, in Washington, shared background with one of the Cleveland franchise backers, Bill Bancroft, as both owned arenas. Lynn and Bancroft were similar to the original Basketball Association of America (BAA) owners in professional background.

The ABL strove to present a different game than the NBA played. The league instituted a series of rule changes from the NBA's version, including changing the shot clock from 24 to 30 seconds, widening the lane to 18 feet (which was the Olympic standard), and awarding three points for a shot 25 feet from the backboard and 23 feet, 9 inches from the center of the hoop. Finally, a defender could use his hands when facing an offensive player. The league would "bring back defense to the game," said founder Saperstein. Saperstein implied that defense did not exist in the NBA's version of basketball. Since the adoption of the 24-second shot clock during the 1954–1955 season, average scoring rose for all teams in the NBA. Prior to the implementation of the shot clock, Boston led the league, with an average of 87.7 points a game. After the shot clock, Boston again led the league, with an average of 101.5 points a game. The averages for all teams rose, while only Boston topped 100 points the first season with the clock, three teams broke 100 points the next year. Four years later, in the 1957–1958 season, all eight teams averaged more than 100 points a game. The average points per game continued to climb during the remainder of the decade.[5]

While a major factor, the institution of the shot clock was but one change that led to increased offense. The game's equipment, particularly the balls, improved significantly. The conditions in which the game was played improved as well, with new arenas and better flooring. Finally, transportation improved, so players started games less fatigued from arduous treks to get to the arena. As Neil Isaacs notes, the Pioneer Era of NBA basketball had ended.[6]

Saperstein stuck by the ABL product of "defensive" basketball. Asked by a reporter if there would be any 125- or 120-point totals in his new league, Saperstein quipped, "If there are, someone will be shot at sunrise."[7] Given the improvements in conditions and equipment and the implementation of a 30-second shot clock, it was unclear how the ABL would be able to create a different basketball product from the NBA version. If it did, would this version of the game attract customers? The ABL leader thought the league's teams would survive through sharing gate receipts, as opposed to the NBA method of allowing home teams to keep the gate proceeds. Washington's owner expressed a clear-eyed assessment, observing that Saperstein was handling the television arrangements for the league and that this national television package would provide the revenue that would establish the league financially.[8]

The sports press assessed the situation for the ABL. After acknowledging that population growth and increased leisure time made sports expansion seem smart, the situation for the leagues was not too bright. A few of the AFL teams struggled financially during the early years, and a basketball league thought it could compete with the NBA when attendance for the league dropped by 30%. *Sports Illustrated* staff summed up the situation, saying, "The ABL is trying to pass off its own inferior product as big league in a sport where the established big league is still crawling out of the bushes."[9]

The ABL had not officially completed its roster of teams. Rumors emerged that teams would join the league representing Baltimore, Pittsburgh, and Portland; however, only Pittsburgh and, later Hawaii, came to fruition. The additions of these two teams late in the process created a headache for the new league, as these two teams had a difficult time finding dates to hold their games in the arenas in their cities. This trouble, and a desire to give all the teams a relatively equal start on finding players, led to the ABL leaders' decision to postpone the start of the league for one year, until the fall of 1961.

Lynn had to work around this delay in establishing a Washington basketball franchise. A vice president with a national buyer for the Kay Jewelers chain, Lynn purchased Uline Arena from Mike Uline's family for $1 million at the end of 1959. Mike Uline died in February 1958, leaving two daughters, several grandchildren and great-grandchildren, and an estate of $235,000. One of Uline's daughters, Mrs. Jean Paul Pratt, the wife of a Detroit physician, ran the businesses for a year and then returned home after the sale to Lynn. Although Lynn had no experience in either ice manufacturing or the arena business, he made the purchase because his family loved living in Washington. "My main objective was to find a business that would enable us to remain here."[10] He retained the executives already in place to help him run the businesses. Lynn aimed to study the sports picture to promote the newly renamed Washington Coliseum.

The new owner also faced certain challenges. By 1961, the inner city lost 5% of its population from the high in the late 1940s and early 1950s. Most of those who moved to the suburbs had a higher disposable income. Still, the median family income in the city averaged $1,500 above the national figure. The "Near Northeast" neighborhood retained its vibrant commercial area around the H Street, NE corridor; however, almost a quarter of the housing in the section received a label of substandard, lacking private bathrooms and in need of major repairs. The neighborhood attracted more crime than a decade earlier.

The new team also faced detriments that the Capitols from a decade before did not experience. The customers the team wanted to attract had more activities to fill their leisure time with and spend their dollar on. More people used their free time to participate in sports and games, for example, bowling leagues and various card games. Others spent more time watching television, which by now was broadcasting more channels and during more hours of the day than in the late 1940s.[11]

The New American Basketball League

When Lynn met with the ABL owners and general managers at the league draft in the spring of 1961, eight teams participated. The postponement allowed Pittsburgh and Hawaii to join the inaugural six franchises. The ABL would consist of Eastern and Western divisions, with the Capitols in the Eastern Division, along with Chicago, Cleveland, and Pittsburgh. The Western Division would include Hawaii, Kansas City, Los Angeles, and San Francisco.

The draft tested the ABL's contention that there were plenty of good basketball players around. The league quickly learned that few current NBA players wanted to jump to the new league. Would draftees make an NBA squad or be interested in playing for an ABL team? Washington's draft selections included Doug Moe and Roger Kaiser, two strong collegiate players. Similar to the NBA draft of the era, the draftees did not congregate in one location for a ceremony. Kaiser was in class at the Georgia Institute of Technology when a radio announcer on the campus informed him of his selection. The previous year, Tom Sanders became the first draft selection for the Boston Celtics, a fact he discovered when one of his friends told him that he had heard the news on the radio. Could Washington sign either or both to contracts? Who else would be on the team? Who would be their coach?

Lynn consulted with Saperstein regarding a coach and took his recommendation of Elmer Ripley to lead the new Washington Capitols. The former star with George Preston Marshall's Palace Laundry had served as coach of Georgetown University on three different occasions. Others considered for the job were Bones McKinney, Matt Zunic, and another former Capitol, Sonny Hertzberg. The Touchdown Club greeted the news by holding a luncheon for Ripley. The Capitols began signing a few of the local collegiate stars, which they thought would help generate interest among local basketball fans. In the summer, the owner settled on a nonbasketball person to be the team's general manager and appointed Charlie Brotman, a 33-year-old worker in the public affairs department of the Washington Senators baseball team.

The league schedule, which came out in late summer, included several interesting features. The league would play a series of doubleheaders, some of which included a league game and an exhibition game featuring the Harlem Globetrotters, who were a big gate attraction. Other doubleheaders featured not two teams playing each other twice, as in baseball, but four different teams playing two league games. Like the NBA schedule, many teams played consecutive games against one another; for example, the Hawaiian Chiefs would play the Capitols on November 7 and November 9 at the Washington Coliseum. The NBA would schedule the two games to be played at one team's home and then at the other team's arena when the teams were geographically close to one another, such as Chicago and St. Louis.

The opening games for the ABL started at the end of October for most teams, but the Tapers started during the first week in November. The Capitols received 31 home dates. Three of these home dates included doubleheaders, with two in the first month of the season. Unfortunately, the Caps were slated to play against the same team, Hawaii, in both doubleheaders. After having home dates throughout the first month, the team would not return to the Washington Coliseum until the middle of December. Then after five games split between Cleveland and Los Angeles, the team went on the road until the middle of January. The length of time between the clusters of home games made it hard for any team to develop interest among local fans.

The Washington Coliseum was 20 years old and needed significant improvements after a 10-year dry period without professional basketball. Lynn identified parking as his top priority and provided more through leasing a nearby lot directly across the street for 750 cars, doubling the former capacity. Then he put a new face on the entrance of the arena. Inside, Lynn applied a fresh coat of paint on the walls and hung new flags from the ceiling. For the upcoming college basketball season, the coliseum had a new floor laid on supports to keep it a few inches above the arena's permanent floor of ice. New paint on the wooded seats and new spotlights brightened up the building. One columnist suggested that Lynn's investment approached $100,000. Additional proposed changes included remodeling the lobby and adding a balcony. The latter move would increase the seating from 6,700, the smallest in the ABL, to 10,000.

Uline shared with the Cleveland Arena and Kansas City's Municipal Auditorium as a place designed for housing sports. Some other sites in the ABL originally started as spaces for various events, shows, and exhibitions. The

Chicago International Amphitheater, built in 1934, started as a hall to show livestock. The appropriately named Cow Palace in San Francisco also served this function. Pittsburgh's Civic Arena was built for an opera company and Memorial Sports Arena in Los Angeles featured boxing, as well as political conventions.[12]

Shortly after completing many of the improvements, the team announced the firing of coach Elmer Ripley. Lynn sold half of the ownership of the team to Paul Cohen, the president of Technical Tape Corporation, of New Rochelle, New York, for $85,000. The move seemed necessary to Lynn, who stated, "When I saw what some of the other teams in the league had in the way of talent I knew we needed more money, better players, and somebody at the top who knew more about basketball. I didn't know enough myself."[13]

The revised team underwent numerous changes. The team name became the Washington Tapers. Elmer Ripley received an offer to stay on and serve as the team's director of training and personnel. Charlie Brotman became Lynn's personal assistant, as Paul Cohen assumed the general manager position. The Tuck Tapers played in the National Industrial Basketball League for two years. The league emerged around the end of the National Basketball League (NBL), which, as discussed in the previous chapter, occurred with the formation of the NBA. The Tuck Tapers finished in last place both years. The champions from the league's last year, the Cleveland Pipers, also joined the ABL.

The Tapers employed a unique coaching system. Their three-coach strategy featured Paul Cohen running the defense and Stan Stutz devising strategy and handling the offense. Mario Perri handled issues related to personnel and recruiting. Stutz played three years in the BAA as a middling-shooting guard. He eventually served as the primary coach and carried a reputation of cursing every other word. No other team in the ABL employed this type of coaching structure. Most of the ABL teams took their coaches from the ranks of the NBA. Neil Johnston, Pittsburgh's coach, formerly coached the Philadelphia Warriors. Ephraim "Red" Rocha of the Hawaii Chiefs coached the Detroit Pistons for the three previous years. Chicago's coach, Andy Philip, was a great player who coached St. Louis in the NBA for a portion of a year. Two other teams recruited players with championship pedigrees. The Kansas City Steers chose Jack McMahon, who won with the St. Louis Hawks. The Los Angeles Jets and, later the Cleveland Pipers, selected Bill Sharman, Hall of Fame guard and four-time champion with the Boston Celtics.

Cohen realized that his team needed to find players with more abilities to create a winning team. The team had only a few strong players, and they recently lost two, guard Paul Neumann and forward Lee Schaffer, to the

Syracuse Nationals of the NBA. The Tapers held an open scrimmage for the local collegiate stars that the team had signed and other interested players. Several of the local players seemed to offer great fan support, which would help bring fans to the coliseum.

Other teams in the league made moves to improve their squads. One of the few NBA players to join the new league, the New York Knicks' Kenny Sears, signed to play for San Francisco. Chicago picked up former Knick Nat "Sweetwater" Clifton, and Los Angeles inked former Fort Wayne star George Yardley. The Pittsburgh Rens signed former Knick Phil Rollins, and the Cleveland Pipers lured Dick Barnett away from the Syracuse Nationals. The Tapers' management looked for players from the professional ranks as well. The team picked up Syracuse National Connie Dierking to also play a forward/center position. The newspapers considered the blond-haired center a sure hit with the lady fans. The Tapers sought another player from the NBA ranks.

Professional baseball and basketball player Gene Conley had been drafted by the expansion Chicago Packers from the Boston Celtics during the expansion draft. A pitcher with the Boston Red Sox, Conley chose not to go to Chicago and instead entered into negotiations with Cohen. Three weeks before the beginning of the ABL season, the Tapers announced that Conley signed with them. The 6-foot, 8-inch man would be a key player at forward and center. The Red Sox worried that the pitcher would lose his eligibility to play Major League Baseball (MLB), because the ABL had signed some players who had associations with gambling. MLB commissioner Ford Frick stated that his office would not take any action about Conley and left the concern in the hands of the Red Sox.

Almost all major league sports professionals worked at another job during their sport's off-season. The salaries that players made in their sport were not high enough to forgo additional money. The reserve clause attached to the contracts of professional sports enabled owners to maintain control of the player and kept the player from marketing their talents to any other teams in the league. Additionally, the expectations of the sport regarding athletic condition for players were not so exacting that players needed to use the off-season for training and improving their bodies.

Conley played both sports during the same year, as did Waite Hoyt, the Yankee pitcher who played one season in the ABL of the 1920s. A select group of others also accomplished this feat. Pittsburgh Pirates shortstop Dick Groat played guard for the Fort Wayne Pistons in 1953. Detroit Pistons and New York Knicks forward Dave DeBusschere pitched in 36 games for the Chicago White Sox in 1962–1963. Charles "Cotton" Nash, who played forward for various teams from 1964 through 1968, manned first base and outfield for the White Sox in 1967, and again for various teams in 1969–1970. Another Pistons forward, Ron Reed, accomplished this sports cross-pollination from 1965 to 1967, while pitching with a variety of teams from 1966 until 1984.

In the majority of the cases, players who played two professional sports usually dropped one sport and focused on the other. As salaries increased, organizations were less accommodating with what they considered "assets." In 1981, Guard Danny Ainge gave up playing infield with Toronto after three years and moved on to a highly successful career with the Boston Celtics. Pitcher Mark Hendrickson started pitching with Toronto in 2002, after playing from 1996 through 2000 with four NBA teams. Few of these skilled players sustained their presence in both sports, as Conley did. More recently, Bo Jackson and Deion Sanders played both professional football and baseball, the former hurting his baseball career with a football injury.

Signed by the Boston Braves in 1951, Conley, an Oklahoma native, pitched and played basketball during the 1952 season; however, when the Braves moved to Milwaukee the next season, Conley did not play with the Celtics again until the 1958–1959 season. "Long Gene" moved closer to Boston after a trade to the Philadelphia Phillies before the start of the 1959 baseball season, and into Boston after a trade before the beginning of the 1961 season. He averaged six points and seven rebounds a game in his last three seasons with the champion Celtics. The Tapers inked Conley for a $20,000 salary.[14]

Both Conley and Dierking joined the Tapers without significant opposition from their former NBA teams. This same noncontentious manner occurred for Phil Rollins, who had bounced around the league, and the 38-year-old Nat "Sweetwater" Clifton, who had not played in two years; however, a few of the other former NBA players that ABL teams signed sparked resistance from NBA club owners. George Yardley made six consecutive All-Star Games. Kenny Sears had played in the All-Star Game for two of the preceding three years. Dick Barnett made a name for himself as a sharpshooting youngster. The NBA teams, including the New York Knicks, Boston Celtics, and Syracuse Nationals, sought to retain their players. The teams turned to the legal system to uphold the reserve clause, which enabled them to control the professional basketball career of the players and keep salaries lower.

The three teams sought court injunctions to stop the men from playing with the ABL teams. A federal judge in San Francisco dismissed the Knicks' motion to restrain Sears from playing. The Knicks and Sears had competing damage suits still to be decided. A common pleas judge in Cleveland granted Syracuse a permanent injunction that barred Barnett from playing with the ABL Cleveland Pipers. Boston not only sought the courts to restrain Bill Sharman from playing with the Los Angeles Jets, they or the NBA league office withheld the playoff money that Sharman had earned. Before the end of the second month of the ABL season, Sears and Barnett played with their ABL team, and the NBA franchises presumably received cash settlements while asserting the validity of their contractual agreements.

The ABL teams also had the chance to build their team through signing their draft choices. An intense competition with NBA teams for these players ensued, with the more established league winning most often. Like the other ABL franchises, the Tapers were unable to sign their top pick, Doug Moe. Cleveland and Hawaii were the only teams to successfully sign their top choices. The Tapers leadership did manage to sign Roger Kaiser, the handsome Indiana-born Hoosier who played basketball for Georgia Tech. The Tapers wanted his services and pursued the 6-foot, 2-inch, 190 pounder to take the position of the team's shooting guard. They outbid the expansion Chicago Packers of the NBA. Washington proved to be one of only a few of the ABL teams that signed their second pick, including Hawaii.[15]

Kaiser tried out with the expansion Packers. They were coached by former Minneapolis Laker star Jim Pollard. Kaiser noted that the players spent more time in camp running sprints than playing basketball, and a few guys thought they may have been trying out for track. The experience was not that unusual.[16] After leaving Indiana University and its spacious athletic facilities and then serving time under the mandatory military service, guard Bob "Slick" Leonard went to the Lakers training camp and entered the small storefront, where one secretary sat with a big closet behind her. He was told to go inside the closet and grab some gear. He found himself going through uniform pants and shirts with the names Jim Pollard and Slater Martin on them. After running, the camp turned into a battle, because guys would fight to hold on to their positions when new "All-Americans" out of college came in every year.[17]

Another first-round draft pick from the era also experienced the storefront business circumstances of the NBA teams. After finishing his college career at the University of Maryland, Gene Shue had no idea he had been selected in the 1954 NBA Draft until he received a call days later from the owner of the Philadelphia Warriors, Eddie Gottlieb. Knowing he could have made $10,000 if drafted by the Knicks, Shue went to the small storefront office of the Warriors, met Gottlieb, and received a small piece of paper. Gottlieb instructed him to write what he thought he was worth and then walked out.

When he returned, Gottlieb looked at the paper, laughed, and threw it in the wastebasket. Shue got up, understanding that this was the end of the negotiations. Later, when the Knicks played their annual Milk Fund Game against the college all-stars, Shue was named the most valuable player. Gottlieb met him and offered him a $500 raise. Shue played the first year for $5,500. Teams were frugal and players had little option, and they had the awareness that new rivals for positions would be coming in every year.[18]

The leverage in these negotiations resided so strongly with the teams that little had changed five years later. The St. Louis Hawks used their territorial selection option to make Bob Ferry, from Saint Louis University, their top selection in the 1959 NBA Draft. The team called him right after making the choice and invited him to their offices. Owner Ben Kerner gave Ferry a contract to sign for $6,000 a year, only $500 more than Shue's eventual contract. Ferry intentionally took the summer before providing a response. Meanwhile, he joined a company that had an industrial league team. The company began providing him work training and flew him out to their San Francisco location. The Hawks raised their offer slightly, which Ferry rejected, as he had the leverage of feeling comfortable working and playing basketball in their industry league. Finally, the Hawks asked Ferry what he would play for, and he told them and the parties signed for that amount. Interestingly, St. Louis traded Ferry to Detroit at the end of that first season.[19]

Washington's owners originally invited Kaiser to a country club in West Virginia, but the guard declined out of disinterest in going to that kind of place. He went to Washington during the annual cherry blossom season and was told to meet the team's lead negotiator at Uline Arena. Kaiser and the team's negotiator, Harry Lynn, met outside of a Ray Charles concert. Lynn invited Kaiser to his house in a residential part of the city, where the vice president, Lyndon Johnson, had his home. Kaiser found Lynn to be nice and sought a no-cut contract, because in his mind he wanted to play professional basketball for three years. Lynn called back and explained that he had taken on a partner and asked Kaiser to travel to New York to meet Paul Cohen. The first Jewish person Kaiser had ever met, Cohen impressed him with his nice personality. The team and player negotiated a no-cut deal for three years at $9,000 to $10,000, with a $1,000 signing bonus.

The quality of the players for the new league did not impress the sporting press. The major sports magazines thought that few players in the ABL would have made teams in the NBA. Five of the teams had standout players, including Ken Sears with San Francisco, Connie Hawkins with Pittsburgh, and Dick Barnett with Cleveland. Tony Jackson and Cal Ramsey were the two top players associated with Washington.

The marketing aspects also received attention from team leaders. The team considered linking a ticket plan to the purchasing of groceries at area supermarkets, among other gimmicks. They offered individual season-ticket purchasers a free parking spot. Tapers owners realized that they needed to generate ticket sales. While they had radio coverage, the ABL teams were also able to secure local and regional coverage for their games and received about $1,000 for the programming; however, the ABL had been unable to secure a national television deal. This was not surprising, as one NBA executive observed with its own broadcasts, "sponsors still aren't knocking down the doors to buy it."[20]

Let the Games Begin

For the opening game, team management brought out lights for the outside of the Washington Coliseum. They hired the Bourbon Street Dixieland Band to start the festivities. Miss America, Maria Beale Fletcher, of North Carolina, arrived and threw out the first ball. The Tapers hosted Chicago in the opening game, and, before 4,100 people, the Tapers held on to win the game, 65–64. Several newspapers across the country carried the game description but focused on negative aspects. The *Baltimore Sun* stated that the game resembled a comedy of errors in the last half. Unseasonably warm weather brought moisture through the basketball floor from the ice rink below, resulting in a slippery playing surface. Other newspapers noted the slippery conditions and mentioned that Chicago coach Andy Phillip filed a protest with the commissioner of the league. Although Abe Saperstein served as commissioner and owned the Chicago franchise, he upheld the result. The game earned the name "the sliding loss."[21] Roger Kaiser noted that one of the Chicago players mentioned to him while they were on the icy surface, "I always hated dancing."[22]

The good fortune did not continue for the Tapers. The Chicago team defeated them in the next game, and the Hawaii Chiefs built up a huge lead that sparked many in the crowd of 1,200 to boo and mock cheer Washington's lack of teamwork. The Tapers did come back to win the next game against Hawaii. During the first sets of games, the Tapers received scoring from several players. Warren Spraggins; Tony Jackson, a holdover from the Tuck Taper players; Sy Blye, a forward from California; and Roger Kaiser led the team in total points. The former NBA players were less productive, with Gene Conley faring better, as he sometimes reached double digits in scoring.

The majority of the players in the ABL came from working-class families from all over the country. They attended colleges, usually smaller institutions rather than top basketball NCAA Division I schools. The Washington club fit this profile, as they had nine African American and three white players who got along well. The roster had several outside shooters and was somewhat smaller in stature than several of the other teams. The team could benefit from building chemistry, which would come in time. Since he played at Georgia Tech, several people perceived Kaiser as a Georgian who might be prejudiced. He said one of the worst examples of prejudice he saw occurred in Washington. The wholesale food center of the city sat near Uline and included restaurants, and several players went out for dinner. The guys complained about an $8 charge for a sandwich. "You can't read," Kaiser joked with a few of his black teammates. "It's $4 for a sandwich," Kaiser saw on his menu. His teammates had a different menu.[23]

The Tapers and other ABL franchises faced attendance difficulties. The doubleheader with the Hawaii Chiefs only drew 1,935 fans. By mid-November, the Tapers had a 2–6 record and drew 1,775 fans to their doubleheader. A few days later, a loss to the Kansas City Steers occurred in front of 300 spectators. The Los Angeles Jets reported way under the break-even figure, and other sources viewed Hawaii as set for trouble because of overscheduling due to transportation issues.

The ABL followed the NBA's lead in scheduling games at neutral arenas in a city near one of its franchises. For example, the NBA might have slated a game involving Syracuse in Rochester, New York, or the Boston Celtics at Providence, Rhode Island. The second game of the Washington versus Kansas City matchup took place in Richmond, Virginia. The game drew a significantly larger crowd but left the team with a 5–9 record.

As the first month neared its end, the Tapers pared down the roster to reach the ABL requirement of 10 players per squad. The team prepared to leave on their longest road trip, on which they would be playing 11 games, starting in Pittsburgh. They then played five against the Hawaii Chiefs on successive nights. After two games against Los Angeles, they would play the Hawaii team again, this time in Los Angeles, before completing the trip with a game against San Francisco in Los Angeles.

Kaiser became the team's most prominent scorer over the course of the season. His jump shot helped the Tapers win in Hawaii and also one of the games against Los Angeles. Conley, who earlier in the season had missed games because of sickness, broke his hand in one of the games against Hawaii, a fact that was widely covered in the newspapers. According to his roommate on the team, it happened in a bar altercation. Conley had friends in every city and enjoyed going out, often into the wee hours of the morning. When the trip came to a close, the team had won only four of 11 games.

Kaiser (figure 3.1) ranked third in the league in scoring. Part of the issue was that the team traded away other viable scorers, including Tony Jackson, who, "Coach Stutz did not like and viewed him as 'soft.' Jackson was a heck of a player and a jump shooter with great range."[24] Yet, they traded him to Chicago for another jump shooter, who was less accurate and shorter. The

Figure 3.1. Roger Kaiser shooting over a player on the Los Angeles Jets, 1961. Reprinted with permission of the D.C. Public Library, Star Collection, @ *Washington Post.*

saying in the ABL became as follows: "As Roger Kaiser goes, so go the Tapers." The truth of this became evident in a home loss to Cleveland, when he scored only 12 points.[25]

The team continued to play before near-empty houses at the Washington Coliseum, but this situation appeared throughout the league. The Los Angeles Jets could not fill a house, even with handing out free passes. The Hawaii Chiefs struggled to draw, particularly for the second game in a row against the same team. Even the first-place Kansas City Steers did not draw well. Needing 3,000 paid attendees to break even, the Steers averaged only 1,500 fans. Several owners could not withstand the losses and sought a way out of the ABL.

Tapers co-owner Paul Cohen continued to monitor his "hobby," traveling to games in a $100,000 land-cruiser bus. Most of the team's players drew salaries from basketball, as well as from a job with the Technical Tape Corporation. Sy Blye worked as a plant supervisor, and Tony Jackson served in the accounting department, while coach Stan Stutz enjoyed being a salesman. Roger Kaiser and Gene Conley all expected to become a part of Cohen's company in the off-season.

Most of his co-owners did not share Cohen's financial circumstances and had little interest in continuing to absorb financial losses. The ABL leadership met in Chicago before the close of the year to discuss the fate of the Tapers. The Los Angeles Jets also teetered on disbanding. Harry Lynn made the announcement that the owners agreed for the Tapers to move to Commack, New York, on Long Island. The team drew poorly in Washington, partly due to the Tapers not playing as well as expected. Lynn expected to lose $50,000 in the first season, but losses had totaled more than $100,000. According to Lynn, "If we continued and tripled our attendance from here on out, we'd still lost $150,000." He noted that the team had fine cooperation from the newspapers and that the team's promoter did a fine job. The team's 13–22 record undermined the efforts.[26]

Despite the move, Lynn retained his interest in the club, at least until the end of the season. The new arena seated 4,000 fans for basketball, and in the past the occasional basketball program had drawn well there. By mid-January, the arena was attracting 1,000 to 1,600 fans, even for doubleheaders, and the team continued to lose on the court and on the financial ledger. Most of the team received the news happily, as they had come down from New York to play, and now they returned home.[27]

The Washington franchise served as a trendsetter. It began the relocation that hit several of the league's franchises during the second season. The Tapers moved to Philadelphia for the 1962–1963 campaign. Hawaii moved to Long Beach, California, and San Francisco moved to Oakland. The season concluded before the end of 1962. Some of the players never played professional basketball again. Kaiser felt disappointment but noted that, "I never wanted to be a traveling salesman, and that's what it is like, except I was playing basketball. I was going to play but three years."[28] Team owners claimed more than $1 million in losses. The league did not die in vain. Its innovations brought about the adoption of the wider foul lane in the NBA within a few years and the adoption of the three-point shot much later.

Saperstein lost a significant amount of the money lost within the ABL. When he died in 1966, the Harlem Globetrotters were highly popular. After making a few movies and many televised appearances, the team expanded as a cultural phenomenon, including becoming a television cartoon show from 1970 to 1973.[29]

The Washington Coliseum became an arena catering to the arts rather than sports. Circuses and ice shows remained regular visitors throughout the 1960s. The Bolshoi Ballet and Ballet Folklorico of Mexico appeared there. The Beatles opened their U.S. tour there in 1964, and Bob Dylan played a concert there in 1965.

The NBA remained steadfast in its requirements for a city to acquire a franchise. The city needed an arena seating more than 12,000 people. The owner had to submit a fee for entry of $200,000. They also had to have the wherewithal to cover the cost for the players that the team would take in the expansion draft and all nonbasketball operations. Meanwhile, the league continued its practice of playing games in nearby cities that lacked a team. The Washington Coliseum hosted several games over the years from 1965 through 1967, which featured a team from Baltimore that took the name of the old BAA-NBA franchise, the Bullets.

Notes

1. Seymour S. Smith, "Arena Again Costs Quintet," *Baltimore Sun*, April 28, 1960, S25; Robert Cromie, "Pro Basketball League Adds Two Cities," *Chicago Daily Tribune*, May 11, 1960, C4.

2. Mario R. Sarmento, "The NBA on Network Television: A Historical Analysis," Thesis, University of Florida, 1998, 10–18.

3. Jack Walsh, "Lynn Says New League Banking on TV Deal," *Washington Post*, April 23, 1960, D7.

4. Paul Zimmerman, "Sportscripts: New Loop Spirs Action by NBA," *Los Angeles Times*, April 23, 1960, A1; Paul Zimmerman, "Sportscripts: AFL Yelps over Cannon Premature," *Los Angeles Times*, April 29, 1960, C1.

5. "1953–54 NBA Season Summary," Basketball-Reference.com, www.basketball-reference.com/leagues/NBA_1954.html (retrieved February 14, 2011); "1959–60 NBA Season Summary," Basketball-Reference.com, www.basketball-reference.com/leagues/NBA_1960.html (retrieved February 14, 2011).

6. Neil D. Isaacs, *Vintage NBA: The Pioneer Era, 1946–1956* (Indianapolis, IN: Masters Press,) 1996.

7. Leonard Koppett, *24 Seconds to Shoot: The Birth and Improbable Rise of the NBA* (New York: Total Sports, 1999), 136–38.

8. Jack Walsh, "Washington Awarded Pro Basketball Team," *Washington Post*, April 22, 1960, C5.

9. "Scorecard," *Sports Illustrated*, July 31, 1961, 4; "Scorecard," *Sports Illustrated*, November 6, 1961, 10.

10. Jack Walsh, "Sports Arena Sold By Ulines," *Washington Post*, December 18, 1959, C1.

11. Jack Walsh, "Lynn Says New League Banking On TV Deal," *Washington Post*, April 23, 1960, D7; Richard O. Davies, *America's Obsession: Sports and Society Since 1945* (Fort Worth, TX: Harcourt Brace College Publishers, 1994), 24–41; Boyd and Ball Consulting, "A Historical Study of Near Northeast Washington, D.C.," H Street Community Development Corporation, July 15, 2001, section V.

12. "Capitols Sign Markowitz, Willie Jones," *Washington Post*, May 11, 1961, A18; "Jack Sullivan, Area Star, Signs With Caps," *Washington Post*, June 13, 1961, A18; "Golbert, Brotman Appointed By Senators, Caps," *Washington Post*, July 13, 1961, B6; Roger Kaiser, interview by author, February 16, 2012.

13. Dave Brady, "Ripley Fired, Caps, Now Tapers, Get New Money, Coaches, Players," *Washington Post*, September 22, 1961, C1.

14. "1960–61 Boston Celtics Roster and Statistics," Basketball–Reference.com, www.basketball-reference.com/teams/BOS/1961.html (retrieved February 14, 2011); "Gene Conley Jumps NBA Signs wth Washington," *Hartford Courant*, October 13, 1961, 21.

15. Robert D. Bradley, "Major Legal Cases in Pro Basketball History," Association for Professional Basketball Research, www.apbr.org/forum/viewtopic.php?t=3505&start=25 (retrieved February 14, 2011).

16. This and other details and quotes by Roger Kaiser were obtained during an interview with the author, February 16, 2012.

17. This and other details and quotes by Robert (Bob) "Slick" Leonard were obtained during an interview with the author, February 24, 2012.

18. This and other details and quotes by Gene Shue were obtained during an interview with the author, March 5, 2012.

19. This and other details and quotes by Bob Ferry were obtained during an interview with the author, March 17, 2012.

20. Bob Addie, "Basketball Begins," *Washington Post*, October 27, 1961, C3; "Petition to Stop Ken Sears fom Playing Denied," *Washington Star*, October 28, 1961, B1.

21. "Capital Five Nips Chicago," *Baltimore Sun*, November 3, 1961, S16.

22. Kaiser interview, February 16, 2012.

23. Kaiser interview, February 16, 2012.

24. Kaiser interview, February 16, 2012.

25. "Kaiser Talk of League a Tapers Come Home," *Washington Post*, December 15, 1961, D4.

26. Robert D. Bradley, "History of the American Basketball League," Association for Professional Basketball Research, www.apbr.org/ablhist.html (retrieved May 12, 2011).

27. Howard Bleier, "Taper Five Moves To Long Island: Pro Club To Operate At Commack Arena," *New York Times*, January 1, 1962, 18; Howard Bleier, "Troubles Beset Debut of Tapers," *New York Times*, January 17, 1962, 54.

28. Kaiser interview, February 16, 2012

29. "Harlem Globetrotters Celebrate 75 Years Anniversary Gala in Chicago," *Jet*, vol. 99 (January 20, 2001), 46–49.

CHAPTER FOUR

~

Earl Foreman, Arnold Heft, Abe Pollin, and the Baltimore Bullets

The Chicago Packers shared much in common with the Washington Tapers. In the last chapter, we saw the two "expansion" teams purchase their franchise for about $200,000. The Chicago and Washington teams tried to sign some of the same players. Both struggled to draw fans into their respective arenas. They met the same fate, as each team moved on to another city in the hopes of developing a larger and more interested fan base.

The Packers received the top player in the college draft for the 1961 season. With that choice, they selected the player considered to be the best of the draft, Indiana University center Walter Bellamy. He did not disappoint. Bellamy became rookie of the year, averaging 31 points a game; however, his teammates were not strong performers on the court. With the mediocre support, Bellamy and the Packers managed to win 18 games and lose 62. The team drew poorly, and the league as a whole did not see much of an increase from its 2 million in attendance from the 1960–1961 season. The power of scoring ceased to excite the viewing public.

Part of the loss of its power came from the frequency of the high-scoring game. The league played fast-paced basketball. The run-and-gun style meant teams sped up and down the court. During an average game, each team had the ball in its possession about 152 times. With this many chances, even with a fair amount of turnovers, teams averaged about 115 points.[1]

A plateau in attendance represented only one result from the public having seen this style of game in the five years since the use of the possession clock. After years of ratings near nine million viewers, NBC decided to drop its Saturday afternoon National Basketball Association (NBA) telecast. The absence of tight races for the championship, seeming monotony of the game, and constant complaining about referee calls hurt the telecasts. The Boston Celtics won their fourth championship in a row. They perfected a game suited to the 24-second shot clock. The team created fast breaks to maximize scoring attempts, and they did this through controlling the rebound and making a quick pass to a floor general, who would direct the play down court. That player could then either take a shot himself or find one or two of the team's other sharpshooters for a layup or mid-range jump shot.[2]

The expansion Packers struggled to play with this style and level of success. After drawing poorly in their first season, the team changed their name to the Zephyrs and moved up from the International Amphitheatre to the Chicago Coliseum for the 1962–1963 season. One player observed that the arena was horrible and that they were lucky to get a shower, but he felt good about what he was doing because owner Dave Trager was a warm person who made everyone feel good. While attendance increased from 100,000 to more than 150,000, Trager reportedly lost $500,000 over the two seasons and had enough. The owner sought a purchaser for his franchise.[3]

The Syracuse Nationals moved south to become the Philadelphia 76ers for the 1963–1964 season. With this move, the NBA had all of its teams in major cities. New league president Walter Kennedy took over from the retiring first commissioner Maurice Podoloff, who led the NBA through its formative years. Kennedy saw the value of television and worked hard to convince the television networks to broadcast a national game every week. Finally, he succeeded in convincing the ABC network to purchase the rights for $650,000 for the first year of four years. They would air the games in prime time for 11 weeks.

After an attempt by former basketball player and businessman Dick Klein to keep the Zephyrs in Chicago, Dave Trager sold the Zephyrs franchise at the beginning of the 1963–1964 season. Three men from the Baltimore–Washington area, Arnold Heft, Earl Foreman, and Abe Pollin, made the purchase for a record $1.1 million. The value of NBA teams had risen. Three years earlier, the Philadelphia Warriors sold to a San Francisco group for $850,000. Abe Pollin took on the role of president of the renamed Baltimore Bullets. A graduate of George Washington University in 1945, Pollin built a successful construction company and ran the business side of the team. A native of Baltimore, Earl Foreman specialized in real estate law in the District of Columbia. In early 1964, he became minority owner of the Philadelphia Eagles with his friend, builder Jerry Wolman. He took the position of vice president of the Bullets and focused on NBA relations and the Board of Governors. A graduate of

Central High School, in Washington, D.C., Arnold Heft experienced a loss of his ability to pitch while in the Boston Red Sox farm system. In March 1947, while operating a butcher shop on George Avenue, he received an invitation to referee a local basketball tournament. He became an NBA referee for many years. As the team's secretary-treasurer, he told the media, "We plan to give Baltimore a championship basketball team."[4]

The NBA Board of Governors expressed their problem with the relocation that occurred after the sale. Neither the old Chicago ownership nor the new Baltimore ownership received the board's approval for the franchise shift. The NBA initially fined the company that operated the Bullets $25,000 for failing to live up to the agreement of remaining in Chicago for three years. Upon request, the Board of Governors received the case and reduced the assessment to $5,000, which the Bullets' ownership paid.

The owners' desire to move the franchise quickly made economic sense. The team did not draw well in Chicago. In addition, they played in two arenas in two years. In Baltimore, the Greater Baltimore Committee, an organization of commercial, industrial, and professional leaders intended to improve downtown Baltimore, had recently completed the construction of the Baltimore Civic Center. The 14,000-seat arena, located in Westside Baltimore, sat near the city's department stores and shopping strips, which had been losing patronage to the suburbs. Years later, according to Foreman, the location was good, but people didn't come. The players enjoyed the arena too, particularly compared to the "old barns" like the old Madison Square Garden and Boston Garden.[5]

The Bullets became the latest team in the NBA to relocate. NBA franchises moved frequently during the era from 1950 through the early 1970s. Seven teams had moved prior to the Chicago team, and the majority moved to a place with a larger population and higher per capita income. The Bullets were the exception, as Chicago, with the second-largest population in the country, would be hard to outpace. Baltimore ranked sixth, with nearly one million residents, to Chicago's three and a half million. The median income for families in Chicago outdistanced Baltimore's income by nearly 20% ($7,404 to $6,199).

The new owners entered a league that encountered labor strife. In 1955, the players formed the National Basketball Player's Association (NBPA), and the union obtained a more generous playoff pool for players to split and increase in per diem, limits on fines, and an appeal structure during the late 1950s. With concerns over retired player's pensions, NBPA president and Boston Celtic forward Tommy Heinsohn, as well as the league's top players, threatened to strike at the 1963 All-Star Game if concessions were not worked out. League commissioner Walter Kennedy promised to work out a deal if the players gave up their threat. The players did so, and the next year they attained modest gains in pensions.[6]

The New Baltimore Bullets

Arnold Heft's proclamation about bringing a championship to Baltimore seemed premature during that first season. The team the trio bought finished with 25 wins and 55 losses the preceding season. The former Chicago franchise had a legitimate All-Star in center Walter Bellamy, the rookie of the 1962–1963 year, and Terry Dischinger, and a total of 17 players had been on the team's roster over the course of the year. Only seven players moved with the team, and six rookies started for the Baltimore Bullets. The team remained where Chicago had been in the Western Division, with the Los Angeles Lakers, St. Louis Hawks, Detroit Pistons, and San Francisco Warriors.

The owners decided to retain the team's coach, Bob "Slick" Leonard, and the recently hired general manager, Paul Hoffman. The two Indiana natives had been guards in the NBA for 7 and 10 years, respectively. Hoffman played with the Basketball Association of America (BAA) champion Baltimore Bullets in 1948, before finishing his career with the New York Knicks and Philadelphia Warriors in 1955. He coached at Purdue University for several years, before taking the reins of Dave Trager's team in August 1963. Slick Leonard played for the Minneapolis, later Los Angeles, Lakers, before being selected by Chicago in the expansion draft in the spring of 1961. In the middle of the franchise's second season, Leonard took over for Jack McMahon as the team's coach, guiding them to 13 wins and 29 losses.

Hoffman and Leonard worked closely together on improving the team. They engineered two early season deals. The team leadership traded forward Larry Staverman to the Detroit Pistons for guard Kevin Loughery. The first-year pro from Brooklyn, New York, went on to be a staple of the Bullets for years. After playing for several years during the 1960s, he returned to as coach in the 1980s. The Pistons traded Staverman after half a season, and he was out of the league at the end of the season. Hoffman also dealt one-year veteran Bill McGill for two men who ended their careers with the Bullets: center Paul "Duke" Hogue and guard Gene Shue.

The first two months of the first season in Baltimore proved brutal. The team endured two long losing streaks and found itself with a record of 3 wins and 12 losses. As one player noted, the squad lacked a nucleus of players and needed to rebuild. Still, the scrappy unit stayed in most of the games, losing a few by one, two, or three points. They won four in a row but quickly gave those games back with a four-game losing streak. The team played its best ball in the middle of the season, winning six in a row in January. In some games, with such a young team, the Bullets used a very short bench, only seven or eight players. They could keep up the energy, as against the Philadelphia 76ers, when Walter Bellamy scored 42 and Gus Johnson added 29, to lead the team to its highest point total ever, 131 points.

Baltimore ranked in the middle of the league in both scoring and defense. As the season neared its close, the team reached a record of 30–40, six games out of the last playoff spot with 10 games to play; however, the Bullets lost nine of their next 10, most of them resoundingly. Still, the first season in Baltimore proved successful. The team improved by six games in the standings and drew almost 200,000 fans.[7]

The Bullets' six-game improvement on their win-loss record ranked among the top of the positive changes for NBA teams that relocated. The Lakers won eight more games the season they moved to Los Angeles, and the Hawks won seven more games the year after moving from Milwaukee to St. Louis. While three teams experienced little change, the San Francisco Warriors lost 18 more games the year they left Philadelphia, and the Syracuse Nationals lost 14 more games when they moved to Philadelphia and became the 76ers.

The 20% attendance growth that the Bullets experienced was in the middle of the attendance changes that relocated basketball teams experienced in their first season. The Fort Wayne Pistons made a similar gain when they moved to Detroit half a decade earlier. The Lakers jumped up by 30% with their move, and the Hawks more than doubled their attendance in the first year in St. Louis; however, the Rochester Royals declined in attendance during their first year in Cincinnati, and both the Warriors and 76ers took significant drops, both losing a third or more.[8]

The ending to the season sparked Paul Hoffman and the team ownership to make a few changes. In May, the team drafted 14 guys. Only four went on to play professional basketball. With the third pick in the 1964 draft, they chose Gary Bradds, a big forward. A month later, the Hoosier pair pulled off a blockbuster trade with the Detroit Pistons. The Bullets traded Terry Dischinger, Don Kojis, and Rod Thorn for Bob Ferry, Bailey Howell, Leslie "Les" Hunter, Wally Jones, and Don Ohl. The Bullets gave up their second-leading scorer on the team, as Thorn had just completed an amazing rookie season, and Kojis could shoot the ball when he got playing time. The Pistons felt elated, according to their coach, Charley Wolf, because he thought that Howell and Ohl did not play enough defense and were too plodding. Wolf was later fired after his team started the next season at 2–9. Slick Leonard summed up the deal, saying, "I really got a lot of good guys out of that."[9]

After the trade, Dischinger made two more All-Star Games and had three solid seasons with Detroit. Kojis bounced around a few teams and did not make an All-Star Team until his eighth year in the league. Thorn never scored as many points as he had in his first year. The Pistons traded the guard to St. Louis before the end of the next season. He ended up being selected by Seattle in the expansion draft, where he played only one year as a regular and three more as a part-timer.

Meanwhile, the Bullets did well with the veterans they got in the deal, but the two youngsters did not measure up to expectations. Les Hunter played only 24 games before the team cut him after extending him a no-cut contract. Hunter returned to college and honed his game, which he showed off in a new league that started in 1967, the American Basketball Association (ABA). Wally Jones played one season with the Bullets, during which the rookie averaged a field goal percentage and assists per game slightly below the league average. Bob Ferry served decently as a center forward until retiring five years after the trade. He moved into the assistant coach and scout positions before assuming the mantle of the Bullets' general manager from 1973 to 1990. According to Ferry, he had mixed feelings but saw it as another new beginning. His son, Danny Ferry, later had an excellent career with the Cleveland Cavaliers. The veteran Bailey Howell served as a solid scorer and rebounder for two years. And Don Ohl had three high-scoring All-Star years as a guard with the team.

The sports magazines expressed positive assessments regarding the Bullets after the exhibition season. Per one magazine, "This should be the most improved team in the league. The corners and pivot are a match for anyone, with Walter Bellamy, Bailey Howell, Gus Johnson, and at least four strong subs."[10] The question mark for the team was finding a playmaker to set up that front line. The team auditioned Si Green and rookie Wally Jones for the role.

Unfortunately, later in the summer the team replaced coach Slick Leonard. While the newspapers blamed an impasse in contractual negotiations—the team wanted to give a one-year deal and Leonard wanted a three-year deal—others offered different reasons. Leonard thought the new owners wanted someone who was more popular in Baltimore, and so they selected Buddy Jeannette, the star and coach when the Baltimore Bullets won their one championship in the BAA and NBA. A few players believed that the coach offered expressions of intolerance toward two ethnic groups. While perhaps a sign of the times, the comments were also unacceptable to the new owners. The trio of owners hired Jeannette, who for a few years had been running a liquor store that he owned in the city.

The players had no idea about this change. As one noted, members of the team received a telephone call on a Friday and were told to be in Baltimore the following Monday. When they arrived, they discovered the coaching change. The game had fewer offensive and defensive plays, so coaches had less to do than they would in the future NBA. The Xs and Os were less important, as the players were playing the game and would develop the play, like point guard Don Ohl and Bailey Howell would have, or Gus Johnson with a hand or head signal. As a coach, the most significant thing was for them to make sure the players felt motivated. Still, several players believed that the game had passed Jeannette by. One thought that Jeannette had simply been away from the game too long, while another felt that he had older methods of teaching, but the guys liked him as a person because he was a character. Gene Shue argued that Jeannette was the face of the Bullets and a good choice in an effort to sell basketball to the city.

During the 1964–1965 season, the team played inconsistently. They surprised by winning against top teams and disappointed by struggling to win against several of the weaker ones. The Bullets liked to play offense, as they were second in most points scored per game, but they finished dead last in defense, allowing the most points per game. Adding two more rookies to the team and receiving strong performances from youngsters Kevin Loughery and Gus Johnson, the team flirted with a .500 record two-thirds of the way through the season; however, the grind started to get to the crew as they attained a record of 11 wins and 16 losses for the remainder of the season. Various players griped over who got the most shots and not getting enough touches of the ball. Coach Jeannette did not address the situation, as he simply felt "pretty disgusted with dealing with these modern prima donna athletes."[11] He came from old-school 1940s players.

Observers believed that the inconsistency hurt the team at the ticket booth. Attendance declined by 15,000 between the first and second seasons in their new city. Despite the Baltimore Civic Center's 12,000 seating capacity, the team averaged 4,000 spectators per game. In addition, the Bullets earned $80,000 from both the local television contract and the league's national television money. Yet, the team was losing money, and in the NBA only San Francisco and Philadelphia were in the red as well. Arnold Heft explained that the revenue did not cover the Bullets' payroll. "We would like to have a regional TV network as extensive as the Redskins had before they became part of the league television package. We already have a sizable radio network."[12] The Bullets charged $1.50, $2.25, $3, and $4 for regular-season games.[13]

Playoff Team

The team did have an additional revenue source. Their record of 37 wins and 43 losses placed them in third place in the Western Division, ahead of the Detroit Pistons by six games. For the first time in its existence, the team made the 1965 NBA Playoffs. Ownership raised the prices for the playoff tickets, scaled from $2 up to $5. As the third-place team in the division, the Bullets played the team that finished second in the Western Division semifinals.

The Western Division semifinals began March 24. In front of 5,320 fans, the Bullets fought off a late rally from the St. Louis Hawks to win by a score of 108–105. With less than a minute to go, the teams exchanged fouls in a time possession game, with Walter Bellamy knocking down two free throws for the victory. The Hawks tied the series, as they romped over the Bullets in the second game by a score of 129–105. The third game had the teams returning to Baltimore and proved to be the biggest draw of the series, with 6,358 fans in the crowd. The Bullets never trailed in the game, as all five starters added double-digit points. Don Ohl, Walter Bellamy, Kevin Loughery, and Bailey Howell all had at least 20, while Gus Johnson scored 19.

Johnson represented the team's most successful draft choice in their first year in Baltimore. The 1963 draftee, Johnson expressed that he felt fatigued at season's end. While the team traveled to St. Louis to continue the series, reports arose that Johnson was "tired" and wanted to be traded. Toward the end of the season, he was fined multiple times for late arrivals and missing practices, a factor that might have contributed to his shooting woes down the stretch. "I've felt this way since about half way through the season," he said. "So if I feel this way I might as well get it off my chest."[14]

A seesaw battle ensued in game four. The Hawks pulled to within a basket, at 105–103, with 37 seconds left. The Bullets then scored four unanswered points to finish them off. Loughery shined again in St. Louis, scoring 31 points and leading the Bullets past the Hawks, 109–103, into the Western Division finals to face the Los Angeles Lakers. The Bullets overcame a 14-point deficit early in the game, as well as a late rally, to get within two points with 37 seconds to play. Ohl made two baskets, one a breakaway off of a loose ball, to finish off the Hawks season.

Baltimore met the Los Angeles Lakers in the Western Division finals, with the series opening in Los Angeles. In game one, the Bullets came close to pulling out a victory but lost in the final seconds. The Lakers went on to "hold serve," winning both games in front of large, star-studded crowds. Jerry West, the Lakers Hall of Fame guard, had huge scoring games. The

Bullets' management looked to expand the crowd attending these games at the Civic Center. Washington, D.C., residents could purchase tickets and transportation to the game at the D.C. Transit Sight Seeing Office in the city's downtown. Baltimore won the first game of the series, played in front of their home crowd of 7,200 fans. Howell, Ohl, and Bellamy each scored more than 20 points to lead the Bullets.

Despite the team's status of being Baltimore's third team, behind the National Football League's (NFL) Colts and Major League Baseball's (MLB) Orioles, excitement grew. A crowd of more than 10,000 made it to game four. West ran up a total of 48 points. The Bullets received balanced scoring again from Ohl, Bellamy, and Johnson. With West missing four shots in the final two minutes, the Bullets triumphed, 114–112. Intriguingly, despite this success, the team had internal troubles. According to Charles Hardnett, "We didn't have a good locker room, even when we were two games from playing the Celtics in the championship. So many issues on the team. So many things happening that impact how the players' feel."[15]

Back in Los Angeles, the Lakers regrouped. They prevailed in a high-scoring affair, 120–112. The teams returned to the Baltimore Civic Center for game six. The game started well for the Lakers, and the team kept rolling behind their star guard. With half of the fourth quarter remaining, the Lakers led, 105–92. The Bullets climbed on the backs of Don Ohl and Walter Bellamy, whose barrage of buckets cut the deficit to six points. West scored four quick points, but Baltimore clawed back to within four, with Wally Jones hitting a big bucket. Jerry West forced a foul and made the two free throws, but Walter Bellamy dropped in a deuce to cut the lead to 117–113. With 27 seconds remaining, the Lakers passed the ball around to waste 24 seconds. Bailey Howell hit a shot with the buzzer sounding, giving the Lakers a 117–115 victory. The Bullet players had their bags packed before the game, but not necessarily in case they had to go back to Los Angeles for the seventh game. Money situations were tight for players so, "as soon as the season was over you moved back to where you came from because you didn't want to pay rent and other expenses in the place you stayed during the season."[16]

Regrettably, the Bullets followed the same pattern as the Capitols after they had a long playoff run. The team spent less energy promoting its accomplishments and focused more on picking itself apart. While the Capitols lost their head coach, the Bullets allowed their head coach to move into the general manager position. This meant that the team needed to hire a new coach, who would bring in a new system. It also meant that Buddy Jeannette, as the new general manager, would want to put his stamp on the team's personnel. He could do this by hiring his man as a coach, and he chose to hire Paul

Seymour. The three-time All-Star guard with the Syracuse Nationals had ended his playing career five years earlier. He successfully coached the St. Louis Hawks to first place in the Western Division in his first year of retirement. The next season, the team slipped to five wins and nine losses, when a schism between the coach, star players, and management led to his dismissal.

Coach Seymour and general manager Jeannette made personnel decisions. During the off-season, Jeannette had to address the salary of one of the team's stars. Walter Bellamy had slipped from his tremendous rookie year numbers but remained one of the best big men in the game. As one of his friends noted, Walt needed to be motivated, as many athletes do, but Bullets' leaders tended to criticize Bellamy for not measuring up to Bill Russell and Wilt Chamberlain. Chamberlain and Russell each earned $100,000 as the epitome of the big center, and Bellamy received both of these men's respect as a strong adversary. The team currently paid their star less than one-third of what the other men received, and this caused Bellamy to feel disrespected and to view the criticism he received as unfair. The leaders made the situation worse, as they reportedly offered Bellamy a decrease in salary, from $30,000 to $25,000. Unfortunately, feelings on both sides became public. Bellamy felt insulted by the offer because he led the team deep into the playoffs. Jeannette claimed that Bellamy was most uncooperative in dealings over his contract. The Bullets' management choice to play "hardball" in negotiations seemed excessive, particularly since, in October, Bellamy signed a contract for the same amount he made the previous year.[17]

Bellamy remained one of the highest-paid players on the team. During every off-season, many players needed to get second jobs. Many of the guys on the team, particularly the sixth through tenth or eleventh players, received a little above a teacher's salary. If they could not find a job, they received financial support through welfare and food stamps. Generally, the team mailed each player their contract with the expectation that the player would sign the document and mail it back; however, a player could not sign the document and perhaps get an incremental increase in their salary. If they elected not to sign the contract, the reserve clause ensured that their career in the NBA was over and that they needed to move on with their lives.

Meanwhile, just before Walter Bellamy signed, the team picked up another center. The Bullets received Johnny "Red" Kerr from Philadelphia. The 33-year-old, 6-foot, 9-inch, 230-pound 11-year veteran was once a good player, but when he signed with the Bullets, he was shooting 40% from the field in an era when big men were averaging 50%. Consequently, the Bullets gave up one of the assets they acquired from the Detroit trade a year earlier. Guard Wally Jones had made the All-Rookie Team with Baltimore and took his decent shooting and solid free-throw shooting to Philadelphia. While Kerr lasted one year with the Bullets before being selected by the expansion Chicago Bulls, Jones played six strong years with the 76ers, including winning the championship in 1967.

The escalation of the Bullets–Bellamy contract dispute in the media resulted in emerging trade rumors. The team shopped their All-Star with St. Louis, offering very little in return. The season started poorly, with two wins and six losses. The issues between players and team management were known by all. After the fourth game of year, the team had demonstrated to coach Paul Seymour another way to lose. The coach walked into the locker room and heard whistling. Without a second thought, Seymour yelled for Bellamy to stop. The team owners called the hiring of Seymour their best move to date, yet the team looked bad, as its starters appeared deaf to Seymour's instructions, pleas, and even rages. The team barely ran its offense, and its defense was painful to watch.

Unfavorably, the dissention on the team received media coverage in the sports magazines. The experts noted that Gus Johnson and Walter Bellamy had whined the previous season because Don Ohl, Bailey Howell, and Kevin Loughery allegedly refused to pass them the ball. They said that the two frontcourtmen seemed to act as if getting an assist was painful and they thus appeared to avoid it. The observers also quipped about the team's attendance woes, noting that the Bullets drew fewer fans than stripper Blaze Starr down at the 2 O'Clock Club a few blocks away. As one historian noted, among the white working class of Baltimore, the track ranked first among spectator sports. At the beginning of November, the team traded their All-Star center to the New York Knicks for Johnny Green, Jim Barnes, and guard Johnny Egan, as well as cash. Both Seymour and Jeannette made unfavorable public announcements about the former Bullet, labeling Bellamy selfish, incommunicable, and uncoachable.

The trade disrupted the team. Bellamy no longer made the All-Star Team, but he maintained his top 10 position in the league in games played, free throw attempts, rebounds, and a field goal shooting percentage. His solid scoring touch and rebounding presence led to voters electing him to the Naismith Memorial Basketball Hall of Fame in 1993. Meanwhile, the Bullets return on the deal had limits. According to Bailey Howell, the team now had six forwards and no natural center. Johnny Egan had three decent years in Baltimore before being taken by the Milwaukee Bucks in the expansion draft before the 1968–1969 season. Two years after acquiring him, the Bullets left Johnny Green unprotected in the expansion draft, and the San Diego Rockets selected him for their inaugural season in 1967–1968.[18]

The Western Division had weak teams. Despite the Bullets' slow start, they remained in contention for a playoff spot. Since only the Los Angeles Lakers won more games than they lost, both Baltimore and St. Louis made the playoffs while losing at least four more games than they won. Since the Bullets finished in second place, they had a home-court advantage over the Hawks. The teams squared off for the first two games at the Civic Center.

The Bullets went into the first game without star forward Gus Johnson and guard Kevin Loughery. Meanwhile, St. Louis player-coach Richie Guerin decided to play his "iron-man five," as the majority of the team's starters played every minute of the game, with Cliff Hagan as the team's sole substitute. Behind the sextet, St. Louis held off the Bullets, who received 38 points from Don Ohl in a losing cause, 113–111. Loughery came back for game two, and the Bullets received balanced scoring from Ohl, Barnes, Egan, Ferry, and Howell to take a 56–45 halftime lead; however, a few of these main players started getting into foul trouble. St. Louis edged back into the game and closed to within three by the end of the third quarter. A 12–1 run helped the Hawks take their first lead in a long time, at 93–91. The Hawks held a one-point lead with 2:50 on the clock. Baltimore tried to play defense, but two more buckets put the game out of reach.[19]

The teams received a three-day respite as they traveled to play in St. Louis. The first off day, Paul Seymour surprised the Bullets' brass and fans with an announcement that he planned on quitting as the team's coach after the playoffs. He said, "I don't know how to get into this. I usually don't resign. I usually get fired. I have obligations to my family and my businesses, and they come first."[20] The coach's family and business remained in Syracuse, New York. The team stated that they had no time to consider a successor. While some team members thought that Seymour spent too much time promoting himself through the sportswriters, most thought he did his job well because he knew how to handle players and got the right guys in and let them play. That Seymour quit made people wonder about the organization and what was going on.

With a lame duck coach, the Bullets limped into game three. They managed to hold on to a one-point lead at halftime. St. Louis came out of their locker room and outscored the Bullets by 14 in the third quarter. The Bullets, behind Ohl's 15 points and Howell's timely shooting, made a run to close the deficit to three points in the fourth quarter, but St. Louis responded and took the game, 121–112, to sweep the series.

In the off-season, the Bullets continued their coaching merry-go-round. The fourth coach in four years arrived and brought with him another offensive and defensive system. The organizational instability due to the numerous coaching changes wrecks havoc on teams, no matter the sport. As soon as the team lost in the playoffs, speculation about the identity of the new coach began, with Al Bianchi and Alex Hannum heading the list. The former retired as a player at the end of the season and had never coached. The latter coached for a decade, spending the last three years in San Francisco before leaving at the end of the regular season.

Neither of the early favorites landed the job, as the ownership trio and general manager settled on a surprise new coach. They selected Mike Farmer, former assistant coach and chief scout of the St. Louis Hawks. One of the first activities involved Farmer conferring with vice president Earl Foreman about which Bullets players to make available for the new Chicago franchise expansion draft.

Each team had the opportunity to protect up to seven players and had to submit that list to the league for approval. The expansion draft allowed the Chicago Bulls to select two players from each of the existing nine franchises. The two selected from the Bullets were Johnny "Red" Kerr and Jerry "Spider" Sloan. Kerr transitioned to the head coach of the new franchise. Sloan ranked among the top of the Bullets most successful draft choices in the 1964 and 1965 college drafts, so it was difficult to lose him. Sloan became a two-time All-Star and an All-NBA Defender over his 11-year career. He later became the only head coach to have 1,000 wins with one team (the Utah Jazz) and a Hall of Famer in 2009.

The new expansion team in Chicago, the Bulls, took a spot in the Western Division. This enabled the NBA brass to move the Bullets to the Eastern Division for the 1966–1967 season, joining the Boston Celtics, New York Knicks, Philadelphia 76ers, and Cincinnati Royals. Instead of playing each team in the league 10 times over the course of a season, the teams now played each team 9 times. The playoffs would now include four teams per division. Unfortunately for the Bullets, they moved to a division with stronger teams.

The basketball pundits saw the Bullets as an inspirational model for the Bulls and forthcoming teams. "The Bullets inspiration to expansion teams [rose] in five years from 18 to 38 wins. Then the proverbial shoe dropped. [The Bullets] accomplished [this] despite turnovers in ownership, management coaches, and players, [which] may well have destroyed continuity."[21] The sports observers expressed concern that the team's improvement would not continue. They moved to the tougher Eastern Division. They traded their All-Stars. Two top players, Gus Johnson and Don Ohl, had been holding out for contract changes. Jeannette would not give Ohl a $30,000 contract, believing that it was too much to pay for a player. The general manager told Ohl, "Jack Twyman doesn't make that much." Ohl said, "So what, I'm better than him."[22] Pollin secretly met with Ohl and promised to make up the $5,000 difference if Ohl would sign the contract for $25,000. Their recent draft choices had not made the NBA or were with other teams. Finally, the players had not warmed up to the new coach.

Under the guidance of ABC Sports president Roone Arledge, the NBA began to increase its national television ratings. The climb from a 6.0 rating to an 8.2 rating from 1965 to 1968 showed that the sport had gained a following on television. The contract's value with ABC climbed to about $1 million for the last year of broadcasting. Arledge doubled the number of cameras to 10, and captured the ballet and power of the game with close-ups and replays. The Bullets' ownership continued to seek more revenue. They added more televised games in the Washington market. Now 12 road games per season were televised on WTTG-TV in Washington, D.C., for the next three years. "We estimate that 10% of our attendance last season came from D.C.," said Arnold Heft.[23]

The team management engaged in other activities that would shape the product they showed to their fans. During the preseason, the team traded solid veteran forward Bailey Howell to the Boston Celtics for the 7-foot center Mel Counts. Buddy Jeannette said, "In Counts we have acquired a promising young giant who could step in and take over. To get a center with some ability and size we knew we'd have to pay dearly and we did."[24] Reportedly, Boston general manager Red Auerbach sold the Bullets on Counts, noting that he was a great center whose way was blocked by Bill Russell. Bailey Howell assessed the situation, saying, "Auerbach kinda smoked them on that deal."[25] The team had a strong center in Walt Bellamy and then acquired youthful forward-center Jim Barnes in the trade for Bellamy. Barnes ranked fifth on the team in scoring, averaging 12 points and 10 rebounds per game, but he was not a true center. After acquiring Counts, the Bullets shipped Barnes off to the Los Angeles Lakers for Leroy Ellis, who provided decent rebounding and an average of 10 points a game for four seasons.[26]

Slipping into Last Place

The 1966–1967 season became one of the roughest in the franchise's history. The team started out winning only one of their first nine games. Beat reporters claimed that the team appeared to get completely out of hand. Earl Foreman decided to fire coach Mike Farmer, who some observers speculated seemed like too nice a guy to command the respect of the team. Buddy Jeannette stepped in and did little better, leading the team to a 3–13 record.

While working with the owners to find a new coach, Jeannette, in his capacity as the general manager, traded the recently acquired Mel Counts. The center averaged six points and six rebounds in the first 25 games played with the Bullets. The Lakers took the big man off the Bullets' hands in exchange for Detroit's forward, Ray Scott. Detroit acquired a draft pick from the Lakers after the original player traded, Rudy LaRusso, refused to report to Detroit. The 6–foot, 9-inch Scott gave the Bullets 19 points and 13 rebounds a game that first year and a declining rate over each of the next three years before the expansion Buffalo Braves selected him from the Bullets at the end of the 1969–1970 season. When the dust settled, Bailey Howell gave the Celtics more than the Counts/Scott combination provided to the Bullets.

Buddy Jeannette and the owners selected a new coach with one-third of the season gone. A Baltimore native, Gene Shue's 10-year playing career ended with the Bullets' first year in Baltimore. He brought an emphasis on defense to the team, a tough task when the team had the most porous defense in the league during the previous two years.

Midseason, the new coach, general manager, and Herb Heft, brother of Arnold Heft and the Bullets' vice president and publicity director, discussed the team with the local sports reporters. They admitted that the current club did not have enough talent to win consistently. Marketing switched to making the games fun and, as did the New York Mets, promoted seeing the best players in the league on other teams. The conclusion everyone arrived at was that it was difficult to build a winning team in the current sports climate when you make money and almost impossible to do if you always lose money. The team received roughly $130,000 as part of the Chicago Bulls entry fee, but this did little to offset losses. During their first three years in Baltimore, the team ranked in the middle of the league in attendance figures. Basketball observers noted that the Bullets' average attendance was 3,100 before December 18, 1966 and 6,000 afterward.[27] Fans tended to become more interested in basketball after the Colts season was over; however, with the 1966–1967 season, the turnout dropped to just more than 40,000 people and placed the team last in the league in attendance. One former player noted that the team reached out to the community very little, although he observed that players generally split for home as soon as a season ended.

The cost of the team's basketball operations would increase. In January 1967, the new NBPA president, Oscar Robertson, used the All-Star Game platform to express a variety of concerns. The players sought increases in pension benefits and changes to the number of exhibition games and the standard contract. The sides attempted to negotiate, but in March the owners threatened to cancel the playoffs if the players did not promise to comply with their contracts. The union threatened to involve the National Labor Relations Board and to strike during the playoffs. Shortly thereafter, the sides agreed to a pension increase for players with 10 years of service and further discussions about exhibition games and the standard player contract. The contracts were increased to minimums of $10,000 to $13,000 for rookies between 1968 and 1971, and to $13,500 for veterans by the 1969–1970 season.

The Bullets' owners faced several challenges. How could they account for the increased business costs, improve the quality of the team they fielded, and increase the interest of fans? Certainly, poor trades played a role in the limited talent on their roster. In addition, a few uninspiring collegiate drafts played no small part in that process. The team again received the second choice in the first round for the 1967 collegiate draft. The Bullets choose a dynamic player in guard Earl "The Pearl" Monroe; however, the owners faced a new challenge in getting Monroe signed. Basketball players had more choices, as an alternative league emerged in 1967.

In February, a group of investors from California started the American Basketball Association (ABA). Sports promoter Dennis Murphy, Gary Davidson, and other investors had initially focused on a second football team in Los Angeles; however, the American Football League (AFL) and NFL reached a merger agreement, so the NFL's Los Angeles Rams would not want another team in their market. Murphy turned his consideration to a second hockey or basketball team and chose the latter because of his own love of the sport. Despite professional basketball's third place in popularity to baseball and football, this group insisted that sports generated money and saw a market for a second league. The slow grind of finding owners to back franchises in various cities took months.[28]

The new league aimed to distinguish its product from the NBA with a more wide-open style of offensive play. Since the NBA averaged more than 117 points a game per team, it was hard to imagine how they could have created a more offensively minded game. Interestingly, their approach was the opposite of what the American Basketball League (ABL) promoted half a decade earlier. The ABA did adopt facets of the ABL's rule changes, including a 30-second shot clock and the three-point shot. Then they added two fun innovations: a red, white, and blue basketball and, in the final season, a slam dunk contest to the All-Star Game festivities.

The league gained instant credibility through hiring George Mikan to be its first commissioner. Known as "Mr. Basketball" while playing in the NBA, Mikan provided a big name in the industry and cache to the league. The ABA started with 11 teams. The five in the Eastern Division included the Pittsburgh Pipers, Minnesota Muskies, Indiana Pacers, Kentucky Colonels, and New Jersey Americans. The Western Division consisted of the New Orleans Buccaneers, Dallas Chaparrals, Denver Rockets, Houston Mavericks, Anaheim Amigos, and Oakland Oaks. As with the ABL, most of the franchises were not located in cities where they came into direct competition with existing NBA teams; however, the owners of the ABA stated that they would compete with the NBA for the top players, including raiding existing rosters.[29]

While trying not to recognize the existence of a competitor, the NBA partially countered the development of the ABA with a continued effort to expand on its own. Prior to the 1967–1968 season, the league added two teams, the Seattle SuperSonics and the San Diego Rockets. They both joined the Western Division, and the Board of Governors shifted the Detroit Pistons into the Eastern Division to create two six-team divisions. The entrance fee for the two new teams resulted in each existing franchise receiving $350,000, money that could help them in their battle to sign important players.

The two leagues each held college drafts and drafted many of the same players, igniting a competition for their services. As happened with most of the NBA teams, Baltimore beat the Pittsburgh Pipers for the services of their top draft choice, Earl Monroe. They were able to sign the rookie to a contract, offering him about $20,000 a year. Like many of the other teams, Baltimore lost the services of several other draft picks for that year, including Jimmy Jones, who played with the New Orleans Buccaneers in the ABA; Al Salvadori, who played for the Oakland Oaks; and Dexter Westbrook, who played with the New Jersey Americans for one year. Ron Perry played three years in the ABA, and Bob Riedy played one year. The most exciting gain for the new league was the signing of San Francisco Warrior All-Star Rick Barry to an Oakland Oaks contract. The Warriors protested in court, and Barry was forced to sit out the first season. Quite remarkably, their last pick in the draft, in the 20th round, Roland West, actually made the team but was cut after playing in just four games. West was the highest-round draft choice to play in the NBA.[30]

The Bullets proved to be a high-scoring, weak defensive squad. The roster included five rookies, just as it had in the team's first year in Baltimore. After a few good games, they endured a six-game losing streak, with a loss to Philadelphia, in which the 76ers scored 20 straight points in the second quarter, proving indicative. The team righted itself and crawled close to .500 with wins like a thrilling beating of the NBA's perpetual top dog, the Boston Celtics, behind 58 points from Don Ohl and Gus Johnson, with Kevin Loughery chipping in 17 more. Unfortunately, however, another tailspin awaited.

The team lost another six straight, including a revenge win from Boston. By mid-season, the team hit a low point of 14 games under .500. Soon, Buddy

Jeannette traded Don Ohl to the St. Louis Hawks for Tom Workman, who rarely played with the Bullets during the next season before being waived. Years later, Ohl interpreted the trade as part of a salary clearance to pay for Earl Monroe's services. The guard noted that his new team ran a higher-class operation; the organization ran their team better, with nicer travel arrangements and higher salaries and no quibbling over the contracts.

The Bullets performed a little better in the second half. A few three- and four-game winning streaks took the team's final record to 36 wins and 46 losses. The record represented a significant improvement over the previous year. The team also had the NBA Rookie of the Year, as Earl Monroe won the honor, averaging 24 points and dishing out nearly 5 assists a game.

The financial situation for the team did not make great strides. While attendance regained the 50,000 it lost the previous year, the Bullets finished with slightly more than 170,000 in total paid. This total attendance amounted to less than they had achieved during their first two years in the city. The team ranked 10 out of the 12 franchises in the league, finishing ahead of only the Chicago Bulls and Cincinnati Royals. The average of 4,000 or less fans a game resulted in the three owners losing a good deal of money. The trio had to wonder, as the entire NBA garnered 3 million attendees and the ABA about 1 million fans.[31]

Ownership Change

As the season ended, rumors of potential movement of the team hovered about. The trio denied the rumors of the franchise moving to another location. A syndicate from Houston, Texas, reportedly placed a bid to purchase the Bullets. This offer came despite the presence of an ABA team already in the city and playing at Houston Coliseum, which seated 11,000. Earl Foreman expressed his interest in moving to Miami, but many of the other NBA owners thought that the city would be a poor location. That potential location disappeared when the ABA ownership allowed the former Minnesota Muskies to become the Miami Floridians before the start of the 1968–1969 season.[32]

Regardless of the Bullets' financial shape, they had particular advantages over their ABA counterparts. The ABA had three more franchises relocate, with the Anaheim Amigos franchise becoming the Los Angeles Stars, the New Jersey Americans, the New York Nets, and even the champion Pittsburgh Pipers becoming the Minnesota Pipers. The league leaders did not secure a television contract to create that revenue stream for the league. The NBA owners also knew that they would be receiving additional income through the addition of expansion teams to the league.

The owners needed the money as the two leagues engaged in a continuing bidding war for players. The Bullets received the second selection in the annual draft after losing the coin flip. Two camps existed among the team's leadership about whom to select. Gene Shue and Bob Ferry wanted Westley "Wes" Unseld from the University of Louisville, while others wanted to choose another center, Bob Kauffman, from Guilford College. Knowing that the ABA's Kentucky Colonels also sought the local star's services, Ferry and Shue flew down to Louisville to meet with Unseld. Earl Foreman met the coaches at the airport and said, "Gene, what do you want. Thankfully, we chose Unseld."[33] The Bullets second-round pick, forward Bob Quick from Xavier University, also stirred the interest of the ABA's Indiana Pacers.[34]

The Bullets made a total of 21 selections in the draft. Most of their later round draft choices did not make the team. Several opted to play with various ABA teams. Jack Thompson signed with the Indiana Pacers and Dallas Thornton played with the Miami Floridians for two years, while Ron Nelson played with them for a year. Wayne Chapman played with Kentucky.

However, the team owners secured their top picks. The Bullets succeeded in signing their top player, as did five of the eight teams that made a selection in the second round. Bob Quick played a small number of games during two seasons with the team before being traded with a draft pick to the Detroit Pistons for guard Eddie Miles. Miles played a few seasons with the Bullets and had one of the best nicknames in franchise history: "The Man with the Golden Arm."

Most important, the Bullets outbid the Kentucky Colonels and secured center Wes Unseld. The team signed the 6–foot, 7-inch center-forward to a deal worth $440,000. Reportedly, Kentucky offered the center $500,000. Like every other NBA team, the top draft choice elected to play with the NBA team rather than the ABA team. At Unseld's signing, owner Earl Foreman claimed that, "This contract represents the most attractive and rewarding contract that has or will be signed by any player in the NBA this year."[35]

This might have been the trio's last gleeful moment. Arnold Heft had been hurt by the tight money market in his building business. In addition, his brother, team publicity director Herbert Heft, had recently died. Newspapers reported that Arnold had to sell his share of the team. Earl Foreman had been the partner who exerted the greatest influence on the direction of the team, and people speculated that he would purchase Heft's shares. In addition to his share of the Bullets, Foreman already had a 42% share of the NFL's Philadelphia Eagles.

Similar to the previous off-season, outside groups also made efforts to purchase the team. A New York group placed a bid for the Bullets in early May

1968. Options about moving received consideration, as the Washington, D.C., metropolitan area of Northern Virginia, Fairfax County, had plans for constructing an area and getting an expansion NBA team. The Bullets considered the Washington area within their territorial rights and would have objected to the location for any basketball team.

Two months later, Arnold Heft leaked information about negotiations among the trio. Heft said one of the owners would be in Baltimore to run the club. He claimed that the remaining partner would make a good profit if the sale was completed. In addition, he noted that the sale would eliminate the disagreement among the owners. Earl Foreman and Abe Pollin reportedly disagreed over the team's future location. Baltimore provided some concessions when the team originally moved there, so Foreman claimed that the team owed the city to not forget that help. Pollin felt disgust over the team's limited fan support in Baltimore. When Foreman signed the team up for a lease renewal at the Civic Center, Pollin expressed his outrage. Pollin bought out Foreman and Heft for $900,000, $400,000 more than the original $500,000 investment. Heft needed the money, and Foreman chose to opt out for the money, although he said it was ironic that Pollin bought them out because Pollin was the one who first wanted to sell his share of the team.[36]

Pollin established that few things would remain the same. The Bullets signed up for three years at the Civic Center for $1,000 a game, $100 more than their last contract with the arena. The newly solo owner declared that, "The Bullets are here to stay in Baltimore," and that, "The image of the Bullets as a losing and lackadaisical organization on the court and at the box office—all that is over with. Starting today, it's going to be a successful organization."[37]

Pollin quickly revealed what he had in mind for changes. He fired several of the main administrative employees, including the team controller, ticket manager, public relations man, and head scout. His biggest decision came shortly thereafter, as he fired general manager Buddy Jeannette. In Pollin's opinion, Jeannette did not fit the total qualifications that were necessary for a general manager to make the Baltimore Bullets a big-league franchise.

The new sole owner needed to put his organization together quickly, as the season was only two months away. Pollin opted to retain Gene Shue as the team's coach. Within a week of firing Buddy Jeannette, Pollin hired a new general manager, Jerry Sachs, formerly a public relations director for the Baltimore Orioles of MLB. Other things remained outside of his control. The addition of two more new franchises in Milwaukee and Phoenix created two seven-team divisions, from which four teams made the playoffs. Together, the teams provided $4 million for the existing teams to split for their entry fees. The ABA continued to remain a nuisance, and, for Pollin, that presence would soon be too close for comfort.[38]

Notes

1. Jerry Mittleman, "Has NBA Shooting Really Gone South," InsideHoops, www.insidehoops.com/shooting-121503.shtml (retrieved January 13, 2010).

2. Mario R. Sarmento, "The NBA on Network Television: A Historical Analysis," Thesis, University of Florida, 1998, 15–36.

3. This and other details and quotes by Charles Hardnett were obtained during an interview with the author, February 24, 2012.

4. Mark Asher, "New Owners Keep Bullets In Baltimore," *Washington Times Herald*, November 24, 1964, D2.

5. This and other details and quotes by Don Ohl were obtained during an interview with the author, February 26, 2012; this and other details and quotes by Earl Foreman were obtained during an interview with the author, May 4, 2011.

6. Alan Goldstein, "Bullet Sale May Be Near," *Baltimore Sun*, October 16, 1964, 22; Bob Maisel, "The Morning After," *Baltimore Sun*, November 24, 1964, S21.

7. 1963–64 Baltimore Bullets Roster and Statistics," Basketball-Reference.com, www.basketball-reference.com/teams/BAL/1964.html (retrieved October 10, 2010).

8. Frank P. Jozsa and John J. Guthrie, *Relocation Teams and Expanding Leagues in Professional Sports: How the Major Leagues Respond to Market Conditions* (Westport, CT: Greenwood, 1999), 34–40.

9. This and other details and quotes by Bailey Howell were obtained during an interview with the author, February 23, 2012; this and other details and quotes by Robert (Bob) "Slick" Leonard were obtained during an interview with the author, February 24, 2012.

10. "The Pack Closes in on Boston," *Sports Illustrated*, October 26, 1964, 50.

11. Bailey Howell interview, February 23, 2012.

12. Dave Brady, "Pleased Bullets' Officials Plan More TV Exposure," *Washington Post*, March 26, 1965, D4.

13. "Bullets Trade 3 for Five Pistons," *Washington Post*, June 10, 1964, D4.

14. Bill Gildea, "'Tired' Johnson Wants to Be Traded by Bullets," *Washington Post*, March 30, 1965, C3.

15. Charles Hardnett interview, February 24, 2012.

16. This and other details and quotes by Bob Ferry were obtained during an interview with the author, February 24, 2012.

17. "Bullets Trade Walt Bellamy," *Chicago Daily Defender*, November , 1965, 8; A.S. Doc Young, "Good Morning Sports," *Chicago Daily Defender*, November 10, 1965.

18. "A Round-up of Sports Information of the Week," *Sports Illustrated*, May 17, 1965, 110; Mark Kram, "Lost Bullets in Disasterville," *Sports Illustrated*, November 8, 1965, 26.

19. "Hawks Whip Bullets," *Washington Post*, March 28, 1966, D1; "WTTG Plans Carrying 12 Bullets Games' on TV,"*Washington Post*, May 17, 1966, D3.

20. Alan Goldstein, "Bullet Post Still Open," *Baltimore Sun*, April 10, 1966, A-7; "Paul Seymour Quits; Bullets, Celtics One Game Away from Elimination,"*Washington Post*, March 29, 1966, C2.

21. "Scouting Reports," *Sports Illustrated*, October 24, 1966, 40.

22. Ohl interview, February 26, 2012.

23. "WTTG Plans Carrying 12 Bullets Games on TV," *Washington Post*, May 17, 1966, D3.

24. "Bullets Get Mel Counts for Howell," *Washington Post*, September 2, 1966, E4.

25. Howell interview, February 23, 2012.

26. Bob Maisel, "The Morning After," *Baltimore Sun*, January 6, 1967, C1.

27. "Scouting Reports," *Sports Illustrated*, October 24, 1966, 40.

28. Terry Pluto, *Loose Balls: The Short, Wild Life of the American Basketball Association* (New York: Simon & Schuster, 1990).

29. Peter Carry, "Having a Ball with the ABA," *Sports Illustrated*, March 18, 1974, 34; Frank Deford, "The Last Hurrah in Hyannis," *Sports Illustrated*, June 28, 1976, 64.

30. "Noon Today Is Deadline for NBA Row," *Washington Post*, March 14, 1967, D1; Hardnett, interview, February 24, 2012.

31. "1967–68 Baltimore Bullets Roster and Statistics," Basketball-Reference.com, www.basketball-reference.com/teams/BAL/1964.html (retrieved October 10, 2010).

32. Seymour S. Smith, "Westley Unseld of Louiville Signs Rich Contract With Bullets," *Baltimore Sun*, April 19, 1968, C1; Alan Goldstein, "Offers Made For Bullets," *Baltimore Sun*, May 12, 1968, A1; Alan Goldstein, "Houston Syndicate Bidding for Bullets," *Baltimore Sun*, June 2, 1968, SP4.

33. "Bullets Sign Unseld, Claim Contract Tops Hayes' $440,000 at San Diego," *Washington Post*, April 19, 1968, D4.

34. Ohl interview, February 26, 2012; Foreman interview, May 4, 2011; Gene Shue, interview by author, March 5, 2012.

35. Seymour S. Smith, "Westley Unseld of Louiville Signs Rich Contract with Bullets," *Baltimore Sun*, April 19, 1968, C1; Alan Goldstein, "Heft Looks, but Can't Find Any Takers for Bullets," *Baltimore Sun*, June 30, 1968, A6.

36. *"Bullets' Stock Sale Near Final Stages," Chicago Daily Defender*, July 18, 1968, 41; Alan Goldstein, "Bullets Sign LeRoy Ellis to Three-Year Contract," *Baltimore Sun*, August 17, 1968, B1.

37. Seymour S. Smith, "Pollin in Sole Charge of Bullets," *Baltimore Sun*, July 24, 1968, C5.

38. Edward Kiersh, "The Two Faces of Abe: Both Sides of Washington's Legendary Sports Impresario," *Regardie's Magazine*, 10 (March 1990), 66, www.accessmylibrary.com/article-1G1-8986101/two-faces-abe-both.html (retrieved September 12, 2011).

CHAPTER FIVE

Earl Foreman and the Fourth Washington Capitols

The American Basketball Association (ABA) finished its inaugural season with the Pittsburgh Pipers winning its first championship behind former American Basketball League (ABL) star Connie Hawkins. The ABA then resumed its competition with the National Basketball Association (NBA) teams for signing the best of the collegiate basketball players, as well as raiding the NBA teams for stars. The biggest star to leave the older league's orbit was former San Francisco Warrior Rick Barry. Barry completed his mandatory one-year ban from playing professional basketball and then suited up for the team across the Bay, the Oakland Oaks, as the league began its second season.

Oakland topped the six-team Western Division, with a 60–18 record. They finished 14 games in front of the second-place New Orleans Buccaneers. The team had five winning streaks of six games, including a 16-game streak that lasted nearly two months. Barry ranked fourth on the team in scoring because he played in less than half of the team's games due to injury. The team's leading scorer, Warren Armstrong (later Warren Jabali), opted to sign with the Oaks rather than the Knicks. Doug Moe, the second-leading scorer, was originally a draft choice of the ABL's Washington Tapers. Third-place scorer Gary Bradds played two seasons with the Bullets before they let him go.[1]

The Oaks excelled at the ABA's supposedly "wide-open" offense. Despite the claim, the NBA teams averaged only 2½ fewer points per game than their ABA counterparts (114.8 to 112.3) and shot more accurately from the floor (44.1 percent to 43.6 percent). Perhaps the proponents of the NBA style of game offered a more accurate description of the ABA product, referring to the ABA game as a more "unscripted" style of basketball. The ABA displayed more running and wide-open offenses, with less-physical defenses. In comparison, the NBA used the more traditional plays on offense, like the pick-and-roll and cut-and-screen. On defense, players in the older league often used a grab-and-hold style of play, where ABA players were looser in coverage and less clogged in the foul lanes. The ability to shoot the three-point basket offered more room to all pure shooters, including shorter guards, like the Oaks' Larry Brown, who is now renowned for his 30 years as a coach in college and professional basketball, including his induction into the Hall of Fame in 2002.

The Oaks squeaked past the Denver Rockets in the Western Division semifinals in a seven-game series. They swept New Orleans in four games to win the division finals. Meanwhile, in the Eastern Division, the regular-season champion Indiana Pacers defeated the Kentucky Colonels in seven games and then Miami for the right to face Oakland for the league championship. The Oaks defeated the Pacers for the title in five hard-fought games.[2]

While the ABA drew nearly 1.5 million fans, several teams struggled financially. The high cost of the players and operations, combined with the low ticket prices, made long-term sustainability of the teams in the league difficult. Indeed, according to Indiana Pacers' owner Dick Tinkham, the league's goal was to force a merger with the NBA. After the second season, this had not happened, nor had they obtained the television contract they needed to generate revenue. The team owners hired CBS director of sports Jack Dolph as the league's new commissioner with hopes of getting the league on television.[3]

After the second year of operation, the league added a franchise in Carolina, which created a six-team Eastern Division. In the Western Division, the Houston Mavericks were sold to North Carolina businessman Jim Gardner, who moved the team to Carolina. The owners of the championship Oaks team faced financial difficulties. Owned in part by singer-entertainer Pat Boone, the team took on a great deal of debt to make it function. The proximity to the San Francisco Warriors of the NBA also hurt the team's efforts at drawing fans. They averaged about 2,800 per game, significantly below the 4,000 to 5,000 necessary to break even. Having accumulated a debt of about $1.4 million, the owners sought to sell the franchise before the Bank of America foreclosed on the operation to get its $1.2 million.

Former Baltimore Bullets coowner Earl Foreman reportedly had an interest in bidding for the majority share of the National Football League's (NFL) Philadelphia Eagles after the conclusion of the 1968–1969 season.

Majority owner Jerry Wolman needed to sell his holdings as a result of his own indebtedness. When businessman Leonard Tose won the team's shares with a bid of more than $16 million, Foreman accepted his share. Shortly thereafter, Foreman received a phone call gauging his interest in investing in an ABA franchise.

Purchasing the Oakland Oaks

In the late summer of 1969, Earl Foreman and business partner Tom Shaheen put in a bid to purchase the Oakland Oaks for $2.5 million. As the new owner later described in a book on the ABA, buying the Oakland franchise was a great business deal for him, and it did not cost him a cent. In an interview, he explained that he actually made money with his 75% share. While preparing to maintain the team, Foreman also knew that he would move them to his adopted hometown of Washington, D.C. This new Washington franchise, like eight other franchises in the ABA, would experience a change in ownership. The new Washington owner knew that his relocation would violate the "territorial rights" of his former team, the Baltimore Bullets. He viewed that sticking point as a key to getting him a NBA franchise.

The other ABA owners realized that the Washington move would create friction with the Bullets. Foreman's action would halt the possibility of the NBA–ABA merger. Foreman told the owners that he must be able to move the team to Washington or he would back out of the Oakland purchase. The NBA had offered a merger that would have enabled five or six of the current ABA teams to enter the NBA at a cost of $1 million apiece. Foreman convinced the other ABA owners that they should not "play dead for the NBA, to swallow the offer like lambs sacrificed up for the kill." Moving the team to Washington would give the ABA a better bargaining position he argued, and the others agreed.[4]

The new Washington owner won that battle; however, the other owners did the new owner and his team a disservice. Because more teams existed in the Eastern Division than the Western Division, the ABA opted to keep the new Washington team in the Western Division. This created a scheduling and logistical nightmare for the team and other league members.

The new owner faced extensive works on both coasts. A few key members of the Oakland Oaks did not want to continue to be associated with the team. Coach Alex Hannum balked at the prospect of heading east to Washington, D.C., so he quit the team. One of the guards, Doug Moe (who had been drafted by the Washington Capitols/Tapers of the ABL), also switched teams rather than play for Washington. The team's superstar, Rick Barry, also did not want to leave the Bay area. Foreman visited with Barry and tried to woo him to stay with the team. Barry insisted that his contract, which had two years remaining, allowed him to quit the team if it relocated. Barry negotiated with his first team, the San Francisco Warriors of the NBA, and signed a five-year contract to join the other league. Foreman sought redress in court, planning to sue Barry, the Warriors, and the NBA for $10 million in damages, while obtaining a temporary restraining order preventing Barry from playing with the Warriors.

Despite the legal issues, Foreman worked to address other areas of team needs. The owner changed the name of the team from the Oaks to the Capitols. The name intentionally harked back to the team that played in the early years of the Basketball Association of America/National Basketball Association. Foreman hired Al Bianchi as his team's new coach for the 1969–1970 season. The former guard for Syracuse and Philadelphia for 10 seasons was a scrappy player who began his coaching career with the expansion Seattle SuperSonics two years earlier. He left to join the Capitols after amassing a 53–111 record during the course of two seasons.[5]

Foreman also added personnel to the team. The club signed a few of its top draft choices, including Jack Gillespie, Ron Taylor, Bill Bowes, Joe Cromer, and George Tinsley. Unfortunately, Gillespie played for New Jersey in the ABA, and Bowes and Cromer did not make the team. In addition, the Capitols received Garfield Smith, who would soon be released from the armed forces. Al Bianchi reached out to a sportswriter friend, who told the coach that Roland "Fatty" Taylor tried out with the Philadelphia 76ers but was released prior to the season due to roster constraints. Bianchi called Taylor and invited him down to Washington and signed him after a few tryouts with the team. Foreman announced a major signing, inking big-name guard and Washington native Dave Bing to a contract for the 1971–1972 season. The Washington Capitols, like other ABA teams, raided the NBA for established stars. As Oakland did with Rick Barry and Carolina did with Billy Cunningham, Washington signed Bing before his contract ran out with the NBA. This prevented Bing from playing immediately, so they would have to wait to actually benefit from the player's services.[6]

The Capitols' team faced a schedule unlike any other team in the ABA. Since they were a team on the East Coast playing against teams in the Western Division, the travel burden was enormous. Most of the teams in the ABA played 41 of their 84 games on their home courts, with two or three games slated for a neutral site to promote the game in a nearby state or big city. The Washington Capitols played only 31 games on their home court in Washington, D.C. They played 40 games at the opponents' arena, and the remaining 13 games were played at "neutral" locations. The Capitols neutral games did not happen in neighboring Delaware or York, Pennsylvania. They happened in places including Los Angeles, California; Wichita, Kansas; and Albuquerque, New Mexico. Unfortunately, these neutral locations often had little to do with where the team had played its previous game or where the team would be playing its next game.

The Capitols' owner needed to make arrangements for the team's home court. The choices involved two existing arenas and a couple that were expected to be built in the near future. Reports immediately leaked that Foreman had spoken with Ted Lerner, who would ultimately buy a Major League Baseball (MLB) franchise in 2005, about the latter's progress on his $20 million arena and convention center in neighboring Oxen Hill, Maryland. This arena had originally been slated to be completed in the fall of 1971. Foreman soon learned that additional delays would bump the project back a year.[7]

The Capitols' owner received another jolt from Congress. A subcommittee on the House of Representatives' District Committee conducted hearings on the possibility of building the Dwight D. Eisenhower Memorial Arena. The plan would have destroyed the existing area around the Mount Vernon neighborhood in downtown D.C. Foreman offered one of many positive testimonies to the House. The bill's sponsor, Representative Joel Broyhill (R-Virginia), agreed with Dr. Leslie Glasgow, assistant secretary of the interior, that a one-year study to determine economic feasibility would be in order.

Foreman realized that he faced two alternatives, using the D.C. Armory or the Washington Coliseum, the 50-year-old former home of the original Washington Capitols and the Washington Tapers. The armory held fewer spectators than the coliseum but had a location near RFK Stadium, placing it within the city's main sporting orbit. The stadium/armory complex also offered easy access for suburbanites coming from areas in Maryland and Virginia. Foreman also said the D.C. Armory was "out front" as the site for the team's home games, despite scheduling issues. Unfortunately, armory manager Dutch Bergman stated that the Capitols could not be fit in to the D.C. Armory's schedule. The arena was clogged during the upcoming basketball season with various exhibitions, including auto, health, boat, and flower shows.

The Washington Coliseum appeared to be the Capitols last option. Foreman started talks with the arena's owner, Harry Lynn. As noted in chapter three, Lynn made some refurbishing efforts on the building in the beginning of the decade; however, the area around the coliseum had rapidly declined. With obsolete and substandard housing and a commercial decline as residential blockbusting occurred, both residents and businesses experienced devastation from the three days of looting, arson, and vandalism that occurred after the assassination of Dr. Martin Luther King Jr. in April 1968. The total population in Washington, D.C., had dropped only 7,500 people since 1960, but 135,000 white residents, many with significant disposable incomes, left the city. Even worse, many perceived the city as being dilapidated and dangerous to visit.[8]

The Capitols accepted the circumstances and arranged to play at the coliseum. The arena received criticism from locals for being in a bad area, with inadequate policing, lighting, and parking. Indeed, off-street parking at the coliseum could accommodate little more than 500 cars. The owner addressed some of these concerns, arranging a deal with the department store Woodward & Lothrop to use its parking lot within two blocks of stadium, which could handle 300 cars and was well-lighted. The team investigated the possibility of providing bus service to the arena from parking areas at Catholic University, Carter Barron, RFK Stadium, and American University.[9]

As the season neared, the Capitols began promoting the Washington Coliseum as a safe environment for fans. The team arranged for free shuttle buses from 10 locations to a new parking lot less than two blocks from the coliseum. The Metropolitan Police offered protection similar to that at RFK Stadium. The District of Columbia Government added their assistance by starting general improvements in the vicinity of the coliseum, including improved lighting, roadway repairs, and a sidewalk on the west side of Third Street between Florida Avenue and M Street, NE. Foreman also made attempts to improve the conditions of the locker rooms for the two teams and referees. He asked Harry Lynn for improvements. Lynn looked at him with a cigar in his mouth and stated, "Kid, you got four walls—that's what I give you, that's what you got."[10]

The Washington Coliseum shared many characteristics with other ABA arenas. The locations had small seating capacities and proved to be second-rate arenas. Denver played in an arena constructed as an auditorium in 1908, while Louisville's 6,000-seat multipurpose armory opened in 1905. The New York Nets moved into the 4,000-seat Long Island Arena that the Washington–New York Tapers of the American Basketball League had called home in 1962. One Capitol noted that they needed to use blankets on the bench to keep themselves warm during games in Long Island. In the case of Miami, some games took place in the Dinner Key Auditorium, the name for two airplane hangers. The players offered a split decision on the coliseum, remembering it as okay, or decent, but with condensation coming up from the ice rink at times during practices. Coach Bianchi stated, "Our schedule saved us from the coliseum, while the travel killed us."[11]

Before the new season began, the leadership of the two leagues conversed about a potential merger. Now, the ABA owners responded with a change of attitude, "as if the doves became hawks," former owner Ken Davidson noted.[12] The owners appeared to be looking forward to the beginning of their third season rather than seeking a way out. NBA president Walter Kennedy led the break off of the meetings, saying, "The NBA does not contemplate having further meetings with the ABA."[13] The new Washington franchise sat at the center of the dispute, its location in Baltimore's territorial area, combined with its insistence on keeping Rick Barry, demonstrating in the minds of NBA officials that the ABA was not negotiating in good faith.[14]

The NBA owners apparently held differences of opinion on how to deal with the upstart league. Two weeks later, NBA officials returned to meeting with their ABA counterparts and made a merger offer. The conditions included a merger with 10 of the ABA's 11 teams, with Washington being bought out of existence. Foreman was set to receive more than the reported $2.6 million he paid for the purchase of the Oakland Oaks. Three of the NBA's most powerful franchises, New York, Philadelphia, and Los Angeles, pushed for a merger before the season began. The ABA owners had received the better deal that Foreman had promised, but it was not consummated. The two leagues began their respective 1969–1970 seasons in October.

Local newspaper columnists offered their opinions on the new team's possibility for success. Long-time columnist for the *Washington Post*, Bob Addie, noted that the city had failed to support two basketball teams in the past. Addie figured that Foreman must be gambling on losing money or struggling to break even while awaiting the construction of a new arena or for a merger between the two leagues.[15] An editorial page commentary called Washington a basketball town and argued that the city was becoming a place looking for the best in sports. The thought was that the Capitols should have no trouble capturing the same fans who support the Senators and Redskins. Foreman agreed, noting that the Capitols were a championship team and that basketball was a fast-growing sport. The owner offered a prediction that, "we will outdraw at least 50% of the NBA teams. I think Washington is that good a sports town." The team's tickets sold from $2 to $5 at the gate, and Foreman aimed to fix the basic problem of getting people in the community to come to games and see how the coliseum had been made a safer place.[16]

Newspapers and special interest sports magazines alike offered their predictions for all professional sports leagues before the beginning of the seasons. Newspapers ranging from the *New York Times* to the *Washington Post* wrote brief articles projecting the ABA winners in each division. Both thought that the Capitols would not fare as well as the Oaks. The article in

Sports Illustrated described the competition in the league as stimulating and second best. Oakland was described as too good for the rest of the league, so the probable decline in fortunes for the team relocated in Washington was viewed as fine for the league. The Denver Rockets were viewed as a potential threat to the Caps winning the Western Division.

The Season Begins

The team opened up with a game at the coliseum on Saturday, October 18, 1969. The crowd of 3,400 witnessed a close game for three quarters. The Caps committed a large number of turnovers, but the strong play of Rick Barry and Warren Armstrong kept the team in the game for the first half. Bench scoring from guard Mike Barrett enabled the team to pull away from the New Orleans Buccaneers late for the win, 110–104. The squad hit the road and lost two out of three before returning to Washington. The team often had to scramble to find places to practice because the coliseum was booked up with other events. Native D.C. residents Roland "Fatty" Taylor and Bernie Williams often sought out local schools and other facilities for the team. The struggle sometimes showed at game time, as Washington went on to lose two of three home games.

The team hovered around the .500 mark when they played their first two neutral-site games. They lost to the Dallas Chaparrals in Los Angeles and two days later defeated New Orleans again in Memphis, Tennessee. The team then played five consecutive road games, a seven-game road trip, according to the newspapers. The team won only two of seven, losing four in a row when their defense proved porous as teams scored more than 120 points per game. Coach Al Bianchi dismissed the notion that travel caused fatigue, instead insisting that the team was lazy and out of position on defense. An accurate assessment or not, Bianchi's view raised questions about the relationship between coach and players, which indicated potential distance and dysfunction.

At home throughout the Thanksgiving and Christmas seasons, the Capitols ripped off four consecutive wins to reach a record of 13–11. Playing without an injured Rick Barry, the team relied on Warren Armstrong and Gary Bradds for scoring up front and the guard combination of Larry Brown (figure 5.1) and Mike Barrett. Defensive woes continued to undercut the team's firepower, resulting in the Capitols finishing that home stand only one game over .500. The team played without a trainer on staff, resulting in Bianchi taping up all the players (figure 5.2).[17]

While the team remained around an average record, the off-court results were less positive. The team averaged only a little more than 2,000 fans per

Figure 5.1. Washington Capitols guard Larry Brown on the floor, 1969.
Reprinted with permission of the D.C. Public Library, Star Collection, © *Washington Post.*

game after 18 home dates.[18] The perception of the area around the Washington Coliseum was blamed for the poor turnout. "I wish I could show a picture of some of the people who have been to every one of our games," Earl Foreman stated. "It would prove that there are no knife wounds, no black

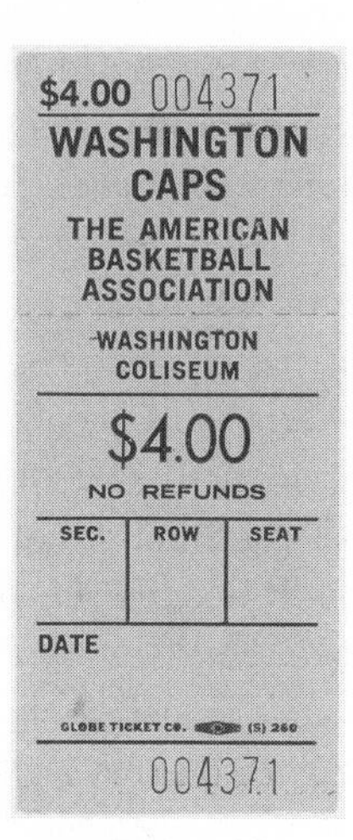

Figure 5.2. Washington Capitols ticket.
Courtesy of the author.

eyes, nor bruises from being mugged." The owner remained optimistic about the turnout for the remaining 12 home games in the season. "I'd like to hope the longer we play here, the more people will become interested, and this roadblock on the coliseum will be overcome to a greater degree."[19]

The Capitols situation matched that of many of the teams in the ABA. Compared to the rest of the league, 5 out of the 10 teams were struggling with attendance. The Indiana Pacers led the league, with an average of more than 7,000 per game. The Kentucky Colonels, Carolina Cougars, and Denver Rockets drew relatively well over the course of the season. After a rough start, the New York Nets' drawing power increased. The Capitols found themselves with half the other teams as part of the league's "have-nots."

The home attendance raised concerns over the team's financial condition. Foreman explained that the team had an $800,000 budget, about the same as for any other basketball team, except for the Los Angeles Lakers and New York Knicks. The Capitols' owner hinted that he was willing to sustain a loss of $400,000 and stay in operation. Foreman highlighted the expectations of such stars as Rick Barry and Dave Bing to almost ensure an upswing in home attendance. Ironically, the coliseum, the supposed biggest problem for the team, was in great playing condition. Former Washington Capitol player and coach Bones McKinney stated, "It's better now than when we played here."[20] The Capitols owner and the owners of the Carolina Cougars, Indiana Pacers, and Kentucky Colonels all planned on continuing to pursue NBA defectors to bring in more star power and help motive the older league to merge.

The commissioner of the ABA had succeeded in achieving his main goals. Five months after he took office, Jack Dolph had the ABA presenting its first nationally televised games; however, the contract provided limited revenue for the teams because the ABA teams played in smaller television markets. The league's home-team markets were considered the primary viewers for the games, so advertisers paid the network less in revenue to purchase slots. Thus, the network paid the league less for the contract to broadcast the games.

Dolph and his NBA counterpart, Walter Kennedy, continued efforts to forge a merger agreement. Dolph observed that there remained two sticking points in the discussions. The first involved the ABA's antitrust suit against the NBA, while the second featured the continued existence of the ABA's Washington Capitols. Dolph assured Kennedy that there was room to move on the antitrust suit. The younger league learned that the NBA, particularly Bullets owner Abe Pollin, offered no room to maneuver regarding the existence of the Capitols in Washington infringing of the Bullets' territorial rights.

The NBA owners faced consideration of another expansion or merger with the ABA. As a member of the NBA's expansion committee, Abe Pollin pushed for continued expansion in the NBA rather than a merger with the ABA. Two new teams would be added to the 14-team league, and they would be located in Buffalo, Cleveland, Houston, or Portland. Each would pay a $3 million entrance fee. A merger, however, offered the dropping of the ABA's multimillion dollar antitrust law suit against the NBA and the savings of thousands or millions of dollars in bonuses and salaries for players by avoiding the current bidding war for player services.

The NBA expansion committee completed a proposal and sent it on to a vote for the league owners. At their meeting, the group voted 12–2 to expand into all four of the locations; however, the new franchises would have to pay $3.5 million each to gain admittance into the league. The initial proposal for only two teams to enter was squashed by opposition from seven NBA owners. After a change in the personnel on the expansion committee and acrimonious meetings that lasted from Monday morning through Tuesday evening, the new approach to include four teams and raise the entrance fee won support. The bidders for the expansion teams abruptly left town after the announcement without comment.[21]

The ABA owners held their own meeting while the team played its All-Star Game. Four owners and the league commissioner served on the expansion committee and looked into possible franchises in Louisiana and Florida. New teams in the ABA would pay $1.5 million for entrance.[22] Commissioner Dolph admitted that the NBA rebuffed the latest merger efforts and stated, "The Caps will be in Washington as long as I can foresee."[23]

Just before the All-Star Game, the Capitols left on another long road trip, which featured three neutral-site games. After starting out with double-digit victories over Pittsburgh and New York, two of the weaker teams in the Eastern Division, the team lost five in a row. Despite the return of Rick Barry and his averaging 20 points and 10 rebounds, the team dropped all three neutral-site games by 10 or more points. In the five victories, their opponents averaged 130 points per game.

While the Indiana Pacers had a stranglehold on the Eastern Division, with a 32–7 record, four teams battled for the top positions in the Western Division. The Dallas Chaparrals led with a 22–20 record, followed by the Denver Rockets at 21–21, the Capitols at 20–22, and the Los Angeles Stars at 18–21. The Capitols had an excellent chance to gain ground on these teams, as they played them six times in the next 11 games. They would have to do this without Warren Armstrong, who injured his foot and would be out for the remainder of the year. The loss was great, for Armstrong and Barry were the only Capitols truly capable of dominating a game. During a short stopover in Washington, they faced off against Los Angeles and Dallas. Emblematic of the season, they lost the first game before rebounding to eke out a victory over Dallas, 122–121. Then the team embarked on a nine-game road trip beginning in Los Angeles. They split the games with the Stars and then dropped the game to Denver before coming back to trounce the Rockets, 142–125, the next time the teams matched up.

Personnel issues emerged as the team reached the conclusion of the road trip in early February. Center Ira Harge walked out on the team as they prepared to play in Albuquerque, Harge's adopted hometown. The center had been unhappy with playing on his previous years' salary of $18,000. During negotiations, Foreman told Harge that he was his second-best player behind Barry. In response, Harge asked Foreman to pay him half as much as what given to Barry. Foreman said he could not do that. A related factor for Harge centered on what he termed "undue criticism" he received for the team's lackluster 24–25 record. Foreman claimed that he offered Harge a contract worth $27,000 at the beginning of the season, which the player turned down. Harge claimed that he would return to the University of New Mexico and finish his master's degree in education. The dispute lasted one game. Replacement center Jim Eakins had a great game, and Harge returned before they really missed him. Harge returned to the lineup with a $35,000 salary against the New York Nets. Behind Barry's 35 points and George Carter's 22 points, the Caps stayed with the Nets but fell four short, losing 114–110. The loss dropped the Capitols into fourth place in the Western Division.

The game proved to be a turning point in the season. With solid scoring from all the team's key players, the Capitols went on a tear throughout the remainder of the month. The team cruised to 11 wins in 14 games, despite playing mostly on the road. Their record of 35 wins and 29 losses moved the team up in the Western Division standings. The Capitols took their hot streak to Denver, who had just won six games in a row. The battle went decidedly for Denver, as the home team pulled away to win by nine, 137–128. The Capitols found themselves looking up in the standings behind Denver and Dallas.[24]

Merger?

If the Capitols faced a struggle in the division, the off-court merger situation posed as many questions. Earl Foreman offered no comments while sitting with more than 4,000 fans for a doubleheader at the Washington Coliseum. He knew that his most important opportunity awaited, as he scheduled a meeting with the merger committees for each league at the beginning of March. The Capitols owner argued that, "We've got a team here we want to keep it in Washington, and we feel the fans deserve it."[25] Abe Pollin, a member of the NBA's committee, did not want the team in Washington, preferring to keep the territory open for his Bullets should a major-league arena be built in the city.

The ABA merger committee offered the NBA merger committee four proposals. According to Foreman, "Each one of them concerned having a franchise in Washington." He added, "I felt each [proposal] was equitable and fair, with something to placate Baltimore."[26] Pollin was reportedly in the Virgin Islands. The NBA owners planned a telephone discussion of the proposals before the next meeting of the league's merger committee.

The NBA owners met soon thereafter in Chicago for 12 hours to address all concerns. The group failed to accept any of the ABA plans for a merger. Instead, they instructed their committee to resume negotiations with the ABA. The NBA realigned itself into four divisions, with three of the divisions receiving one of the expansion franchises for the upcoming year. In addition, they moved the date of their college draft up one week earlier in March.

Foreman and his fellow ABA owners responded that the NBA owners' decision did not surprise any of them. The action to make the draft date earlier did not deter their efforts to sign some of the best college players. Foreman announced that the Capitols signed Charlie Scott to a $500,000 contract.

The 6–foot, 5-inch guard from the University of North Carolina had also been selected by the Boston Celtics in the seventh round of the NBA Draft. Washington proved one of the few ABA teams who signed All-Star caliber players who were chosen in the later rounds of the NBA Draft, including the Kentucky Colonels (forward Dan Issel, eighth round by Detroit) and the New York Nets (center Billy Paultz, seventh round by San Diego). Most of the players on the Capitols' roster attended college and many graduated.

The four teams played 20 games in the season's final month. The Capitols faced the largest hurdle, playing 14 of the games on the road. They had only two games left with Denver to try and catch the top team. The Capitols also had two games left with Los Angeles, with which to bury the team that sat right behind them in the standings. Three games remained with second-place Dallas, including one near the close of the season.

Denver played the best basketball down the stretch. Their 15–8 record enabled the Rockets to win the division by six games. The other three positions remained up for grabs. While Dallas embarked on five win and five loss streaks, Washington vaulted into second place, with a 9–6 record, and Los Angeles zipped off two six-game winning streaks and narrowed the distance between second and fourth place to two games with four games to play. Both Dallas and Los Angeles finished with two wins and two losses, but Washington lost their last four, barely holding on to third place. As seen in earlier losing streaks, the Capitols defense let them down. The team finished with the second most points per game but dead last out of the 11 teams in team defense.

A few scholars have analyzed the data related to team performance and drawing power when a team has changed franchise locations. The ABA experienced 11 team relocations during its years of existence. In six of the cases, the team's performance on the court dropped during the regular season, and the Capitols had the most precipitous decline, from winning at a nearly .800 clip in Oakland to winning at a .523 clip in Washington. Owners do not move teams with playing performance in mind, instead focusing on financial benefits. They usually think that attendance will improve. This was the case in 7 of the 11 ABA cases, while a near draw existed when Minnesota moved back to Pittsburgh during the 1969–1970 season. The Capitols were an oddity for the league and for the general relocation of sporting teams. The team experienced a drop from 223,000 to about 170,000 in turnout. This decline of nearly 25% was both substantial and highly unusual in the first year after a franchise relocates. Only Carolina's move to St. Louis five years later came close to that level of decreasing fan support.

The ABA playoffs included the top four teams in each division. The first-place team played the third-place squad, while the second-place team played the squad that finished fourth. The NBA had used this same system, beginning with the 1966–1967 season, when the Chicago Bulls joined. The league planned on changing this system with the latest expansion and creation of divisions in the upcoming year, the 1970–1971 season.

The Capitols started this series with the odd knowledge that they would be moving from Washington at the close of this season. The ABA and NBA leaderships reached an agreement regarding the merger of their leagues. Before they could merge the businesses, the leagues needed to receive approval from the Federal Government that their merger did not violate the Sherman Antitrust laws. Alternatively, the leagues could turn to Congress, as the two professional football leagues did a few years earlier, and ask to receive an exemption from the laws.[27]

The Playoffs

For one of the few times all year, the Capitols had their top players ready for the first-round playoff series; however, the team had a below-average season against Denver, winning only 5 out of the 12 games. The Rockets had the Rookie of the Year and the Most Valuable Player in forward Spencer Haywood. Haywood topped the league with an average of 30 points and 20 rebounds a game. The Capitols had superstar Rick Barry, the ABA's top assist man; guard Larry Brown; and a solid shooting guard in Mike Barrett. Local reporters expressed concern over the Capitols recent slump and the strength of Denver on its home court.

In game one, the Capitols jumped out to a big lead in the first quarter behind the play of Mike Barrett. The team adjusted its starting lineup, placing Frank Card at the forward position. This might have weakened the bench, and the Rockets overtook the Capitols in the second quarter. The Rockets then poured it on in front of their roaring crowd and won going away, 130–111. The weakness of the Capitols returned to hurt the team's effort in game two. The Rockets scored 143 points on the way to beating the Capitols by 10. This was the most the Rockets scored in the three years that they had been in the playoffs and was the fourth-highest total for a playoff game in ABA history. Ironically, the Oakland Oaks gave up the most, allowing the Indiana Pacers to score 150 points in the only game that the Pacers won in the 1969 finals.

The Capitols returned to the Washington Coliseum and prepared for game three. Behind Rick Barry and Mike Barrett, the team took a 14-point lead into the locker room at halftime. Denver returned to the court on fire and cut the lead in half behind their rookie Spencer Haywood's barrage of points. Larry Brown took control and dished out a record 14 assists to give the Capitols a five-point victory, 125–120. Both Barry and Haywood scored 45 points, only two shy of the ABA record for points in a playoff game. Mike Barrett added 31 points, and Gary Bradds, Larry Brown, and Frank Card also scored in double figures for the home team. The crowd in attendance numbered less than 2,000 people.

A large crowd of nearly 5,500 attended game four. The home team rewarded them with a big victory to even the series at two games each, winning 131–114. Rick Barry and Mike Barrett each scored 30 points. Backup center Jim Eakins added 20 points in the victory, helping to offset Spencer Haywood's 41-point performance (figure 5.3).

The teams flew to Denver that evening. The next day, they hit the court in the high altitude. The Rockets took the lead and held on to romp over the Capitols, winning by 22 points, 132–110. The teams returned for a Saturday game at the Washington Coliseum. The lead zigzagged through the first half, with the teams ending up tied at 55 points. Denver again game out of the break strong. They jumped to a five-point lead, receiving scoring from Spencer Haywood and the guard tandem of Larry Jones and Jeff Congdon. Washington charged hard in the final period. Rick Barry finished with 40 points, and Larry Brown added 17. Mike Barrett scored 28 points in the second half, including three three-point buckets. The Capitols took the game 116–111, tying the series at three games apiece.

While the two teams prepared to traverse the country once again, the other playoff series neared their ends. The Los Angeles Stars maintained their winning ways in the playoffs, defeating Dallas in six games. In the Eastern Division, the Indiana Pacers swept the Carolina Cougars, and the Kentucky Colonels dispatched the New York Nets. No team in the Denver–Washington series had won on the road. Denver's publicity director, Bill Gullion, noted that the fans in Denver were boisterous, and the crowd's backing made the Rockets play at peak efficiency. The Capitols still thought they stood a chance. The team fell behind by eight points at the half. Denver did not give them a chance to make a comeback. The Rockets outscored their opponent by 11 in the third quarter. Haywood was on his way to 42 points, backed by Jones's 27 points and four others in double figures. Barry dropped in 52 points, with Barrett adding 23 and Brown 14. Frustration broke out in the final two minutes. Barry and Denver's Lonnie Wright got into a fight. Denver prevailed over Washington, 143–119.[28]

The Capitols' season ended, but the off-season offered nearly as much drama. The Capitols' coach, Al Bianchi, provided a detailed post mortem, stating that the team did not have a close unity. "Everybody on this club was

Figure 5.3. Spencer Haywood shooting over Ira Harge of the Capitols, 1970.
Reprinted with permission of the D.C. Public Library, Star Collection, @ *Washington Post.*

concerned with what the other guy is making. . . . There is little loyalty to the organization."[29] Clearly, Barry's unwillingness to come east and Harge walking out midseason showed that. But the players could not be faulted for the seeming internal disorganization that appeared at times. The team's general manager, Bruce Hale, already announced that he took a job coaching at St. Mary's College in California. The entire team had to take responsibility for not playing much defense, including the coach, as he could not get the players to implement his strategy. Bianchi promised to fix things for the upcoming season. The team had All-Stars in Brown, Barry, and Armstrong, but there were also other players who would complain that some guy hogged the ball, or would not pass the ball, because they wanted the ball.[30]

Congress and the Merger

The team would not start its next season in Washington, D.C. The Capitols owner, Earl Foreman, agreed to move his team to the tidewater area to become a regional franchise, with games in Norfolk, Hampton, Roanoke, and Richmond, Virginia, or to St. Louis. The owner received a few perks for ending his territorial disagreement with the Baltimore Bullets and their owner, Abe Pollin. The ABA agreed to cover the losses that the Capitols sustained during the 1969–1970 season, amounting to about $400,000. The NBA agreed that the team would have a free ride into the newly merged league, as they waived the $1.25 million indemnity price that each of the ABA's other 10 franchises would have to pay to become part of the NBA.

The merger received opposition from the National Basketball Player's Association (NBPA). The union took the issue to federal court, where they argued that a merger would involuntarily bind them to one team throughout their basketball careers. The players argued that the merger eliminated competition for talent and removed their right to determine whether they were dissatisfied with their current employer and had the ability to do something about their dissatisfaction. The NBA players were fighting a similar battle to the one that Curt Flood fought against the reserve clause in professional baseball during the same year. In the era of minority groups protesting for recognition of their rights, now athletes stood up for their rights to have control over their labor and to be able to negotiate for the best salaries for that labor.

The first court granted a temporary restraining order prohibiting the leagues from discussing the merger. Two weeks later, in early May, Judge Charles A. Tenney, in New York federal court, granted a preliminary injunction barring the merger without the approval of Congress; however, he approved of a stipulation that allowed the basketball leagues to resume their merger negotiations and preparation for seeking congressional exemption from the Sherman Antitrust laws. Earl Foreman expressed his satisfaction. "We now have a shelter under which we can work and not be afraid of someone putting up a lawsuit while we are talking to Congress. We're at the point we wanted to be."[31]

The editorial board of certain sports magazines and the general public seemed to support a merger. *Basketball Weekly* wrote that, "The American basketball public is clamoring for a merger. So are the NBA and ABA owners, the two commissioners, and every college coach. The war is over. The armistice will be signed soon."[32] This expectation soon appeared premature. Congress can move deliberately. Some within the country's most powerful legislative body had begun to look at professional sports less as a game and with a more jaundiced eye that sports are a business, a business that they need to regulate.

Congress enacted nearly 300 pieces of legislation related to professional sports between 1950 and the 1970s. Nearly two-thirds of this legislation had antitrust issues as the focus. This battle between competing perspectives in Congress existed since the late 1950s, when Congress held hearings on the antitrust exemption that MLB had since the 1920s. As the Continental Baseball League began to emerge as a possible competitor and the Supreme Court ruled that professional football was subject to antitrust laws, Congress faced pressure to deal with baseball's different treatment. The efforts that passed the one chamber of Congress without reaching the floor of the other in 1958, and again in 1965, would apply federal antitrust laws to professional sports, while exempting how the sports were played, how the leagues were organized, and how the team dealt with the players.[33]

The NFL and the American Football League (AFL) sought exemption from antitrust laws from Congress in 1966. The leagues sought a merger and faced opposition to their effort from Emanuel Celler (D-New York). As justification, the NFL argued that the bidding war between the two leagues would lead to financial harm and potential doom for the sport. They achieved passage of the bill in the Congress. The situation looked awkward, when shortly after the vote the NFL awarded New Orleans a franchise.

A series of senators introduced a bill to authorize the merger between the two professional basketball leagues along the same lines as the one that worked for the professional football leagues in July 1971. Senator Roman Lee Hruska (R-Nebraska), who introduced S. 2373, commented on the success of the earlier football merger authorization and noted that the two basketball leagues risked financial difficulties without the authorization to merge. Senators ranging from John Varick Tunney (D-California) to Gordon Llewellyn Allott (R-Colorado) congratulated Hruska on the bill. Hruska listed six advantages to the merger, including preservation of job opportunities in professional basketball, stability, restoration of competitive balance, and having an undisputed champion of professional basketball. The Senate referred the bill to the Committee on the Judiciary.

Unfortunately for the team owners, including Earl Foreman, the heads of the House and Senate judiciary committees sought an end to all pro sports monopolies. Representative Emanuel Celler and Senator Sam J. Ervin Jr. (D-North Carolina) jointly announced their perspective that the players were treated like "chattel" and that the bill authorizing the merger of the two professional football leagues was "railroaded" through Congress. Their joint press release argued that the common draft abridged the players' freedom to contract their services, as did the option clauses in the players' contracts. If the antitrust exemption was granted to enable the sport to operate as a monopoly, then professional sports would become a public utility and a federal commissioner to oversee them would be necessary. During testimony before the House subcommittee, former Baltimore Bullet Kevin Loughery and current Bullet Archie Clark explained that the existence of the ABA helped the players win concessions from the NBA owners, including a minimum salary and health, accident, and life insurance.

The leagues expressed optimism regarding the passage of a bill authorizing their merger. They figured that the changes could go into effect for the 1972–1973 season. The ABA sought a new Commissioner whom they thought would be a better person to carry their view to the Congresspersons. The ABA owners hired New York corporate lawyer Bob Carlson, a man with close ties to the NBA and an appearance like MLB commissioner Bowie Kuhn, which they felt was likely to impress Senators.

Bob Carlson would be making an appearance with the commissioners of the other professional sports. When the bill reached the floor, it contained a proposal for a federal sports commission. Senator Marlow Cook (R-Kansas) thought that the sports world appeared to be in turmoil. He declared that fans of the various sports had the right to a stable system and viewed the commission as a way to address the problems, including the mass commercialization of sports; however, the commissioners of baseball, football, and basketball went to Washington and objected to taking a path toward overregulation.

More than a year later, the Committee on the Judiciary issued its report. The report authorized the merger between the two leagues, as written in Senate Bill 2373 and the Act of September 30, 1961, with several significant amendments. First, the act obliterated the reserve clause, with the stipulation that teams could sign a rookie for two years and extend the contract for an additional year through individual negotiations. Second, it required that instead of the home team keeping all television revenues, they had to provide at least 30% to the visiting team. Third, the bill imposed a blackout on broadcasted games on Tuesday and Friday nights, and Saturday, when contests appeared within 75 miles of a high school or college basketball game. Fourth, all teams would be required to move into the combined leagues. Fifth and last, the indemnity payment from ABA teams to NBA teams of $1.25 million would be payable in $125,000 allotments during a span of 10 years and could be paid only out of television revenues. If the revenues did not exist, then the team would not have to make the payment for that year.[34]

NBA commissioner Walter Kennedy noted that the league had issues with the proposed bill. He claimed that the league could not live with many of the proposed amendments. In particular, owners expressed opposition to gate receipt sharing. The second least popular proposal for the owners centered on the plan for indemnity payments. The NBA owners expressed little support for this legislation.

Senator Cook's perception of sports in turmoil had advocates among sportswriters and the general public. The games, which had provided haven for some from the Vietnam War and its protests, and the civil rights activities of the African American, Native American, Chicano, and gay and lesbian social movements, experienced disruptions. While the Summer Olympics in Munich provided cheating and murder, and tennis contended with feuding factions, the basketball merger illuminated the business aspects of sports as prominently as the Supreme Court ruling on the Curt Flood versus Bowie Kuhn case did earlier in the year. As players jumped basketball teams, club owners raided other clubs for talent, and the courts made decisions on what team legally had the right to a player's services, for many observers, the fun was squeezed out of sports.

The Supreme Court ruling in *Flood v. Kuhn*, which upheld the reserve clause, presumably shaped the expectations of the basketball owners that the next Congress might grant them an antitrust exemption without undoing the clause. In April 1973, a new bill reached the floor of the Senate in the next Congress. Introduced by Senator Birch Bayh (D-Indiana) and Senator Cook, the legislation removed several of the amendments that appeared in the last version; however, the legislation still freed players from the reserve-clause restrictions. According to this law, a team could sign a player for a year with a one-year option or for a multiyear contract with no option. While the ABA owners supported the measure, the NBA owners appeared to have little enthusiasm for the bill. As Walter Kennedy later explained, "The stumbling block remains the option clause. Our owners feel the option clause is a must for the future of the NBA."[35]

As the bill languished in Congress, the owners returned to the court system. The federal judge recently issued a revised ruling that permitted the leagues to discuss a merger without congressional approval, but those talks would have to include the players. Kennedy noted the positives with the change but argued that unless there was agreement on the option clause, no merger will occur.

The Virginia Squires

The two leagues continued operating separately. The Washington Capitols moved to Virginia and became the Squires for the 1970–1971 season. The plan called for the Squires to be a regional team that played home games in Hampton, Norfolk, and Richmond and a few games in Roanoke. Earl Foreman now viewed the choice as a unique, perhaps desperate, idea that did not work for many different reasons.

Several major changes in personnel also occurred. Earl Foreman and Al Bianchi made decisions together, and they traded their rookie spark plug and major outside shooter, Warren Armstrong, to the Kentucky Colonels for cash in return. The Colonels sent the guard to Indiana. The Pacers and Armstrong made it to the ABA finals later that season. Rick Barry apparently did not want to play in Virginia. In the cover story for *Sports Illustrated* a month before the beginning of the upcoming 1970–1971 season, Barry said that he thought the South was a dreadful place to live and knocked Virginia's Southern heritage. This ruined him as a spectator draw and forced Foreman to deal him. Team management then sold Barry to the New York Nets for the Nets' number one draft choice and an undisclosed amount of cash, reported to be around $250,000.

Despite the roster changes and shuffling around the state of Virginia, the team performed well on the court. They excelled during the regular season, winning the six-team Eastern Division by 11 games over the Kentucky Colonels. Rookie Charlie Scott led in scoring, with more than 2,200 points. His performance stood out so much that the leadership began introducing the team at home games with the phrase, "Charlie Scott and the Virginia Squires."

The Squires won the Eastern Division semifinals against the New York Nets, four games to two. The Squires won the first two home games pretty thoroughly then lost two squeakers in New York. Back home, Virginia held off the Nets to win by three points. The teams returned to West Hempstead, Long Island, and the Squires won the final game by four. Then they lost in the Eastern Division finals to the Colonels, four games to two.

The team succeeded on the financial ledger as well. The owner made money from the aforementioned trades. The team proved very popular in their new home. The Virginia Squires weren't playing to packed stadiums, but the arenas weren't empty, either. While the Capitols drew 170,000 fans, the Squires drew 361,000 fans in their first year. "The fans continued to come see the team. They did ok. It wasn't like empty arenas."[36] Center Jim Eakins recalled good crowds in Norfolk and Hampton and poor attendance in Roanoke.[37]

The Squires signed Julius Erving to a four-year, $500,000 contract for the 1971–1972 season. With Erving, the team had the most electrifying player in the ABA, a man who would become synonymous with the league. Julius Erving and Charlie Scott made a dynamic frontcourt pair, scoring nearly half the team's 10,000 points, the second-highest team total for the league. As was true with the Capitols, the team's defense remained porous, ranked 9 out of the 11 teams. The team's home announcement moved to "Charlie Scott, Doctor J, and the Virginia Squires," but shortly thereafter it became, "Doctor J and the Virginia Squires." Erving enjoyed his time with the team: "The two years I was there were wonderful. They set the stage for everything."[38]

The Squires finished second in the Eastern Division by 23 games. Near the season's end, Charlie Scott left the team. Much speculation surrounded the decision, including Scott not wanting to put up with subpar ABA travel and arenas or his inability to get along with Doctor J. His roommate, Fatty Taylor, noted that after one game in New York, Scott handed Taylor his uniform and said, "I'm going to Phoenix." Said Taylor, "Two days later we see him on TV playing with Phoenix."[39] The team that drafted him, the Boston Celtics, traded him to the Phoenix Suns for Paul Silas.

Despite the loss of one of their key scorers, the Squires played well in the playoffs, taking the first round in a sweep. They were the epitome of the ABA style of game: younger, faster, and slicker, with less-patterned offensive play. The game had a looser officiating style, with freer use of hands and fewer elbows on the inside and more "steps" allowed on the outside. The Squires represented that style, with one of the league's best players showing it off. They took Rick Barry's Nets to a seventh game in the Eastern Division playoff finals before losing.

Meanwhile, Squires owner Earl Foreman pushed the limits of the basketball establishment in other ways. Unlike the NBA, the ABA allowed for a college player to invoke the "hardship" clause to permit himself to be hired to play professional basketball before his class graduated. The federal judge hearing the Spencer Haywood case in Los Angeles enjoined the NBA from enforcing its wait until the player's class graduated. During the second phase of the ABA's 1971 draft, Foreman drafted three underclassmen without invoking the hardship clause: Tom Riker, a junior from the University of South Carolina; Barry Parkhill, a sophomore from the University of Virginia;

and Jim Chones, a sophomore from Marquette University. Foreman gambled that this injunction issued by the judge would be made permanent. This did not happen, and the three men were eventually drafted with their class in 1973, Riker by the New York Knicks, Parkhill by the Squires, and Chones by the Capitol Bullets.[40]

While attendance improved for the Squires, they, like many other teams in the league, operated on a tight budget. A few teams, like the New Orleans Buccaneers and the Los Angeles Stars, relocated to Memphis and Utah, respectively, to save the franchise. The Miami Floridians and Pittsburgh Condors tried several actions to remain solvent. Miami traded several of its key players, including Donnie Freeman, Les Hunter, and Simmie Hill, to various teams from the 1969–1970 season through the 1971–1972 season for players and cash. Pittsburgh could not retain its superstar, Connie Hawkins. Instead, Hawkins settled his lawsuit against the NBA and joined the Phoenix Suns. Neither the Floridians nor the Condors remained in the ABA for the 1972–1973 season.

Like its older sibling organization, the league experienced other challenges. Most of the ABA teams had more African Americans on their rosters than those in the NBA. Still, players sometimes heard particular sob stories from team leadership. One recalled that an executive took him aside and explained the need to cut him from the squad as a focus on what his patrons thought and that most people wanted to see people who looked like them on the floor. The expansion of drug use also began in this period. While many players had seemingly always drank, frequently and in quantity, using bennies (amphetamines) and marijuana also increased. Many guys reportedly smoked marijuana, and it did little to change their play, but those who snorted coke did not last in the game of professional basketball.

By the 1972–1973 season, guard Fatty Taylor, known for his pesky defense and numerous steals, and center Jim Eakins, were the only Squires players who also played with the team that sojourned in the nation's capital. Despite signing an exciting new rookie, George Gervin, the Squires faced a major player defection. Julius Erving was looking for a way out to improve his earnings and play elsewhere. Erving had the opportunity, as he became eligible for the 1972 NBA Draft. The player and owner became frustrated with one another, as Erving went to Foreman and asked that some of his deferred salary money be moved up. Foreman disliked that Erving said that he did not want to spend his entire career with Virginia and removed his offer of a contract modification from consideration. In April 1972, the Milwaukee Bucks drafted Julius Erving as the 12th choice during the first round.[41] As Erving later noted, "I was naïve when I decided to turn pro. I didn't know much about contracts."[42] He felt that he had been taken advantage of by the owners and representatives.

With the apparent loss of their superstar, basketball observers gave the Squires little chance to succeed on the court. Several predicated the team to finish in fourth or last place; however, Erving did not sign with Milwaukee, but signed a contract with Atlanta. Squires' owner Earl Foreman won an arbitration clause through the federal courts, requiring Erving to play the season with Virginia. Meanwhile, the NBA fined the Atlanta Hawks $25,000 for the three exhibition games that Erving played with the team because the Milwaukee Bucks owned the rights to Erving as an NBA player. Foreman fortunately also had a good head coach as an asset. "You'd run through a brick wall for Al Bianchi," guard Dave Twardzik said.[43] Behind Erving's 2,200 points, the Squires finished in third place, with a 42–42 record. The team lost to the Kentucky Colonels in the Eastern Division semifinals, the first round of the league's playoffs.[44]

Their on-court play proved to be only one of the disappointments as the team struggled financially. The Squires could not pay their rent for their regular arena. They also owed nearly $7,000 to Scope Coliseum for six games that the team played in February and March in Norfolk. Earl Foreman decided to trade Julius Erving to the New York Nets for forward George Carter, a one-time member of both Washington Capitols and Virginia Squires, and $1 million.

As the 1973–1974 season dawned, things looked difficult for the ABA. The second merger bill died in the Senate, as the NBA owners would not support it. Commissioner Bob Carlson resigned. The television contract disappeared, and income and morale were low. The ABA owners hired former Bullets and Pacers executive Mike Storen to take the commissioner's reins. The league had several strong teams and a few owners willing to spend, something that Storen himself did to build powerful Indiana and Kentucky teams.

The basketball writers expected little from the Squires in the 1973–1974 season. One writer thought that the team seemed to stay in business selling off some of the game's best players. They noted that the Squires would quickly discover Erving's worth on the court and in attendance. The Squires dropped to fourth place in the division. The team won one of every three games but still made the playoffs. The team scoring proved more balanced than in prior years, with George Carter, George Gervin, and long-time center Jim Eakins ranked among the top shooters. Virginia also had the Rookie of the Year, Swen Nater, at center, providing solid rebounding and defense. The team lost in the first round of the playoffs to the Julius Erving-led Nets. The Nets went on to win the first of their two league championships.

Virginia returned to selling off more assets, trading Swen Nater to the San Antonio Spurs for $300,000.

Commissioner Mike Storen attempted to steer the league through this period, when a merger seemed unlikely. Several ABA owners needed the drive to continue. Through fining franchises, suspending referees, and snarling at owners, Storen provided the league with the will to survive. During the early part of the 1973–1974, season San Antonio Spurs owner Angelo Drossos arranged to buy George Gervin from the Squires. He agreed to a delay of the move until after the All-Star Game in Norfolk, at Foreman's request. Storen vetoed Virginia's sale of high-scoring Gervin to San Antonio on grounds that the Squires, who were up for sale, would be rendered an incompetent team by the deal. The Spurs challenged his action in a Texas court, and the court ruled that Storen had overstepped his authority. Drossos won final permission during a meeting with fellow owners. Memphis franchise owner Charley Finley said, "You crazy sons of bitches. Instead of bringing up Angelo on charges, you should be congratulating this man. In this weak-kneed league of ours, here's a guy willing to spend money to improve his team. I'm voting with Angelo."[45] Other owners followed Finley.

Despite the sales of their top players, the Squires finished in fourth place. They made the playoffs, with a 28–56 record, but the Nets quickly dismissed them in five games. The assessment of the ABA teams for the 1974–1975 season appeared in the newspapers and sports magazines. The Nets were viewed as young and gifted, solid with superstar Julius Erving. The Virginia Squires and St. Louis Spirits were seen as the bottom-feeders of the division. As one magazine noted, former owner Earl Foreman set a world record for unloading talent before finally unloading his team.[46] Foreman argued that owning a basketball team in those days, in either league, was a losing proposition. Even the Celtics didn't make money then—they made it in the playoffs. Foreman sold the Squires off to Van Cunningham, who came by his money through the Stewart Sandwiches Company. They finished the 1974–1975 season at 15–69, 12 games below the next closest team in the standings. On top of the worst record in the league, a Chesapeake policeman shot the team's center after catching the latter stealing $14 from a gas station.

The Squires nearly duplicated their record the following year. The new owner thought it best to replace Al Bianchi as coach and did so early on. A series of men led the Squires from the bench, including Mack Calvin (0–6), Bill Musselman (4–22), Jack Ankerson (1–1), and, finally, Zelmo Beaty (9–33). This team bested the previous year's record by losing one less game.

After two years of inactivity, the NBPA received a new hearing after judge Robert L. Carter picked up the case. In *Oscar Robertson et al. v. Na-*

tional Basketball Association, Carter ruled that the players had a valid complaint on antitrust grounds. The owners settled right before the case went to court. The settlement eliminated the "reserve" clause in the NBA's player contract, removed the four-year waiting rule for players to join the league, and provided players with $4.3 million.[47]

The owners of the franchises in the two leagues met to discuss establishing peace between the two leagues. In Hyannis, the owners sought to create a single league. The NBA owners eventually accepted a proposal that allowed only four of the eight existing ABA teams to join their league. While the New York Nets, Indiana Pacers, Denver Rockets, and San Antonio Spurs joined the NBA at a cost of $4.5 million each, they also had to buy out the owners of two of the ABA teams not included in the merger, the Kentucky Colonels and the former St. Louis Spirits, for about $3 million each. The Virginia Squires existence came to an unceremonious end. They shared this fate of going out of existence before the merger meetings with fellow ABA members the San Diego Conquistadors and the Utah Stars and were excluded from any of the considerations. Nonetheless, among most of the players the ABA was a close-knit family. "All the teams, we all got along. You played hard on the court and partied after the game. We keep in touch even today."[48]

Like his fellow NBA owners, Bullets owner Abe Pollin could now put the competing leagues behind him. The team that had moved into his territory was now gone. While New York had a second team because of the deal, the New York metropolitan area had more people and size than Baltimore and Washington, and the New York Knicks received a $4 million special reparations payment. Pollin could enjoy the $700,000 indemnity payment and look forward to the forthcoming dispersal draft for the ABA players left without a team.

Notes

1. "1967–68 Oakland Oaks Roster and Statistics," Basketball–Reference.com, www.basketball-reference.com/teams/OAK/1968.html (retrieved February 14, 2011).

2. Frank Deford, "The Last Hurrah in Hyannis," *Sports Illustrated*, June 28, 1976, 34; Leonard Koppett, *24 Seconds to Shoot: The Birth and Improbable Rise of the NBA* (New York: Total Sports, 1999), 181–90.

3. Peter Carry, "Having a Ball with the ABA," *Sports Illustrated*, March 18, 1974, 65.

4. Mark Asher, "This Man and His Red, White And Blue Basketball Have Plently to Laugh about," *Washington Post*, November 22, 1970, 265.

5. Mark Asher, "Bid Made to Move Oaks Out of Oakland," *Washington Post*, August 19, 1969, B1; Mark Asher, "Bid to Bring Oakland Oaks Here hits Scheduling Snag," *Washington Post*, August 20, 1969, D1; Mark Asher, "Foreman Brings ABA Kings here," *Washington Post*, August 21, 1969, B1.

6. This and other details and quotes by Roland "Fatty" Taylor were obtained during an interview with the author, March 4, 2012; this and other details and quotes by Al Bianchi were obtained during an interview with the author, February 28, 2012.

7. Steve Guback, "Armory Schedule Biggest Obstacle," *Washington Star*, September 13, 1969.

8. "NBA Quits Merger Talk after ABA Breech of Faith," *Washington Post*, August 26, 1969, D1; Kenneth Denlinger, "Superstar Reportedly Joining Caps,"*Washington Post*, September 2, 1969, D3; Shirley Povich, "This Morning," *Washington Post*, September 5, 1969, D1.

9. Mark Asher, "30 Home Games of Caps Head for Coliseum," *Washington Post*, August 22, 1969, D1; Steve Guback, "Armory Schedule Biggest Obstacle," *Washington Star*, September 13, 1969.

10. Foreman interview, May 4, 2011.

11. Bianchi interview, February 28, 2012.

12. Terry Pluto, *Loose Balls: The Short, Wild Life of the American Basketball Association* (New York: Simon & Schuster, 1990), 177–99.

13. Tom Yorke, "Caps Schedule in 16 cities with 30 games listed here," *Washington Star*, October 14, 1969, C-4.

14. Tom Yorke, "Caps Will Outdraw Half of NBA-Foreman," *Washington Star*, October 15, 1969, C-3.

15. Bob Addie, "The Ball Bounces," *Washington Post*, August 22, 1969, D1.

16. Mark Asher, "30 Home Games of Caps Head for Coliseum," *Washington Post*, August 22, 1969, D1; Tom Yorke, "Caps Will Outdraw Half of NBA-Foreman," *Washington Star*, October 15, 1969, C-3.

17. 1969–70 Washington Capitols Roster and Statistics," Basketball-Reference.com, www.basketball-reference.com/teams/WSA/1970.html (retrieved October 10, 2010).

18. Morris Siegel, "Foreman Hopeful Roundballing Caps Don't Foul Out," *Washington Star*, December 21, 1969, S-8.

19. Tom Yorke, "Caps' Average Attendance of 2,012 Shakes Foreman," *Washington Star*, December 23, 1969, C-1.

20. Morris Siegel, "Foreman Hopeful Roundballing Caps Don't Foul Out," *Washington Star*, December 21, 1969, S-8.

21. 1969–70 Washington Capitols Roster and Statistics," Basketball-Reference.com, www.basketball-reference.com/teams/WSA/1970.html.

22. "NBA Meeting Seighs Expansion," *Washington Star*, January 19, 1970, C-1; Tom Yorke, "City Seen as Pro Cage Battleground," *Washington Star*, January 22, 1970, C-1.

23. "ABA Boss Says Caps Aren't about to Leave," *Washington Star*, January 24, 1970, A-13.

24. This and other details and quotes by Ira Harge were obtained during an interview with the author, February 22, 2010; this and other details and quotes by Warren Jabali were obtained during an interview with the author, February 22, 2010.

25. Tom Yorke, "ABA Eying Caps for Norfolk Area," *Washington Star*, March 8, 1970, C-2; "Merger Units Hear Foreman," *Washington Star*, March 10, 1970, A-19.

26. Mark Asher, "ABA Proposes Four Plans for Merger," *Washington Post*, March 11, 1970, D1.

27. "ABA Head Makes Peace Bid to NBA; Caps One stumbling block," *Washington Post*, January 9, 1970, D1; "Players hoping to block merger," *Washington Star*, January 19, 1970, C-1"Caps' Prexy mum about club's future," *Washington Star*, February 16, 1970, C3.

28. "Rockets overtake Caps for 1-0 lead," *Washington Post*, April 18, 1970, F-3; Mark Asher, "Barry scores 45 Caps dump Denver," April 20, 1970, D-1; "Rockets rout Caps and capture series," *New York Times*, April29, 1970, 68; Taylor interview; March 4, 2012, Bianchi interview, February 28, 2012.

29. Mark Asher, "Petty Jealousies Cause Caps' Fall," *Washington Post*, April 30, 1970, F1.

30. Asher, "Petty Jealousies Cause Caps' Fall," F1.

31. "Million-Dollar War," *Newsweek*, April 6, 1970, 63–64.

32. Sam Palermo, "More ABA–NBA: The fans speak Out," *Basketball Digest*, http://en.wikipedia.org/wiki/ABA%E2%80%93NBA_merger.

33. Arthur T. Johnson, "Congress and Professional Sports, 1951–1978," *Annals of the American Academy of Political and Social Science*, vol. 445, (September 1979): 102–15.

34. Committee on the Judiciary, *Report Authorizing the Merger of Two or More Professional Basketball Leagues, and for Other Purposes*, U.S. Senate, 92nd Congress, Rep. No. 92-1151 (1972).

35. "Merger Seen No Closer," *New York Times*, August 15, 1973, 30.

36. Don Harrison, "A League of Their Own," *Virginia Living*, vol. 6 (April 2008), 153

37. Harrison, "A League of Their Own," 157–59.

38. Harrison, "A League of Their Own," 157–59.

39. Taylor interview; March 4, 2012.

40. Martin Kane, "Scorecard," *Sports Illustrated*, March 29, 1971, 11.

41. Vincent M. Mallozzi, *Doc: The Rise and Rise of Julius Erving* (New York: John Wiley & Sons, 2010), 54–74.

42. Mallozzi, *Doc*, 74.

43. Harrison, "A League of Their Own."

44. Harrison, "A League of Their Own," 159–61.

45. Terry Pluto, *Loose Balls: The Short, Wild Life of the American Basketball Association* (New York: Simon & Schuster, 1990), 301.

46. Pat Putnam, Jane Gross, "The NBA Said No Way," *Sports Illustrated*, October 28, 1974, 68.

47. *Oscar Robertson et al. v. National Basketball Association*, 556 F.2d 682 (2d Cir. 1977), U.S. Court of Appeals for the Second District.

48. Taylor interview, March 4, 2012.

CHAPTER SIX

~

Abe Pollin and the Baltimore Bullets

Abe Pollin began the 1968–1969 National Basketball Association (NBA) season, his first as majority owner of the Baltimore Bullets, with decisions to change all of the team's major leadership, except Coach Gene Shue. The team's annual operating costs were nearly $3 million, and the owner would need for the Bullets to make the playoffs to even have a chance at recouping his expenditures. While the sports media ranked Boston, New York, and Philadelphia as tier one, they put the Bullets in tier two and thought they were one guard away from being a playoff team.

Led by last season's Rookie of the Year, Earl Monroe, fellow guard Kevin Loughery, and rookie center Wes Unseld, the Bullets got off to a fast start, winning 15 of the first 20 games. After the surprising quick start, the team kept on winning. Their nine-game winning streak through the Christmas holiday game left the team in first place in the Eastern Division. The Philadelphia 76ers trailed the Bullets by three games, and the world champion Boston Celtics sat in third, four games behind.[1] The team became the surprise of the basketball world. News magazines mentioned how the season was turning the recent past on its head, almost like the promotional campaign Pollin launched at the beginning of the season promised, "We've got a few scores to settle."[2] The words resonated in a league that had certain players whose jobs, as New York Knick guard Walt Frazier described it, as enforcers were to push the other team's guys around and protect their own teammates.[3] Nevertheless, small problems remained, as Earl Monroe declared, "The less I have to stay in Baltimore, the better."[4]

The teams remained close through the winter months. The Bullets completed two five-game winning streaks and two four-game streaks leading up to the final two weeks of the season. With nine games left before the playoffs at the end of March, the Bullets led the Celtics by seven games. Philadelphia won two games to climb to within one game of the Bullets. After losing four in a row on their longest road trip of the year, the Bullets faced the expansion Phoenix Suns at the Arizona Veterans Memorial Coliseum. The Bullets ran up 140 points on the Suns to take the final game of the trip. The team then won four games in a row, including one-point victories against the Knicks and Celtics to bury the 76ers and finish on top of a division for the first time in franchise history.

Coach Gene Shue stressed that his team needed to perform well on defense. During the course of the year, the team finished in the middle of the pack in that realm, seventh in the 14-team league, as they allowed 112 points a game. The Bullets had a high-flying offense that averaged more than 116 points, finishing second only to Philadelphia. A sizable portion of the team's offense emerged from the ability of Wes Unseld to control the defensive boards. Unseld would snare the rebound and quickly throw an outlet pass down the court to one of the team's guards, similar to the Boston Celtics with Bill Russell at center during the early 1960s.

For the first time in several years, attendance rose at Bullets games. The team drew more than 290,000 fans to the Baltimore Civic Center, nearly 100,000 more than the previous high. The team placed fifth in the league in attendance, behind the Knicks, Lakers, 76ers, and Celtics. All the teams benefitted from the additional revenue coming from the new ABC television contract. The network paid almost $1 million a year, roughly $55,000 a year to each team. Combined with what they earned from local broadcasting rights, the Bullets earned slightly more than they had a few years earlier. The NBA contract compared unfavorably with the television rights for Major League Baseball (MLB) ($16.5 million in the course of a few years) and the National Football League ($22 million a year). Journalists noted that the NBA's erratic officiating, long road trips, small arenas, and expansion hurt its attempts to become a major league. ABC made razor-thin profits from its broadcasts and faced a barrage of criticism for its productions, including lame halftime shows and lack of skill in appreciating the action of a basketball game.

The Bullets played the season with a stable roster. The starting five of Earl Monroe, Kevin Loughery, Wes Unseld, Gus Johnson, and Jack Marin played nearly 35 minutes a game. Forward Ray Scott and center Leroy Ellis came off the bench for the front line and played about 20 minutes a game. The top reserve guard was John Barnhill, who played about 17 minutes. Boston, Philadelphia, and New York substituted a little more, using seven-, eight-, or nine-man rotations that averaged playing 20 minutes per game

While the NBA had expanded from 10 to 14 teams during the last two years, the league retained the same playoff structure. The top team in each division played the team that finished in third place, while the second- and fourth-place teams met in the other division semifinal. As the Washington Capitols had 20 years before, the Bullets faced the New York Knicks in the first round of the playoffs; this time in a best-of-seven series. The top team hosted the first game, and the home court alternated after each game.

The Rivalry Begins: Baltimore versus New York

The Knicks came down to the Civic Center for the first game. The Bullets faced a disadvantage, as their two top scorers played with nagging injuries. Earl Monroe had bursitis in his knees, while Kevin Loughery sustained an injured adductor muscle. In addition, Gus Johnson could not play due to his knees. Slowed by these factors, the Bullets scored only 101 points and lost by 12, 113–101. The Knicks hosted the second game of the series and outmuscled Baltimore on the boards and contested the outlet passes that led to many of the Bullets' quick points. Holding the Bullets to 91 points, the Knicks won game two by 16 points, 107–91.

Back home, the Bullets played a dogged game three in front of a crowd of nearly 10,000 fans. The Bullets held on to a nine-point lead with less than seven minutes to play in the game, but the Knicks made their move behind guard Walt Frazier and took the lead when he made a driving move to the basket for a layup with a minute and a half remaining. Both teams exchanged misses, and then Frazier dropped in a free throw to up the lead to 116–114. With Bill Bradley hitting a shot and Willis Reed making a free throw, New York took game three, 119–116.

Behind three games to none, the Bullets traveled to Madison Square Garden with hopes of salvaging at least one game. Eyeing a sweep, the Knicks realized that they could end the series quickly and did not let up. Coach William "Red" Holzman continued his strategy of utilizing New York's superior bench with key substitutions. To the roars of their nearly 20,000 faithful, the Knicks held on to a 111–100 lead with about two minutes remaining. Led by Ray Scott, Wes Unseld, and Earl Monroe, the Bullets cut the lead to three within a minute. The Knicks defense, particularly center Willis Reed, cut off the Bullets' last chances, and the Knicks took the series with a 115–108 victory, sending the first-place Bullets home for the summer.

The Boston Celtics went on to win the 1969 championship, their eighth during the 1960s. If they were to repeat during the 1969–1970 season, they would have to beat stronger squads in the division. The Milwaukee Bucks drafted center Lew Alcindor (later Kareem Abdul-Jabbar) and improved with him in the lineup. The Knicks rookies now had a year of seasoning. The Bullets drafted two guards, Mike Davis, in the first round, and Fred "Mad Dog" Carter, in the third, to expand their bench. Baltimore's second-round choice, Willie Scott, like 7 others out of the 14 chosen in the round, had never played a game in the league.

One of the longer-term Bullets, center Bob Ferry, retired and took a job as assistant coach and scout. The Bullets followed the trend mentioned with Mike Farmer in chapter four, and Al Bianchi, the Capitols' coach described in chapter five. These former players left the rosters to take a new position that helped the team's head coach and general manager. This hiring expanded and strengthened the Bullets' organizational structure and capabilities.

Like Baltimore, the majority of the teams in the league generally had small scouting staffs. The year before, the Bullets had one main scout, Jerry Krause. A few teams moved to a more regional scouting system, which included a few people, sometimes hired only on a part-time basis. The slight improvement made sense because of the fierce competition among the American Basketball Association (ABA) and NBA, as well as the increase in the number of teams in the NBA from 9 to 28 during the 1960s. Professional basketball scouts now regularly attend the National Association of Intercollegiate Athletics championship. These 32 "small colleges" did not get the attention of the bigger colleges, but scouts saw the benefits of attending the championships. The Knicks were among the leaders in this scouting niche, signing Walt Frazier, Willis Reed, and Dick Barnett, three of their starting five, while observing these games.

The contest over players grew more hectic, as colleges and universities began to have to fight to retain players. Spencer Haywood, who we saw lead Denver to a playoff win over the Washington Capitols in the last chapter, could not play in the NBA until the four years of his collegiate eligibility had elapsed, per the NBA's draft rules. Haywood brought suit, and federal judge Warren Ferguson ruled that the four-year rule violated the Sherman Antitrust Act, enabling Haywood to sign with a professional team rather than having to wait until his four-year collegiate period elapsed.

In its annual preseason prediction issue, which had been appearing since 1958, the staff of *Sports Illustrated* declared that the old balance of power had disappeared. Perennial power Boston might be dislodged from the top spot that they seemed to have held since the magazine started printing this review. The staff predicated a change, as they expected Baltimore and New York to battle for the top positions.[5]

The Bullets had to overcome last season's failure after being swept out of the playoffs as the top seed. Heading into the season, the offensive style featured plays for individuals. "We have lots of plays, but they are geared to create one-on-one situations," Gene Shue stated. This high-scoring and fast-paced style was also the trademark of the Philadelphia 76ers, who at times employed a three-guard offense to maximize the running style. Yet, unlike Baltimore, they did not have set plays for one guy. The offense ran with continuity, and as more of a pattern, with players taking certain spots on the court based on the play. New York employed a style of moving without the ball and passing to the open man. As Bernie Bickerstaff noted, "The New York Knicks of the 1970s were a great passing and one of the greatest shooting teams of all time." Cincinnati, Seattle, and many other squads used a version of the older style of using a set play offense. Los Angeles chose to use its big center to set picks to create open shots.[6]

Throughout the league, shooting improved on a team and individual basis. Teams' averages rose from 44% to 46% during the 1960s, while ball possessions dropped slightly. Individual shooting percentages also rose during this time. Of the top 20 scorers, the twentieth player on the list shot at a 43% clip during the 1961–1962 season and improved to shoot 46% by the end of the decade.

With the improvements in offense across the board, the range of magazines covering the NBA predicted 10 top teams, all mostly because of their fire power. The Bullets numbered among them because of their speedy offense and Wes Unseld's rebounding (figure 6.1). The Lakers had a team full of guns but would have to play better defense to win. The Knicks were the consummate team. The 76ers had plenty of scoring. The Warriors and Hawks had strong inside and outside shooting games. The Bullets finished another strong regular season with a record of 50–32, but with two of the league's top teams in the Eastern Division, the Bullets' 50 wins only placed them in third, behind the New York Knicks and Milwaukee Bucks. Earl Monroe led the team in scoring again, but the team also received more balanced offense, with five players scoring more than 1,000 points, and seven contributing at least 500 points. While team scoring averages rose across the league, the Bullets jumped up four points, to 120 a game. Again, the total placed them in second, behind Philadelphia. The team defense slipped to 10th in the league.

The Bullets did not have a traditional general manager that ran basketball operations. Instead, they had Jerry Sachs in an executive president position,

Figure 6.1. Wes Unseld grabbing a rebound against the Philadelphia 76ers.
Reprinted with permission of the D.C. Public Library, Star Collection, @ *Washington Post*.

handling organizational matters. Coach Gene Shue made most of the basketball personnel decisions. Shue made a few trades toward the second half of the season. He shipped forward Ed Manning to the Chicago Bulls for forward Al Tucker. The Bullets gained a slight rise in scoring and rebounding. Two years later, Tucker would not make the team, while Manning moved on to the ABA. In February, guard Bob Quick went to the Detroit Pistons for

Eddie Miles, trading younger for older. Miles shot better but received little playing time. The next season, Miles played quite a few minutes but made small contributions in assists and ranked in the lower middle of team in field goal percentage. He would also not make the team by the 1971–1972 season. Meanwhile, Quick was also out of the NBA by the 1971–1972 campaign. Neither trade proved that significant.

The biggest trade was the one that the team could not accomplish. The Bullets and the Cincinnati Royals arranged a trade for the Royals' All-Star guard, Oscar Robertson. The Bullets planned to send forward Gus Johnson to Cincinnati. The rumors expected the team to trade guard Earl Monroe to the Phoenix Suns in exchange for their forward, Paul Silas. Robertson demanded a three-year contract for $700,000, and the Bullets offered a $350,000 pact for two years. Robertson exercised his veto power on trades and went to Milwaukee instead.

Then, right before the playoffs, the Bullets made another move. Mike "Crusher" Davis, the team's back up guard, went to the expansion Buffalo Braves for their first-round draft pick, center George Johnson. The move made Fred Carter and Eddie Miles the guards coming off the bench. Of Baltimore's other draft choices, guard Gary Zeller played one year with the Bullets, and the next year with the Bullets and the Nets of the ABA. The 6-foot, 11-inch Johnson signed a lucrative four-year contract despite concerns about the health of his knees. The Bullets hoped that Johnson would be the answer to their attempts to find the right big man to carry the team deep into the playoffs.[7]

Round Two with the Knicks

Finishing third in the Eastern Division set up a rematch of last year's division semifinals with the Knicks. The Knicks began the season winning 23 of their first 24 games, and pundits and fans expected them to become the league champions. The Knicks won 60 games and featured the stingiest defense in the NBA, holding their opponents to less than 110 points a game. The season series between the teams did not bode well for Baltimore, as they lost five of the six games played.

As the top team in the conference, the Knicks hosted game one at Madison Square Garden in front of a capacity crowd. The teams waged a battle, and the game remained tied after regulation and through the first overtime period. Both teams squeezed minutes out of their bench players to keep the starters' legs as fresh as possible. Despite Earl Monroe's 39 points and Fred Carter's 21, the Knicks prevailed for a 120–117 victory in double overtime.

Spectators, ranging from Don and Henny Margolin to sports columnist Leslie Matthews, thought the game ranked among the top sporting events of the year. The Bullets played like champions, but the Knicks still had the winning fever.

The two teams traveled to Baltimore and played game two, two nights later. Walt Frazier loved playing in Baltimore because of its knowledgeable fans and carnival atmosphere; however, the team did not fill the arena for this playoff game. Earl Monroe played 41 minutes on his arthritic knees but only managed 19 points. Frontcourt teammates Gus Johnson and Jack Marin tried to pick up the slack, scoring 28 and 22 points, respectively, but the Knicks received their usual big game against the Bullets from Willis Reed (27 points) and timely contributions from substitutes Mike Riordan and Cazzie Russell to win, 106–99.

Reporters began talking about the Bullets needing blindfolds, for they might get blanked again, two series in a row in which they won no games. In an attempt to find trends and draw meaning from past experiences, other statistics appeared, for example, the Bullets losing 11 straight playoff games since 1965; however, the players knew that the game was about the play on the court.[8] "I'd be thinking about four straight, but it's gonna get rough," said Walt Frazier.[9]

The third game in the series appeared on national television, as ABC broadcast it as their Sunday afternoon featured game. Kevin Loughery, playing with a corset harness to protect his cracked ribs and punctured lungs, took off the brace after the team fell behind in the first quarter. The guard then chipped in 17 points the rest of the way. Fred Carter hounded Knicks ace guard Walt Frazier with his tough defense. The Bullets took the game, 127–113, and headed to their home court down by one in the series.

Gus Johnson summarized his team's feelings in their steamy, noisy dressing room after their 102–92 defeat of the Knicks in game four. "It's a new series now. We're both starting from scratch." Exultant Coach Gene Shue grinned, "Our defense has been really tremendous." Earl Monroe hit 14 of his 26 shots to give the Bullets a lead, and clutch scoring from other veterans held off the late charge by the Knicks. Wes Unseld, who contributed 24 rebounds and forced the Knicks to think twice about shots as they attempted to penetrate the lane, sat quietly in front of his locker. "We've got to wait until this thing is all over before I can get excited."[10]

Wes Unseld's opposing number at center, Willis Reed, starred in game five. Reed scored 36 points and grabbed 36 rebounds in the contest. After three quarters, the game remained close, with the Knicks leading, 76–69. Then, the Knicks broke open the game with a 13–2 run over the first half of the final quarter to put the game out of reach. This time the Knicks defense stifled the Bullets, holding their opponent to a mere 11 points during the last 12 minutes, winning the game, 101–80 (figure 6.2).

The two teams brought their tough defenses to game six. In front of the largest Baltimore crowd of the series, near the capacity of 12,500, both teams missed many shots during the first period. At halftime, the Knicks went into the locker room with a 43–41 lead. The Bullets came out strong in the second half. Forward Gus Johnson and guard Earl Monroe combined for 28 points, as the Bullets took a 71–66 advantage. The pair added another 12, half of the team's total, in the fourth quarter, as the Bullets walked away with a 96–87 win. Coaches Gene Shue and Red Holzman expected a decidedly physical game in store for the do-or-die game in New York. "Both teams are tough and talented. . . . It should be a real battle, full of emotion and hard play," Holzman added.[11]

The Knicks jumped out to an early lead. Behind the scoring of Dave DeBusschere and Dick Barnett, the team led by five at the close of the first quarter. The pair and others off the bench, including Mike Riordan and

Figure 6.2. Wes Unseld and Jack Marin battle Phil Jackson for the ball.
Reprinted with permission of the D.C. Public Library, Star Collection, @ *Washington Post.*

Cazzie Russell, expanded the lead to 15 by halftime. Despite consistent scoring by the Knicks and their own foul trouble, the Bullets summoned the energy to cut the deficit to 88–82 by the end of the third quarter. Earl Monroe and Gus Johnson led the way back with help from Jack Marin, but the Knicks remained hot on offense and supplied enough defense to pull away and take a 127–114 victory.

The Knicks drew the Milwaukee Bucks for the next round of the playoffs. The Bucks, with Rookie of the Year Lew Alcindor, dispatched the Philadelphia 76ers in five games and had nearly a week off before meeting the Knicks. The New Yorkers bested the Bucks in five games and then took the NBA Championship with a four games to three victory over the Los Angeles Lakers.

The NBA expanded during the 1970–1971 season. Franchises in Buffalo, Cleveland, and Portland joined to create the 17-team league, and the organization's leadership took the opportunity to restructure the divisions. The NBA moved from two divisions of seven teams to four divisions, three with four teams and the Western Division with five teams. The schedule also changed significantly. Instead of playing each team six or seven times a year, teams now played each other anywhere from four to six games per year. The divisions remained linked with the Eastern and Central divisions forming the Eastern Conference, and the Midwest and Pacific divisions linking to create the Western Conference.

Expansion or Merger?

As a member of the NBA's expansion committee, Bullets' owner Abe Pollin pushed for continued expansion in the NBA rather than a merger with the ABA. As we learned in the last chapter, he asserted that the ABA's Washington Capitols infringed on the Bullets' territorial rights. He refused to reconsider his position, and the Capitols moved the franchise to southern Virginia as part of the merger efforts. While Pollin insisted that the 40 miles between the cities enabled Baltimore and Washington to root for the same team, other opinions differed. The dean of Washington's sportswriters, Shirley Povich, said, "Semifranchises won't work in Washington. Let Baltimore have their own teams, Washington has shown its big-league style a long time ago." Povich's position seemed unassailable when considering the NFL, but questionable when examining MLB (two Washington Senators franchises moved from the city in 1961 and 1972). It would not have been possible with a NBA team.

Despite all the changes, the league kept the playoffs limited to four teams, the first- and second-place finishers from each of the divisions. The team with the best record would play the second-place team from the other division, while the remaining first- and second-place teams would also meet in the conference semifinals.

Baltimore moved from the Eastern Division into the Central Division, joining Atlanta, Cincinnati, and Cleveland. The Central Division was a weaker division: Cleveland was an expansion team, Cincinnati played 10 games under .500 the previous season, and the Atlanta Hawks won fewer games than the third-place Bullets did the previous year. Still, the experts expected Atlanta to win the division. Baltimore had several players struggling with bad knees, including first-round draft pick George Johnson, who had such mobility issues an observer wondered if he could guard anything more mobile than a tree.

Most of the roster returned from the tough series loss to the Knicks for the opening of the season in October 1970. The team lacked a second-round choice, and their third- and fourth-round choices did not play in the NBA. Most of the teams in the NBA shared that experience. Still, three rookies, including two of the Bullets 1970 draft choices, joined the team; however, free agent forward Dennis Stewart did not last, and the team purchased onetime Bullet Jim Barnes to replace him. Coach Gene Shue also traded second-round draft choices for the 1971 and 1972 seasons to acquire more help in the frontcourt. The Bullets picked up Dorie Murrey from the Portland Trail Blazers and longtime pro John Tresvant from the Los Angeles Lakers. Both brought rebounding and a decent shooting touch to the team.

The team hovered around the .500 mark until early December. A four-game winning streak at home put them at 18–12, solidly in first place in the Central Division. Cleveland had won only two games at that point, and Cincinnati, with a record of 12–16, sat in second place. A six-game win streak to begin the new year represented the team's longest burst of winning for the season and put them at 26–16. By the end of February, the Bullets had nearly clinched the division title. While other veterans suffered from knee injuries, rookie George Johnson returned from his troubles to play in 24 games. Even with a 4–10 record during their last 14 games, the Bullets finished six games ahead of the Atlanta Hawks.

The team expected their captain, Gus Johnson, and center, Wes Unseld, to return for the start of the playoffs. Johnson predicted that the Bullets would defeat the 76ers in five games based on the return of himself and Unseld to the team's lineup. The Bullets split six regular-season games with Philadelphia, so Coach Shue expected a closely contested series.

Baltimore started poorly. The Bullets committed 27 turnovers, as the 76ers defense hounded the team's ball handlers. Johnson and Unseld appeared rusty, and Earl Monroe sustained a bruised rib, which kept him out of the game after the first half. The less-than-half-capacity crowd witnessed a 126–112 defeat of the home team. At the Spectrum in Philadelphia two nights later, the Bullets played like a team that knew it needed to win. Behind forward Jack Marin and Earl Monroe's combined 48 points, the Bullets rolled to a 119–107 victory before a crowd that filled a little more than half of the Spectrum.

In game three, the team found their stride. Before fewer than 6,000 fans and a national television audience, the Bullets played a tough, physical game, dominating the boards. The 76ers battled—an elbow in Monroe's sore rib during the second quarter sent him to the locker room, where smelling salts and codeine tablets took the glaze out of his eyes and slowed the cold perspiration rolling off his body. Scoring from the 76ers guard tandem of Hal Greer and Billy Cunningham reduced the Bullets lead to four points before Monroe scored eight points to put the game away. In game four, the Bullets kept up their running game and continuously drove to the basket, drawing fouls on Philadelphia. While the teams were tied at 62 apiece by halftime, Philadelphia's star guard, Billy Cunningham, had to sit out the start of the third quarter with four personal fouls. Baltimore went on a 12–5 run and kept it up despite having Unseld on the bench with five fouls himself, holding on to win 120–105.

The 76ers showed no desire to quit despite being one game away from elimination. In game five, they took a huge halftime lead into the locker room behind good shooting and a suffocating defense. The Bullets mounted a comeback from a 17-point deficit. With the score 104–103, Baltimore's Wes Unseld passed the ball to Jack Marin on the sidelines with five seconds left. The ball slipped through Marin's fingers, and the game ended.

The defending champion New York Knicks had already defeated the Atlanta Hawks in the other Eastern Conference semifinal, so they could sit back and watch the Bullets and 76ers run each other ragged. The 76ers did just that, evening the series at three games apiece with a seesaw home court victory, winning 98–94. The game slipped away from the Bullets when they could only score one field goal during the last three minutes of the game.

The deciding game seven was played in Baltimore, and both teams scored well during the first quarter. The small crowd quickly became energized, as the Bullets broke open a 31–30 game, scoring 43 points in the second quarter. The Bullets rested a few of their players toward the end, with both Kevin Loughery and Gus Johnson playing through the help of painkilling injections. The Bullets advanced to the next round of the playoffs, winning game seven by a score of 128–120.

It was then another year and another matchup with New York, and, as with last year's playoffs, the Knicks and Bullets were rated evenly matched at several positions. The major pairings were Reed-Unseld, DeBusschere-Johnson, and Frazier-Monroe. The latter pair appeared together in a report that the Dallas Chaparrals of the ABA were interested in purchasing their services. The discussions between the team and a sports player management company named Sports Productions Unlimited featured a $3 million deal including both Frazier and Monroe.

The story seems credible in the environment of the NBA–ABA war over players. As noted in the last chapter, more teams created more opportunities for players. The better players with higher salaries could leverage the possibility of playing for another team, or another league, into lucrative contracts. For example, the Chaparrals wooed the Bullets' top draft choice, forward Stan Love, with a big contract. Other NBA players had jumped leagues using that leverage, including Billy Cunningham of the 76ers, Dave Bing of the Pistons, and Joe Caldwell of the Hawks.

Neither Frazier nor Monroe was thrilled with their current contracts. Frazier had talked with Knicks management about his $25,000 annual salary after the Knicks signed guard John Warren, their top pick in the 1969 draft, for a guaranteed three-year, $100,000 contract. Monroe also expressed salary complains to the Bullets' management, as his salary contained some of the same elements of Julius Erving's Virginia Squires' contract. As noted in the previous chapter, Erving had a large portion of his salary deferred until years later; Monroe made $35,000 yearly but had $200,000 due to him during the course of 10 years, beginning a decade from the day the contract was signed. The deferred compensation might save a player on taxes and help him save money, but it also kept the player beholden to the team, in addition to the existing reserve clause, which the players were fighting to remove from contracts because it restricted their ability to bargain.

Earl Monroe had other concerns about continuing to play with the Bullets. The earlier trade rumors during the failed attempt to acquire Oscar Robertson set the relationship off. Monroe and the Bullets both realized the he was not a drawing card for fans, despite being a superstar, which made the guard wonder about all of Baltimore's basketball fans who did not come to see the team. Two months earlier, he had attended a high school basketball game between predominantly black Dunbar and mostly white Mount St. Joseph. A fight erupted after Dunbar's overtime loss, and Monroe tried to break it up. When Monroe explained his actions to the city's police, they still arrested him, along with 22 others. The team later threatened to fine the guard if he played in a NBA–ABA All-Star Game at the Astrodome, which the players arranged.

As their series with Philadelphia came to an end, the Bullets expressed their frustration over the schedule for the Knicks series. Usually, home courts are switched after every game in the playoffs. The Bullets argued that playing in New York on Tuesday night and then traveling to Baltimore for the Wednesday night game was too harsh a travel schedule. The Bullets believed that they could not play well under the current schedule and requested that the Knicks agree to the change.

The Knicks sought to maintain the current schedule. The NBA brokered a compromise, which changed the schedule to move the second game to Friday afternoon in New York. The third and fourth games would be played in Baltimore. If the series continued, the remaining games would alternate home courts, with New York hosting the fifth and seventh games.

Despite the changes, the Knicks held a distinct advantage going into the series. While the Knicks had the rest before the playoffs, Baltimore played two extra games. The Knicks had depth and used eight players on their roster nearly every game. Three others played in at least five games and averaged six minutes, or an eighth of a game. Meanwhile, the Bullets played six men nearly every game. Gus Johnson played when he was healthy. Two others substituted in for an average of five minutes. The Knicks won four of the six contests between the teams during the regular season. They held a 19–7 advantage during the course of a three-year span. More significantly, the Knicks won both of the playoff series the teams played during the previous two postseasons.

The first game recalled the thrilling double overtime opener from the previous year's series. The Knicks won game one, 112–111, as the Bullets played without their star forward, Gus Johnson. Before another capacity crowd in Madison Square Garden, the teams ended the first half of game two tied at 48 points apiece at halftime. Then Walt Frazier and Dick Barnett brought hot hands into the second half of the game. With Baltimore committing a number of turnovers, the Knicks ran away with the game, winning 107–88.

The reeling Bullets returned home to play before a crowd filling two-thirds of the Civic Center. Could the Bullets come back from a two games to zero deficit, like last year? As they warmed up, stars Gus Johnson and Kevin Loughery sat on the bench unable to play, and Earl Monroe hobbled on a twisted ankle. Walt Frazier, Dick Barnett, and Cazzie Russell had the Knicks ahead, 40–39, with five minutes left before halftime. Fred Carter, playing for the injured Kevin Loughery, and Earl Monroe began pouring in shots. By the halfway point of the third period, the Bullets led, 75–53. Soon thereafter, Knicks coach Red Holzman pulled his regulars from the game, and the Bullets took the Sunday afternoon nationally televised game, 114–88, to climb back into the series.

The Bullets began the fourth game with the same energy they had in the game three. Earl Monroe and Fred Carter received scoring help from forward Jack Marin and center Wes Unseld. The frontcourt hustled and beat New York on the boards, enabling the team to take a 10-point lead with only six minutes left to play. Willis Reed, New York's key defender and rebounder, took several shots to his sore right shoulder, further crippling his ability to reach up and grab rebounds. Meanwhile, New York lost is rhythm on its motion offense and shot less than 40% from the floor, while Baltimore made nearly half of its attempts. The Bullets won the game, 101–80, and tied the series at two games apiece.

Back in New York, the teams returned to a bruising defensive battle. The Knicks sparked their offense with consistent movement and multiple passes, which freed up Walt Frazier and Bill Bradley to make shots. After seizing an eight-point lead, Jack Marin and Earl Monroe replied to cut the lead in half at the close of the second quarter. Willis Reed, playing with his sore shoulder, battled Wes Unseld to a near draw in points and rebounds. Fellow frontcourt mate Dave DeBusschere hauled down 17 boards, while scoring 15 points, but the Knicks started missing their shots, and the Bullets' hustle led to six free throws that pulled them to within 86–84 with 30 seconds left on the clock. Walt Frazier hit a clutch jump shot, and Willis Reed grabbed the rebound after Kevin Loughery's miss to enable the Knicks to grab the series lead by a score of 89–84, as the teams returned to Baltimore.

The seesaw nature of this series continued. While Willis Reed's shoulder and knees limited his effectiveness, the Bullets received a boost from the return of their forward, Gus Johnson, from his knee problems. With Johnson contributing 10 points to the scoring of Earl Monroe and Jack Marin, the Bullets took a 56–43 halftime lead. A surprising 20-point contribution from reserve John Tresvant helped the Bullets win, 113–96. The two teams would return to New York for a game seven, and, with the six games so far being won by the home team, the Knicks had to feel they had the advantage.

The final game featured all the top players on both teams. Gus Johnson was prepared to play more minutes than in the last game. Willis Reed took painkilling shots in his bad knee and came out on the court with better movement. Behind his scoring and that of Dick Barnett, the Knicks held a four-point lead at halftime. The Bullets regrouped and came out of the locker room with renewed energy. Earl Monroe and Jack Marin, plus Fred Carter and Wes Unseld, propelled their team to a 30–21 third-quarter to overtake the Knicks; however, the Knicks battled back. With less than three minutes remaining, New York took an 88–87 lead. Monroe would not let the Knicks seize the game, as they had done so many times before. He scored, and then

Marin put in a rebound off a Monroe miss. His backcourt mate, Fred Carter, hit a 20-foot jumper to close the Bullets scoring. The Knicks took the ball down and had Bill Bradley set for a shot. Unseld partially deflected it. Johnson saw the ball coming down off the boards and said, "I was going to get that one no matter what; I never wanted the ball so much in my life."[12] He did so, and his rebound sealed the 93–91 victory for the visitors.

The theme of Baltimore's individuals against New York's team appeared even after the series win. "We're a one-on-one team, and we can't change that," Earl Monroe said. He continued, "But now we're taking more time, getting better shots."[13] Jack Marin noted that while he and Earl were considered great offensive players, they did not always help in other ways. Their teammates (and coach) were not always pleased. Said Marin, "Over the last 18 games, there's rarely been a time when I've been unhappy with a teammate. And the feeling shows in our defense."[14]

A Zero for the Finals

While the Bullets outlasted another opponent in seven games, the Milwaukee Bucks dispatched the Los Angeles Lakers in five games in the Western Conference finals. Oscar Robertson, one of the best guards of all-time, joined Lew Alcindor, now Kareem Abdul-Jabbar, for the season, and the Bucks finished the campaign with 66 wins and only 16 losses. They dispatched their playoff opponents, while losing only one game each series. Walt Frazier analyzed the series, saying, "If the Bullets play the Bucks the same way they played us, they can beat them. If they go back to their one-on-one stuff, though, they won't beat them."[15] Coach Gene Shue, more of a strategist than any previous Bullets coach, continued to preach team defense and a more structured offense. The strategy paid off in the postseason, up until the NBA Finals.[16]

In game one of the NBA Finals, the duo of Kareem Abdul-Jabbar and Oscar Robertson seemed too strong for the aggressive but undermanned Bullets. Gus Johnson sat out again because of his knees, leaving the small-sized center, Wes Unseld, to battle the seven-foot, two-inch Bucks' center alone, but Abdul-Jabbar picked up three personal fouls and had to sit out most of the first half. Robertson took over and enabled Milwaukee to take a small lead at halftime. Abdul-Jabbar returned to score 18 points in the third quarter, six on tip-in baskets and four more off missed shots that he rebounded. Earl Monroe and teammates plugged away, narrowing the Bucks lead to six points before the Bucks pulled away for a 98–88 win.

The capacity crowd hoped for the Bullets to even the series. The home team held tough in the first half. Unseld played Abdul-Jabbar to a near draw, grabbing 17 rebounds and scoring 6 points against his opposing number's 14 points and 14 rebounds. Monroe, Marin, Carter, and Loughery all scored to pull the Bullets to within four points at halftime. Unfortunately, the team had little left for the remainder of the game. Milwaukee burst out on a 19–2 run, and, as Abdul-Jabbar controlled both sets of boards, the Bucks went on to win easily by a score of 102–83.

The Bullets were crippled with injuries leading into game three. The scrimmage held in the off day between games only had seven players in uniform able to play. Neither team played well in the third game of the series, although Milwaukee performed fine in short spurts, particularly with Bobby Dandridge shooting the ball. The guard scored 29 points, and Oscar Robertson chipped in 20. The Bullets struggled to hold the Bucks down defensively, and their offense lulled. The team missed 54 out of 81 shots, a shooting percentage of only 33%, before finally making an attempted comeback. The end result was a 107–99 loss that left the team facing the potential to set a negative record, the lowest points per game in a final series since the advent of the 24-second shot clock in 1954.

The Bullets started slowly in game four. Milwaukee moved the ball with precision and shot nearly 60% from the field. In a 13-point hole at halftime, Baltimore tried to mount a rally to get back into the game. Fred Carter led the attack, with 28 points, and Kevin Loughery added 18, but the Bucks continued making their shots, and the Bullets only chipped away a single point from the lead after three quarters. The fourth quarter seemed little better, as the Bullets closed the margin to 7 points before Milwaukee raised it back up to 12 on their way to a 118–106 win.

While the ending to the playoffs was obviously disappointing, the Bullets players and management earned important income from making the NBA Finals. Columnists believed that it was the first season Pollin's team would turn a profit. One sports columnist predicted that the playoff run would boost the Bullets as an attraction the following year, hopefully filling their 12,000-seat arena more often. The Civic Center ranked among the bottom third in capacity among NBA arenas.

The Bullets had a large potential fan base throughout their territory, yet they seemed to draw mostly from their home city. Baltimore ranked seventh nationally in city population in 1970; however, it had lost 35,000 people, or 4% of its population, from a decade earlier. Although it ranked eighth among cities in real per capita income in 1970, the city had begun the process of having the income decline during the 1970s. The team saw the need to expand its appeal to nearby Washington. The team planned to play a few more home games at the University of Maryland's Cole Field House

Figure 6.3. The Bullets play at Cole Field House, at the University of Maryland, College Park.
Reprinted with permission of the D.C. Public Library, Star Collection, @ *Washington Post*.

as part of an effort to increase the team's fan base (figure 6.3). Survey results from spectators indicated that nearly 12% of their audience came from the Washington, D.C., area. Few viewed the Civic Center as unsafe, although most fans found the high ticket prices and long driving time prohibitive to regular attendance. Most of the spectators were white males, and Pollin and his marketing department sought ways to increase those groups' attendance. The Bullets did manage to set a record for season ticket sales, with a total of 1,738, an increase of 154 over the previous year.[17]

Even without the limited attendance, some sports pundits wondered how NBA teams could be financially successful. One pointed to the million-dollar contracts being given to unproven rookies to sign them. Another pointed to teams having to pay the players, when NBA salaries averaged $36,000 per man and each team carried 12 players. In addition, team travel expenses increased significantly. Only New York continued the policy of having players room together, so hotel costs increased. Per diem meal costs also rose.

Personnel Changes

The Bullets faced greater hurdles in assembling a team in the 1971 off-season. Wes Unseld slowly recovered from his knee operation, and Gus Johnson had off-season knee surgery on both knees. When asked when Johnson would be ready to play again, guard Fred Carter asked, "Ready to play what? The harp?" Even with the limits on their top two frontcourt players, the team waived their top draft pick from two years earlier, center George Johnson.

Most of the new draftees looked like they would not make the team. Besides Stan Love, it appeared that the Bullets would keep guard Phil Chenier, who they drafted as a hardship case in the first round of the 1971 draft. Veteran guard Eddie Miles received his release. Coach Gene Shue made a bold trade that would dramatically alter the team's makeup. After unsuccessfully trying to trade Earl Monroe to Philadelphia, the Bullets traded guards Kevin Loughery and Fred Carter for guard Archie Clark and a second-round draft pick in the 1973 draft. The Bullets gave up their excellent shooting guard and defensive spark plug for a good defender with one-on-one offensive skills. Loughery happily played for the 76ers and their coach, Jack Ramsey, but he only lasted two more years. Carter played for several years on a few woeful squads before a new 76ers coach, who, ironically, was Gene Shue, traded him away from a winning squad during the 1976–1977 season.[18]

Sportswriters wondered how Archie Clark and Earl Monroe would function together. Soon, the open secret that Monroe was playing out his option and pressuring the Bullets to trade him emerged. "The Pearl" chose to sit out the opening games, as did Clark, who engaged in a contract dispute with his new team. Clark soon returned to the team. Monroe; his lawyer; the National Basketball Player's Association's general counsel, Larry Fleisher; and owner Abe Pollin accused one another of irresponsible behavior and a lack of loyalty for two months. Did Monroe want a better contract? If so, did Pollin offer an increase plus more deferred money, as he claimed? Did Monroe inform Pollin about his desire to be traded months prior, or just before the season started?

Many athletes considered Baltimore the last outpost for gaining national attention. Teammates cited how much money Monroe would make in endorsements if he played in New York. Most of his teammates supported Monroe, everyone except forward Jack Marin, who said, "The club ought to tell him to get a job somewhere—sweeping streets or something. Management will only hurt itself in this predicament by patronizing him." The law student cited the sanctity of the contract and that the situation made professional basketball look bad.[19] Monroe appeared prepared to sit out the option year, as Rick Barry did during the 1967–1968 season to join the team of his choice.

The Bullets knew that they would have to trade Monroe to acquire value back for their team. Gene Shue tried to trade the superstar, but the Bullets received rejections or unacceptable offers of players that did not match Monroe's ability. The team eventually accepted an offer from the Knicks for small forward Mike Riordan and Dave "The Rave" Stallworth for Monroe. While the new concern was whether Walt Frazier and Monroe could play well together, the players the Bullets received seemed to fit into Shue's mold.

Riordan was a defensive specialist, and Stallworth ran from his forward position. While Baltimore's main sports columnist told readers that both players were hustlers and unselfish, Frazier later characterized Stallworth as "having lots of potential but [with] a heart problem and [he] liked to party a little too much."[20] Stallworth's minutes and contributions dropped each of the three seasons with the Bullets before the team traded him and a 1975 second-round draft pick for Clem Haskins in 1974.[21]

The disarray in personnel hurt the Bullets on the court; however, the Central Division earned the nickname "The Comedy Circuit" from sportswriters. Despite signing superstar guard Pete Maravich, the Atlanta Hawks, two weeks into the season, were tied with the Bullets in first place, each team winning one of every three games played. Cincinnati kept winning at slightly above that clip for the season, while Cleveland did worse. The Hawks made a strong run at season's end to win 36 games, two short of Baltimore's total of 38.

The team's play presumably hampered attendance. The Bullets drew more than 272,000 spectators, placing the team in its familiar position in the lower half of the league (11th of 17 teams). The 8 games at the University of Maryland averaged nearly 9,000 fans, while the remaining 34 games in Baltimore drew an average of 5,300. Only two games drew more than 10,000, a doubleheader featuring the Harlem Globetrotters and the return of Earl Monroe with the New York Knicks in November. The Bullets' Jerry Sachs argued, "Something has to be done to put more emphasis on the regular season." He added, "There are too many regular-season games."[22] Sachs' comments reflected the sentiments of the small-market teams. New York and Los Angeles sold out every game and so would not want any reduction. Chicago also followed the pattern of the big-market clubs; however, both Seattle and Milwaukee placed in the top five, so winning teams could generate great fan interest in certain smaller cities.

Despite both teams having low winning percentages, each made the playoffs. Boston won the Eastern Division, so they played fourth-place finisher, Atlanta, and dispatched them four games to two. Baltimore and New York met again in the playoffs. But *Sports Illustrated* staff claimed the matchup bordered on irrelevancy, as the three strongest clubs, Chicago, Los Angeles, and Milwaukee, all played in the Western Conference.[23]

Round Three

As the first-place team, the Bullets opened at home against second-place New York. Before the sellout crowd, the teams engaged in their usual war of tight defense and clutch shots. The Knicks overcame a fourth-quarter deficit to force the game into overtime. Behind Archie Clark's 38 points and key free throws by Jack Marin, the Bullets won game one, 108–105. At Madison Square Garden two days later, the Bullets went into the arena highly emotional, shouting encouragement to one another. Knicks coach Red Holzman made the bold move of starting Earl Monroe in the place of Dick Barnett. "The Pearl" got the Knicks off to a quick 13–7 lead and a 13-point bulge in the second quarter. Helped by Walt Frazier's 31 points, with Dave DeBusschere contributing 29 points, the Knicks never led by less than 11 points on their way to a 110–88 thumping. Home cooking continued to matter, as Baltimore took the third game in the series, 104–103, with Archie Clark hitting for 35, Wes Unseld for 19, and Phil Chenier for 16 points. In the Knicks' game four 104–98 victory, Bill Bradley hit for 25 points, and his backcourt mates combined for another 45, to offset strong games from Archie Clark, Phil Chenier, and Mike Riordan.

The two teams faced the familiar. The winner needed to win two of three, and this time Baltimore had the home court advantage. Earl Monroe again staked the Knicks out to an early lead. The Bullets could not hit their shots, and, at halftime, Coach Shue thought that things could have been worse, as the team trailed by only seven points and the Knicks had foul trouble. The Knicks made just 36% of their shots in the third quarter, and the Bullets fell behind by 22 points. The Bullets scored 12 points in the quarter, four more than Knick Phil Jackson, playing for foul-troubled Bill Bradley, scored during the same period.

After the 106–82 debacle, the teams returned to the Garden. The teams engaged in their usual rugged contest, with bodies banging, off-balance shots, and tough fouls. The Knicks seized the early advantage and extended it to 10 points by the first quarter, but Baltimore battled back and took the lead, 93–88, with four minutes remaining in the game. Jerry Lucas, playing for injured Willis Reed, made a driving basket and the ensuing free throw to cut the lead to seven. The Bullets' shots did not go in. New York missed a few too, but Lucas hit another basket and picked up two rebounds, which led to a Bradley jumper that put the Knicks in the lead, 97–95, with two minutes remaining. The Bullets came down the court and failed to get a shot off, violating the 24-second rule. The Knicks missed a shot during their possession, and Archie Clark brought the ball down the court to the top of the key. Frazier stole the ball from Clark's hands and then drove to the other basket and was fouled. His two free throws put the Knicks up by four with a minute remaining. The teams swapped a few points, and the Knicks closed out the Bullets with a 107–101 win.

As the lease on using the Civic Center came to an end, Abe Pollin considered where to base his basketball team. Earlier in the year, he had engaged in discussion with officials about potentially playing in Columbia, Maryland. He viewed the area as an appropriate location, halfway between the two major cities. Maryland's governor, Marvin Mandel, met with executives from Baltimore's professional sports teams and discussed building a new arena and stadium for them. Meanwhile, the arena that key members of the House of Representatives' District of Columbia Committee had been advocating since 1969 awaited President Richard Nixon's advocacy for the Eisenhower Center. The president's aid was needed, because Congress would not approve of the arena in the Mount Vernon neighborhood of Washington, D.C.

The Civic Center compared unfavorably to most of the NBA arenas throughout the country. While only a decade old, only seven of the other 16 active NBA arenas were older. Of those older stadiums, the Boston Garden, Chicago Stadium, and Buffalo Memorial Stadium all had a much larger seating capacity. Out of the 16 locations, only Cleveland Arena, Milwaukee Arena, Portland Memorial Coliseum, and Houston's Hofheinz Pavilion seated fewer people.[24]

A New Arena

As the 1972 playoffs neared the end, Abe Pollin announced his plan to build a $15 million arena on the Capital Beltway in Prince George's County, Maryland. Pollin's former coowner, Arnold Heft, had spent four years acquiring the 50-acre site. Heft brought Maryland democratic legislator Leonard Blondes into his Potomac Sports, Inc., company, which controlled the 20-year lease on the government land. They could not acquire a franchise from the ABA or the required financing to build the arena.[25] Pollin raved about the advantages of the new site. "The site . . . will serve 3 million people within a 45-minute drive. There will be parking for 5,000 cars, and a Metro station is planned within 1,000 yards of the project."[26]

Before they could begin construction, the new arena had certain contingencies. Pollin knew of the economic need to have an area to service both basketball and hockey franchises. He bid on acquiring an expansion National Hockey League (NHL) franchise for the 1974–1975 season. The NHL Finance Committee had 10 bids for two franchises, and if Washington was selected it would be contingent on building the arena. On the fourth ballot, Washington and Kansas City received the nod of the NHL Board of Governors.

The development on open park land created opposition to the arena. The county executive supported the development and launched an attack on the group that sought to block the $2 million in county bonds to pay for the related roads and water and sewer services for the complex. The executive focused on the reported $1.5 million in tax revenue expected to be generated annually. The circuit court dissolved its temporary injunction against the issuance of a building permit on the basis that continuing it would hurt the public through higher ticket prices. Then, the Prince George's County Zoning Board issued a variance to allow building on 55% of the land, instead of the usual 25%. Local newspapers, weary of the county's land-dealing history and the involvement of Blondes, who had been convicted of bribery in a different case, thought citizens should be skeptical of this development and the possibility of it being used as a wedge to promote more development of park land.

The environmental groups and other protestors acquired signatures to place the use of the county bonds up for a referendum vote. The court then ruled that the county officials could allocate funds for the development under emergency legislation. Maryland's House of Delegates approved legislation that authorized the county to issue tax-free bonds to finance construction of the sports arena. Pollin would save approximately $300,000 a year by using these bonds for his financing rather than commercial bonds.[27]

With the new arena plan set to launch, Coach Gene Shue and others in the Bullets' leadership worked on the team. In the annual 1972 NBA Draft in April, longtime Bullet Gus Johnson was traded to the Phoenix Suns for their second-round pick. Said Johnson, "The club had a decision to make and since I'm the oldest one on the club, I guess I was prime bait."[28] This pick, the team's first in the draft, resulted in the Bullets selecting forward Tom Patterson. With the third-round pick, the team selected guard Kevin Porter. Of the 14 men selected, these two made the club for the 1972–1973 season. Patterson played 100 minutes during the course of one and a half seasons before being waived. Porter was the sixth or seventh man off the bench during that first year before becoming the team's key assist man for the next two seasons. Bob Ferry heard about a small tournament in southeast Virginia, so he drove down to the Portsmouth Invitational Tournament and saw Porter playing there. For three or four years, Ferry stood as the sole NBA scout in attendance. Porter's success in the league, along with that of Len "Truck" Robinson, helped make the tournament in Portsmouth a must for all NBA teams later in the 1970s.

In mid-summer, the team made a blockbuster move. Jack Marin went to the Houston Rockets in exchange for forward Elvin Hayes. Hayes carried a reputation as a difficult, selfish, and uncoachable player, which he said was a result of playing on losing teams. "It will be nice having an atmosphere of winning people around who know what's going on."[29] Coach Gene Shue planned on using a double-post offense, along with three guards, or two guards and a fast small forward, with his big-man pair.

But the team's executives needed to bring one of the guards back into the ranks. Archie Clark walked out after he and the Bullets were miles apart over contract negotiations. Despite a fine of $350 a day for missing training, Clark argued that he would not be pressured into caving. Jerry Sachs said the Bullets could not afford the salary Clark requested. Clark flirted with another one of Abe Pollin's former co-owners, the owner of the Virginia Squires ABA team, Earl Foreman, but the Bullets were granted an injunction, stopping Clark from playing anywhere else. The team revealed that they offered Clark as much as $175,000 annually, but his payments would be spread out over six years. Clark wanted $200,000 a year. Two superstar NBA guards made $300,000 (the Los Angeles Lakers' Jerry West and Atlanta's Pete Maravich). Some other teams faced these contract struggles, as Wilt Chamberlain did not sign until a last-minute accord with Laker management produced a deal worth $1 million.

The Bullets played without their premier guard for half of the 1972–1973 season. The team swapped wins and losses through the middle of December. Wes Unseld, one of two members left from the 1971 finals, along with John Tresvant, declared that the new team jelled into a cohesive unit during January. The team won 12 games and lost only two that month, and their 33–18 record placed them five games ahead of the second-place Atlanta Hawks and 13 in front of the Houston Rockets, who had moved from the Pacific Division to the Central Division. The Cincinnati Royals became the Kansas City-Omaha Kings and moved into the Midwest Division, pushing the Phoenix Suns from into the Pacific Division.

The Bullets continued to play good basketball. Executives and other basketball men admired the job Gene Shue did with transforming the team. Within two years, he had changed the squad from a helter-skelter fast-break outfit to more of a set offensive structure. The second-ranked offense moved down to number 12 of 17. The team that once ranked in the middle of the league on defense had moved up to the fourth-best defense in the league, holding teams to slightly more than 100 points a game.[30]

The claiming of the Central Division crown made the Bullets the number two seed in the Eastern Conference playoffs. First seed Boston, with a record of 68–82, took on fourth-seed Atlanta, while the Bullets and Knicks met again for the fifth year in a row. New York won five more games than the Bullets during the season, so the first two games took place at Madison Square Garden. As in past playoff games, matchups were the key to victory.

Willis Reed now faced fellow Louisianan Elvin Hayes in the pivot, while Wes Unseld moved over to forward to guard Dave DeBusschere. Mike Riordan covered Bill Bradley; Walt Frazier drew the prodigy, 22-year-old Phil Chenier; and Earl Monroe again faced Archie Clark. They finished the six-game regular-season series 3–3.

The visitors jumped out to a six-point lead after the first quarter of the first game and held a 45–43 halftime lead. Mike Riordan played dogged defense against Bill Bradley, holding him to one field goal, while Archie Clark and Phil Chenier poured in some key jumpers. In the second half, Earl Monroe and Walt Frazier each hit major shots, and Jerry Lucas came off the bench to make eight of nine field goals. The Knicks took a nine-point lead against the Bullets substitutes and expanded it in the last quarter to win by 12.

The second game went worse for the visitors. The Bullets played defense to work against New York's patterned offense and clamped it down. The Knicks switched to Monroe and Frazier each playing one-on-one against their man. Frazier hit for 29, and Monroe generated 32 points. When Baltimore moved to shut down the lane, it took the defenders away from the Knicks' outside shooters, who began making the less-contested jump shots. This barrage led to 123 points and a 20-point victory over the Bullets, 123–103.

Down two games to zero, the Bullets returned to the Civic Center for what might be the last games they played there. The construction crew worked hard on the Capital Centre in Landover, Maryland, and appeared to be close to making the deadline of holding the first Bullets game there on October 20. Before a capacity crowd, the Bullets rode Elvin Hayes's 36 points to keep within range of the hot-shooting Knicks. They trailed 60–59 when the Knicks ran off six unanswered points. The Bullets had watched films of each of the first two losses, but they did not prove useful, according to Wes Unseld. The star forward, who Dave Debusschere had neutralized in the series, had a point. The Knicks made more than half of their shots again this game, on their way to a 103–96 win.

Facing elimination, the Bullets regained defensive form in game four. Coach Shue switched his big men. Unseld now covered Reed, and Hayes moved over to DeBusschere. Clark now guarded Frazier, and Chenier took on Monroe. The team held the Knicks down to only 89 points. Hayes again made big baskets, as did guard Clark, to provide Baltimore with the offense to take an eight-point victory, winning by a score of 97–89. Back on their home court, the Knicks fell behind in the first half before dominating the second quarter with a 14 point spurt, while keeping Baltimore's offense at bay. Monroe brought his wizardry and scored 20 first-half points. The Knicks took the series behind a 109–99 victory.

The Baltimore Bullets were only able to manage one series victory in six tries against the Knicks in the playoffs. Maybe Jerry Lucas summed up the last series in particular, but perhaps all the series, when he said about the Knicks, "We're the smartest team that has ever played pro basketball."[31] The Bullets and owner Abe Pollin finished their decade in Baltimore. The Bullets experienced much success, even as they seemed to have New York limit their time in the playoffs. As the team moved south in Maryland, they did so without Gene Shue, who had sparse negotiations about the renewal of his contract. He believed that Abe Pollin must have thought that he did not want to continue with the team. Instead, Shue thought he would continue to live in Baltimore and commute the 40 minutes to the new arena. The move surprised Bob Ferry, who had no idea that the owners were not going to rehire Shue. Shue landed on his feet, obtaining a coaching contract with the woeful Philadelphia Sixers for four years and $800,000. He became the highest-paid coach in the league. In the nation's capital, basketball personnel decisions now would now become mainly the domain of Ferry, as the assistant coach took over as the team's general manager that summer.[32]

Notes

1. 1967–68 Baltimore Bullets Roster and Statistics," Basketball-Reference.com, www.basketball-reference.com/teams/BAL/1968.html (retrieved May 7, 2010); "1968–69 Baltimore Bullets Roster and Statistics," Basketball-Reference.com, www.basketball-reference.com/teams/BAL/1969.html (retrieved May 7, 2010).

2. "Speeding Bullets," *Newsweek*, January 20, 1969, 61.

3. Walt Frazier, with Neil Offen, *Walt Frazier: One Magic Season and a Basketball Life* (New York: Time Books, 1988), 97–106.

4. Milton Gross, "Baltimore Not Pearl's Oyster," *Baltimore Sun*, October 30, 1971, B1.

5. "Central," *Sports Illustrated*, October 26, 1970, 39.

6. This and other details and quotes by Bernie Bickerstaff were obtained during an interview with the author, March 17, 2012.

7. Alan Goldstein, "Upstart ABA Claims 'Who Needs NBA' Crows Jim Gardner," *Baltimore Sun*, March 18, 1970, C4; "Three Contests Start NBA Playoffs," *Baltimore Sun*, March 25, 1970, C1; Alan Goldstein, "Bullet Search for 'Giant' Set to Begin New Chapter," *Baltimore Sun*, June 1, 1970, C4.

8. "Results," *Washington Post*, March 29, 1970, 37.

9. "Bullets Go After Playoff First," *Washington Post*, March 31, 1970, D2.

10. Thomas Rogers, "Embattled Knicks Are Strong Again," *New York Times*, April 1, 1970, 71.

11. Thomas Rogers, "The Pearl Happy to Let Mate Carry Load in Bullets' Victory," *New York Times*, April 6, 1970, 69.

12. Leonard Koppett, "Bullets Eliminate Knicks 93-91," *New York Times*, April 20, 1971, 55.

13. "Bully for the Bullets," *Newsweek*, May 3, 1971, 91.

14. "Bully for the Bullets," 91.

15. Peter Carry, "Winner Gets to Play Alcindor," *Sports Illustrated*, April 26, 1971, 22.

16. "Bully for the Bullets," *Newsweek*, May 3, 1971, 91.

17. U.S. Census Bureau, *U.S. Decennial Census, 1970* (Washington, D.C.: U.S. Government Printing Office, 1950); "For the Record," *Sports Illustrated*, April 19, 1971, 101.

18. Peter Carry, "Playing the Comedy Circuit," *Sports Illustrated*, November 8, 1971, 62.

19. Carry, "Playing the Comedy Circuit," 62.

20. Frazier, with Offen, *Walt Frazier*, 36.

21. Frazier, with Offen, *Walt Frazier*, 172–82.

22. Mark Asher, "Regular Season Hurting NBA," *Washington Post*, April 2, 1972, F2.

23. "First West, Then the Rest," *Sports Illustrated*, October 16, 1972, 54.

24. "NBA Arenas," NBA Hoops Online, http://nbahoopsonline.com/History/Leagues/NBA/Arenas.html (retrieved May 13, 2010).

25. Mark Asher, "Pollin Bids for NHL," *Washington Post*, March 14, 1972, D3.

26. Kenneth Denlinger, "Basketball Disputed," *Washington Post*, May 3, 1972, D1.

27. Eugene L. Meyer, " His Approval of NW Arena Held Dim Despite NHL Grant," *Washington Post*, June 10, 1972, B1; "Mr. Pollin Picks Largo," *Washington Post*, August 3, 1972, A22; Philip A. McCombs," The Offer Prince George's Couldn't Refuse," *Washington Post*, August 20, 1972, B1.

28. Leonard Shapiro, "Knicks Prepare for Showdown," *Washington Post*, April 13, 1972, G8.

29. Mark Asher, "Hayes Paints Rosy Future," *Washington Post*, August 4, 1972, D4.

30. "Basketball: In the Money," *Newsweek*, October 23, 1972, 72.

31. Gerlad Strine, "Knicks Great; DeBusschere Superb," *Washington Post*, April 6, 1973, D2.

32. This and other details and quotes by Gene Shue were obtained during an interview with the author, March 5, 2012; this and other details and quotes by Bob Ferry were obtained during an interview with the author, March 17, 2012.

CHAPTER SEVEN

~

Abe Pollin and the Capital-Washington Bullets

Abe Pollin, along with the construction crew he hired, nearly completed most of the Capital Centre in 15 months for a total of $18 million. Several other arenas emerged between 1972 and 1976, including the Omni Coliseum in Atlanta, the Coliseum at Richfield in Ohio, Detroit's Pontiac Silverdome, Market Square Arena in Indianapolis, the Summit in Houston, and Kemper Arena in Kansas City.

Pollin used private funding to construct his arena. The Atlanta Hawks' owner also built the Omni with his personal money a year before the Capital Centre. The arena served as one part of a larger downtown development that became the CNN Center. The Coliseum at Richfield, completed in 1974, also involved private funding by the team owner. The Summit in Houston went up a year later for $18 million, led by the Houston Rockets' ownership group Texas Sports Investments. The Summit's 16,200 seating capacity placed it on par with the Omni, but 2,500 seats smaller than the Capital Centre and 5,000 less than Cleveland's Coliseum.[1]

The desire to have a team and revitalize downtown areas also resulted in some cities using public money to construct basketball arenas. The larger sports of baseball and football had numerous owners of professional clubs enjoying this benefit. As a smaller, less-established professional league, basketball owners received this gift much less frequently. While Pollin received public investment in infrastructure, the owners of the Pistons benefitted from the city of Pontiac's interest in hosting the National Football League's Detroit Lions. The Pistons moved in as cotenants in the $85 million arena with a

33,000 seating capacity in 1975. Kemper Arena combined a private donation and public funds to cover its $22 million price tag. The 16,000-seat arena sat on top of former stockyards and housed the Kansas City Kings. The American Basketball Association (ABA) Pacers, who would soon join the National Basketball Association (NBA), played in Market Square Arena. This 1974 public construction sought to bring activity back to a part of downtown Indianapolis. The arena seated 16,500 and cost $223 million to erect.[2]

The Capital Centre set the standard for these arenas. The facility contained more than 1,000 special seats, with a nearby restaurant. Another section included a private club and then another large room with a cocktail lounge, private dining room, mammoth kitchen, and small dining room for VIP guests. Above it all was a four-sided, 16 foot by 20 foot projection screen that beamed 40 feet above the sunken floor. The Capital Centre and these other arenas represented a new style and size for this type of facility, sprinkled generously with amenities, which sparked the NBA's growth into the multibillion dollar entertainment industry that it is today.[3]

The ownership complemented the new arena with team changes. The Bullets changed their name from Baltimore to the Capital Bullets. They unveiled new uniforms that featured an American color scheme. The home uniforms included red horizontal stripes on white jerseys and blue stars on their white shorts with red and blue trim. Blue with white and red trim decked the simpler road uniforms. Abe Pollin sought a new coach after not rehiring Gene Shue. He called K. C. Jones, a former member of the Boston Celtics championship teams who had coached the ABA's San Diego Conquistadors to a playoff berth the year before, and offered him the job. Jones, an African American, became one of the few blacks with a head coaching job in professional sports, his former teammate with the Celtics, Bill Russell, Al Attles, and Ray Scott being the others.

The new coach brought with him a friend from his days in San Diego, naming Bernie Bickerstaff as the team's new assistant coach. Jones hoped to influence players while creating a relaxed atmosphere. "I like to fast break and play tenacious defense. If a player does something well, I believe in giving him the freedom to do it."[4] As the assistant, Bickerstaff would do advanced scouting, coming back after watching every team in the league, preparing the scouting reports, and returning to sit along the sidelines and help out during the games.[5]

The NBA players shared a few characteristics. Most hailed from working-class families, and even the small salaries that many would earn during their early basketball careers enabled them to buy the first new car that the family had ever owned. Nearly all played basketball in college. The dream of playing in the NBA and getting paid to play started taking shape. Most of the older players preferred alcohol as their drug of choice, while marijuana slowly came into the league with some of the younger players. According to Walt Frazier, the league maintained an informal limit regarding the race of players. He viewed white men as composing 60% of most squads, while more than half of the blacks playing in the league did so as starters. While a few stars earned high salaries, most of the players did okay financially and took jobs during the off-season.[6]

New Leaders

The new general manager and coach of the Bullets made several personnel changes. First-round draft pick Stan Love was traded to Los Angeles for a second-round draft pick in 1974. John Tresvant also netted a draft pick in a trade with the Chicago Bulls. Several other Gene Shue draft picks were waived off the squad, including Tom Patterson and Rich Rinaldi.

The "new" Bullets started slowly and were homeless, as the Capital Centre would not be ready to host the team until December 1973; however, after their 1–5 start, the team took six games in a row. Still, there was no room for euphoria, as they hovered near the .500 mark for the first month and a half of the season. Several of the team's key contributors sat out with injuries, including Wes Unseld and Nick Weatherspoon.

The Bullets proved to be very streaky. During the Christmas holiday season, they won five in a row and then dropped three games. They won another four, then lost two, won another two, and then dropped four in a row. Their 27–23 record at the close of January placed the team six games ahead of their nearest competitors in the division, the Atlanta Hawks. The biggest decision centered on Unseld, whom the team sent to Canada to have a specialist examine his knee.

Coach K. C. Jones sought to install a fast-break offense and tough defense. The team struggled to produce on offense, averaging 102 points, which placed them near the bottom of the NBA. The defense, however, proved fantastic. They limited opponents to 100 points, fifth best of the 17 teams. The Bullets closed out the remainder of the season winning 20 games and losing 12, with wins in four of their last five games. The team set a record for attendance, bringing in more than 414,000 spectators, finishing fifth in the category.[7]

The league added a wrinkle to the system for the 1974 playoffs. Instead of like the prior years, when the top two teams from each division in a conference made the playoffs, the top four teams based upon their win-loss record earned the slot. In both conferences, three teams from one division and only one from the other made the playoffs. The two first-place teams received the number one and number two seeds based upon the higher winning percentage. The remaining two teams became the third and fourth seeds. As the first-place team with the lower winning percentage, the Bullets became the second seed and took on the third seed, which was, surprise, the New York Knicks.

The prognosticators saw no clear favorite for the NBA title. While Milwaukee and Boston had the typical dominant centers who anchor a title winner, each had key injuries. The Knicks seemed to thrive on playoff atmosphere, and they were the defending champions. The experts made New York a prohibitive favorite over the Bullets. Would the Bullets, under K. C. Jones, prove more successful against their rival as they had under Gene Shue? Jones had a four-pronged strategy, playing disciplined position defense against the Knicks' pattern offense. The idea was to keep their big guys from getting offensive rebounds and work for the open shot on offense and always get back on defense. Bernie Bickerstaff explained, saying, "In any playoff series we (coach) will take you (any opposing team) out off your game plans, so to win in the playoffs a team needs a guy who can make plays on the court."[8] A team may have one or, if they are lucky, two of those guys, or a guy who can create plays for others; however, the NBA also remained a game of matchups, and some teams had the right combination of players to give an otherwise winning team fits.

The best-of-seven series began in New York. Elvin Hayes scored 40 points, on 19 of 29 shooting. The ever methodical Knicks used their backcourt tandem of Earl Monroe and Walt Frazier to score six more than Hayes and relied on their key substitutions to drop in another 22 points, as opposed to the Bullets, whose subs provided zero points, to take a 102–91 victory.

The Bullets turned the situation to their advantage. Back home, for the Capital Centre's inaugural playoff game, the Bullets' defense began to clamp down on the suddenly old-looking Knicks. The offense scored off the defensive stops. The second game went to the Bullets, 99–87. They took the same intensity to Madison Square Garden and shut the Knicks down again for an 88–79 win in game three. The Bullets returned home again and sped off to a lead, which they expanded to 10 points midway through the fourth quarter. The only remaining Bullet from these earlier matches, Wes Unseld, battled Dave DeBusschere to a standstill, limiting the Knicks' ability to drive to the basket and popping in a few buckets of his own. Despite giving away three inches in height, Kevin Porter smothered The Pearl. Monroe seemed destined to be contained for the third game in a row. Then he and the Knicks regained their verve. The team shut down Baltimore's offense and crept back into game four. With 30 seconds remaining, the Knicks trailed 87–85, as Monroe had the ball, backing Porter down toward the hoop. Monroe swiveled and took a 15-foot jump shot that went in. The teams went into overtime, and Monroe drew the foul on Porter, which made the pesky guard foul out of the game. Ten more points from the Knicks' star guard earned his team the win and evened the series at two games each.

The Knicks' other superstar guard carried his team the next game. The Sunday televised game was full of the usual drama for these two teams. They matched one another shot for shot. Despite the resurgence of Walt Frazier and Earl Monroe as the Knicks' big offensive threats, scoring from Mike Riordan, Phil Chenier, Wes Unseld, and Elvin Hayes helped the Bullets down the stretch drive into the fourth quarter. But Frazier would not be denied. Carrying his team with seven field goals and assists on the Knicks other two buckets, he made everything from layups around the big hand of Elvin Hayes to long bombs, ranging out to 25 feet. The Knicks took the win, 106–105.

The Bullets showed amazing poise in game six. They gave the sellout crowd much to cheer about as they battled back from an early deficit and scored 41 points in the fourth quarter to take game six 109–92. Game seven came down to Earl Monroe scoring 30 points, with Elvin Hayes able to score only 12. The Knicks outrebounded the Bullets and iced the tough series, 91–81.

Despite losing, Jones felt that the team had earned the respect of the league. He formed a good working relationship with Bob Ferry and a friendship with Abe Pollin. The end of the playoffs brought the annual draft. Washington made 10 choices during the course of 10 rounds. The first four picks eventually had NBA careers. The draft proved deep, and the majority of the teams had their top two or three selections play in the NBA. Unfortunately, Washington did not get a great deal of benefit on the court. University of Maryland's Len Elmore, the team's top pick, forsook the Bullets and signed with the ABA's Indiana Pacers. He entered the NBA when the Pacers did two years later. Forward Len "Truck" Robinson gave the Bullets a backup at center and forward for two and a half seasons. He appeared to be reaching his potential when the team dealt him to the Atlanta Hawks. The remaining two players had nominal playing days.

The expansion draft also cost the team their second-round pick from the 1973 draft. The New Orleans Jazz drafted guard Louie Nelson from the Bullets' unprotected player list. Nelson averaged five points a game in his only season with the team. He played four more seasons in the league, two with New Orleans. The new team began the 1974–1975 season as a member of the

Central Division, which now had five teams, as opposed to the four based in the Atlantic Division of the Eastern Conference.

The Bullets' brass made several more changes to the personnel during the summer. Shooting guard Phil Chenier received a reward for his solid season. The team signed him to a seven-year contract for more than $1 million. Archie Clark, who received less playing time with the emergence of Kevin Porter, joined the SuperSonics, as the newly christened Washington Bullets received Dick Gibbs and a third-round draft pick in return. Clark played two more seasons, and his teams advanced to the semifinals of the playoffs. Gibbs served in a reserve player role, and the team traded him to the Buffalo Braves the next year for a first-round draft pick. Meanwhile, the Bullets cast off Dave Stallworth and a second-round draft pick for the Phoenix Suns' Clem Haskins. Stallworth's career ended with two teams waiving him that season. Haskins played a little more than Gibbs during a span of two seasons before his career finished.[9]

Basketball on Television

The NBA owners viewed their product as great entertainment and thought that the ABC network executives' broadcasting of their product hampered its appeal. Roone Arledge, who had nursed the league back to broadcasting help, perceived the league's owners as misguided and ungrateful. ABC received a great deal of criticism for the style of its coverage from newspapers and sports magazines. The criticisms ranged from announcers who did not know the game to bad camera work and vapid halftime shows. The NBA shopped its games, and CBS bought the rights for $27 million for three years. ABC sued the league for not negotiating in good faith but lost that battle, so they waged a war of counterprogramming with a fluff program called *The Superstars*. NBC put college basketball against CBS' Sunday NBA game. In an era in which the three networks dominated, the battle over the sports ratings and the big dollars for winter sports began in earnest.[10]

The CBS sports executives chose to show regional games rather than a single national weekly game. The Bullets got themselves on television, as they played fantastically throughout the 1974–1975 season. After winning their first seven games, they endured a few wins and losses before running off another six-game win streak as the second month began. More long streaks of winning began to occur every month. Observers noted that after years of second-billing status, this Bullets team featured a strong starting five and a deep and able bench. "You must have that dimension to win," noted Hayes.[11] The Bullets set a new franchise record for number of wins in a season, with

60, besting the 1968–1969 team's win total by three games. Jones attributed the success to everyone knowing their roles and being happy with them. This total would remain the franchise record. The team topped 50 wins only one time after that, in 1978–1979.

Ten men averaged at least 10 minutes per game. The depth of this rotation rarely occurred in the NBA, because individuals thought too much about their statistics and there had been a large gap between the sixth and 10th man on the roster. This deep team also shared the ball well. Elvin Hayes and Phil Chenier topped the scorers, but Mike Riordan bested and Kevin Porter nearly topped 1,000 points. The squad improved their offensive production by two points per game and moved up to rank fifth in the league. They gained on the defensive end as well, ranking as the second-best defense in the league, behind the frenzied, harassing defense that Coach Dick Motta preached to his Chicago Bulls. "We believe offense is for shooters and defense is for all five guys," said K. C. Jones.[12] As with the 1971 team, the media portrayed the Bullets as a disparate collection of individuals. This time Jones received credit for forging them into a team. "[Coach] brought us a championship attitude. He's not a yelling, screaming kind of coach," Wes Unseld explained.[13]

The winning teams highlighted different versions of basketball on the offensive end. The Celtics ran fewer fast breaks and relied on scoring from forward John Havlicek and guard Jo Jo White. New York moved the ball around to the open man. The Bulls used two forwards for their offensive thrust. Golden State played run-and-gun, with forward Rick Barry as the primary scoring option. The Warriors also used a 10-man rotation and declined to use the word *subs* for players coming off the bench. As noted in the last chapter, the 10-man rotation, while not used very often, had been an approach of the 1971 Bullets team under Gene Shue. The Bullets, like most teams, relied on scoring from a big center and a shooting guard, using either Elvin Hayes or Phil Chenier. Milwaukee had Kareem Abdul-Jabbar and Lucius Allen, Detroit had Bob Lanier and Dave Bing, and the Buffalo Braves had Bob McAdoo and Randy Smith.

New Format, New Results

The NBA added another round to the playoffs. The two teams that finished with the fourth- and fifth-highest winning percentages in each conference would play one another. The winning team from this first-round match would draw the highest-ranked team in the conference semifinal round. Meanwhile the second- and third-ranked teams would play in the other semifinal. The Bullets' nemesis, the New York Knicks, finished fifth and lost to the fourth-seeded Houston Rockets two games to one in the first round. As the top team in the Eastern Conference, Boston drew the Rockets.

The Bullets took on the Buffalo Braves. The two teams split their four meetings during the regular season. The Braves had the league's Most Valuable Player in center Bob McAdoo; a good shooting guard in Randy Smith; and, at forward, one-time Baltimore Bullet Jack Marin, who finished third on the team in scoring.

The Bullets felt rested and relaxed. "We match up pretty well with them, it's just that we can't match up with McAdoo. But who can?" asked K. C. Jones.[14] The question seemed prescient after the first game. McAdoo picked up 35 points, and, with 24 points each from the tandem of Gar Heard and Randy Smith, Buffalo beat the Bullets on their home court, 113–102. In Buffalo for the second game, the Bullets faced a must-win situation. The Bullets' big men, Elvin Hayes and Wes Unseld, controlled the glass and outrebounded the entire Buffalo team, helping the Bullets to the win, 120–106. The domination kept the Braves from getting into their running game and getting easy shots. Phil Chenier noted, "We did a better job on the boards, and that enables us to control the tempo."[15] The Bullets' guard had a big game the next evening. The sold-out crowd at the Capital Centre watched Kevin Porter and Phil Chenier control the tempo of the game and make the big plays. Chenier dropped in 18 of 28 points, as the Bullets took over the game during the third quarter. Hayes chipped in 30 points in the 111–96 victory.

Before a national television audience, the Bullets continued their strong team play; however, Bob McAdoo and his teammates scored above their average for the series, as the Braves took a 108–102 victory at home. The pivotal game five started with the Braves jumping out to a five-point lead in the first quarter. Elvin Hayes helped lead a rally in the second quarter, as he scored 18 points in a row to help his team lead 42–39 at the half. The Braves came out of the locker room strong and limited the Bullets' ability to find good shots. The Bullets scored only 19 points in the third period and fell behind by four going into the final quarter. The Big E took over and netted 46 points, yet the Bullets led by only one point, 94–93, with a minute left. Hayes shot and missed. Wes Unseld grabbed the rebound and put the ball in to widen the lead. Buffalo missed, and Unseld snared the rebound to seal the game.

With the series in their hands, the Bullets faced an inspired Buffalo effort. Bob McAdoo scored 37 points, but he received timely support from Randy Smith and Jim McMillian. The Bullets went minutes without hitting a field goal and made many costly turnovers, with three of the starting five chipping in thirteen of them and two more of the team's regular substitutes adding another seven. The Braves won game six, 102–96.

The Bullets' great season came down to one game. They seized the moment, with great shooting and smothering defense enabling them to take a 28–13 lead after one quarter. The backcourt duo of Phil Chenier and Kevin Porter kept it up, giving the Bullets as 56–38 lead at halftime. The Braves could get no closer than 13 points, as small forward Mike Riordan chipped in 16 points and Elvin Hayes provided another 24 to advance the Bullets to the Eastern Conference Finals against the defending champion Boston Celtics.[16]

The Celtics and Bullets played four games during the season, with each winning two. The Celtics hosted game one, and the "Celtic machine" passed the ball with brilliant efficiency, generating 15 assists during the first half. With his team trailing by as many as 12 points, the Bullets' head coach lit into his team at halftime. "K. C. wasn't as quiet as usual," Elvin Hayes said. "We deserved the few choice words he used."[17] Washington ran off a 14–2 spurt as the third quarter began, getting three baskets off of the fast break. The Celtics restored some of their lead on baskets from John Havlicek, Jo Jo White, and center Dave Cowens, but the Bullets came on and scored the first ten points of the fourth quarter to take an 80–73 lead, as Porter made passes into Hayes, who then made his shots. Boston clawed back but, the Bullets stayed with their main scorers, and Hayes and Chenier carried them to victory, 100–95.[18]

The Bullets' big guns got the team off to a good start in the first quarter of game two. Chenier dropped in 12 points, and Hayes tallied 29 for the game. The Celtics carried over the cold shooting that hampered them at the end of the first game. Boston's coach, Tom Heinsohn, observed the poor play, stating, "Christ, we had wide-open shots from 15 feet and we were missing, everyone."[19] After leading 60–44 at the half, the Bullets cooled during the third quarter as Hayes missed shots, partly due to the Celtics opting to double-team the big man when he had the ball. The Celtics narrowed the Bullets' lead to eight, when Hayes got his hot hand back and Washington pulled away, scoring 33 points during the final period to Boston's 18, taking a 2–0 series lead with the 117–92 victory.[20]

Back home in Boston for the crucial game, the Celtics and Bullets locked in a good-shooting first half. The Celtics held on to a 60–57 lead, but the team then adopted a high-pressure defense as a way to thwart the Bullets. The quickening of the tempo caused the Bullets to struggle with their ball handling. The visitors began turning the ball over or taking rushed, low-percentage shots. The Celtics expanded their lead to 14 points. "Our defense takes care of our offense," guard Jo Jo White explained, as he pulled off three steals during this crucial portion of the game.[21] When both teams' shooting eyes went cold in the last quarter, the Celtics got additional shots, as Dave Cowens and forward Paul Silas dominated the offensive glass for their team.

Now holding a 2–1 lead, the Bullets recognized their weak points from game three. The team concentrated on running their offensive patterns, the ball movement enabling a variety of guys to get open and get a less-contested shot. The Celtics made their shots as well, so the teams remained close throughout most of the first half. Holding a narrow 41–40 lead, the Bullets had Elvin Hayes, Phil Chenier, Wes Unseld, Nick Weatherspoon, and Jimmy Jones on the court. Passing brilliantly, each man scored four points, enabling the home team to engineer a 20–6 run. The swift movement led to the Celtics' big men, Dave Cowens and Paul Silas, picking up fouls. Each spent a significant amount of time on the bench, so Wes Unseld ruled the boards, grabbing 25 rebounds in the game. En route to this 119–108 result, Bullets' guard Jimmy Jones, an experienced shooter and first guard off the bench, tore ligaments in his right knee, forcing him out for the remainder of the playoffs.

But the Celtics would not go away easily. The teams engaged in a virtual mugging, playing an intense, physical match in game five. The referees whistled a total of 54 fouls on the players, generating falling debris from the stands as the crowd showed their displeasure. Boston jumped out to an 11-point lead during the second period, but Washington charged back and closed to within a basket by the start of the last frame. Phil Chenier scored his 32nd point to give his team the lead with about three minutes remaining, but Kevin Porter fouled out while trying to block Jo Jo White's jump shot. White tied the game with a foul shot. The teams traded misses before forward Don Nelson drained a 15-foot jump shot to give Boston the lead. The Bullets turned the ball over, and when Dave Cowens put Boston up by four, Washington was unable to protect the ball, as the Celtics executed two steals to seal their win, 103–99.

The Bullets opted for a running attack in the early stages of game six, and it worked. Their defense caused nine turnovers by the Celtics in the first quarter and a total of 14 for the half. Meanwhile, the Bullets made more than half of the shots they took and led by 15 at the half. The Bullets' big assist man, Kevin Porter, exclaimed, "We wasted no time getting to them early."[22] Champions do not quit, and the Celtics charged back with a strong third quarter, which reduced the deficit by half. "We were unprepared and too relaxed," Porter noted. "But when we had to give it to them, we did."[23] His teammates regained composure and their shooting accuracy and matched the Celtics in scoring to win the game and the series, 98–92. As the Celtics coach Tom Heinsohn and others noted, the Celtics came back hard against the Bullets, and they didn't crack, they held their poise.[24]

Another Zero in the Finals

Washington started the finals as the prohibitive favorite to win. The Golden State Warriors won 12 fewer games during the regular season than the Bullets. They lost three of the four head-to-head games with the Bullets as well. Washington got off to a great start, scoring 27 points each quarter to take a 14-point lead into the locker room. The Warriors made a switch, bringing on their fourth and fifth guards, who brought youth and aggressiveness to the floor. The lead evaporated to one by the end of the third quarter. The Bullets received little help from their big scorers in the second half and watched the Warriors take the lead. They increased it to 94–86, with scores off of steals and offensive rebounds. The Bullets went on a brief run to narrow the score to 97–95. The Warriors brought the ball down the court with 40 seconds left. Their play broke down, and Rick Barry got the ball and launched a 20-foot jumper that dropped in to give the underdogs a 99–95 win.

Game two took place in San Francisco. The blueprint looked similar. After falling behind by 13 points, the Warriors battled back, this time through their running game. The team took a 90–84 advantage and slowed up their game to run the game clock down. This took them out of their shooting rhythm at the same time that the Bullets gained accuracy. A shot by Phil Chenier and a driving shot by Mike Riordan put the Bullets in front by one. After Rick Barry and Truck Robinson traded misses, the Warriors threw an outlet pass to Barry, who Riordan fouled before he could shoot. Barry's two free throws put his team ahead by 1 point with 23 seconds left. The Bullets failed to get off a makeable shot and went down two games to none in the series, losing 92–91.[25]

The Warriors happily discussed the circumstances of game two with the media. While the Bullets concentrated on trying to reverse the circumstances for game three. For the first time, the Warriors got off to a good start and took the early lead in game three. Barry put in 19 points to lead his team during their early burst. When the Bullets narrowed the advantage to one, Barry and crew rolled off eight straight points. Hayes and Porter kept the Bullets close, scoring 24 and 21 points, respectively. Golden State rode Barry's next 19 points to an 8-point victory, 109–101. "They thoroughly outplayed us," Riordan said. "They've been the best basketball team so far."[26]

The Capital Centre did not help the home team. The Bullets took a big lead early on and then nearly squandered it by making 18 turnovers before halftime. The Warriors again used their deep bench. The team seemed to be able to roll out fresh legs, which pressured the dribbler, and cover the Bullets' key shooters. They generated offense through defensive pressure and run-and-gun style. Despite the efforts, the Bullets once again remained locked in a close game. The Bullets led the game with less than two minutes remaining but then promptly turned the ball over. The Warriors did the same. Then the Bullets obliged again, as they had throughout the series, and the Warriors sunk two free throws to grab the one-point victory, 96–95, winning the NBA Championship.

The series ended quickly and unexpectedly. A newspaper article featured a photograph of a ticket for the fifth game at the Capital Centre, now useless. The media hammered away at Coach K. C. Jones, referring to him as either stupid or a dirty coach, partly as a result of CBS' television cameras showing assistant Bernie Bickerstaff drawing up a play. The play was part of Coach Jones's playbook, and he asked Bickerstaff to draw it up so that Phil Chenier could see it diagrammed.[27] When columnists did praise the Bullets and their fantastic season, they noted how little they could do right in the finals. The team drew nearly 384,000 spectators during the season, a decline of about 8% from the previous year's crowd. The attendance placed them in the middle of the league, underwhelming for a team that won more than 70% of its games. The ownership observed that making the playoffs enabled the team to make money for the season. Each home game during the playoffs earned the team 55% of the gate, nearly $50,000 when the games were sold out. Two of the Buffalo, three of the Boston, and two of the Golden State games sold out.[28]

The fact that the Bullets needed to make the playoffs to break even illuminated the precarious financial position of most NBA teams. Washington had a sizable market with disposable income, within the top third of the cities in the league. The situation for at least half of the other teams who played in smaller cities and brought in fewer fans during the regular season had to be troublesome. That financial situation would be even worse when the club did not make the playoffs so it had no additional revenue stream. The costs to run a NBA club had increased. Of the increased costs, the largest was player salaries, which had increased greatly due to competition with the ABA. They rose exponentially with the settlement of *Oscar Robertson v. National Basketball Association*, which led to the dissolution of the reserve clause in player contracts and the start of free agency.

Washington also had an additional advantage of the owners' relationship to the arena. The Bullets and the arena in which they played were owned, in part, by the same person, Abe Pollin. Thus, even if Pollin lost money with the team, the team played a role in helping the arena that he partially owned make money. The arena did well during the basketball season, and it also profited from the playoffs. The Capital Centre's management brought in $12,000 per evening from parking and about $8,000 per game from its share of concession revenue. Atlanta, Cleveland, New York, Houston, and Los Angeles all had similar arrangements.[29]

The playoffs had additional advantages other than simply increasing revenue during a single year. The wins helped the team grow the confidence and interest of its fan base and of people in the Washington and Baltimore areas. The team received many season ticket renewals much more quickly than in other years. In addition, season tickets sales increased by several hundred from the 3,900 pass holders that the team had during the 1974–1975 season.[30]

Ticket holders saw one solid new player who the team picked up from the college draft: top pick, forward Kevin Grevey. As the previous few years had demonstrated, the top two rounds generally produced the players with the longevity in the league. The team traded their second-round pick but held selections in rounds 3 through 12. The seven later-round picks did not make the team for the next year. The team saw their third-round pick, Tom Kropp, at the National Association of Intercollegiate Athletics tournament, one of 10 teams that had scouts approach the player from the University of Nebraska at Kearney. Despite the attention, Kropp did not give a thought to a NBA career and told the scouts who invited him to camps for tryouts that he would play at the Portsmouth Invitational, so they could see him there. The Bullets signed Kropp for the minimum contract of $35,000, and he also received a $10,000 signing bonus. Kropp played one year with the Bullets before being traded to the Chicago Bulls for a 1977 third-round draft pick.

Despite winning so many games, the Bullets' general manager, Bob Ferry, did not stay with the same team. Only Kevin Porter had to receive a new contract, and the guard was definitely going to receive a raise from his $45,000 annual salary; however, Ferry made a big trade of guards in the summer, swapping Kevin Porter for the Detroit Pistons' guard, Dave Bing, and a first-round draft pick for 1977. The native Washingtonian regularly made the All-Star squad as a top assist man in the league. Bing, while six years older, shot better and played better defense than Porter. Ferry explained, "You can't wait around for players to develop while your big men get old. . . . Dave Bing was brought here to be our quarterback." K. C. Jones offered the following prediction: "He'll fit right in."[31]

The teams that lost in the NBA Finals usually made changes to their roster the next season. The Los Angeles Lakers made several changes between the team that reached the 1970 championships and the 1971 squad, including two purchases and two trades. The 1971 team lost in the Western Conference Finals. The last chapter discussed how much the Bullets changed between the 1971 Finals team and the 1972 team that only reached the semifinals. The New York Knicks made few changes between the 1972 finalist and the 1973 team that won the NBA championship. The Lakers team that lost to the Knicks and the team the following year retained but seven players and lost again in the semifinal round. The Milwaukee Bucks lost key player Oscar Robertson and traded two players from their 1974 finalist to 1975 also ran club. Most changes during the offseason ended up causing a worse performance the next season. In the instance that changes were not made, the team returned to the finals and won.

The NBA teams generated more scoring during the 1975–1976 season than the year before; however, the Bullets played less effective offensive basketball. With Elvin Hayes, Phil Chenier, and Mike Riordan all scoring fewer points than the previous year, the team floundered around the .500 mark until early January. Most of the teams sat bunched near the top of the Central Division, including the Bullets, the Hawks, the Rockets, and the traditional doormat of the division, the Cleveland Cavaliers. By February, Atlanta had several long losing streaks that dropped them from contention. Houston hovered around the .500 mark. Cleveland rode an 8-game winning streak to a virtual tie with the Bullets with less than 20 games remaining, at 38–25. The Bullets struggled as both guards, Jimmy Jones and Dave Bing, lost time to injuries. Bob Ferry had to defend his decision to trade Kevin Porter. In turn, Ferry lost confidence in K. C. Jones, and the coach often found himself having to explain personnel decisions in the general manager's office. Still, basketball experts expected the team to pull away from Cleveland and win the division.

This seemed to be occurring in March. For the first time in the 1975–1976 season, the Bullets played like they had in 1975. A streak of nine wins in 10 games knocked Cleveland to two and a half games behind. The Bullets went to Cleveland and lost a tight game, 95–92. The two teams spiraled in opposite directions. Washington won only four of their remaining 12 games, while Cleveland won 8 of 13. The Cavaliers finished with a 49–32 record, which put the Central Division crown out of Washington's reach for the first time in its six-year existence.[32]

The second seed, Cleveland, drew the third seed, Washington, in one of the Eastern Conference Semifinals. The Cavaliers won four of the six games between the two teams during the season. As the playoffs started, K. C. Jones admitted that he thought his future with the club was on the line. He said, "I've heard my job has been in jeopardy since the third week of the season."[33] Players and coaches mentioned that the team lacked cohesion, as three or four players expressed more concern with playing time or getting shots than teamwork. The team did not use the analysis of film to break down the way the games played out in the series. The Chicago Bulls would later incorporate this item into their arsenal when they made the playoffs in the 1976–1977 season.

The team seemed to belie that attitude during the first game with the Cavaliers. The Bullets started the game hitting their shots, with Dave Bing driving the lane, Phil Chenier hitting jumpers off of Elvin Hayes's pick, and the team picking up the rebounds from Cleveland's long-range shots and starting the fast break. The home team never recovered from going into the locker room down 21 points at halftime, and the Bullets won, 100–95.

Neither team looked sharp or effective in the second game. Players launched shots that turned into air balls, dribbled off their feet, and struggled to build any positive momentum. The Bullets led by 10 points at the half, and the home crowd thought that if they could get a lead under those conditions, then they would surely win when they played better. The teams played a little better, and the Bullets held a one-point lead with less than a minute to go. Wes Unseld committed a three-second violation. Bingo Smith came down the court and committed a traveling violation. Washington took the ball out with 29 seconds left. They stalled, and, with seconds left, Dave Bing turned down the left baseline and double dribbled. With five seconds remaining, Smith received the inbounds pass and launched a bomb that dropped through the net to give his team an 80–79 victory.

The two teams moved back to Cleveland for the third game. The visitors' offense appeared disordered. Players stood around or bumped into one another on the offensive end. The 24-second clock often ran down, leaving the team a long-range shot as their only option. Team "quarterback" Dave Bing observed that, "We're not patient enough to run through our offense and get the good shots."[34] Fellow guard Phil Chenier shot a horrid 4 of 15 from the floor. The missed shots and long-range bombs generated easy rebounds that the Cavaliers turned into three-on-one and four-on-one breaks down to the other end of the court.

After that rout, the Bullets played two solid games. They won the fourth to even the series and battled back from a late deficit to take a one-point lead with seven seconds remaining in the fifth game. Elvin Hayes had the ball, and Cleveland's Campy Russell fouled him. Hayes stepped to the line having made 9 of 12 in free throws on the evening. He missed on his first attempt. The second rolled around the rim and fell off. Cleveland moved down the court, and Bingo Smith threw up a shot that hit nothing. Guard Jim Cleamons snatched the ball and, with three Bullets surrounding him, dropped it in the basket as time expired.

The Bullets returned to the Capital Centre after the 92–91 loss. In game six, the team seized an early lead, but the Cavaliers came back and the two teams fought to a tie at the end of regulation. The Cavaliers lost forward Bingo Smith to an injury, and Washington rode the strong play of guard Jimmy Jones to score first in the overtime. After Jones's shot, his teammates dropped in three more buckets, and Washington held on for a 102–98 victory that sent the series to a deciding seventh game.

The teams traded leads throughout the final game. With more than a minute and a half to go, the Bullets trailed by two points. Elvin Hayes stood at the free throw line. He missed them both. The Bullets tied the game as Cleveland came down the court for the last shot. With four seconds left, Dick Snyder hit to give Cleveland an 87–85 victory and the series win.

K. C. Jones's contract as coach of the Bullets expired. Jones remained hopeful of returning to the Bullets' bench based upon his personal relationship with the team owner. Abe Pollin called Jones in to see him and fired his coach.[35] Jones understood that Pollin faced pressure from the fans, the media, and general manager Bob Ferry to let him go. Several players expressed frustration over the firing, explaining that they were responsible for the team losing in the playoffs, not the coach. As one explained, "You played your tail off for him because you wanted to please him."

Meanwhile, Ferry concentrated on the draft; the Bullets had two first-round draft picks. Both selections provided immediate impact on the court. With the 13th pick of the draft, the Bullets selected forward Mitch Kupchak. The team then made the next selection in the draft and chose guard Larry Wright. Both guys would play in the vast majority of the team's regular-season games and during the playoff run later that fall. Second-round pick center Joe Pace also played immediately, in about a third of the team's games, and he lasted two seasons with the Bullets. The remaining eight selections did not play in the NBA.

Indicative of the status of the NBA Draft even up to this era, the rankings of players and mock drafts did not exist. Mitch Kupchak recalled that the draft occurred midweek. He did not know what ranking he had, only that he was one of three big men that would be drafted early in the first round. He did not hear about his selection until the next day, and he received a telegram with the news from the Bullets later that day.[36]

Did the Fat Lady Sing?

The Washington Bullets, Chicago Bulls, and seven other teams fired coaches that spring. The Bulls had a poor season under tough, disciplined coach Dick

Motta, yet Bob Ferry and Abe Pollin chose Motta to run their team. The experts wondered if the pampered Bullets could find happiness with the tough guy. "I'm not going in with my six-guns drawn," noted Motta. "There is a lot I have to learn about these players, and there is a lot they have to learn about me."[37] The beat reporters expected that the Bullets would become less of a finesse team and more about exerting muscle and running picks.

While Motta brought a change in offense and defensive ploys, he and Ferry maintained an important consistency. Motta kept K. C. Jones's assistant coach, Bernie Bickerstaff. Assistant coaches often ran aspects of practices, but, more importantly, they drew up the work on the blackboard before games and discussed with the players the other team's plays during the morning shoot around. In addition, many played an important role as a link between the head coach and the players when team members had concerns about on-court issues. The amount of work, combined with the age-old desire to find a place for a retiring player, led to some teams hiring a second assistant coach. Jerry Sloan tried to come back from a debilitating injury during the 1976–1977 season, but when he could not he served on staff with his old team, the Chicago Bulls. The same season, John Wetzel joined Al Bianchi as an assistant coach in Phoenix to John MacLeod. Aside from the aforementioned duties, the pair broke down film and showed it to the players for many games.

The NBA also experienced significant changes for the upcoming season. The merger with the ABA occurred, bringing four franchises into the league. Each team paid a $3.2 million expansion fee to the NBA, which was split among the existing 18 teams. Two of the teams joined the Midwest Division, one joined the Atlantic Division, and the San Antonio Spurs joined the Central Division. The playoffs expanded, and the conference first-round series featured two sets of games, between the third and sixth seeds and the fourth and fifth seeds, with the winners taking on the first or second seeds in the conference.

A few interviewees mentioned the Five-Star Basketball Camps as showing their influence in this era. Players coming into the league from the ABA, like Moses Malone, had participated in the camps during their high school years. Founded during the mid-1960s, Howard Garfinkel and Will Klein brought in coaches to offer training to the 11- to 18-year-old boys who had the desire to improve their skills and play basketball in college and maybe professionally. The first year they ran a camp with 70 children, and enrollment kept doubling. Coaches from collegiate and professional basketball taught technical, athletic, and psychological skills. The repetition of skills, game situations, and workouts to improve agility and quickness enabled these players to bring these abilities into the NBA. The camps' influence continued to expand over the years as more teenagers received the training.[38]

The relationship between owners and players underwent the most significant change. The resolution of the Oscar Robertson/National Professional Basketball League suit against the NBA enabled the merger to occur. In exchange, the resolution granted players free agency, with the teams receiving compensation through 1980. Afterward, the player's former team held a right of first refusal on any free-agent signing. Teams had one year to sign their draft choices before they returned to the draft pool. Finally, the players received an increase in pension benefits; per diem; insurance coverage; and minimum salary, up $10,000, to $30,000.

During the first month of the 1976–1977 season, media experts filed reports offering their assessment of the league. Most complaints focused on the players, arguing that their allegiance appeared to be to their egos and their agents. Their salaries, ranging from the average guy making $150,000 to the $3.5 million made by Doctor J. and the $3 million made by his teammate, George McGinnis, made one wonder about the intensity that they gave on a nightly basis. The coach who was supposed to get these two big stars to share the ball was former Bullets coach Gene Shue.

This chronic selfishness had hit the Warriors, who had been the epitome of the word *team* with their 10 men. Heading into the season, they had players perceived as either shooting too often or sulking. The Denver Rockets and Portland Trail Blazers appeared to be paragons of teams who exhibited unity and hustle and played with missionary zeal. Meanwhile, the rising salaries resulted in high ticket prices ($12 a ticket), which had led to a drop in attendance (even Madison Square Garden remained half empty for games). Even with the collection of the nearly $13 million in expansion fees and the raising of ticket prices, franchises claimed to be suffering financially. The NBA Board of Governors decided to impose a cost-saving measure and reduced the number of players on the roster from 12 to 11.[39]

The complaints about stars, prima donnas, and their high contracts in the NBA appear in chapter 4, when Bullets' coach Buddy Jeannette made the claim a decade earlier. Each generation appeared to dislike the style of play of the latest generation and cited it as indicative of a lowering standard of performance. Expansion of the league into a greater number of teams always served as a reason for the watering down of the quality of the game; nevertheless, during this season, the league average in shooting percentage climbed 1% from the start of the decade.

As the team did the previous year under K. C. Jones, the Bullets started out slowly. They struggled through two months before reaching the .500

plateau. Guard Jimmy Jones struggled to recover from his latest injury. In December, Bob Ferry traded forward Nick Weatherspoon. The team's 1973 top draft choice never felt happy with the Bullets, always believing that he did not receive enough playing time. "It's a relief to get out of here," he told the press in response to hearing he had been shipped to Seattle for forward Leonard Gray.[40] "Spoon" played with three more teams during the next few years, while Gray played only the remainder of the 1976–1977 season in the NBA. Another recent top pick expressed similar frustration. Kevin Grevey started wondering aloud before the Bullets made another trade, swapping forward Truck Robinson and the team's 1977 top draft pick in exchange for guard Tom Henderson and the Atlanta Hawks' 1977 or 1978 top draft pick. This move gave the team the guard they sought and let go of Robinson, who was about to become a veteran free agent after the season.[41]

The last deal occurred during the middle of the team's first sustained winning streak of the year. The Bullets won eight in a row, only a game behind both the Cleveland Cavaliers and Houston Rockets for the top spot in the Central Division. During the second half, the Cavaliers struggled playing .500 ball, and the Bullets took over first place in the division as the calendar moved into March. Then the Rockets took off, winning nine in a row, and 12 of 14 games, giving them a 45–28 record. The Bullets failed to keep close, dropping to five games behind with 11 games left on the schedule. Houston won their last home game and then went on the road for four games. They lost three in a row, heading in for a showdown at the Capital Centre. Houston held only a game and a half lead over the Bullets. The Rockets summoned their skills and defeated the home team, 91–85.

Houston won the division with the second-best record in the conference. They waited for the winner of the Bullets and Cavaliers first-round series. Coach Dick Motta observed that there were 12 good teams in the playoffs and that his team would be its own worst enemy. They would have to play right to win. The Bullets defeated Cleveland three out of four times during the season. The Bullets took the first game at home rather easily, 109–100. The Cavaliers trailed by 25 and 17 points at various stages of the game as the Bullets got everyone into the game.

Eleven players got into the second game as well. This time the Bullets sought someone with a scoring touch. After being held to 14 points in the first quarter, they made a run and cut the deficit to only two points by halftime. Campy Russell opened the third quarter with several key shots, and the Cavaliers sprinted out to a 16-point lead. Washington started to crash the offensive boards and work to get better shots, which enabled them to tie the game at 68 with half of the fourth quarter remaining. The Cavaliers enjoyed another offensive spurt, but two driving layups by Tom Henderson put the Bullets back to within three. They could get no closer, as the Cavaliers made big baskets down the stretch, tying the series at one game apiece, and they won game two, 91–83.

Before a half-filled Capital Centre, the home team came out determined to set the tempo for the series-deciding game. Running at every opportunity, the Bullets got layups and short jump shots to take a 23–8 lead. Cleveland showed the poise that they had throughout the series and battled to within nine points by halftime. Tom Henderson, Elvin Hayes, Phil Chenier, and Kevin Grevey all contributed timely shots during the huge-scoring third quarter; however, the Cavaliers matched their production behind Elmore Smith, Campy Russell, and Jim Chones.[42] As the fourth quarter began, the Cavaliers made a run, and the Bullets went scoreless for five and a half minutes. "Our concentration just wasn't there," Wes Unseld observed.[43] A thirteen-point lead evaporated, and, with three and a half minutes remaining in one team's season, each team had 94 points. Henderson drove to the basket for a quick two. Hayes blocked Russell's shot, and Henderson went the length of the floor for a layup. As the Cavaliers missed their shots, they had to foul the Bullets to stop the clock. Henderson added four free throws, which gave his team the series, 104–98.[44]

After making it past the first round of the playoffs for the first time, the Bullets returned to the Eastern Conference Semifinals to face the Houston Rockets. The Rockets had owned the Bullets during the regular season, winning three out of the four games the teams played by an average of 13 points. The series began at Houston's Summit with everything going right for the home team. They jumped out to a 26–13 lead on a 16–0 run. Led by rookies Mitch Kupchak and Larry Wright, the Bullets outscored Houston 19–4 toward the end of the second quarter to level the game at 46 apiece by halftime. Kupchak's 13 points helped his team to take the lead, 83–77, going into the last quarter. Houston's guard, Mike Newlin, stepped up his play, scoring 12 points to narrow the Bullets' lead to two points. Tom Henderson responded with an underhanded layup. Newlin banked in a 20-foot jumper. Elvin Hayes scored four points, and Washington scored four more, to create a 10-point bulge with under a minute and a half left to play.

His team down one game, big center Moses Malone put the Rockets on his back for game two. Malone dropped in 31 points and cleared 26 rebounds, including 15 offensive boards. His domination of the rebounds on both ends enabled Houston to shoot 114 shots to Washington's 83 attempts. The Bullets countered with 37 points from Phil Chenier and 21 from Mitch Kupchak. These 31 extra shots outweighed the 5% advantage that the Bullets had in accuracy of shooting.

The two teams reversed roles from game one at the beginning of game three. The Bullets jumped out to the early lead, only to have the Rockets wage a big second-quarter comeback behind one of their rookies, John Lucas. The game became physical and the tempo slowed. The physical struggle was nothing new to basketball in the late 1970s. The 1976 Warriors–Suns series even featured a punching match. The intensity of the battles between the Rockets and Bullets continued to escalate during the series. With two referees, there was a blind spot on the backside where play got very physical, and the referees tended to let play go a little more then.

The teams battled to an 86–86 tie with three minutes left. Hayes moved to the basket and dropped in his shot as he was fouled. After converting the free throw, the teams swapped missed layups and turnovers. Malone drew a foul and converted two free throws to narrow the Bullets' lead to one. After another turnover, Malone grabbed a missed shot and threw in a dunk to give his team the lead. Hayes missed a layup, and Malone seized the rebound. Lucas came in on a drive and pulled up for a jump shot, which Henderson rejected. The Bullets inbounded to Chenier, who faced a double team and dumped the ball off to the open Kupchak. He went up, and, as Malone rejected his shot, the big center bumped into Kupchak, drawing the foul call. The near-capacity crowd went crazy and continued celebrating as the rookie's two free throws put the home team on top by one. The Rockets drew a play for guard Mike Newlin, who made his way around Chenier but bumped into Kupchak, drawing the offensive foul that sealed the Bullets' game-three victory.[45]

The Bullets and Rockets engaged in another closely fought game two nights later. The capacity crowd watched as the teams traded leads throughout the first quarter. Both shot well in the second quarter, going into halftime with Houston ahead by one point. The Rockets extended their lead to a pair during a third quarter in which neither team shot well. Elvin Hayes scored 10 points to begin the last frame, and the Bullets jumped out to a 91–90 lead. Then the Bullets endured a four-minute scoring drought. Rudy Tomjanovich hit two baskets, Calvin Murphy dropped in a bucket on a fast break, and Moses Malone capped it off with a slam dunk that gave the Rockets a six-point bulge. The Bullets retaliated. Phil Chenier converted a three-point play, and Mitch Kupchak made one of two free throws to narrow the margin to two with more than a minute left. Malone came up short on a jumper, and Hayes followed with his own miss. When Mike Newlin made a long jumper, the Rockets sealed the victory. "It's a two-out-of-three series now, and we have the home court advantage," noted Tomjanovich.[46]

The Rockets looked to take advantage of the home court. The team started well and led by four points early on. Coach Dick Motta inserted

Mitch Kupchak and Larry Wright, and the pair scored 10 and nine points, respectively, during the second period. Washington led by 55–52 at halftime. "I thought at halftime we had the game completely under control," observed Motta. Houston used its small guard, Calvin Murphy, and big center Moses Malone to seize a 14-point lead during the first few minutes of the last frame. The Bullets came back behind the shooting of Dave Bing, Elvin Hayes, and Larry Wright, while the Rockets endured four minutes without a point. Kupchak countered with a basket, which made the score Rockets 108, Bullets 105, with three minutes left. Murphy hit a jumper. The Bullets missed, and Murphy came back down and hit another jumper. "[Murphy] was hot, and he just went at it. We weren't with him at all," said Motta.[47]

The Bullets showed calm and poise facing sudden death in game six. They jumped out quickly with evenly distributed scoring to take a 35–28 lead. They expanded this total by one in the second quarter. After halftime, Houston spread the floor and passed the ball around until a man got the open shot. Regardless of the distance from the basket, these jumpers seemed to go in. The Bullets continued to battle, putting in missed shots to keep themselves behind by only two points. But Newlin drove down the court and cut to his left, and his off-balance shot went in to restore Houston's four-point lead with 30 seconds left. "If a team is going to beat you like that, they're supposed to win. And there's nothing you can do about it," observed Hayes.[48]

The coach, the owner, and the media began the annual response to the team's playoff defeat. Although Motta made the observation after the game that Houston just beat the Bullets, he believed that the team was inconsistent and that some players did not want to be taught how to play but would rather be left alone to play. Pollin expressed his disappointment in not winning the championship but refused to comment on the performance of any player. The team's low turnout for home games during the playoff frustrated Pollin. "Our playoff attendance was probably the lowest in the country. It's baffling," he stated.[49] The media questioned which players would be returning for the 1977–1978 season. They zoned in on those who might leave due to age, specifically Bing and Unseld, and those who might be traded, particularly Hayes. Bing offered a criticism of Motta, saying that he had a difficult time communicating with his players. He said, "I'm not the only player who is upset or has some bad vibes as far as Dick is concerned."[50] Hayes felt that he took the criticism for the team's playoff failures and announced to the media that he had had enough of it, saying, "For myself and for my nerves, maybe another place will be better for me."[51]

This degree of public venting usually occurs in the country's largest media markets. The Knicks faced some of this to an extent. The Los Angeles Lakers and Chicago Bulls also faced the continuous questioning about playoff performance. The Boston Celtics, because of their championship past, also heard criticism when they fell short of expectations. Few other teams in the league experienced this focus on playoff failure in the public venue.

The 1977 NBA Draft offered the Bullets another opportunity for two selections in the first round. The team basically knew that Dave Bing would not return, so it was expected that they would seek a guard. Instead, the Bullets drafted two forwards: Greg Ballard of Oregon and Maurice "Bo" Ellis of Marquette. Dick Motta and Bob Ferry had visited Ballard before drafting him, although the forward was still uncertain if the team would select him. The selection of Ellis with the 17th pick left at least three guards who were not chosen at the time: Anthony Roberts, Norm Nixon, and Mike Glenn. Ellis was traded by the Bullets to the Denver Nuggets before the start of the season for a first-round draft pick in 1978. While Roberts had a five-year career, Glenn was a solid shooter for nine years, and Nixon made the All-Rookie Team, won two championships with the Lakers, and made two All-Star Teams during his long career.

The Bullets' second-round selection proved to be a one-year player, hurting the team's opportunity to build a deep bench. This placed Washington in a minority among the league. Out of the 22 selections in the second round, six other teams also received less than 100 games from their choice, and three selected a person who never suited up for a league game. Of course, most of the 12 choices enjoyed long careers with other teams, including a guard from Rutgers University named Eddie Jordan, who would go on to play a large part in the Washington Wizards' history.

Teams now had another method to improve in the standings. The new process of free agency provided a second way. First hailed as the most sensible labor-management solution in sports, the program developed a hitch. Only a few teams, like the New York Knicks, Buffalo Braves, and New Orleans Jazz, engaged in signing veteran free agents during the 1976–1977 season. The National Basketball Player's Association's general counsel, Larry Fleisher, wondered about the lack of interest. "It's unconceivable to me that a team that finishes 22nd or 21st or 20th in the league isn't interested in signing or even talking to one of these free agents."[52] The fear involved what a team had to give up as compensation for signing a veteran free agent.

Sufficient examples appeared to reduce the anxiety, so many more teams engaged in the process during the 1977–1978 season. During the summer, Washington made its first big splash with the signing of Bobby Dandridge, formerly of the Milwaukee Bucks. A forward on the team that defeated the Bullets during the 1971 finals, the three-time All–Star, nicknamed "Greyhound," brought another scoring option to his new team.

Preseason picks for the Central crown wearers included last season's winner, Houston, the San Antonio Spurs, the Atlanta Hawks, and Washington. The *Sports Illustrated* cover featured an article on the "Enforcers," glorifying the role of the guys who intimidated and sometimes fought to maintain the safety of their teammates.[53] The Portland Trail Blazers' Maurice Lucas received credit for turning the 1977 finals around with a brawl in game two. The attitude of the fans and the league changed shortly, as Kurt Benson and Kareem Abdul-Jabbar exchanged elbows and punches, which led to the former breaking his jaw and the latter breaking his hand. A month later, the Lakers and Rockets engaged in a brawl that ended with the incident known as "The Punch," when Kermit Washington broke Rudy Tomjanovich's face. Public condemnation of the violence came in newspaper editorials and television national news.

Coupled with the rumors of drug usage, these incidents damaged the league's public image significantly. These fights between and among white and African American men occurred in the years after the civil rights and other movements, and during the tumultuous period of equal opportunity for African Americans, Latin Americans, gays, lesbians, bisexuals, and women.[54]

The veteran Bullets and their old-school coach ran a physically aggressive training camp. They relied on their veterans to play most of the minutes during the season. The team started slowly in 1977–1978, with a .500 record during the first month, yet Houston fell to the bottom and barely rose up throughout the season. As the players began to gel, Washington won five in a row, and nine of 11 games, to move slightly ahead of both the Atlanta Hawks and San Antonio Spurs, but the winning did not continue. Washington fell back to the .500 mark as the month of March began. San Antonio had a five-game lead over the Bullets, seven games over Cleveland, and eight and a half over Atlanta. The Spurs stepped up their play, winning 15 games and losing six the remainder of the season to cement their hold on first place in the Central Division. Cleveland won 12 and lost eight, and the Bullets' 13 wins and nine losses enabled them to maintain their edge over Cleveland to finish as the third seed in the upcoming playoffs. Atlanta won six of their last eight to take the last playoff spot against third-seed Washington. Cleveland played against the New York Knicks in the two first rounds of the series in the Eastern Conference.

The Championship Run

In other playoff action, the Knicks played well, knocking out Cleveland in two straight games. They went up against number-one seed Philadelphia, eventually losing in the semifinal round. For Washington, a small crowd at the Capital Centre watched Atlanta use a zone defense that draped itself around Elvin Hayes and Mitch Kupchak, offering the big men little room to maneuver and shoot. This forced them to find the open man on the perimeter and left Washington's guards and small forward no choice but to launch long-range shots. Along with Charles Johnson, who was picked up midseason as a free agent, Larry Wright, Kevin Grevey, and Bobby Dandridge made those shots, accounting for 63 of the Bullets' 103 points and giving the team a nine-point victory, 103–94. Dandridge suffered a neck injury, which restricted his ability to turn his head. He commented, "I just have to hope that heat and rest can help it."[55] The Bullets played without Dandridge in the second game of the series. The teams battled through regulation tied. In overtime, the Bullets took the lead and held on to win by four, 107–103, and the team moved into the semifinal series against the San Antonio Spurs.

The quick dispatch of Atlanta set a precedent, as the Bullets beat the Hawks on three of four occasions. The team split its four games with the Spurs, an omen for a hard-fought series. San Antonio had great quickness and finesse to match against Washington's big bodies and strength down low. The Spurs looked to push Washington outside of its comfort zone of inside the foul line. Dick Motta believed that the Bullets could play good defense but would yield a lot of points because of the accuracy of the Spurs' shooters, George Gervin and Larry Kenon. "We have to hit our open shots and take advantage of what they give us," Motta commented.[56]

Playing inside the HemisFair Arena on the grounds of the 1968 expo, the Bullets ran a highly constructed set of offensive plays during the first half. San Antonio overplayed and doubled teamed the player identified as the primary option of the play. This left guys wide open, and the Bullets made less than half of these shots. Still, they led 49–48 at halftime. In the second half, Gervin pumped in several shots on his way to 35 points. The Bullets became lax about running their organized plays. Motta, screaming at his team to stop playing barnyard basketball, looked ready to pop veins in his neck. Poor shot choices led to San Antonio getting down the court and Kenon making shots to add 22 points. The Spurs took game one by 11 points, 114–103.

The Bullets' offense ignited throughout the first three quarters of the second game. Kevin Grevey and Elvin Hayes scored 29 and 28 points, respectively, and Bobby Dandridge returned to action and provided a key spark. They held a 21-point lead that dropped to 17 points as the final quarter began. San Antonio would not quit and inspired the home crowd by whittling the deficit to two points with a minute and a half remaining. George Gervin, who already had 46 points, made a big steal but then lost the handle on the ball and it rolled out of bounds. After the reprieve, Tom Henderson and Mitch Kupchak made shots to give the Bullets a big win. Back at home, the Bullets continued their accurate shooting, making 50 of their 92 shots, a 54% clip that enabled them to play fast break basketball with the run-and-gun Spurs. Dandridge, Hayes, and Johnson outpointed Kenon and Gervin, who received little scoring help from their teammates. The Bullets won game three, 118–105.

Game four proved a contrast. While neither team shot particularly well, San Antonio took a six-point lead, with the Bullets scoring mostly from fast breaks they generated from San Antonio's misses. After the half, the Bullets' outside shooting improved, enabling Elvin Hayes and Wes Unseld to score more on the inside. The Spurs led by one in the fourth quarter, but Bobby Dandridge took control. He'd drive past his man to the basket, drawing another defender over and leaving Unseld or Hayes open for the easy layup or dunk. The 98–95 victory put the Bullets on the verge of the Eastern Conference Finals against the Philadelphia Sixers, who swept the Knicks.

The Bullets took advantage of San Antonio's undisciplined style to outscore, outrebound, and outthink them. Dick Motta told the media, "I've said there are five solid teams in this league and that we are one of them. We can stay in there with the others—especially under playoff conditions, when there is more rest, more specific preparation, and more scouting."

The Spurs opted to push the Bullets with their running style for the fifth game. It worked. San Antonio shot well from the floor, and the speed and pressure of the defense forced the Bullets guards into several turnovers. While the teams were separated by only two points at the half, the Spurs kept up the speed and their hustle play paid off with an eight-point bulge at the close of the third quarter. The final score was 116–105, as Washington did not have a comeback in them. "They seemed to want the game more than we did, and they played like it," Bobby Dandridge said.[57] The Bullets also had to play without Mitch Kupchak, and the forward did not suit up for game six either.

The Spurs played with the same approach, but the Bullets met their pace and held the lead at halftime. Gervin led his team's charge, as the Spurs scored 10 to the Bullets' three to edge in front, 62–61. Then the Capital Centre's lights went out. It took eight minutes to relight the scene and get play going. The Spurs and Bullets exchanged several baskets, and the visitors led, 84–82, during the last quarter. Then Larry Wright and Elvin Hayes each scored twice to give the home team a lead they would not relinquish. The Bullets advanced with a 103–100 victory. "I think [the Spurs] tried too many different things and were not used to it," Hayes said, ironically because the basketball experts predicted that Washington would have to change its way of playing when they met Philadelphia in the conference finals.[58]

The Sixers were well rested. The winners of the most games in the Eastern Conference, Philadelphia featured All-Stars Julius Erving and Doug Collins, high-scoring forward George McGinnis, guard World B. Free, and, at center, "Chocolate Thunder," Darryl Dawkins. The deep bench enabled them to rotate in 10 players on a regular basis. The Bullets also used as many as nine players during the Spurs series, so they could have been able to match up with the Sixers to sustain their energy level.

The hosts had a great season on their home court, going 38–4 at the Spectrum. The two games they won against the Bullets also came on their home court. The experts predicted that the Sixers would easily run past the aging and infirmed Bullets. The Bullets came out fast, taking a 26–19 lead, as the Sixers appeared slow, perhaps from the layoff, but Philadelphia regrouped and tied the game at halftime with a good-shooting second quarter. The Sixers rode the shooting of Julius Erving and World B. Free to open up a four-point lead, and Wes Unseld went down with an injury to his right ankle. The Bullets kept their poise behind the scoring of Bobby Dandridge, Elvin Hayes, and Kevin Grevey and grabbed the lead near the end of the fourth quarter. The Sixers closed the gap to two on a Darryl Dawkins stuff of a Julius Erving miss. Tom Henderson tried to dribble out the clock, but George McGinnis drew a jump ball by pinning the ball to Henderson's chest. McGinnis won the tap back to Doug Collins, who let go a 20-foot shot that dropped through the net to tie the score. Despite being pushed into overtime, the Bullets scored the first six points, as the Sixers missed three wild shots. Collins and Erving scored to narrow the lead to two, but Hayes made three straight shots to lead his team to victory in overtime, 122–117.

Already without Wes Unseld, the team suffered another loss when Kevin Grevey felt a crick in his neck while blow drying his hair after showering. The Sixers used speed and muscle to take the second game, 110–104. The home team broke the close game open with a 32-point third quarter, which included several fast breaks off of blocks by Darryl Dawkins and Caldwell Jones. The visitors viewed the Sixers as "trying to bogart us . . . trying to be intimidating," according to coach Dick Motta,[59] while Elvin Hayes said that the roughhouse tactics "show [that] they are saying we are a better team. They couldn't beat us the regular way, so they had to resort to dirty stuff."[60] "We have to drag ourselves down in the trenches and battle them on the boards," said forward George McGinnis.[61]

The shoving match started again at the Capital Centre with both teams shooting 91 free throws on 71 personal fouls. When the game got into tempo,

Bobby Dandridge blanketed Julius Erving, keeping Dr. J to 12 points while scoring 30 of his own. Kevin Grevey returned to the lineup and added 21 points. Rookie Greg Ballard replaced Wes Unseld again and contributed 12 points and 15 rebounds to help the Bullets romp, 123–108. Elvin Hayes outplayed George McGinnis. Sixers forward Steve Mix said after the game, "I know what, if we try any more of that bleeping one-on-one stuff we could lose by 40 on Sunday."[62]

The afternoon game two days later started the Sixers way, with them clogging up the inside to deny Tom Henderson the ability to penetrate and dish off to the Bullets' inside men. Down 42–33, Coach Motta went with Kevin Grevey and Charles Johnson at guard, with Elvin Hayes, Mitch Kupchak, and Bobby Dandridge up front. The outside threat opened things up for Hayes, who scored nine of the team's 19 points to give the team a six-point lead at the half. A Sixers run midway through the third quarter cut the lead in half, but Coach Motta made constant player substitutions to keep the matchups favorable. The Bullets extended the lead to 10 before the starting group returned midway through the fourth quarter and poured it on to give the home team a 121–105 victory and a three games to one lead in the series. "We should all be talking," said World B. Free in the Sixers' locker room. "To each other. Not having arguments."[63]

Back home at the Spectrum, the Sixers adopted their run-and-gun game. Under the speed and defensive pressure, the Bullets committed 27 turnovers and shot less than 40% from the field and won, 107–94. "We never settled down and got into our patterns. That disturbs me," said Motta. The Sixers received 24 points from both Erving and Collins and showed less selfishness on offense while playing fired-up defense.

The Capital Centre crowd tried to spark the home team, cheering the Bullets as they warmed up and booing the Sixers. The will of the crowd could not stop the hot shooting Collins, who had 29 points, but it helped Hayes make his turnaround jumpers. The lead seesawed between the squads throughout, when, near game's end, the Bullets had to play without Dandridge and Wright, who had fouled out. The score remained tied at 99, as Unseld missed a shot. He went up and grabbed the ball and then let it roll off his fingers toward the hoop. It dropped in. The Sixers' Free dribbled down the court and took an errant last-second wild shot. The Bullets won the game, 101–99, and would again play for the NBA Championship. While their coach had reached his first NBA Finals in 10 years of trying, the franchise made it to their third and had yet to win a single game. Still, defeating the highly talented Sixers demonstrated that Washington played better as a team, on offense, on defense, and in thinking. As one veteran put it, the Bullets hit their stride.

Dick Motta preached running the offense through his main patterns. Since Motta's entry into the league during the late 1960s, the more freelancing style diminished, as many coaches, including the Bullets' Gene Shue and K. C. Jones, instituted offensive patterns. Motta insisted that his five patterns took three years to learn correctly, so he unveiled three parts to the Bullets the previous year and two more parts during the current season, with one remaining. "The whole offensive is designed to create one-on-one situations. . . . The first rule is that we try to get half of our shots within what I call the 50% shooting area. That's the area inside the foul circle."[64] The guard dribbling the ball up the court was the initiator of one of the five plays, or what Motta called "automatics." He starts them by where he throws the ball once crossing half court and which direction he runs after throwing the ball. The coach wanted to allow for the players' ability and stated that he designed plays for players like Chenier because of his high shooting percentage from the outside. Motta further stated that, "In this era, a lot of other teams ran their players through the three spot, like the Sixers with Doctor J."[65] Bickerstaff noted that the Bullets did not follow that pattern, using their point guard.[66]

The Seattle SuperSonics opened with the home game and surprised the basketball world with a win. The Bullets had won the muscle game inside and took an 84–65 lead. Then Seattle started its running game, scoring the final eight points of the third quarter. Washington launched into a deadly combination: poor shooting and no rebounding. The frontcourt produced only a few baskets, and the team shot 30%. They only pulled down one offensive rebound. Soon, Seattle's guards, Fred Brown and Dennis Johnson, dropped in big shots and led the team to an amazing comeback and a 106–102 win. With the loss of game one, the franchise had lost nine straight finals games, and everyone offered an opinion. Hayes pointed to a lack of inside shooting and Motta to bad shooting. The discord spread among the players, who bickered.

In the suburbs of Washington, D.C., for game two, the Bullets again leapt out to a big lead but watched it dwindle by halftime. The Bullets' Hayes and Dandridge kept up the scoring, totaling 59 for the game. Without adequate outside shooting from Grevey, who was playing with a sore ankle, the Bullets got reliable penetration from guard Tom Henderson to relieve pressure from the team's big men. Seattle closed to within six before Unseld's lay in shot gave the team a cushion that held up, by a final score of 106–98.

Every expert proclaimed that the Bullets needed to win game three at home because of Seattle's long home winning streak. Motta proclaimed that it was the "most important game in the history of the franchise." The Bullets missed too many shots, hitting on only 34% for the game. Shaky defense contributed to Seattle holding a slim lead. The SuperSonics sagged in on defense to keep Hayes and Dandridge from getting the ball to shoot. The Bullets' outside shooters did not help, and the Bullets lost, 93–92.

The Bullets' guard play did not improve significantly during the fourth game. The Bullets' big men outplayed Seattle's Marvin Webster and Jack Sikma to keep the game close. In the last quarter, Charles Johnson and Larry Wright hit their outside shots to bring the Bullets past Seattle. With just seconds on the clock, Fred Brown made a long-range jumper to tie the game and send it into overtime. Charles Johnson and Tom Henderson took over. Johnson scored six points, and Henderson grabbed an offensive rebound and then made two free throws to give the Bullets a 120–116 win.

Seattle bounced right back in game five, as the teams crisscrossed the country again. Key shooting from the two guards enabled them to win by another narrow margin, 98–94. Seattle jumped out to a lead and then scored only 14 points during the second quarter. Dandridge lit the scoreboard. In the third quarter, Hayes, Johnson, Kupchak, and Ballard produced big shots and pounded the boards, leading to an advantage of 20 more rebounds for the home team. Seattle hurt its cause with 22 turnovers and only 34% shooting. Washington won game six in a blowout, 117–82.

Back in Seattle for game seven, the two teams waged a battle. The Bullets' forwards put them ahead, 54–45, at halftime. Seattle remained close despite the inability of their guards to make their shots. This time Webster and Sikma generated the team's offense. The Bullets added to their lead in the third quarter and then went wobbly. Webster and Sikma led the SuperSonics on a 12–4 run to narrow the lead to 98–94. Johnson came down the court and fired up a jumper that fell short of the rim. Henderson dove on the ground, knocking the ball between Webster's legs. Kupchak grabbed the loose ball and made a layup as Webster fouled him. After putting in the free throw, the Bullets led by seven with 90 seconds remaining. Seattle scored three points and then fouled Unseld. The center had made about half of his free throws but missed both. A Paul Silas putback of Fred Brown's miss made the score 101–99, and Seattle immediately fouled Wes Unseld again. He missed the first shot, but, since it was a backcourt foul, he had two more attempts remaining. Unseld made them both. Dandridge scored the last basket on a break, pushing the score to 105–99, and the Bullets won the championship (figures 7.1 and 7.2).

With their victory, the Washington Bullets joined the eight other franchises that won in the decade. The 1970s proved to be the most competitive and wide-open period of any era in the league's history. Owner Pollin, Coach Motta and team captain Unseld joined in the team's celebration in

Figure 7.1. Owner Abe Pollin holding up the championship trophy.
Reprinted with permission of the D.C. Public Library, Star Collection, @ *Washington Post*.

the locker room. Of the 12 men, only Dandridge and Johnson had won prior championships. Only Kupchak would go on to win another as a player, with the Los Angeles Lakers in 1985.

This was one of the finals that appeared on a tape delay. Television and sports analysts found a lot to dislike with CBS' NBA coverage. Halftime

Figure 7.2. The NBA Championship ring of the Washington Bullets.
Reprinted with permission of the D.C. Public Library, Star Collection, @ *Washington Post*.

coverage and announcers again headlined the noted problems. The NBA provided CBS with flexibility in its coverage, so the network could show regional games and one national game, and also stage doubleheaders or switch to the most exciting game. The ratings rose and hit their peak during the 1977 NBA Finals. Then they dropped significantly during the 1978 season and plummeted by 22% during the Washington–Seattle Finals. Sunday afternoon games drew 34% less viewers, while Friday evening games drew 13% less. By the beginning of the next season, both ABC and NBC's program beat the ratings for CBS' first regular-season telecast. Speculation for the drop included people not wanting to stay indoors during the springtime and less excitement over the sport, particularly due to its problems of drug usage, which affected its image. The CBS network and the NBA wanted to find a resolution to the sinking situation, especially since the contract brought in $1 million a year to each team.

The showing of the NBA Finals on tape delay had been a much-featured element of NBA discussions of this era. The move to showing the game on tape delay occurred for a few different reasons. First, the finals occurred during the sweeps period, when television networks maximized their ratings to earn more advertising dollars. Second, with only three major networks, those networks aired programming that appealed to the greatest number of people to achieve high ratings. The networks learned back in the late 1940s that putting on a variety program, situation comedy, or drama appeals to both sexes and to more people than a sporting event. Despite the increasing popularity of sports in general, little had changed. The era still offered limited viewing options and required least common denominator programming.

The Bullets had problems with fan interest since their days in Baltimore. Even with the new arena, losses in the playoffs during past seasons had led to people losing interest in the team. The attendance declined during the regular season from 1976 through 1978, despite the team regularly making the playoffs. The turnout for playoff games dropped from close to capacity during the 1976 semifinals to lukewarm reception in 1977 and an even smaller turnout in 1978. The fans apparently did not judge the first round worthy of paying playoff prices to see. Others chose to stay home and raised a protest over the attempt to blackout the local broadcast of the game on television. When the local station showed the game, they also opted for tape delays as a drive to push people to attend the games in person.

This limited turnout to some of the big games gave the team's leadership headaches. It hurt the team financially, as they appeared to be losing money again, despite winning the championship. The situation perplexed Abe Pollin, as he loved the team deeply and could not understand why the city had not embraced them to the same degree that most other cities embraced their professional sports teams. The most frequently offered reason involved the transient nature of the city's population. As the nation's capital, Washington drew people from all over the country, and they had their team allegiances already formed; however, that ignored a sizable number of residents and the fact that the Washington Redskins football team was immensely popular. A local columnist argued that the city had a specific style of recreational basketball that they loved to play and watch, but the Bullets did not play that improvisational style. One D.C. high school coach asserted that he was not sure too many people inside the Beltway had "'Bullet Fever,' because the team is no-nonsense . . . they're not talented players so much as skilled players."[67] To appreciate the Bullets, one needed to appreciate basketball and understand its values, but if someone liked basketball because it's exciting, then they might want to root for some other team.

Within a week of the triumph, the Bullets' front office went to take part in the 1978 NBA Draft. The team traded first-round pick Bo Ellis for the ability to select a first-round pick in this draft. The Bullets had two picks, and they selected Roger Phegley, a guard and forward, and Dave Corzine, a center, with the 14th and 18th picks of the draft. Phegley noted that the team might have seen him play during the college senior basketball all-star games, for example, at the Pizza Hut Basketball Classic, which started in 1973, contests that were crammed into the two months between the end of the National Collegiate Athletic Association's basketball tournament and the NBA Draft on June 9, 1978; however, the team never contacted or interviewed him, and he was not at all certain which teams had an interest in him. The rookie hired an agent from his hometown in Illinois to negotiate for him and felt satisfied. His salary ranked somewhere in between the $200,000 that the top draft pick, Mychal Thompson, received and the $50,000 that several first-round draft picks from 1978 earned.

This draft became the second problematic draft in a row for the Bullets, despite having two first-round choices. Roger Phegley came off the bench for a season and a half before being traded to the New Jersey Nets for guard John Williamson and a 1981 second-round draft pick. Dave Corzine played two seasons with the Bullets before being traded to the San Antonio Spurs with a 1981 and 1982 second-round draft pick. Other choices remaining on the board while the Bullets picked these players were forward Mike Mitchell, who played several strong years with Cleveland and San Antonio; forward Terry Tyler, who enjoyed five good seasons with Detroit; and guards John Long, again with Detroit and Maurice Cheeks, a four-time All-Star with the Sixers. Michael Cooper and Gerald Henderson were each late third-round selections. Only one of the remaining nine picks the team made during this draft spent any time in the league.[68]

Holy Land

In mid-summer, the team went on a trip to Israel. Every member of the organization traveled, except for Phil Chenier because of back surgery, and Charles Johnson because of prearranged obligations. The team would play one exhibition game, and the expectation was that the revenue would pay for the trip, with Abe Pollin paying the remainder of the costs. NBA teams had traveled to Brazil and other countries and played exhibition games to promote the game and the NBA brand.

The Bullets were featured in a documentary about the trip, which the organization intended to sell to commercial television and use for other promotional purposes. The seriousness with which the opponents played the game, the flag-waving crowd, and the intensity of the televised event surprised the Bullet players. They had not practiced and were not prepared to win what they thought would be a relaxed game. After the game, Abe Pollin apologized to the team for the circumstances. The players then spent a week sightseeing in Israel, including going to Jerusalem. The trip appeared to be a great opportunity for Pollin to thank his team and also to attempt to make the team into more of a family unit. K. C. Jones and others had mentioned that the Celtics felt like a family during their years spent making title runs. The attempt to forge this type of bond turned out to be a good choice by the Bullets' ownership and management.

During visits to several religious sites, some degree of family building occurred. Unfortunately, upon the team's return to the United States, certain business activities undercut some of that bonding. The Bullets signed Elvin Hayes to a three-year, $1.3 million contract extension a year before his contract expired; however, Bob Dandridge, who had two years remaining on his contract, tried to get a renegotiation accomplished and the team refused. Dandridge expressed his disappointment and felt underappreciated. Negotiations with Coach Motta on a new contract also hit an edge when the team offered him a two-year extension when Motta wanted three. How that affected the coach awaited the passage of time. Even to insiders, the team appeared very businesslike, concentrating on winning while on the court, but, off the court, the team lacked camaraderie.[69]

The league officials and Board of Governors made several important changes to the game for the upcoming 1978–1979 season. The number of referees per game moved from two to three to increase the ability to arbitrate the game. The rules against hand-checking were tightened, which made the touching that impedes a player's progress into a foul. This change had as its impetus a desire to improve the NBA's image by reducing the threat of violence. Most of the professionals thought that the change reduced the differences between the pro game and high school and college basketball. The board also voted 20–2 to experiment with the three-point shot for the exhibition season. If things went out well, the shot from 25 feet would be included in games starting with the 1979–1980 campaign.

The NBA also tried to address the financial problems plaguing some franchises. All teams benefitted from a reduction of gross receipts due to the league. The NBA also voted to take 7% rather than 8% of the total gross receipts from each club. The expectation was that an increase in gate receipts would help generate more income for all. The league also decided to allow the Buffalo franchise to seek permission to move to San Diego, which they did. The Detroit Pistons moved from the Midwest Division to the Central Division, and, the dominant team in the Central Division for years, the Washington Bullets, moved into the Atlantic Division.

The Bullets started the season as their streaky selves. They won their four games and then lost five in a row. Basketball columnists began questioning the team's abilities. They cited others who said that the Bullets were too slow, too old, and too dependent on a pattern-oriented offense. Some even referred to the team's championship as a "fluke" title. Their play silenced some of the critics.

Winning streaks of five and nine games gave the team a 23–9 record right before the Christmas holiday season. Throughout the season, they would embark on two winning streaks for each losing streak they had. Newcomer Roger Phegley noted that the team practiced infrequently because of the team's age and being so banged up from the season. On those infrequent occasions, guys usually drove to the facility in their practice gear and then threw on sweatpants and drove home to shower after the practice ended. Their 54–28 record topped all teams in the NBA. The team generated four more points on offense, while their defense per game remained roughly the same. Yet, this number of 109 points per game ranked ninth out of 22 teams, three places up from the previous season. Hayes, Dandridge, and Grevey all scored more than 1,000 points during the season, while Kupchak tallied 961.[71]

The Bullets first-seed position placed them in the Eastern Conference Semifinals against the Atlanta Hawks, who had beaten the Houston Rockets in the first round of the playoffs. Atlanta brought a hustling, fast-paced style to the Capital Centre, and the Bullets had all they could handle. The tight game burst open when Hayes and Dandridge combined for 37 points in the second half, leading the team to a game-one win by a score of 103–89.

The Hawks used a sagging, aggressive defense in game two to shut down Hayes, but Dandridge kept the Bullets close. With the game tied at 83, the Hawks started a 16–4 spurt by sharing the ball on offense and denying the Bullets the ability to pass the ball down deep inside to their big forwards. Atlanta won game two, 107–99.

The scoring dropped precipitously in game number three. The two teams sat at 61 points at the beginning of the last quarter. With neither team shooting well, the Bullets put pressure on Atlanta by dominating the glass, restricting the Hawks to one shot each time down the floor. Grevey regained his shooting touch and made three key baskets in a scoring burst that enabled Washington to win, 89–77. Game four proved a real nail bitter for fans of both teams. They tied after regulation and played a tense overtime, which the Bullets won by one basket, 120–118.

The Bullets promptly lost the next two games in the series. The Hawks turned the series around by winning the battle of the boards. They started to rely on their bench more, and their substitutions outplayed the Bullets' bench players. They received key shooting and defense from these players, and Hubie Brown did an amazing job as coach. The Bullets summarized this situation coming down to a game seven, saying, "One of these days, we are going to cut it too close. We are going to lose a seventh game because of injury or a cold performance, and we'll have no one to blame but ourselves." A sold-out crowd, including President Jimmy Carter, watched another tight game. The two teams went to halftime only two points apart. Hayes and Dandridge regularly made their shots, and the Bullets outrebounded the Hawks by 13 to win the game, 100–94.[71]

The Eastern Conference Finals featured the first-and second-seeded teams. The San Antonio Spurs and their run-and-gun game went up against the slower, structured offense of the Bullets. As each team played its game, the Spurs held a four-point lead into the third period. Then the Bullets started turning the ball over, and the Spurs got out and ran down the court for easy baskets. The 43–26 burst enabled the Spurs to win going away. Wes Unseld summoned his 11 years of experience for a 26-point and 22-rebound performance during the second game. Complemented by Kevin Grevey, who scored 18 points, and better defense from the team's guards, the Bullets won, 118–97.

The Spurs returned home and relied on their scoring tandem of George Gervin and James Silas. The pair built a 14-point bulge with only seven minutes remaining, but the Bullets, behind Bobby Dandridge and Kevin

Grevey, narrowed the deficit to one. After swapping baskets and San Antonio making a free throw, the Bullets' Charles Johnson had a jump shot from the corner that rimmed out as the buzzer sounded, enabling the Spurs to win, 116–114.

Game four came down to a singular performance in a single period. Gervin, San Antonio's "Ice Man," poured in 20 points in the third quarter, and Washington did not have the offense to counter. Incensed, Coach Motta complained that "this is not my team," because the Bullets would not run his offense. The Bullets were not working the ball inside "to the guys who got us here." Only two teams in NBA history had won a series after falling behind three games to one, the task the Bullets faced.[72]

Back home, the Bullets eked out a 107–103 win in game five. Now, in San Antonio, the Bullets jumped out to a 30–23 first-quarter lead, despite Elvin Hayes facing a double team every time he touched the ball. The Spurs brought out their speed game and tied the game in the first minutes of the fourth quarter, at 82 each. The Bullets switched to a big lineup, moving Bobby Dandridge to guard and bringing in the 6–foot, 7-inch Greg Ballard at small forward. Hayes started the run with a three-point play. Eight points by Ballard and some other timely scoring let the Bullets embark on a 21–10 run that salted the game away, 108–100.

After two victories, it might have seemed that the team was due for its letdown. Bobby Dandridge and Elvin Hayes, with some contributions from outside shooters Kevin Grevey and Larry Wright, had enabled the Bullets to hang close, but George Gervin dropped in 42 points and Larry Kenon added 23, which allowed the Spurs to hold on to a 10-point lead going into the fourth quarter. The Bullets tied the score and then had the ball with 25 seconds remaining. Coach Motta let Dandridge improvise, and the scorer made a jump shot over three defenders with eight seconds remaining. Guard James Silas drove into the lane and went up for a short jumper, but Hayes came across the lane and blocked the shot into the hands of Kenon. Before he could shoot, Dandridge slapped the ball away, and Greg Ballard cradled it until the buzzer sounded.

The Bullets survived another grueling series, winning game seven at home by a final of 107–105. This time the friction that came from coming close to elimination generated intense tension amongst the team. Dick Motta's denouncement of the team could not have sat well with any of the players. The coach already had a conflict with Bobby Dandridge. Dandridge also had a conflict with the Bullets' management, expressing his frustration at being paid less than he believed he was worth to the team. He demanded that the team renegotiate his contract at the end of the season.[73] Along with this friction, the Bullets also had Mitch Kupchak sidelined with a back injury that required surgery. The team hosted the Seattle SuperSonics for game one, and, like the previous year, the Bullets took a large lead going into the final quarter. The SuperSonics once again caught up, as Washington missed 13 of 15 shots. With seconds left and the game tied, Larry Wright took a shot and official Ed Rush called a foul on guard Dennis Johnson. With no time on the clock, Wright dropped in both free throws to give the home team a 99–97 win. Seattle returned to the sagging interior defense to shut down the Bullets' forwards. The best defensive club in the NBA during the season shut Washington down in the second half and, behind Johnson's 20 points, took game two, 92–82.

Washington brought their rebounding ability to Seattle for the swing game. Unfortunately, however, they made only one-third of their shots. Trailing 55–44 at halftime, the Bullets tried to close the gap, only to have the SuperSonics stay ahead on strong shooting from everyone on the team. Wes Unseld grabbed eight offensive rebounds and scored 23 points to complement Bobby Dandridge's 28. "He's one tough player," noted center Jack Sikma. "Unseld may be the strongest guy I've ever played against." When told of the comment, Unseld replied, "He's young. He hasn't played against too many guys in this league."[74] While not detailed in the local media, Motta gave a lengthy interview to a sports reporter for the *Los Angeles Times*, during which the coach mentioned his interest in coaching the Lakers. This was a highly curious action taken during the middle of his team's battle for the championship.

The two teams engaged in a good-shooting fourth game. The SuperSonics jumped out to a sizable lead, but the Bullets stayed in the game through the shooting of their guards. The team's big men took over, and the lead seesawed between the teams through three quarters. As the fourth began, the Sonics led, 84–81. The Bullets battled back and tied the game at 102 with 18 seconds left. The Sonics brought the ball down, and guard Gus Williams missed; Jack Sikma got the rebound and missed his shot too. Elvin Hayes fouled out of the game at the end of regulation, and Wes Unseld and Bobby Dandridge followed during the overtime, giving Seattle the win, 114–112.

Game five appeared little different. The Bullets held an eight-point halftime lead. The SuperSonics got a burst of scoring in the third quarter from guards Gus Williams and Dennis Johnson. The team used traps and pressure defense to disrupt the Bullets' offensive patterns and make them take low-percentage shots. The Bullets managed only 42 second-half points and lost the game, 97–93, and the series, four games to one.

The home crowd applauded thunderously for both teams' efforts. One columnist noted that the Bullets played the series with several players out with injuries. Another captured comments of the team's main players. Unseld noted that, "They were always one step ahead of us the whole series. We could never seem to do anything to get us going."[75] Does this reflect upon the composition of the team, the inability of the coaching staff to develop alternatives, or the failure of the players to implement alternative strategies to offset the SuperSonics? It involved some of all these factors. Yet, they lost with style and class. Most articles focused on the composition of the team. How would the recently dethroned Bullets look during the 1979–1980 season?

Notes

1. "Silverdome History," NBA Hoops Online, www.silverdomeevents.com/about-us/history.html (retrieved July 14, 2010).
2. American Institute of Steel Construction. *Modern Steel Construction*, XV (Fourth Quarter 1975), 3–9.
3. Mark Asher, "Capital Centre's Bookings Reach 175 for 81/2 Months," George Solomon, "Tremendously Successful Capital Centre Still Has Bugs," *Washington Post*, July 7, 1974, C1; Bernie Bickerstaff, interview by author, March 17, 2012.
4. William Gildea, "Bullets Figure to Hire K. C. Jones as Coach,"*Washington Post*, June 14, 1973, D1.
5. George Solomon, "Title-Minded Bullets Select KC Jones," *Washington Post*, June 19, 1973, D1.
6. Walt Frazier, with Neil Offen, *Walt Frazier: One Magic Season and a Basketball Life* (New York: Time Books, 1988), 24.
7. "Celtics Ponder Strategy," *Los Angeles Times*, April 26, 1974, B16; "Boston Makes All the Right Moves,"*Los Angeles Times*, May 13, 1974, C1.
8. Bickerstaff interview, March 17, 2012.
9. Peter Carry, "A Circus with One Tilted Ring," *Sports Illustrated*, April 15, 1974, 24.
10. Mark Asher, "Balance Shifting in NBA," *Washington Post*, October 15, 1974, D1; Phil Elderkin, "Surprise! Knicks Emerge as Quality Product," *Christian Science Monitor*, December 11, 1974, 9.
11. "The Bullets Are Biting," *Time*, March 10, 1975, 72.
12. "The Bullets Are Biting," *Time*, March 10, 1975, 73.
13. "The Bullets Are Biting," *Time*, March 10, 1975, 72.
14. Pat Putnam, "In the NBA It's Muscle," *Sports Illustrated*, April 14, 1975, 32.
15. Pat Putnam, "A Beaut of a Brawl," *Sports Illustrated*, April 28, 1975, 14
16. Pat Putnam, "In the NBA It's Muscle," *Sports Illustrated*, April 14, 1975, 32; Pat Putnam, "A Beaut of a Brawl," *Sports Illustrated*, April 28, 1975, 14.
17. David DuPree, "Bullets Break Down Celtics," *Washington Post*, April 28, 1975, D1.
18. Kenneth Denlinger, "Did Bullets Win or Celtics Lose?" *Washington Post*, April 28, 1975, D1.

19. "Bullets Rout Celtics," *New York Times*, May 1, 1975, 64.

20. "Bullets Rout Celtics," 64.

21. "Celtics Win 101–90," *New York Times*, May 4, 1975, 227.

22. "Roundup of Week April 21–27," *Sports Illustrated*, May 5, 1975, 78.

23. Pat Putnam, "When Low Down, Go Down Lower," *Sports Illustrated*, May 12, 1975, 28.

24. "Roundup of Week May 5–11," *Sports Illustrated*, May 19, 1975, 87.

25. "Roundup of week May 12–18," *Sports Illustrated*, May 26, 1975, 99.

26. K. C. Jones with Jack Warner, *Rebound: Autobiography of K.C. Jones and an Inside Look at the Champion Boston Celtics* (Boston: Quinlan Press, 1986): 126–28

27. K. C. Jones with Jack Warner, *Rebound: Autobiography of K. C. Jones and an Inside Look at the Champion Boston Celtics* (Boston: Quinlan Press, 1986): 126–28; Bickerstaff interview, March 17, 2012.

28. Leonard Shapiro, "Playoffs Let Bullets Cash in," *Washington Post*, May 13, 1975, D1.

29. "The Collapse at Capital Centre," *Washington Post*, May 28, 1975, A18; David DuPree, "Bullets Qualify for Hardship," *Washington Post*, May 29, 1975, D1; David DuPree, "Bullets Deal Dick Gibbs to Braves," *Washington Post*, July 31, 1975, C1.

30. "Roundup of Week May 12–18," *Sports Illustrated*, May 26, 1975, 99. *Sports Illustrated*, May 26, 1975; "Roundup of Week May 19–25," *Sports Illustrated*, June 2, 1975; Ross Atkin, "Warriors' Sweep of Finals: Fantasyland Comes to NBA," *Christian Science Monitor*, May 28, 1975, 22.

31. David DuPree, "Bing Gives Bullets Inside Track to Title," *Washington Post*, August 29, 1975, D1.

32. "1975–76 Washington Bullets Roster and Statistics," Basketball-Reference.com, www.basketball-reference.com/teams/WSB/1976.html (retrieved July 13, 2010).

33. "Merge Talks Called in Basketball," *Washington Post*, April 13, 1976, D1.

34. "Merge Talks Called in Basketball," *Washington Post*, April 13, 1976, D1.

35. Jones, *Rebound: Autobiography of K.C. Jones and an inside Look at the Champion Boston Celtics*, 130–32.

36. This and other details and quotes by Tom Kropp were obtained during an interview with the author, March 6, 2012; this and other details and quotes by Mitch Kupchak were obtained during an interview with the author, April 25, 2012.

37. David DuPree, "Bullets Seen Nearing Deal on Guard," *Washington Post*, November 5, 1976, D1.

38. Gene Shue, interview by author, March 5, 2012; Casey Mack, "The Architect: The Legendary Howard Garfinkel Reflects on His Legacy in Youth Basketball," Five-Star Basketball.com, http://fivestarbasketball.com/originals/04-01-2011-the-architect-howard-garfinkel-1 (retrieved March 9, 2012).

39. Pete Axthelm, "Why Pro Basketball Is Sick," *Newsweek*, November 22, 1976, 87.

40. David DuPree, "Bullets Deal Weatherspoon," *Washington Post*, December 14, 1976, D1.

41. David DuPree, "Bullets Get Henderson in Trade for Robinson," *Washington Post*, January 21, 1977, D1.

42. Barry Lorge, "Star Back but Celts Still Lose," *Washington Post*, January 15, 1977, E1.

43. David DuPree, "Grevey Says Not Playing Frustrating," *Washington Post*, January 19, 1977, D1.

44. David DuPree, "Bullets Get Henderson in Trade for Robinson," *Washington Post*, January 21, 1977, D1.

45. This and other details and quotes by Greg Ballard were obtained during an interview with the author, April 23, 2012.

46. David DuPree, "Rockets Even Series at 2–2," *Washington Post*, April 27, 1977, E1.

47. Ken Denlinger, "Wright Exit Spells Doom for Bullets," *Washington Post*, April 30, 1977, D1.

48. David DuPree, "Rockets Draw Hot Hand," *Washington Post*, May 1, 1977, D1.

49. David DuPree, "Inconsistent Bullets Face Rockets Today," *Washington Post*, May 1, 1977, 33.

50. David DuPree, "Rockets Draw Hot Hand," *Washington Post*, May 1, 1977, D1.

51. David DuPree, "Bing Upset at Motta's Clean Bill," *Washington Post*, May 13, 1977, C1.

52. Paul Attner, "Free Agent Talks Center of Dispute," *Washington Post*, July 16, 1977, C1.

53. "When the Going Gets Tough," *Sports Illustrated*, October 31, 1977, 38.

54. Douglas McAdam, *Political Process and the Development of Black Insurgency, 1930–1970* (Chicago: University of Chicago Press, 1999).

55. Paul Attner, "Bullets Outlast Hawks," *Washington Post*, April 13, 1978, D1.

56. Paul Attner, "Motta Accuses Bullets of 'Barnyard Basketball," *Washington Post*, April 17, 1978, D4.

57. Paul Attner, "Bullets Stumble 116–105," *Washington Post*, April 26, 1978, D3.

58. Sam Goldpar, "76ers to Renew Drive Today against Bullets," *New York Times*, April 30, 1978, S8.

59. Paul Attner, "76ers Tie It, 110–104, Rouse Bullet Anger," *Washington Post*, May 4, 1978, D1.

60. Paul Attner, "76ers Tie It, 110–104, Rouse Bullet Anger," *Washington Post*, May 4, 1978, D3.

61. Paul Attner, "76ers Tie It, 110–104, Rouse Bullet Anger," *Washington Post*, May 4, 1978, D1.

62. John Papanek, "Another Chapter in the Philadelphia Story," *Sports Illustrated*, May 15, 1978.

63. John Papanek, "Another Chapter in the Philadelphia Story," *Sports Illustrated*, May 15, 1978.

64. Paul Attner, "Motta Patterns an Open Secret," *Washington Post*, May 18, 1978, D1.

65. Bickerstaff interview, March 17, 2012.

66. Bickerstaff interview, March 17, 2012.

67. This and other details and quotes by George Leftwich were obtained during an interview with the author, April 22, 2012.

68. "Pizza Hut Basketball Classic," *Harvard Crimson*, January 9, 1973, www.thecrimson.com/article/1973/1/9/pizza-hut-basketball-classic-pthe-balloting/ (retrieved October 10, 2011).

69. Mark Asher, "Israel Trip Caps Dream Year," *Washington Post*, September 3, 1978, D4; William Claiborne, "Bullets Pilgrims in Jerusalem," *Washington Post*, September 7, 1978, G1; William Claiborne, "Fat Lady Sings," *Washington Post*, September 8, 1978, E1.

70. *Chicago Tribune*, June 16, 1978, D3; *Christian Science Monitor*, November 8, 1978, 10.

71. Paul Attner, "Hawks Proving They Have Heart," *Washington Post*, April 26, 1979, D1; Paul Attner, "Cheap Seats from Furlow Anger Bullets," *Washington Post*, April 28, 1979, D1; Paul Attner, "Bullets Outlast Hawks," *Washington Post*, April 30, 1979, D1.

72. Paul Attner, "Motta Simmers at His Team's Cool," *Washington Post*, May 8, 1979, D1.

73. *Baltimore Sun*, May 2–19, 1979; *Washington Star*, May 2–19, 1979; *Washington Post*, May 2–19, 1979.

74. Sam Goldapar, "Sonics Tie Series,"*New York Times*, May 25, 1979, A19.

75. Paul Attner, "SuperSonics Capture NBA Title 97–93," *Washington Post*, June 2, 1979, D1.

CHAPTER EIGHT

~

Abe Pollin and the Washington Bullets

Before the beginning of the 1979–1980 season, several changes occurred that would significantly alter the way the professionals played and the media covered the sport of basketball. After experimenting with using the three-point shot, the National Basketball Association (NBA) included the shot as part of its rules for the upcoming season. The line on the floor from the basket would be 22 feet from the corners and 23 feet, 9 inches to the top of the arc. League officials knew that the shot made for a more offensively minded and wide-open type of basketball game. NBA brass, struggling with the image of the league, saw the value in making the change, as the shot was also popular with the fans.

While the three-point shot would change how the NBA game was played, the expansion of cable television would alter the league in many other ways. Cable television originated as a transmission method to send over-the-air broadcasting to remote and less-accessible areas of the country. The ability of the cable platform to carry a large number of distinct signals and provide significantly clearer reception to potential audiences helped promote more technological and policy changes. These changes led to the industry providing an expanded amount of broadcast stations.

Some broadcasting television stations took advantage of the cable platform to send their signal around the country. These superstations, including WTCG (Turner Communications Group), became the first of many networks to offer their programs on what was called "basic cable." Other broadcasters with more specialized programming, like the Christian Broadcasting

Network (CBN) and the Entertainment Sports Programming Network (ESPN), soon joined, expanding the appeal of cable television to subscribers in areas that did not have difficulty receiving over-the-air signals. These new stations needed programming to sell their station to the cable companies.

Despite being in the middle of a broadcast contract with CBS, the NBA began negotiations with the networks on basic cable. In situations where the team owner also owned a broadcasting network, those teams had some of their games shown on a cable network. This was the case for the Atlanta Hawks (Turner Broadcasting) and the New York Knicks (Madison Square Garden Network). The Bullets were among the majority of local teams that did not have this synergy of team owner and broadcasting mogul. The league eventually signed a $1.5 million contract with the USA cable network to broadcast games for three years. The contract expanded to $11 million for two years, sharing the rights with ESPN by the 1982–1983 season.

Before ESPN won the rights to broadcast NBA games, they had begun to influence the league. The station's 24-hours-a-day coverage magnified the attention on sports, particularly through the development of special interest and sport-specific programming. SportsCenter and other vehicles for presenting discussion and news about all sports and their personalities began to overtake the local newscasts in presenting sports information. Even with the beginning of the expansion of newscasts throughout the day as part of network and syndicated channel programming, most local markets featured one and a half or two hours of news programming during an entire day. Of that figure, shows devoted a total of 15 to 20 minutes a day to sports. A few programs appeared on local stations or in syndicated production that aired in a number of television markets that featured a half-hour discussion of sports or an hour of discussion accompanied by videos. None of this programming could compare to the two hours of news that ESPN showed and the consequent need to fill those hours that would lead to more interviews with athletes, more dissection of player and team performances, and a significantly increased presentation of the problematic and seamier side of the sporting world.

The platform that ESPN provided for sports to 11 million households in the early 1980s certainly increased the attention paid to all sports and their personalities. The channel also disrupted the previous pattern of fans learning mostly about local teams. Whereas news broadcasts and live sports coverage devoted a great deal of coverage to their local teams, ESPN would send a signal out nationally and internationally. The focus had to be broader, covering all teams and all news events without the previous bias in both time and tone that local stations and newspapers often offered. Despite losing tens of millions of dollars for its owner, Getty Oil, during the first few years, the new media wrought a situation where more people would get more news about every team on a larger scale.

The added sports coverage also created a shift in the scouting and player development strategies. The Portsmouth Invitational Tournament began in 1953, as a way to organize and evaluate 64 of the best college basketball players across the nation. Twelve games were played during four days, with representatives of each team invited to scout potential draft selections. The event garnered attention in the mid-1970s, with players like Dave Cowens and John Lucas playing in the event, and, by the early 1980s, it was the best way to unearth unheralded players from smaller collegiate programs. Later in the decade, players like John Stockton, Scottie Pippen, and Dennis Rodman participated and benefited from the opportunity to showcase their skills on a larger scale.

In the new season, the NBA would have several additional personalities to promote. The two most important would be Earvin "Magic" Johnson of the Los Angeles Lakers and Larry Bird of the Boston Celtics. When they were drafted during the spring of 1979, Johnson signed a contract for $500,000 a year for five seasons, a large sum at the time but only a small amount relative to what college basketball stars would receive a decade later. This rise occurred despite the imposition of a spending limit that each team could expend on salaries.[1]

Motta's Last Stand

In the months before the media landscape changed, local newspapers carried articles with predictions that as many as eight of the 12 current Bullets would not return. Team management faced an unhappy forward (Bobby Dandridge), two free-agent guards (Tom Henderson and Kevin Grevey), two older veterans also as free agents (Charles Johnson and Phil Chenier), and a player attempting to come back from a serious injury (Mitch Kupchak). Bob Ferry recognized that the team had an old roster in basketball years but explained that he did not expect to "break up" the Bullets. Management priced their own free agents and also sought help from other free agents on the market before considering the draft. Then they made their first problematic move later that summer by trading their 1979 first-round draft pick for Phoenix Suns' forward Steve Malovic.

The Bullets approached the 1979 NBA Draft with a diminished selecting position. With their first pick, number 44 (round two), the Bullets selected guard Joe DeSantis from Fairfield University. Two picks later they chose

Andrew Parker from Iowa State University. Charles Floyd rounded out the team's third-round selection. None would go on to play in the NBA. The decision to trade for Steve Malovic was not an epically terrible strategy in hindsight, but there were several players drafted in the later rounds that had productive careers, including center Bill Laimbeer, taken by Cleveland near the end of the third round; center James Donaldson, tagged by Seattle earlier in the fourth round; guard Allen Leavell, whom Houston selected near the end of the fifth round; and center Mark Eaton, chosen by Utah later in the fifth round.

After the draft, the Bullets made a swap of guards. They replaced Tom Henderson, who signed with the Houston Rockets, by inking Kevin Porter to a five-year contract worth $1 million. The team gained a 1980 first-round draft pick as compensation for losing Henderson but gave up a 1980 and a 1982 first-round pick for signing Porter. Abe Pollin wanted the team to sign Porter because he was a popular player, and the owner believed he would increase attendance.

The team and owner Pollin arranged for members of the team and their families to travel to China. In the country, the team would hold basketball clinics and play exhibition games. The Bullets offered the Chinese their first look at a NBA team. Six Bullets regulars, two draft choices, Kevin Porter, front office personnel. and the wives of all who went on the trip formed a 29-person contingent. The members of the team and their families left in the middle of August and also stopped in other parts of Asia and Hawaii.

A large number of players came to the team's camp for tryouts. Despite Mitch Kupchak's difficult recovery from injury, the front office shipped the recently acquired Steve Malovic to the San Diego Clippers for a second-round pick in the 1982 draft. They held out high hopes for starting guard Roger Phegley for the 1979–1980 season, but Bob Ferry sent him to the New Jersey Nets in exchange for six-year veteran John Williamson and a second-round draft pick in 1981. Williamson played 30 games after the trade and nine games the following year before the Bullets waived him. Phegley did not do a significant amount past his remaining five seasons.

After the first three months, the questions about the Bullets' decline increased. Elvin Hayes (figure 8.1) appeared to have lost his enthusiasm. Kevin Porter did not meld well with the team, validating what basketball experts had wondered about the Bullets' choice of Porter. The team showed little cohesiveness on defense, and they had a team of specialist (one-dimensional) players in a league that had increasingly moved toward all-around, do-everything players. The closest all-around player the team had, Bobby Dandridge, played sporadically. The team showed continued disinterest in renegotiating

Figure 8.1. Elvin Hayes and Kareem Abdul-Jabbar battle on the court, 1980.
Reprinted with permission of the D.C. Public Library, Star Collection, @ *Washington Post*.

his three-year, $250,000 annual contract, even after Dandridge's promise to produce during the playoffs. The cold-shouldered approach sat poorly with Dandridge, even though he kept distance from his teammates on occasion. During the season, Dandridge cited various injuries that kept him from being able to play. The problem for some of the Bullets' leadership was that Dandridge had behaved similarly when he was in Milwaukee, so they had no idea what to believe.

All the angst over the team's performance and personal frustrations of various players hid the fact that the Bullets played the game the way the NBA appeared to be moving. The Bullets ran an offense from Dick Motta's set plays, and there were occasional questions about defensive focus. The average team attempted less than 91 shots per game, down more than 15 from the previous decade, in which teams ran more and attempted more shots. The main culprit appeared to be the coaches. As one assistant coach noted, "Coaches are dictators." They wanted to slow the game down and were using defensive changes to do so.[2]

The team played barely more than .500 basketball during the final months of the season; however, their record of 39 wins and 43 losses enabled them to finish the season as the sixth seed in the Eastern Conference and make the playoffs. They drew the Sixers, who finished as the third seed in the first round of the playoffs, and opened up the series in Philadelphia. The Bullets lost, 111–96.

Game two brought more of the same (figure 8.2). As one columnist noted, the Bullets were outmanned, outnumbered, outran, outjumped, and outouted. The series ended, and the post mortem for the Bullets began. Unseld summed things up, noting that the team lost self-confidence and confidence in its coach, who seemed to lose interest. They rarely practiced during the season and lacked intensity.

This perspective would certainly give Bullets' management a great deal of concern. Dick Motta had a contract to coach for one more year. Team management supported Motta in his job, and Motta reiterated his interest in coaching, but that appeared unlikely. "He for some reason wasn't happy coaching the team anymore. He wanted a change, and I helped him go to Dallas," Bob Ferry observed.[3] The executives promoted Motta to a position in the front office, which he soon left to go to Dallas. They hired Gene Shue as the team's new coach.

The new coach had a long history with the franchise. He coached the Baltimore Bullets from 1966 to 1973, and he also played his last season in Baltimore in 1963–1964. Not only was he connected to the team, he was connected to the area, as he had attended high school in Towson, Maryland,

Figure 8.2. The Bullets' bench looks glum after losing in the playoffs, 1980.
Reprinted with permission of the D.C. Public Library, Star Collection, @ *Washington Post.*

and played collegiately at the University of Maryland. The press announcement featured Shue's ability to find talent and his history coaching winning teams. Shue said that on the surface it looked like the Bullets had the nucleus to be successful next season. He highlighted that he did not have a set system, a direct opposite to Motta.

Other team leaders expressed optimism about the Bullets' situation. General manager Bob Ferry observed that Gene Shue was "one of the first guys to coach to the personnel." Shue observed that the team needed help with its backcourt, a problem that had been with the team for several seasons.[4] Guard Larry Wright expected a huge rebuilding effort, noting, "They're going to back a big old moving van up to the locker room and ship out all of the dead weight. That's not going to leave many of us left."[5] Ferry further noted that, "The Bullets had good players but they were starting to get old. Guys usually retired after age 30."[6] The assistant coach reflected, saying, "Sometimes you have to remember that it's a business. We may have waited one year too long to move a player or two on that team."[7]

The NBA brought in another expansion team for the 1980–1981 season, with the Dallas Mavericks joining the Midwest Division as the sixth team. The Bullets made Bobby Dandridge, John Williamson, Jim Cleamons, Ron Behagen, and Lawrence Boston available in the expansion draft, and Dallas selected Cleamons. While the guard opted to retire, Dallas also signed Dick Motta to be their coach, officially ending his time with the Bullets.

Upon Motta's departure, local newspapers proclaimed the end of an era. The articles covered the period of elation, including the championship season, but they also focused on negative stories and claims. They did confirm some of the claims that players had made earlier, including not holding practices. They revealed that Motta had poor relationships with several of his players and appeared to pay limited attention to such factors as team chemistry. Greg Ballard observed that Motta gave up during one game in the 1978 finals, losing the forward's respect in the process. During the 1979 playoffs, with the team still playing, he and management appeared to make personnel decisions for next year. Motta even mentioned his interest in coaching the Lakers during the finals. He treated Charles Johnson with little respect during the 1979–1980 exhibition season, no apparent regard for the man's popularity with his teammates. Motta did have supporters, as Roger Phegley regarded the coach as someone who "coached to the strength of his team" and promoted a workmanlike atmosphere.[8]

That this dysfunctional situation under Coach Motta occurred raised questions about the Bullets' leadership. Had Bob Ferry, or, to a lesser extent, Abe Pollin known about the lack of practices, apparent disinterest, conflicts, and strife on the team? If not, why not? If so, then why not take action to iron out the situation for the better? Ferry called in former coach K. C. Jones to review his actions. Why did he not do the same thing with Coach Motta, particularly when the situation appeared to require this supervision?

During this era, the team, like every other squad in the NBA, traveled commercially, which resulted in much more time spent in transit. Roger Phegley and assistant coach Bernie Bickerstaff described their routine as breakfast at the hotel, lunch at the airport, the game, and dinner after the game. The next day, the team flew out on the first available flight, had breakfast at the airport, went to the hotel, and got ready for the game that evening. The team trainer, as with many other teams in the NBA, also served as the traveling secretary. When teams were slated for an afternoon game, they went from the airport to the arena and, as a result, were often tired and sluggish during the game. The NBA enforced this system through fining those teams who missed the first flights out of cities.

With so much time spent in transit, teams had less time to discuss the details regarding opposing teams and players. The team's assistant coaching staff performed the advanced analysis of the league's teams and broke down game film and video. Bernie Bickerstaff continued his one-man role of scouting all the teams and providing players with insight. The team had a television/

video cassette player combo located in the middle of the locker room that it used to play a copy of the game from the previous night. This was also the case for Golden State and many other teams in the league.

In a few instances, teams had more than a single assistant coach. Al Bianchi was one of two assistant coaches under John MacLeod in Phoenix from 1976 to 1987. During this period, the Suns' organization used rolls of game footage to analyze and break down opposing teams, and then the assistants would make their recommendations to the head coach for review. Later in the decade, a business started selling teams video of all games, which made the acquisition part of the assistant coach's job easier.

The first year with the three-point shot did not significantly alter the structure of offenses. Most, like the Bullets, still ran through the center position. The first season, an average of five three-point shots occurred per game. The success rate of 25% must have been dispiriting. Teams would realize shortly that the offense gained an extra point per position if they made the shot. This placed a premium on having long-range shooters. Outside shooters would continue to draw defenders away from the inside players, still making the center position vital to success, but now they could give the team an extra point each time down the court. The NBA also changed the rules regarding fouling in the backcourt. The change resulted in backcourt fouls being treated as common fouls, encouraging the strategy of a full-court press. Together, these changes put a greater premium on speed and agility. Many teams, particularly in the Western Conference, constructed teams with guys who were mobile, agile, and good long-range shooters, speeding up the pace of the game.[9]

Big-Bruising Basketball

General manager Bob Ferry and coach Gene Shue worked together on assembling the revised Bullets. They aimed to create a running, fast-breaking team for the upcoming season. With the 14th pick in the 1980 draft, they selected Wes Matthews, a guard out of the University of Wisconsin who was expected to bring the skills to run that type of offense. He was known as a crowd-pleasing multitalented player who Shue said, "you love to see with the ball."[10] They selected a big center-forward, Rick Mahorn, with their second pick. Mahorn proved to be one of the most successful players chosen in the second round, as eight selections never played in the NBA and another nine played less than 100 games. Finally, the Bullets made a trade with Golden State to get another big man, forward Jeff Ruland, whom the Warriors selected in the second round. The Bullets gave up a 1981 second-round draft pick, but waited a year, as Ruland opted to play professionally in Barcelona, Spain, before returning for the 1981–1982 season.

Before the start of the season, the team continued to rebuild. In September, they traded a draft pick from 1978, Dave Corzine, to the San Antonio Spurs for a second-round draft pick in both the 1981 and 1982 drafts. Corzine had several additional good seasons in which he averaged 10 points a game and seven rebounds. They lost Larry Wright as a free agent after he signed with Detroit and received a 1981 third-round draft choice and a second-round draft pick in 1983 as compensation. They waived John Williamson and, mid-season, traded their top draft selection, Wes Matthews, to Atlanta. Matthews hung around the NBA for nearly a decade but never materialized into what the Bullets hoped they would get when they drafted him. Meanwhile, the Bullets received Don Collins, an adequate forward whom the team waived two years later.

The preseason experts observed the changes. According to them, the team shifted from old and ugly to ugly. But even if all the new members of the team exceeded expectations, they would not save the Bullets from a dismal season. Indeed, the Bullets amassed a record of 39 wins and 43 losses. While this was the same as the previous year, they finished as the seventh seed in the conference and missed the playoffs by one spot. The team lacked the major young superstar that most of the winning teams had. Larry Bird played with Boston, and Magic Johnson teamed with veteran Kareem Abdul-Jabbar for the Lakers. The Milwaukee Bucks had Sidney Moncrief to complement veteran and future Hall-of-Famer Bob Lanier. The Sixers had Dr. J and Maurice Cheeks. The Houston Rockets had Moses Malone. The men remaining from the championship team had widely different experiences on the new squad. Bobby Dandridge played in 23 games and then signed as a veteran free agent with the Milwaukee Bucks. Wes Unseld played 63 games in his last season, averaging eight points and 10 rebounds. Greg Ballard played every game and ranked as one of the team's top scorers. And Kevin Grevey, Mitch Kupchak, and Elvin Hayes played significant roles as scorers and rebounders, but the latter wanted to leave.

The remaining players from the championship Bullets went separate ways. Wes Unseld retired and took a role as a vice president with the team. The unveiling of his new position occurred on March 29, 1981, during Wes Unseld Appreciation Night. Elvin Hayes sought a return to Texas, and the team worked to oblige him. The 35-year-old went back to Houston, in exchange for a 1981 second-round draft pick and a 1983 second-round pick. A popular figure in the city, Hayes presumably had a few more good years in him, but the team felt that his abilities would not be enough to make the Bullets any better. A younger man who would have improved the team pursued his free agent options. Mitch Kupchak received an offer sheet from the Los Angeles Lakers, and the Bullets did not match it. Kupchak signed as a free agent with the Lakers. In exchange, Washington received Jim Chones, Brad Holland, a 1982 second-round pick, and a 1983 first-round pick. Bob Ferry noted the income disparity between the two teams and said that the Bullets were forced into accepting this move. Chones, a 32-year-old forward, played one season before retiring. The team waived guard Holland during the second month of the season. Greg Ballard and Kevin Grevey represented the remaining pieces from the old guard.

At the June 1981 draft, the Bullets held four picks in the first two rounds. Prior to the draft, the team invited 40 players in to their mini-camp, with only two slots open. First-round pick Frank Johnson, a small guard like Wes Matthews, played seven years with the Bullets and provided that spark plug role in his first two seasons. Forward Charles Davis originally heard that he was going to be the first-round pick during the mini-camp. He watched on television in surprise and then received the phone call seconds after they announced his name as the team's first second-round pick. His agent did not show up for his contract signing, and Bob Ferry offered him a one-year deal for the minimum ($70,000) or a five-year deal with bonus clauses for performance. He selected the latter. The team waived the other two second-round selections, forwards Claude Gregory and Steve Lingenfelter, early in the season.[11]

Ferry continued to be active as general manager. Since the organization did not seem interested in signing big-name free agents, they sought other talent pools, like the free agents playing in European leagues. Ferry signed 13-year veteran Spencer Haywood, who seemed to be maintaining his scoring touch by shooting 47% from the field in 1981–1982, as a free agent out of Italy.[12]

The most lucrative place for the Bullets to find talent seemed to be trading with their most frequent partner, general manager Al Attles of the Golden State Warriors. A year before, the Bullets had acquired center Jeff Ruland from Golden State for a second-round draft choice. Now Ferry's biggest move involved another trade, when the team traded two second-round picks in the 1982 and 1984 drafts for six-year guard John Lucas.

The NBA added more clarity to the zone defense rules. The rules now included specific illegal defensive alignments. These six specific items greatly benefitted the offensive play, as weak-side defenders faced restrictions against being inside the 12-foot lane for more than three seconds and against double teaming a player who did not have the ball. Denying players the ball became more difficult, and players with good cutting and penetrating skills had more room to maneuver. The violations of the rules came with a free throw and continued possession of the ball, which worked as an effective punishment.[13]

The Bullets started poorly, losing two of every three games, confirming the preseason selection to finish dead last. Experts figured the team to be a dud, but the squad made key defensive adjustments to claw their way back to the .500 point near the end of January. Like many of Gene Shue's teams, the Bullets led with their defense. Washington's players had responsibilities for an area on the floor, but their main role was to deny the initial pass that started the opposing team's particular offensive plays. The team ranked second out of 23 teams in limiting the opposition's scoring, but it ranked close to the bottom in average points scored per game. Coach Shue pointed to desire, togetherness, and hustle as the key reasons for the achievements of his team. The basketball writers called the Bullets' personnel a bunch of oddballs and deemed their style a scratch-and-sniff defense. "Every Bullet team I've played against has been physical . . . I wonder if they breed them down there or what," said New York Knicks assistant coach Butch Beard.[14]

The team faced a test of their togetherness when John Lucas publically admitted that he had a cocaine addiction. While the NBA conducted an investigation, the team had known of the situation for some time before the news became public. Ferry stated that the organization was more concerned about the person than the player, although the team fined him for missing games even when he provided an excuse. Lucas's story emerged during a time when the NBA continued to have a tarnished image and wild stories like 75% of its players using drugs could be believed. Lucas thought he represented the one in five players who regularly used "recreational" drugs. Getting the drugs, said Lucas, "It's as easy as making a layup."[15] While Shue had noted that he could not believe a thing Lucas said—and so he would not play him anymore—one could believe Lucas about this.[16]

The illegal and problematic behavior of athletes went unreported years earlier or was buried deep in the newspaper. Despite changes in the media environment, Lucas's actions remained an open secret, but the basketball reporter for *USA Today*, David DuPree, warned Lucas that if things got really bad and obvious, he would have to write about Lucas's drug problems. Dale Murphy, the Atlanta Braves' superstar, said, "It seems to me that athletes are being treated more like average citizens, and I think that's a positive step. We wear this uniform, but I think we should be treated like everybody else because we are like every body [sic] else."[17] While Isiah Thomas asserted that the number of drug users in the NBA was equivalent to the number in the broader society, others, like Golden State's team physician, put the number of users at about 75%. Ultimately, the player's infractions garnered broadcast attention because of their names and social standing. The public perception of the chronically tardy, frequently absent, and extraordinarily rich, yet irresponsible, professional athlete damaged the sport.[18]

The drug use problem was so rampant in the league that many teams, like Denver and Golden State, retained private investigators to probe the off-court activities of their players. These background investigations on players who were under contract would eventually morph into a prime scouting tool used to determine the personal character of not only college draftees, but also of free agents and international players, a practice that is now regarded as normal but was groundbreaking during the 1980s. Teams even hired psychologists to evaluate college players' mental stability. With a higher scrutiny from within organizations but a willingness to protect the player's privacy, teams and unions were involved in a tug of war around this sensitive issue. Under the 1983 Collective Bargaining Agreement, teams were not permitted to administer random or unannounced drug tests without "reasonable cause." While these investigations were agreed upon in theory, it was not a unanimous perspective. Bob Ferry admitted that he did not hire detectives to trail any member of the Bullets or potential draft targets, later stating "if every team goes out and hires detectives, you'll have the investigators out there investigating the investigators."[19]

John Lucas was not the only Bullet with a drug use problem. Forward Spencer Haywood had a great season and received plaudits from Gene Shue and Bob Ferry, and everyone expected that production to continue. Haywood, however, slipped back into his habit a little during the first season and increased his consumption by the beginning of his second season. After several games, Shue informed Haywood that he was a disappointment and needed to play better or the coach would kick his ass. Shortly thereafter, cocaine paranoia led Haywood to believe that the team would release news of his drug problem to the media, so he quit the team.[20] Haywood described the situation in Los Angeles and New York, where power brokers in many entertainment industries, and even government, enjoyed recreational drug use. These problems were similar to those faced by other teams, including the Knicks, with Micheal Ray Richardson. Other players, like Mitchell Wiggins, John Drew, and Lewis Lloyd, could not conquer their addictions despite receiving professional aid. These players received lifetime suspensions from the league. None of these situations compared to the problems of the Phoenix Suns in the mid-1980s, who had six players implicated as involved in cocaine and marijuana possession and trafficking.[21]

About 80% of the players in the league during the early 1980s were African American. As in the recent past, these men hailed from underprivileged and working-class backgrounds. Most went through four years of college, with a slight drop in graduation rates than their peers of 10 years before. They now made a minimum of $40,000 annually, and the average salary climbed to more than $200,000.

There were several drawbacks to the improved travel schedules and situations. The closeness that players from the 1950s and 1960s forged through sharing hotel rooms, traveling in more cramped circumstances, and living closer together during the season had diminished significantly. The Bullets had players living in large homes in Baltimore and throughout suburban Maryland and areas of Virginia. A few players even flew separately at the start of road trips. Some players, like John Lucas, found that the amount of idle time enhanced feelings of loneliness, stress, and sadness. With the structure of the league, playing three to four games in a row and at crazy times with all kinds of travel, basketball changed from a game to a job. Players referred to the NBA as "Nothing But Airports." This easily became a grind unless players adopted the view of seeing the NBA as a profession, and players would then take pride in being the best in their profession. Lucas and others came under the supervision of the Life Extension Institute, which entered into an agreement with the NBA in 1981, to provide counseling and rehabilitative services to players.

On the court, the Bullets followed a seven-game win streak with five losses and hovered around the .500 mark through March. A late winning streak enabled the team to finish four games better than the year before, with a 43–39 record. The team beat the odds, finishing in fifth place to reach the playoffs and facing the fourth-seeded New Jersey Nets in the first round. Dr. J observed that, "Washington always has strong, physical players who play a rough game. That's just their style."[22]

The Bullets were not spectacular, and the fans did not turn out in large numbers. During the season, the Bullets finished in the lower third in league attendance, losing nearly 150,000 spectators compared with the previous four-year span. The NBA's continued expansion played a role in lowering attendance at games. This was particularly true for teams like the Bullets, who had been in the NBA for years. Back in the late 1960s, the Bullets played every team eight or nine times, providing the fan base with the opportunity to see the league's best players on several occasions. This large number of head-to-head matchups enhanced rivalries between teams, as well as the fans. By the 1981–1982 season, with the league now at 23 teams, Washington played every Eastern Conference team five or six times and all Western

Conference teams twice. The reduction in games against the western teams significantly impacted the ability to see both those teams and their top-notch players. Bob Ferry believed that the team could not afford to go through a rebuilding process but needed to remain a playoff team. Ferry said, "I thought if the team did not make the playoffs it would be a disaster, because we were not drawing crowds well at the time as it was."[23]

The Bullets' lack of a superstar and showmanship played a major role in the team's inability to draw fans in greater numbers. The increased coverage of basketball in this era of cable television and ESPN magnified the deficiencies of the Bullets and some other NBA teams. Audience members from around the country watched the games on TBS, TNT, and USA, networks that showed teams with marquee stars or who played an "enjoyable" version of basketball, such as fast break offenses. While the Lakers, Celtics, Knicks, 76ers, and Bulls all prospered with the presentation of their respective superstars, the Bullets and others appeared very little because of their personnel, thus losing the opportunity to build their brand and team support through publicity. ESPN presented 'round-the-clock highlights of every game during the season. Again, teams with big-name players and that played a "fun" game received more coverage of their highlights and additional features about their superstars and teams, resulting in an overall favorable presentation and publicity.

The opportunity to grow the fan base and receive favorable publicity increased exponentially during the playoffs. The small number of teams involved, plus the cache that accompanied playing in the second season for the chance to win the championship, focused the attention of basketball fans and the casual observer alike. The Bullets had returned to the playoffs after missing them in 1981.

Their playoff opponent, the New Jersey Nets, held a four to two advantage in the season series with Washington. Coached by Larry Brown, they had Rookie of the Year Buck Williams at forward and high-scoring guard Ray Williams. The Bullets took the court in East Rutherford, New Jersey, and looked nervous. "We were playing tight in the first half," Rick Mahorn said. Frank Johnson got off to a shaky start, with three missed shots and three turnovers during the first five minutes of the game. The Nets shot very inconsistently and led by 63–55 near the end of the third quarter. The Bullets then set up an isolation game, with Jeff Ruland and Frank Johnson on the left side against Len Elmore and Darwin Cook. If the play worked as designed, Johnson would beat Cook off the dribble and make an easy shot, or dump off to an uncontested Ruland as Elmore came to help defensively. With Johnson and Ruland scoring routinely, the Bullets overcame the deficit and won, 96–83.[24]

The second game featured a similar story. The Nets took another lead going into halftime behind the shooting of Albert King, who was eight for eight from the floor. "We were a little shell-shocked at halftime," Gene Shue admitted.[25] At the beginning of the third period, Frank Johnson and Spencer Haywood combined for 13 points to narrow the Bullets' deficit to 61–60. Then Kevin Grevey took over the final period. He made four for four on three-point shots and 8 of 15 overall to score 23 points and carry the team into the next playoff round. "This team reminds me of our championship team," Grevey said.[26] At least part of the media spread the comparison as they discussed the next opponent, the defending champion Boston Celtics.

During the regular season, the Celtics won all six games the teams played. With a week off, the Celtics needed the first half to warm up. At the old Boston Garden, the Bullets kept the game close through three quarters, slowing the tempo and making the game a battle of half-court offenses. Larry Bird and Robert Parish combined to shoot 33%, but reserves Kevin McHale and Rick Robey entered the game and combined for 26 points. The Celtics won the game, 109–91. While Celtics coach Bill Fitch extolled the games of his substitutes, Gene Shue expressed dismay that Bird and Parish had not been factors and the Bullets still could not manage a victory.

In game two, the Bullets were behind at the half, but, with strong rebounding on the offensive boards, the Bullets got extra shots to make up for poor shooting. After trailing by seven points at halftime, the Bullets outscored the Celtics by 33–23 in the third period. They held on to the narrow lead to win a squeaker, 103–102, and went home tied one game each in the series.

Whatever home court advantage the Bullets had by returning to Washington quickly disappeared in game three. The Celtics matched the physical game of the Bullets with their own and won, 92–83. Parish scored 25 points and had six of the team's 16 blocked shots, noting that he stopped letting the Bullets, "body me out of position [for his jump shots]."[27] The teams then engaged in two games that featured 11 quarters of basketball. The Celtics won the fourth game, which went into overtime by four points, 103–99. Then, game five went into double overtime, with the Celtics winning 131–126. As the local beat reporter described the two battles, the upstarts and castoffs from Washington kept picking themselves up off the floor to give one of the most courageous performances in the history of the franchise.

Heading into the off-season, the team of castoffs needed an infusion of top talent. Unfortunately, the team lacked a first-round draft choice but had three choices in the second round. None of the players drafted made adequate contributions to any team in the league, let alone Washington. The team bypassed several solid contributors, as they played the forward or center position, an area where the Bullets had some of their strongest players; however, drafting the best player available at the time and then working a trade with another franchise was a common tactic. As a team of veterans, the draftees from earlier years did not receive much playing time. "One year I drew Coach Shue's name out of the hat and had to buy him a holiday present. I got him a wind-up clock and said on the card, 'Give me a little more time,'" Charles Davis recalled.[28]

Having a Secret Santa exchange illuminated part of the charm that existed during the era. The front office staff was small and felt connected to the team. General Manager Bob Ferry noted, "Part of the fun in the 1970s and '80s was how players and the front office mingled and got to know each other. Certain players lit up the office and got everybody going. Mahorn, Unseld, Ballard, Adams. Guys would have mail sent to the office and you would do things for them and get to know the players, felt like part of the team."[29]

The team finished the 1982–1983 season in the cellar of the Atlantic Division. Their 42–40 record placed them seventh, one spot out of the playoffs. More roster changes occurred, as the team waived several players, including Spencer Haywood and John Lucas. The team also signed one veteran free agent, Ricky Sobers, and the Chicago Bulls received the Bullets' 1983 and 1985 second-round draft selections as compensation. Lucas went on to provide solid play for San Antonio and Houston for the next three years.

With their first-round picks for the 1983 draft, the team selected guards Jeff Malone and Randy Wittman. The latter had three strong years for the Atlanta Hawks, but a week after the draft, Bob Ferry traded him for veteran forward Tom McMillen and a second-round pick in the 1984 draft. McMillen went on to play three years as a minor contributor. Some claimed that McMillen wanted to switch teams to better prepare for his run to get elected to the House of Representatives. The two second-round draft picks, Michael Britt and Guy Williams, amounted to little. Britt never played in the NBA, and Williams played in less than 100 games. Both circumstances mirrored the norm for other teams in the league. Fortunately, Malone was a solid shooting guard for seven years before moving on to the Utah Jazz.

The Bullets finished the 1983–1984 season with a 35–47 record, worse than the previous year. Columnists described the team as a five-and-dime operation. Abe Pollin continued to follow his personal preference of not spending for big free agents or handing out contracts to big superstars. With his antiquated tactics, high spending teams blew past the Bullets both on and off the court. During the off-season, Pollin told the fan base to forget about seeing Moses Malone in a Bullets' uniform, saying, "The *Washington Post* said I was too cheap or couldn't afford to sign Moses Malone. They might be right on both counts. But I don't think any player is worth that much money [$2 million a year]."[30] Ferry recalled the following:

> Abe was a good owner. We were a club that didn't have or weren't going to spend a lot of money on free agents. You don't have to be reminded all the time that your owner doesn't want to spend a lot of money. You feel like a child going to your father asking him for money. After he says no a couple of times you stop going to ask.[31]

The local media developed their perception of the team's inactivity in the free agent market based on the facts. In the late 1970s, the team signed Bobby Dandridge, and, in 1980, they signed Kevin Porter. From 1981 to 1983, the Bullets did sign one low-level veteran free agent. While that may appear quite inactive, it placed the Bullets squarely in the middle relative to the NBA. During this period, 10 teams had only made a purchase of one veteran free agent. Six teams made purchases of two or more, leaving only six teams inactive in the free-agent market.

Abe Pollin then surprised everyone by announcing that, "I told GM Ferry if we can get a free agent or trade for a player like Larry Bird . . . then do it."[32] Gene Shue described the situation as a treadmill. The team needed offensive help, as they placed in the bottom third in field goal percentage. "We need a good draft, definitely consider a free agent, and then, possibly, a trade to turn it around all at once."[33] Still, the team continued to seek talent from the pool of players on the waiver wire. While it often failed to work out, the Bullets did acquire an adequate bench player, forward Dudley Bradley, and an occasional starting center/power forward, Charles Jones, through this process.

The Bullets played a physical, bruising style of basketball. As noted earlier, some of the best teams played a quicker, all-court game, relying on players with great agility. Detroit started the process of combining some of these elements, bringing strong outside shooting to their adaptation of the bruising style of ball. As with the successful team building that the Bullets did during the 1970s, Detroit's core stayed together and different complementary pieces were added to their specific style of play. The complementary pieces were changed until a successful mix was found. The Bullets went on to become the first-round playoff victims of the Pistons during the final two years of their climb to the top of the league.

First-Round Losses

Despite having a 35–47 record during the 1983–1984 season, the team ranked eighth in the Eastern Conference. The year before, the NBA Board of Governors decided to expand the first round of the playoffs to include the first and second seeds in both conferences. They would play the teams that finished eighth and seventh, respectively, while third place would still play sixth place, and fourth and fifth place would do battle as before. The first-round series became best-of-five games rather than the previous best-of-three. The change enabled the Bullets to sneak into the playoffs as the last seed. Some regarded this as torture, as they drew the Boston Celtics.

Gene Shue brought a game plan to the first round, against the heavily favored Celtics. In the first game, the Bullets played at a snail's pace, limiting the number of shots and the Celtics speed game. Although Boston won, 91–83, longtime NBA man Red Auerbach did not hold his tongue. He commented, "That was about the ugliest-looking game I've ever seen. . . . You almost have to look bad to beat the Bullets, but we don't mind. Much."[34]

The Celtics walked away with a win in tightly contested game two. Washington took a 29–19 lead with a sharp defensive effort, but Gerald Henderson made long-range shots that kept Boston close until the rest of the offense picked up the slack. Larry Bird, Robert Parish, and Kevin McHale scored 40 points, but the game remained close, as Washington cut the Celtic lead to 88–85 with 20 seconds left. The Celtics clamped down defensively, and Washington could not get off a decent three-point shot in an attempt to send the game into overtime.[35]

The Bullets came home and gave the sparse crowd of 8,500 something to cheer about. The teams shot well and stayed neck and neck through three quarters, until the Bullets started running a play designed for Jeff Ruland. Boston finally adapted to the move and battled back to tie the game behind the shooting of M. L. Carr. Ruland and his teammates stayed strong and won the overtime to get back in the series. M. L. Carr and Ricky Sobers had words in the press. "There's bad blood between the two teams. They can be dirty and hit you with cheap shots," Carr said.[36]

In game four, before a much larger crowd, the home team brought their slow-down game and hoped that they could stifle Larry Bird and Robert Parish. The big center had 20 points and 12 rebounds, but his opposite number, Jeff Ruland, scored 30 points and pulled down 15 rebounds. The home team led by three after the first frame, but then the Celtics' bench ran up a 31–17 advantage over the Bullets' second squad. The Bullets tried to cut the deficit but could get no closer than three points. At the buzzer, Frank Johnson and Gerald Henderson wrestled and threw punches at each other. The benches cleared, and everything settled down once the coaches intervened. "Let's just shake hands and go, fellas," Gene Shue said with a forced smile.[37] The Celtics took the series, which Larry Bird described a few years later in his autobiography as containing nothing memorable. The Bullets were the first of four teams vanquished, as the Celtics went on to win the NBA Championship.

The 1984 off-season held a lot of promise for the Bullets. Abe Pollin expressed interest in opening up the wallet for free agents, and more than 60 players were slated to become free agents, with the biggest names being the likes of forward Maurice Lucas, center Joe Barry Carroll, forward Cedric Maxwell, and guard Gerald Henderson. One in the group included Washington's own forward, Greg Ballard, who received a salary of $250,000 when the league minimum moved up to $303,000 for the upcoming season. The Bullets faced a tough decision, weighing the replacement options of the free-agent class compared to retaining Ballard. They chose to hold on to him for the new league minimum. The Bullets also signed journeyman forward Dudley Bradley from Chicago, who did not play in the league during the 1983–1984 season and brought marginal contributions to the team for two seasons.

The free agency market occurred under the new system that the Bullets' owner worked hard to create. The NBA and its players faced the end of their Collective Bargaining Agreement, and the players threatened to strike. The Bullets' owner noted that only seven teams claimed to have made money in 1984, and that 10 were in financial difficulty, including Indiana, Cleveland, and San Diego. As the committee chairman, Abe Pollin worked extensively to reach a new bargaining agreement. With the aid of the National Basketball Player's Association counsel, Larry Fleischer, and the executive vice president for the NBA Commissioners Office, David Stern, Pollin established the salary cap structure on team spending.

The new system served as a modification to the Collective Bargaining Agreement forged during the merger. The cap created a minimum and maximum team salary limit, with a few exceptions. Slated to take effect during the 1984–1985 season, salaries were limited to the larger of either $3.6 million or 53% of the total of NBA gross revenues divided by 23, the number of teams in the league. Washington sat on the low end of the amount of salary expenses in the league, yet its expenses were more in line with the league average. The teams that had their salaries frozen due to their high position above the new limit included Seattle, Los Angeles, Philadelphia, New York, and New Jersey.

The league had several other issues to work out once the parties signed the new agreement. The first franchise relocation under the new commissioner occurred when owner Donald Sterling moved the San Diego Clippers up the coast to Los Angeles. David Stern helped implement a drug testing policy, giving the appearance of a proactive leaguewide approach to the drug problem.[38] Within months of the new labor agreement, Stern moved into the position of commissioner. One of his first objectives was to address the television situation, specifically the network versus cable discrepancy. The cable superstations, including TBS in Atlanta and WGN in Chicago, put their local teams (the Hawks and Bulls) on television, leading to the presentation of more than 170 national games during the 1983–1984 season. This glut caused CBS, who broadcast select games throughout the season, to experience a drop in the ratings. Stern reduced the number of cable games to 55 for the next season, and CBS' ratings climbed. For the 1986–1987 season, the network renegotiated to broadcast the league for four years at a total of $173 million. WTBS also purchased broadcast rights, including the early round playoff games, at a cost of $12.5 million per year for two years.[39]

The NBA was filled with superstars that transcended basketball, and the interest to sell and expand league marketing efforts grew both nationally and internationally. Some of the players whom the NBA went on to market included Michael Jordan, Charles Barkley, and Hakeem Olajuwon, three men selected among the top picks in the 1984 draft. The Bullets tried to improve their marketing. The team brought in some Harvard businessmen to run the team's business operations and expand marketing. Bob Ferry noted that "they wanted to blame the lack of success of the team [on] their failure to market."[40]

While Washington had a top 10 pick, holding the sixth selection, they would obviously miss out on the top talent in the draft. News coverage indicated that the team planned on picking a center, Melvin Turpin, from the University of Kentucky. Bob Ferry and crew selected Turpin but immediately traded him to Cleveland for center Tim McCormick and forward Cliff Robinson. Later in the evening, they traded Tim McCormick and Ricky Sobers to Seattle for 30-year-old guard Gus Williams. The draft essentially netted the Bullets another big-body forward in Robinson, who shot 47% from the field, and Williams, who started for two years and shot 43% and less than 30% from three-point territory. During that era, the majority of players averaged more than 48% from the floor, so the two new players were below average relative to the league. While the Bullets got the veteran Williams, two teams that chose later in the first round nabbed guards Vern Fleming and John Stockton. Meanwhile, the rest of the draft did not improve the team, as none of the three men selected in the second or third rounds made the league. Few of the players on the board made outstanding and long-term contributions. The notable exceptions were forward Jerome Kersey, guard Ron Anderson, and Danny Young.[41]

The team chose to not spend on free agents. The inability to pay for the services of even their own free agents, like Mitch Kupchak, significantly hurt the team's abilities. The preponderance of big forwards made one columnist describe the team as having beef, but it was not prime. The lack of marquee names, combined with the leaden style of play, hurt the team on the court and in the stands.

The Bullets placed 16th out of the 23 teams in attendance. Individuals described the Capital Centre as cold down on the floor and without the intimacy of several other arenas. As already noted, the Capital Centre was often not full, even when the Bullets were a championship team. Other major detriments included limited public transportation, with no Metrorail or Metrobus access to the stadium area, and the prohibitive costs of $24 ticket prices and $3 parking prices. For that era, the combination of style of play, public transit, and cost played a crucial role in attendance figures.

The two newcomers, Cliff Robinson and Gus Williams, acquired through trades, finished among the top four on the team in scoring. In the fourth year of his contract, which would have raised his salary significantly, the team waived Charles Davis. He went on to have two productive seasons as a bench player with a Milwaukee Bucks team that made it deep into the playoffs. Bucks coach Don Nelson made Davis's role clearer to him and to the others so that they meshed well as a team. Under Nelson, the Bucks used video analysis as much as the Bullets. They approached the breakdown with a different defensive philosophy, which was to keep your man out of the paint and follow your guy rather than stay in your assigned section.

Meanwhile, Robinson and Williams each scored more than 1,000 points, despite not having accurate shooting percentages. The pair finished 10th and 12th, respectively, on the team in field goal percentage. The team won regularly early on in the season and sat in third place in the Atlantic Division as late as February. Boston and Philadelphia topped the division, several games in front of the Bullets. The Bullets continued to win, as they had in previous years, with a tenacious defense ranking second in the league, at less than 106 points a game. Unfortunately, the team scored less than 106 points a game, placing them third from the bottom in production. New Jersey eventually passed them in the standings, and the Bullets finished as the sixth seed in the conference.

The Bullets visited Philadelphia for the first round of the playoffs. The Bullets received great news, as they knew that center Jeff Ruland would be in the lineup, providing the team with more inside presence. The Sixers led many times during the game, but Ruland, Robinson, and Williams put together comebacks of eight points early on, nine during the second quarter, and five during the last quarter. The team jumped ahead, 93–92, but then the Sixers ran off a 12–4 run to ice the game. The Bullets tried forcing the ball in to Ruland too often near the end, and the Sixers forced turnovers and scored in transition, winning 104–97. Philadelphia easily won game two, 113–94, to take a commanding two-game lead in the best-of-five series.

After game two, as with the previous season, the Bullets returned to the Capital Centre facing elimination. The team again battled hard, finally limiting their physical and mental lapses. Down 35–28 after one quarter, Washington took advantage of their ability to generate fast breaks off of Philadelphia misses to score 32 points in the second quarter and 30 points during the third. With a lead of as many as 29 points, the Bullets walked away with a 118–100 win.

Game four proved much tougher. The Sixers shot the lights out during the first half. Moses Malone and Charles Barkley outrebounded the Bullets' big men by 17. Julius Erving scored 25 points, and Moses Malone added 18. Yet, in the third quarter, the Bullets put on a run that lifted them from 14 to only four behind. But trailing by six, Erving hit on finger rolls, dunks, and jump shots to expand the lead to 10 and put the game beyond the home team's reach, winning 106–98.

Unlike the previous year, the Bullets did not lose to the eventual champions in the first round. The Celtics beat the Sixers to win the Eastern Conference for the second straight year, although they lost to the Lakers in the finals. As the off-season began, the Bullets sought to make moves once again. They made two major adjustments that appeared to cancel each other out. They again dealt with Golden State, trading forward and longtime team member Greg Ballard for two second-round draft selections (in 1985 and 1987). Ballard had two declining years with the Warriors and then moved to Seattle, before retiring in 1989. The team also traded forwards Mike Gibson and Rick Mahorn to the Detroit Pistons for forward Dan Roundfield. Gibson had not played during the year and only lasted a season with the Pistons. Mahorn's big body and defensive prowess in rebounding, blocking shots, and a physical game enabled him to become one of Detroit's "Bad Boys," the league's 1989 champion. The 32-year-old Roundfield gave the Bullets one good season that fell far short of the numbers he averaged during his nine previous NBA seasons. He played in only half of the teams' games during the next year, his final season in the league.

Despite having the 12th pick, the team had a chance to significantly improve itself. Bob Ferry and crew selected a forward, Kenny Green, out of Wake Forest, whom they traded to the Philadelphia Sixers midway through his first season with the team. The trade yielded guard Leon Wood, who went to the Nets the night before the Halloween evening start of the season for Mike O'Koren. The Bullets waived O'Koren four months later. Thus, the first-round selection, before the start of the 1986 season, resulted in the Bullets getting a man whom they waived one and a half seasons later. Selected by Utah immediately after Green was forward Karl Malone. Bob Ferry explained. "We missed on Karl Malone. I was misled by his college coach, a lot of guys were. The coach said Malone was potential trouble."[42] Joe Dumars, A. C. Green, and Terry Porter also heard their names called later in round one.

With the seventh pick in round two, the Bullets drafted an international player, a trend that would blossom during the course of the next two decades. To be accurate, several Canadians played in the league, and a few players came from Europe, but Hakeem Olajuwon and the Bullets' selection, center Manute Bol, from Sudan, represented an expansion into the world. A humanitarian, the 7–foot, 7-inch Bol became a publicity magnet because of his size, and the Washington team gained from the media attention. He had a good first year, but Bol rarely scored, and he brought down fewer rebounds than anticipated; however, he made the All-Defensive Team during one of his three seasons in Washington and was an amazing shot blocker. Several other impressive players still remained unselected, so the Bullets could have had Tyrone Corbin, a solid guard-forward, for eight years, and center John "Hot Rod" Williams, an imposing big man, for more than nine seasons.

None of the Bullets later-round selections played in the NBA, but Sacramento chose guard Michael Adams and Atlanta took guard John Battle. Most intriguingly, Detroit selected guard Spud Webb and then waived him, allowing Atlanta to sign him as a free agent. Milwaukee selected Mario Elie as the 160th pick and then waived him before the season. After playing several years in the European leagues, the sharpshooter played in the NBA from the age of 27 to 37.

The 1985–1986 Bullets moved personnel around but played much like the versions of the club from earlier in the decade. The team played a plodding half-court offense and trapping defense that pushed everything toward the middle of the court. As in previous years, coach Gene Shue observed that the team needed more quickness and rebounding ability, two of the three top assets in basketball. The team's record stayed close to .500 for most of the season. In March, they suffered two long losing streaks, and the management decided to fire Shue. Kevin Loughery, who played guard for the Bullets from 1963 to 1972, took over the team and finished with a 7–6 record. Loughery's team enjoyed camaraderie with Manute Bol, who coined nicknames for his teammates, ranging from Tom McMillen being known as "Tom Congress" to Jeff Ruland being called "Commando 1."[43]

Again the sixth seed in the conference, despite a record of 39–43, the Bullets drew the Sixers in the first round of the playoffs. The Bullets felt confident and exhibited this when they came back from 18 points down with only four minutes left in the game. Dudley Bradley sank a three-pointer at the buzzer to give the Bullets the startling one-point victory, 95–94. "I guess they thought it was over," said Bullets guard Jeff Malone. "But you can't give up in the playoffs—anything can happen."[44]

Game two was not as kind. Led by forward Charles Barkley, the Sixers evened the series at one game each, winning the game 102–97. The Bullets held the lead through three quarters but failed to score in the final minutes, while Philadelphia mounted its comeback.

Back in Washington, the Sixers won game three, 91–86. Facing elimination in game four, the Bullets won, 116–111, and pushed the series back to Philadelphia. At the Spectrum, the Sixers jumped out to an early lead of 18, while playing strong defense. Rookie center Terry Catledge led the way, with 27 points, and Charles Barkley had a triple-double of 19 points, 15 rebounds, and 12 assists. Philadelphia scored 134 points in the game, winning by 25 and advancing to play the Milwaukee Bucks in the Eastern Conference Semifinal.

In what appeared to be a broken record of off-season public relations, the Bullets owner and management announced that they would do whatever was needed to improve the team. Despite these pronouncements, few significant changes happened. With their continual playoff appearances, perhaps Abe Pollin viewed his team as being good enough to win, despite the advice of others. Sometimes excuses, such as injuries, were viewed as the main obstacle to the team not winning in the playoffs. The team seemed to be in the middle of the NBA pack: good enough to make the playoffs but not strong enough to advance once there. Their mediocre record during the season kept them from having high draft selections. Former Bullet Elvin Hayes advised them to "start all over . . . go through a youth movement. Position yourself for the draft."[45] The team had told Hayes that it was rebuilding when they traded him years before. Kevin Porter agreed, noting that the Bullets last draft choices were minor players. He said that Bol was a "role player, not the player you can build a franchise around."[46]

Middling Team

The Bullets were the middling team of the 1980s. During that decade, they had a 397–423 record in the regular season. They made the playoffs seven times, making it out of the first round only once. Their record in the playoffs was a subpar 9–21. Several teams made the playoffs as the fifth, sixth, seventh, or eighth seed nearly as often as the Bullets. Houston made the playoffs six times and Chicago five times during the same period. Portland and Seattle qualified four times, while Atlanta, Phoenix, Utah, and San Antonio made the second season thrice. However, none of these teams got caught up in the middle-of-the-pack syndrome that the Bullets experienced.

Unlike the Bullets, none of these teams stayed as consistent throughout the decade, winning and losing roughly the same amount of games year in and year out. Houston won 402 and lost 418, but they had two very poor years and two excellent regular-season years. During the playoffs they also enjoyed more success than Washington, making it to the Western Conference Semifinals twice as a sixth seed. Since they had two poor years, they also had the first pick in two consecutive college drafts. Chicago won 369 games and lost 451, and, despite having a worse record during the regular season, the Bulls enjoyed more success in the playoffs than the Bullets. Chicago reached the Eastern Conference Finals at the end of the decade as a sixth seed and the semifinals once as a fifth seed. Chicago, similar to Houston, also had several years in which they selected early in the draft.

Portland's record of 442–378 kept them from selecting high in the draft, but the team had more success than the Bullets, getting a third or fourth seed in the playoffs. They also made it to the Western Conference Semifinals twice as a fifth seed. Portland generally selected toward the middle or end of the draft and once during the decade had a number two selection. Washington's old nemesis, the Seattle SuperSonics, also had several top flight teams and a few that finished near the bottom in the conference. As a seventh seed, managed to reach the conference finals but lost to the Lakers. Seattle had three low draft choices during the decade.[47]

Most tellingly, the club could not take advantage of some of the soft salary cap provisions that existed. The most famous, the Larry Bird exemption, allowed a team to resign one of its players currently on its roster for as much money as agreed upon, even if it exceeded the salary cap. The only provision was that the player needed to be on the team for at least three seasons. This exemption was used to keep a big-name player with the same team, which was perceived as being in the team's and fans' best interest. While Boston had Larry Bird, the Lakers had Magic Johnson, Philadelphia had Dr. J, and Milwaukee had Sidney Moncrief, the Bullets lacked a single player who stood as the face of the franchise. Jeff Ruland came the closest, and his annual salary fell well below the kind of figure that would require concern over exceeding the cap maximum.

Another change in player scouting occurred in 1986, with the advent of the Chicago Combine. This predraft camp mimicked that of the NFL Scouting Combine held annually prior to the draft, measuring the standard height/weight/wingspan/reach statistics, while incorporating such new measurements as body fat, hand length/width, and vertical leap. The combine also measured a player's fitness level, with bench, agility, and sprinting metrics. More players were getting the opportunity to showcase their talents in tournaments other than the Portsmouth Invitational Tournament, which benefitted players and organizations in identifying talent or finding the right fit.

The Bullets not only lacked a superstar, they lacked the big impact player who could make everyone on the team better. The 1986 draft originally offered promise, as Bob Ferry scrambled to make a deal that would enable his Bullets to select earlier in the round. The organization sought Len Bias, a University of Maryland star who had the all-around court ability and local name recognition that would help on and off the court. Even dangling their two first-round choices, the 12th and 21st picks, they were unable to complete a deal to move up. Their first choice was forward John Williams, from Louisiana State University. With their next selection, the Bullets chose guard Anthony Jones out of the University of Nevada, Las Vegas. Williams became an All-NBA rookie team member, but he dropped off precipitously during the course of the next few years. The team waived Jones one month into the season. Other guards, including Johnny Newman and Nate McMillan, were selected later in the draft and had solid playing careers. In the second round, Washington selected Steve Mitchell. He never suited up for a game. Washington ranked among the less successful teams, as only four other teams shared that experience in 1986. All of these teams missed out on Jeff Hornacek, who enjoyed a fruitful career in the league.[48]

Breaking their usual pattern, the Bullets did sign a free agent. Michael Adams had been drafted and then waived by the Sacramento Kings, so the team signed the guard for the 1986–1987 season. The general manager executed a blockbuster trade with the help of Abe Pollin, who met with his Philadelphia counterpart, owner Harold Katz. After Bob Ferry and the Sixers general manager, Pat Williams, ironed out the structure, Pollin and Katz brought together the final pieces to make the Bullets' player salaries fit under the salary cap limit of $4.2 million. The Bullets gave up Jeff Ruland and Cliff Robinson for Moses Malone and rookie Terry Catledge, along with 1986 and 1988 first-round draft picks. The Bullets got a great deal, as Ruland's injuries hampered him and Robinson played only adequately during his three years in Philadelphia. Meanwhile, Catledge gave the team three solid years, and

Malone represented a big-name All-Star scorer and rebounder who immediately boosted the season ticket sales (figure 8.3).

These changes reshaped the Bullets and energized the fan base heading into the 1986–1987 season. The team that had hovered at the bottom of the league in scoring jumped up three places, to number 19, but it still remained way below the average. The two Malones, Jeff and Moses, along with Terry Catledge (figure 8.4), all scored 1,000 points. Only the latter made nearly half of the shots he took, while the team averaged 45%. The team defense declined from fourth to eighth with coach Kevin Loughery. The team started the season losing five of six, but it reached 10–10 in December and hung around the .500 mark until a good winning streak in February. After reaching an apex of five games above .500, the Bullets slipped back and ended the season at 42–40.

Despite the changes in personnel, the Bullets landed in a familiar position as the sixth seed at season's end, playing the third-seeded Detroit Pistons. The biggest change, however, came off the court, as attendance rose to 485,000. While only ranking 14th out of 23 teams, this represented an increase of more than 100,000 spectators from the previous season. Even though Moses Malone was at the end of his playing career, Abe Pollin finally got their "superstar," and he provided more revenue for the franchise.

The Detroit Pistons finished with a 3–3 record against the Bullets during the regular season. The Bullets started the playoffs one man short, as forward Dan Roundfield, who had played only three games near the end of the season, abruptly announced his retirement. The Bullets fined him for his actions, but Roundfield did not want to sit on the bench during the playoffs and accepted the monetary penalty in exchange for keeping his sense of pride.

The front line did not add much to the Bullets' scoring during the first two games in the Silverdome. The biggest news was the play of Pistons' point guard, Isiah Thomas. Thomas scored 34 points and had nine assists, nine rebounds, and four steals in his team's 106–92 victory. The trio of Ennis Whatley, Michael Adams, and Frank Johnson could not stop him, and the three men only scored one basket amongst them.

In game two, Isiah Thomas, Adrian Dantley, and teammates jumped out to a 76–36 halftime lead, and they went on to win by 43 points. The Bullets suffered one of the worst playoff losses in NBA history, 128–85. Back home in game three, the team kept it close but trailed 78–71. Moses Malone scored eight of his 31 to give the Bullets the lead. The Pistons rallied to tie the game at 96, but then former Bullet Rick Mahorn made one of two free throws to seal the win, 97–96. Although Larry Wright's statement about the clean out of the locker room occurred years earlier, the same feeling appeared in the media after this playoff series.[49]

Figure 8.3. Moses Malone and Robert Parish watch a shot go off.
Courtesy Steve Lipofsky, www.basketballphoto.com.

Figure 8.4. Terry Catledge shoots over Larry Bird.
Courtesy Steve Lipofsky, www.basketballphoto.com.

The 1987 draft was deep enough to offer the Bullets a small chance of help. With their 12th pick, they chose 5-foot, 3-inch guard Tyrone "Muggsy" Bogues from Wake Forest. Bogues ran the offense, bringing speed to the oft-plodding offensive attack. All teams had to work these new players and their salaries into the space within their salary cap. The team made an offer, and Bogues held out until he received a contract worth more than $300,000 a year. The top pick in the draft, center David Robinson from the U.S. Naval Academy, received a salary of more than $1 million, which doubled in two seasons. By the seventh pick, the salary averaged $350,000, so Bogues negotiated well.

Bob Ferry and Abe Pollin's most important move involved signing a big-name free agent. The team sought New York Knicks' forward Bernard King. King received an offer, and the Knicks had time to consider whether they would match the Bullets' contract offer. They elected to let King leave, so he inked a two-year contract for $2 million that brought his shooting prowess to Washington. In addition to free agency, Ferry had only begun working with other general managers on potential deals. He found a willing trade partner in the Denver Nuggets and acquired forward Mark Alarie and guard Darrell Walker. In exchange for those two men, Ferry sent Jay Vincent and Michael Adams, whom they had just signed the year prior, to Denver. Adams came into his own as an outside shooter with the Nuggets, but Alarie served as a bench player, while Walker played four seasons with the Bullets. The guard had two of his best seasons with Washington and provided slightly less than 10 points and seven assists per game. With a cap of $6.2 million, players like Alarie and Walker, with salaries less than $500,000, were required to fill out remaining positions, while King and Malone accounted for more than half of the team's salary.[50]

Kevin Loughery decided to bring in Wes Unseld to serve as his assistant coach. The pair did not lead Washington off to a good start, and Loughery offered his assessment of things, saying the following:

> We are very, very small at every position. We don't have a lot of leaders. We're the worst in the league in rebounding. We're worst in shooting percentage. We don't get enough clean defensive rebounds to run the break much. . . . We're not quick. . . . We don't have a single isolation player. . . . We can't jump. . . . The team doesn't have much confidence.[51]

After three home losses during which the number of fans supporting the visiting team made the place seem like a road game, Abe Pollin fired Kevin Loughery. Wes Unseld received the nod to replace Loughery after the 8–19 start to the season. Some in the media focused attention on Bob Ferry. They observed that Pollin expected Ferry to field a team that would make the playoffs every year. Ferry noted that the "hardest team to improve is the team that's playing .500 basketball."[52] He defended his trades and draft choices, but columnists noted, as this chapter has, that Ferry missed on several occasions, the latest example being Mark Jackson, whom the Knicks drafted and who won Rookie of the Year honors, averaging 13.6 points and 10.6 assists per game. Another columnist referred to the Bullets as a misshaped team whose whole amounted to less than the sum of its parts.

A New Coach

Abe Pollin stayed positive about the prospects for his team amid the media scrutiny. As always, he watched from his customary center-court seat at the Capital Centre, catching the latest game featuring his team turning a six-point lead heading into the fourth quarter into a 115–99 loss. "I thought we'd played a good game until that fourth quarter," Pollin said. "I don't know what happened then."[53] The result motivated Kevin Loughery, the assistant coaches, and Bob Ferry to meet. Coaches were often changed for two main reasons. One was that owners consistently asked their general managers or team presidents to start posing questions about how the team performed and if they would be better with another coach. The second involved the coach losing the confidence of the star player. The situation featured the former.[54]

Despite the disadvantages Loughery named, the team played better ball under Unseld. Winning streaks of three and four games were matched by losing streaks of similar length through February. A breakthrough on offensive rebounding during a West Coast road trip enabled the team to run off seven wins in a row. Under Unseld, the team finished 30–25, for an overall record of 38–44.[55]

The Bullets made the playoffs as the seventh seed and for consecutive seasons faced the Detroit Pistons in the first round. Opening in Detroit, the Pistons shot poorly in the first game, shooting 15% in the first half and trailing 30–20. In the second half, the Bullets' front line offered no scoring and allowed the Pistons to grab 14 offensive rebounds. With the many extra shots, the Pistons won, 96–85.

Fortunately for viewers, the shooting improved in game two. At halftime, the Pistons led, 51–46, but the Bullets came out with a resounding effort to create an 18–4 run. They increased their lead to 12 behind the shooting of guard Jeff Malone and forwards John Williams and Bernard King. The Pistons crashed the boards as they had in the first game and cut the lead in half by the end of the third quarter. The Pistons shot only 40% from the floor, but through the second chance opportunities provided by 25 offensive rebounds, they squeaked out a one-point win, 102–101.

The two teams battled to a draw after regulation during game three at the Capital Center. The Pistons improved their shooting, but the Bullets denied them the large rebounding edge gained in the first two games. The Bullets won the eventful overtime game, 114–106, but not without controversy. Labeled the "Bad Boys" for their physical play, Detroit complained about the battling going on with Washington, especially in the paint. Several players had cuts and welts appearing on their bodies from their contact with the Bullets. Darrell Walker, the Bullets' point guard, who received playing time over Muggsy Bogues, responded, saying, "I don't know, everyone's grabbing and holding."[56]

The Bullets rode their overtime victory to another win two nights later. After the Pistons led by a basket after one quarter, the Bullets took the lead going into halftime, riding the Malones, Jeff and Moses. The Pistons evened the score after three periods, with Dennis Rodman and Adrian Dantley leading their scoring. They held a 99–95 lead, but two free throws from Jeff Malone and a steal and the subsequent three-pointer from Bernard King (figure 8.5) gave Washington the lead. "We had the game won," exclaimed Dantley. "There's no way this should have gone this far, if you look at it. It's really frustrating," said Rodman.[57] Back home, the Pistons played their trademark tough defense and watched as Jeff Malone lost the shooting touch he had exhibited throughout the series. The Bullets scored only 78 points and lost by 21, 99–78.

When asked what his plans were, Unseld noted that the team would be looking for help at point guard, wing guard, small forward, big forward, and center, as well as for depth among the reserves. With that much need, was it any wonder that Dennis Rodman thought that the series ought to have been over before five games? With this many holes, the Bullets again turned to the draft to fill the need, holding the 12th pick. They selected forward Harvey Grant out of Oklahoma, one of the best rebounders in the draft. Yet, he was not a lottery pick and lacked the size several teams sought. Their selection in the second round, Ledell Eackles, actually played a few years with the Bullets as an adequate reserve. Unfortunately, there were three players available at the time who played sizable roles in the league: forward Anthony Mason, guard Vernon Maxwell, and sharpshooter Steve Kerr.

The NBA ended the decade the same way it began: with expansion. For the 1988–1989 season, the league increased to 25 teams by adding the Charlotte Hornets in the Atlantic Division and the Miami Heat in the Midwest

Figure 8.5. Bernard King drives against Kevin McHale.
Courtesy Steve Lipofsky, www.basketballphoto.com.

Division. The two teams engaged in an expansion draft, as each existing team could protect eight of the 13 men on their roster and did not have to protect free agents. Since the Bullets had Moses Malone, Frank Johnson, and Charles Jones as free agents, they only had to leave two men unprotected. They chose to offer Jay Murphy, a center who played infrequently, and last year's top pick, Muggsy Bogues, as choices. Charlotte selected Bogues, who played for 13 more years and often ranked among the leaders in assists and steals. One guard they chose to keep, Steve Colter, had been waived earlier in the year, and he provided significantly less offense in his remaining two years with the Bullets. Even the taller, more defensively adept guard, Darrell Walker, wound up being traded two years later for two second-round draft picks.

During the span of two seasons, the media heaped circus allusions on the team as a result of the 5-foot, 3-inch Bogues and the seven-footer, Bol. It was widely speculated that these unflattering perceptions pushed the Bullets to make the moves the team made. In reality, Unseld and Bol did not get along, and the team saw this as a time to get some value for a player who was primarily a defensive specialist. Unseld went to the well his predecessors frequented, trading with Golden State yet again. In a swap of centers, Manute Bol went to the Warriors for Dave Feitl and a second-round selection in the 1989 draft. After one season, the Bullets allowed Feitl to leave as a free agent.

The Swoon Begins

Management had decisions to make about its three free agents. Some outside observers believed that the Bullets had several good players and could do well, but Moses Malone wanted a four-year contract with a team, and Abe Pollin countered with a two-year deal. "Four years is out of the question," Pollin said.[58] Bob Ferry wanted to maintain Malone and believed that he could pick up a few pieces take a chance in the playoffs. People within the organization and the owner wanted to break up the team and start over. The relationship was strained after that. The team chose to sign Charles Jones for a one-year, $300,000 deal. Before the season, management waived Jones, only to resign him to play one more year in the NBA. Six-year veteran Frank Johnson signed with the New Jersey Nets for $375,000, and the Nets promptly traded him to Houston. Malone signed with the Atlanta Hawks for one year and then resigned the next year for $2.4 million. Time would reveal that the 13-year veteran had four solid years left in him, and he played until the 1994–1995 season.

The media discussed available free agents and how each would fit in with Washington's roster and playing style. The more prominent names available included Seattle's Tom Chambers, Detroit's James Edwards, Phoenix guard Walter Davis, and Dallas guard Brad Davis. Dallas resigned their guard, and Denver signed Davis for $600,000. Phoenix signed forward Tom Chambers for $1.8 million and received three All-Star quality years from him. Edwards stayed with Detroit and provided good scoring for that championship squad. Washington signed three small-time free agents, whom they waived before the end of the first half of the season. The Bullets also traded a low-round 1984 draft pick, Jim Grandholm, to Houston for Cedric Maxwell. Maxwell decided to retire from the league prior to the start of the 1988–1989 season and did not play for Washington.

Preseason predictions remained less than optimistic for the Bullets. In an article entitled, "What about the Rest?" the team warranted only a few sentences in *Sports Illustrated's* annual review:

> Congress should do something about this. The Washington Bullets begin the season with Dave Feitl as their starting center. Coach Wes Unseld has installed a modified version of Denver's motion offense, which may free Jeff Malone and Bernard King. Then again, it may close them down.[59]

Clearly, the experts perceived that the Bullets lacked the players to field a strong team. The NBA eras of center dominance had vanished with the arrival of Magic Johnson and Larry Bird. Taller, bigger players; the use of double teams against centers in the paint; and the forcing of players to shoot facing the basket rather than with their backs to the basket all squeezed the center's ability to dominate, but a team could not win with Feitl as their starting center. The strongest teams in the league had very good players with a variety of skills holding down the center position. These men could still shoot from the inside and rebound, but they could also make shots from the perimeter, while possessing more quickness and passing effectiveness.

The Bullets started the season poorly and continued on that roll. After losing 15 of their first 20 games, the team played .500 ball in January and February to pass the Charlotte Hornets and New Jersey Nets in the Atlantic Division standings. They trailed the Boston Celtics and the last playoff spot by four games. The Bullets defeated the Celtics three of five times and had only one game remaining to play against them. Washington went on four winning streaks in March behind the scoring of Bernard King, Jeff Malone, and young center John Williams, the team's top draft choice in 1986. Even playing without an injured Larry Bird most of the season, the Celtics kept pace with the Bullets throughout March.

Four games behind, Washington had an advantage over the Celtics, as they played seven of eight games at home at the beginning of the last month. Meanwhile, Boston played six of eight on the road. The Bullets won the first five games, including beating expansion Miami on the road to reach the .500 mark for the first time all season. Boston went one and one in their next two games, leaving them with a 39–37 record with five games left to play in the regular season. The Bullets lost two home games; the Knicks won by a single basket, and the Pistons blew the Bullets out of their home, winning by 24 points. Their record stood at 37–39. As the veteran Celtics won two more games, the Bullets split their pair to stand at 38–40. The two teams met at Boston Garden with a playoff spot on the line. A Celtic win, or a Bullet loss, would give Boston the last playoff spot. Washington scored 121 points to win by eight, keeping their hopes alive. Back in Washington, they defeated Chicago, but the Bulls exacted revenge the next evening on their home court, ending the Bullets' hopes to qualify for the playoffs.

Washington was one of the last teams to move their travel from commercial to chartered planes. With other teams moving in that direction, this disparity placed more strain on players. Al Bianchi served as the general manager of the Knicks from 1987 to 1991, when they changed their traveling process and moved to employing several assistant coaches, in addition to multiple assistant strength and conditioning coaches and trainers. The Bullets did not have the money to maintain a larger staff. Obviously, the situation was different, with the Knicks being owned by a corporation instead of a solitary owner. Portland and Detroit opted for the use of charter airplanes. The varying business practices between franchises were, in many cases, a matter of the nature of a corporate company versus a mom and pop operation.

While the team had made the playoffs the last few years, they had faced one of the top seeds. The general analysis of the pundits in the magazine and broadcasting world dismissed the Bullets' chances; however, not making the playoffs cost the team the opportunity to have ESPN and other analysts dissect the strengths and weaknesses of the team. The franchises' "face time" was significantly diminished. By the end of the decade, ESPN had become quite profitable, bringing in about $95 million in revenue. The station reached an audience of 3 to 4 million, generally affluent males between the ages of 30 and 45. It was clear that national cable networks outpaced the local stations, and the Washington team suffered from this lack of national exposure.[60]

Washington finished in the middle of the 25-team league in both offensive and defensive production; however, they were well below the league average in field goal percentage, last in three-point shooting accuracy, and below average in creating steals and blocking shots. Most unsettling of all, the team finished dead last in attendance. The 402,000 spectators represented nearly 50,000 less than the viewers of the next lowest-ranking team, the Los Angeles Clippers, who won only 18 games all year. The league schedule continued to limit contests against the Western Conference teams to two games. Washington played its division rivals six times each and members of the Eastern Conference Central Division four or five times.[61]

Management had a few positives to hang on to as they waited for the 1989 draft. The team received solid contributions from Bernard King and John Williams. If Terry Catledge or Ledell Eackles could add rebounding, the Bullets would be headed in the right direction by emulating the successful teams that had adopted a more flexible approach to the play of their frontcourt. This flex approach in current schemes would include a pivot, a center, and a forward. The idea was to have one player with his back to the basket, an outside shooter, and a main rebounder to handle the inside. On the Lakers, for example, Kareem Abdul-Jabbar was the pivot, A. C. Green the center, and James Worthy the forward. For the Celtics, Kevin McHale served as pivot, Robert Parish the center, and Bird the forward. In Detroit's alignment, Adrian Dantley acted as pivot, Bill Laimbeer the forward, and Rick Mahorn or John Salley the center.

The NBA instituted several changes to the college draft starting in 1989. As part of the 1983 salary cap agreement, the league reduced the draft to two rounds. Now, the NBA instituted the first random selection for the draft lottery order. The Board of Governors approved a plan that the seven-team lottery would only apply to the first three selections. The other four teams would be awarded picks in inverse record order. With a 33% chance of getting a top pick, the Bullets' brass watched as the commissioner, David Stern, drew the envelope with their logo on it early, giving them the ninth selection. The lottery order was selected before the end of the postseason, but there was another development that would change the preparation of the front office.

The league decided to expand yet again and added two more teams to increase to 27 squads, adding the Orlando Magic and Minnesota Timberwolves. The Bullets prepared for the expansion draft by submitting their protected roster, and then Orlando took Terry Catledge with their third pick. Catledge appeared uncomfortable at times with the Bullets new passing offense installed under Wes Unseld. In addition, Catledge was arrested for driving intoxicated.[62] According to Unseld, Catledge was someone who they "weren't anxious to lose. . . . It just came down to a numbers situation."[63] As with the Muggsy Bogues situation, there was concern. Why would the team's best rebounder and fifth best scorer have been left unprotected? Could a trade have been used to attain value if the Bullets knew they wanted to move Catledge?

The hope for improving the team hung with a good draft, which was not a strong suit of the team during the decade. The only free agent signing that the team made involved the return of Melvin Turpin, who was originally drafted by Washington in 1984. Turpin was waived by the Utah Jazz in

1988 and did not play in the NBA during the 1988–1989 season. With their first-round selection, the ninth pick, the team drafted Tom Hammonds from Georgia Tech, who was regarded as one of the top 15 players available in the draft. He had a reputation as a strong rebounder and solid scorer. With their two second-round picks, the Bullets chose Ed Horton and Doug Roth. The two forwards and center all made the roster, along with Turpin.

The Bullets won five of their first six games to start the 1989–1990 season, after a brutal training camp. Hammonds mentioned that prior to the season, the Bullets held intense two-a-days for an entire month. The norm in the league was for a week of these types of practices, and Hammonds believed that the added mileage during the preseason led to the diminished play of the team. He commented that "getting into the season was a relief because you didn't have the two-a-days."[64]

But the early success did not last, as the Bullets returned from their first sustained road trip under .500 and continued that level of play through the Christmas holiday. Losing streaks of four, five, and seven games buried the team with a 31–51 final record. Although they finished fourth in their division, they finished two places out of the playoff race. The Bullets maintained a league average scoring output, but their defense ranked near the bottom of the league. John Williams missed all of the team's first 18 games due to injury.

The Bullets benefitted from the vast improvement in the league's financial situation. When Dallas entered as the NBA's 23rd team for the 1980–1981 season, they paid a $12 million entrance fee. When the four teams entered during the 1988 and 1989 seasons, they each paid a $32.5 million entrance fee, a $5.6 million boon to the Bullets and other longtime teams. The league's television situation kept improving as well. Two years earlier, the broadcast rights for cable television sold to TBS and TNT for $50 million. Now TNT paid $275 million for four years. NBC topped the other major networks and won NBA broadcast rights for $600 million for four years, an increase of 340% from the 1986 deal with CBS. By the end of the decade, the NBA was broadcasting games to more than 50 countries. The Collective Bargaining Agreement dictated that the players should receive 53% of all league revenue, complementing the salaries they earned.[65]

While the team's financial fortunes appeared on the rise, its misfortunes on the court continued. Abe Pollin held steadfastly loyal to his leaders during the decade. The disagreement on the issue of Moses Malone prompted a schism between Pollin, much of the staff, and general manager Bob Ferry. Now Pollin approached his longtime employee about the need for a change.

Notes

1. Gerald Eskenazi, "Cable TV Begins to Make Big Changes in Professional Sports," *New York Times*, April 19, 1981, S1.

2. Sean Deveney, "Missing the Points," *Sporting News*, vol. 226 (December 30, 2002), 38–39.

3. This and other details and quotes by Bob Ferry were obtained during an interview with the author, March 17, 2012.

4. David DuPree, "Bullets Hire Shue to Replace Motta," *Washington Post*, May 28, 1980, D1.

5. David DuPree and Paul Attner, "End of an Era," *Washington Post*, May 11, 1980, D1.

6. Bob Ferry interview with author, March 17, 2012.

7. DuPree, "Bullets Hire Shue to Replace Motta," *Washington Post*, May 28, 1980, D1.

8. This and other details and quotes by Bernie Bickerstaff were obtained during an interview with the author, March 17, 2012; this and other details and quotes by Greg Ballard were obtained during an interview with the author, April 23, 2012; this and other details and quotes by Roger Phegley were obtained during an interview with the author, February 27, 2012.

9. Lawrence E. Ziewacz, "Dr. J, Bird, Magic, Jordan, and the Detroit Bad Boys: The NBA in the 1980s," in *Basketball in America: From the Playgrounds to Jordan's Game and Beyond*, ed. Bob Batchelor (New York: Haworth Press, 2005), 244–45.

10. David DuPree, "Bullets Tap Matthews No. 1," *Washington Post*, June 11, 1980, E1.

11. This and other details and quotes by Charles Davis were obtained during an interview with the author, March 14, 2012.

12. Spencer Haywood, with Scott Ostler, *Spencer Haywood: The Rise, the Fall, the Recovery* (New York: Amistad, 1992), 217–26.

13. "NBA Rules History," NBA.com, www.nba.com/analysis/rules_history.html (retrieved February 2, 2010).

14. Alan Goldstein, "Bullets Take No-Frills Flight in NBA Playoffs," *Baltimore Sun*, April 25, 1982, 45.

15. John Lucas, with Joseph Moriarity, *Winning a Day at a Time* (Hazelden Foundation, 1994).

16. Lucas, with Moriarity, *Winning a Day at a Time*, 76–81.

17. Wendell Maxey, "The Suns 1987 Drug Scandal," Hoopsworld.com, reposted on apbr.com, www.apbr.org/forum/viewtopic.php?t=2487 (retrieved September 11, 2010), n.p.

18. Maxey, "The Suns 1987 Drug Scandal," www.apbr.org/forum/viewtopic.php?t=2487.

19. Jack McCallum, "Getting Fooled by Drugs," *Sports Illustrated*, January 26, 1987, 70; Bob Ferry, interview with author, March 17, 2012.

20. Haywood, with Ostler, *Spencer Haywood: The Rise, the Fall, the Recovery*, 227–37.

21. Bill Simmons, *The Book of Basketball: The NBA According to the Sports Guy* (New York: Ballantine Books, 2009), 141–44.

22. David DuPree, "Rick Mahorn," *Washington Post*, April 13, 1982, C1.

23. Ferry interview, March 17, 2012.

24. David DuPree, "Bullets Defeat Nets by 13 in Playoff Opener," *Washington Post*, April 21, 1982, D1.

25. Steve Hershey, "Grevey Scores 23 in 103–92 Victory," *Washington Post*, April 24, 1982, D1.

26. Hershey, "Grevey Scores 23 in 103–92 Victory," D1.

27. David DuPree, "Show of Force Stops Bullets,"*Washington Post*, May 2, 1982, D1.

28. This and other details and quotes by Charles Davis were obtained during an interview with the author, March 14, 2012.

29. Bob Ferry interview, March 17, 2012.

30. David DuPree, "Pollin: 'Everything Possible' to Improve Bullets," *Washington Post*, April 20, 1983, D1.

31. Ferry interview, March 17, 2012.

32. DuPree, "Pollin: 'Everything Possible' to Improve Bullets."

33. David Remnick, "Shue: Bullets On Treadmill, Need Help," *Washington Post*, March 22, 1984, D1.

34. David Remnick, "Bullets Finish Irregular Season," *Washington Post*, April 15, 1984, F9.

35. Remnick, "Bullets Finish Irregular Season," F9.

36. David Remnick, "Bullets Prime for an 'Ugly' Game 2, Too," *Washington Post*, April 19, 1984, E1.

37. David Remnick, "Bullets Beat Celtics in Overtime," *Washington Post*, April 22, 1984, C1.

38. Lloyd C. Bronstein, *Sports Law: Antitrust Suit Fails to Knock off NBA's Salary Cap*, 6 Loy. L.A. Ent. L. Rev. 231 (1986).

39. Mario R. Sarmento, "The NBA on Network Television: A Historical Analysis," Thesis, University of Florida, 1998, 3–66.

40. Ferry interview, March 17, 2012.

41. "1984 NBA Draft," Basketball-Reference.com, www.basketball-reference.com/draft/NBA_1984.html (retrieved February 14, 2011); Eldon L. Ham, *The Playmasters: From Sellouts to Lockouts: An Unauthorized History of the NBA* (Chicago: Contemporary Books, 2000), 161–69.

42. Ferry interview, March 17, 2012.

43. Leigh Montville, *Manute: The Center of Two Worlds* (New York: Simon & Schuster, 1993), 60–61, 168–77. Detroit left Mahorn unprotected, and the Minnesota Timberwolves chose him during their Expansion Draft. Yet, the Pistons repeated as NBA champions.

44. Anthony Cotton, "Bradley's Three-Point Shot Gives Washington Victory," *Washington Post*, April 19, 1986, B1.

45. Anthony Cotton and William Gildea, "Pollin Pledges Effort to Transform Bullets," *Washington Post*, April 13, 1986, D1.

46. Cotton and Gildea, "Pollin Pledges Effort to Transform Bullets," D1.

47. Basketball–Reference.com, all teams, 1981–1986 seasons.

48. Anthony Cotton and William Gildea, "Pollin Pledges Effort to Transform Bullets," *Washington Post*, April 13, 1986, D1; Anthony Cotton, "Bullets Finally Get Their Man," *Washington Post*, June 19, 1986, D1; *Washington Post*, July 23, 1986, D5.

49. Cathrine Wolf, "Roundup of the week April 27-May 3," *Sports Illustrated*, May 11, 1987, 119.

50. Anthony Cotton, "Uncertainties Breed Anxieties for Bullets," *Washington Post*, October 27, 1987, E1; Bob Ferry, interview by author, March 17, 2012.

51. Anthony Cotton, "Loughery Considers Fluctuating Starters," *Washington Post*, December 11, 1987, D1.

52. Thomas Boswell, "Oddball Bullets Might Improve by the Minutes," *Washington Post*, December 11, 1987, D1.

53. Anthony Cotton, "Pollin Stays Upbeat on Bullets," *Washington Post*, December 8, 1987, E1.

54. Ferry interview, March 17, 2012.

55. Jack McCallum, "Blast from the Past," *Sports Illustrated*, March 28, 1988, 44.

56. Anthony Cotton, "Bullets Follow Jeff Malone to Overtime Win," *Washington Post*, May 3, 1988, E6.

57. Anthony Cotton, "Pistons Seek Way of Putting Out Malone's Fire," *Washington Post*, May 4, 1988, C1.

58. David Aldridge and George Solomon, "No 4-Year Deal for Malone," *Washington Post*, June 22, 1988, D1.

59. Jack McCallum, "What about the Rest?" *Sports Illustrated*, November 7, 1988, 96.

60. Geraldine Fabrikant, "For Cable Networks, the Road Gets a Little Steeper," *New York Times*, February 26, 1989.

61. "1988 NBA Draft," Basketball-Reference.com, www.basketball-reference.com/draft/NBA_1988.html (retrieved February 14, 2012); "1988–89 Washington Bullets Roster and Statistics," Basketball-Reference.com, www.basketball-reference.com/teams/WSB/1989.html (retrieved February 14, 2012).

62. David Aldridge, "Bullets Could Face Hard Choice In Lottery: Size or Versatility," *Washington Post*, April 25, 1989, C5; Anthony Cotton, "Green Tabbed No. 1, Mahorn No. 2 in NBA Expansion Draft,"*Washington Post*, June 16, 1989, D1.

63. *Washington Post*, June 27, 1989, E1.

64. This and other details and quotes by Tom Hammonds were obtained during an interview with the author, March 1, 2012.

65. Richard Justice, "Pollin Says He Will Not Sell Bullets," *Washington Post*, January 25, 1989, D1; David Aldridge, "Pollin, Ferry, Unseld: Talent At the Top," *Washington Post*, January 30, 1989, C1; David Aldridge, "Clunk! No. 9 Bullets Aren't Lottery Kings," *Washington Post*, May 22, 1989, C1.

CHAPTER NINE

~

Abe Pollin, the Fab Five, and the Washington Bullets/Wizards

The key leaders of the Bullets mutually agreed that the franchise needed new leadership. After 17 years, Bob Ferry left his position as general manager effective immediately. The best summaries of the era noted that in Ferry's first 10 years, hardly anyone picking later in the draft did better than him. They also observed that he missed some top-notch players and, operating on Abe Pollin's edict of the future, always made trades that cost the team a valuable future draft pick.

Rock Bottom

Within a week of Bob Ferry's departure, the Bullets installed their new general manager. Formerly with the Philadelphia 76ers, John Nash took over with autonomy in the Bullets' basketball decisions. Nash said that he had no single philosophy on how to improve Washington and that he would examine the team's scouting system to see if there were ways to improve it. The new leader immediately faced the college draft without a top pick, because Ferry had traded it away a few years before. Two days before the draft, Nash engineered a three-team deal with the general managers of the Utah Jazz and Sacramento Kings. The Bullets traded Jeff Malone to Utah and a 1991 second-round draft pick to Sacramento, who sent their top pick from 1989's draft, center Pervis Ellison, to the Bullets. Utah shipped two players and two draft picks to the Kings. Ellison had played well in a part-time role with the Kings and came east with high expectations as a starter. Malone continued his good shooting in Utah, leading the team into the conference finals his second year with the Jazz.

Under Nash, the Bullets selected center Greg Foster and guard A. J. English as the 35th and 37th choices. Both played two seasons with Washington. Foster served as a slightly below average backup who went on to play for 10 years after being waived by the Bullets. English received three years of salary from the team but played an adequate backup guard before being released. Washington got more than most teams did out of their second-round selections, as two teams chose people who never played in the National Basketball Association (NBA) and six more had players who played fewer than 100 games. The players remaining on the board after the two Washington selections included a more solid backup guard choice in Bimbo Coles and two very strong forwards, Antonio Davis and Cedric Ceballos.

Nash made a series of moves during the course of the season. The free agents he signed ranked as bench players and generally received their walking papers during the same year. He traded a second-round pick in 1993 for a Washington, D.C., born guard who did not play a single game with the Bullets.[1]

The team retained much of its old-school mentality. Under Coach Wes Unseld, the team went through a month of two-a-days in training camp rather than the one week that most teams did. Tom Hammonds observed, "We beat on each other so we'd have no leg strength when the season started."[2] Sometimes that hard-nosed approach worked, but the Bullets' character did not improve their record. The team lost one more game than the year before and again finished as the tenth team in the conference. Behind Pervis Ellison and Harvey Grant, the team's defense moved up in league rankings, while their offense sank even more impressively. The team continued to lack a real outside scoring threat. John Williams led the team in three-point field goal percentage, and he did not even make one in every four that he took. In addition, for the second year in a row, the young player could not play in two-thirds of the Bullets' games. The team believed in bringing their rookies along slowly, so many did not adapt quickly to the NBA game and could not immediately help the team improve.

Again, the Bullets completed a trade shortly before the college draft. The deal with the Denver Nuggets gave the Nuggets the Bullets' top pick in exchange for the Nuggets' top pick and a 1993 second-round pick. The Bullets also received guard Michael Adams. Denver had the eighth selection in the 1991 draft and chose a player out of Temple University who went on to play 250 games in the NBA. The Bullets did not select until number 19 and chose LaBradford Smith, a tall guard from University of Louisville who went on to play in 183 games. The team lacked a second-round choice and thus did not help itself with this draft.

Before the beginning of the 1991–1992 season, the new front office had made many changes. One step involved trading away veteran players with some value to get more chances at acquiring a top player. John Nash shipped guard Darrell Walker to the Detroit Pistons for two second-round draft choices. Other potentially valuable players, including Michael Adams and Harvey Grant, were not traded. As in previous years, the team signed free agents who had recently not panned out with other NBA teams. Four of the players, Albert King, Tim Legler, Corey Gaines, and Larry Robinson, lasted a total of four months with the team before being released. Local favorite David Wingate played an entire season of adequate basketball at a salary of $250,000. The team lost five more games than in the season before. While improving on offense and playing the same below-average defense, the Bullets finished near the bottom in attendance.

Other recently acquired players began to disappoint. John Williams had not recovered from the injuries that slowed him down the previous two years and made things worse. He earned the nickname "Hot Plate," gaining enough weight to put him at more than 300 pounds. During the span of the entire season, he attempted to lose weight and did not play in a single game. Tom Hammonds had his best scoring year but served as a more effective bench role player than starter. Ledell Eackles, the second-round pick who had been with the team for four seasons, was waived, as his play moved from decent to adequate. After another good scoring year, Bernard King could not play for the entire season. His knees did him in.[3]

The front office faced similar questions to those from the year before. With the sixth selection in the 1992 draft, they chose Tom Gugliotta, a solid forward from North Carolina State University. With the second-round choice, the Bullets selected point guard Brent Price. Other moves the Bullets made reflected two major roster changes. First, the team elected not to resign David Wingate, and then they traded forward Tom Hammonds for shooting guard Rex Chapman. Despite his popularity with Charlotte Hornet fans, Chapman had been injured through most of the previous season, and the Bullets took on the $2 million salary with the thought that he could regain his form. Uncertain about Bernard King's future, the team elected to waive him. They opted to sign small forward Buck Johnson for two years at a total of $1.2 million. Johnson had one less than adequate season and still collected his salary, although he did not make the roster for his second season. Finally, the team gave up on John Williams and traded him to the Los Angeles Clippers for power forward Don MacLean.

Local coaches started traveling basketball teams. Like many of the best players in his era, Don MacLean had joined one while he was in the third, fourth, and fifth grades. As a notable high school player, he received a listing in *Street & Smith* magazine and a few other specific newsletters, alerting colleges to his potential. After four years, MacLean watched his selection on TNT during a draft party at his home. Like most draft choices by that time, the experts had ranked him to be picked within a particular range in the draft, so he knew not to come and sit in the green room waiting to be selected with everyone watching him on television. He hired an agent who talked to the teams to see who wanted him to come to their mini-camp. Teams chose to work MacLean out at their mini-camps based upon their draft position. The highest-ranking team to have him in was the Houston Rockets, who had the 11th pick. MacLean and his agent could not work out a contract with the Clippers, so they traded him to Washington Bullets.[4]

The team started the next season at 0–4 and endured other losing streaks of five, six, and nine games. A newspaper beat writer referred to the losses as numbing in their frequency. "This team doesn't have much confidence," Rex Chapman said.[5] Chapman tried to get his game in order but struggled, and Pervis Ellison had been injured throughout the season. This was the first time in Wes Unseld's five-year tenure that the Bullets did not appear to be working hard. Perhaps play could have improved with a move to incorporate more of the sports science. The Bullets' staff had two assistant coaches and did not regularly review video of games and playing situations. Teams like the Denver Nuggets had three assistant coaches on staff, and one of them had the responsibility of breaking down the tape for the coach and then showing it the players. Washington initially lacked a strength and conditioning man on staff. The leadership forced the trainer to get one, but he hired a buddy instead of putting out a request for the best.[6]

There were other old-school aspects that may have influenced the team's abilities to draw in the best players and generate greater positive feelings from current players. The Detroit Pistons had purchased their own plane for traveling, and other teams had moved to flying chartered airplanes. Washington slowly moved to the chartered airplane approach, using commercial airlines on several occasions during the 1992–1993 season. "It was torture if you didn't get a first-class seat because of my size," said one 6-foot, 9-inch, 215-pound player. Players had to fit into coach seats if they were unlucky enough to not get a seat in first-class or if they lacked seniority. Sometimes the accommodations were less than ideal, for example, if they were located near the airport, causing some sleep deprivation. "You felt like a stepchild," one former player noted. Management frequently deducted certain charges from pay checks, for such expenses as getting uniforms laundered and paying for rooms if a player refused to sleep with a roommate, things that other teams could have made deductions for but usually did not charge the players to do.

At the start of the 1993 off-season, the Bullets' leadership made more moves. In June, they traded another asset, forward Harvey Grant, to Portland for center Kevin Duckworth. Grant played one good and two decent years for the Trailblazers, while Duckworth earned $2.4 million in each of his two subpar years before the Bullets traded him. In the lottery, the team drew pick number six, when the odds had them at number three at the lowest. The Bullets selected Indiana University shooting guard Calbert Cheaney. The top draft picks had become increasingly savvy about their position and potential worth. They hired agents to negotiate their contracts with the teams and, as a result, received better deals. As the sixth selection, Cheaney received a contract that paid him $2 million, with $400,000 increases for the next six years. The choices made by the Bullets for these contracts would go on to haunt Washington, as well as other NBA teams.

The players who knew that they were not going to be selected among those chosen early in the first round, known as "lottery picks," usually did not go to New York. Guys usually knew who the top selections would be based upon their athletic ability demonstrated during the college season, but also from the one or two "all-star" games that they would attend. Other players often received invitations to the gatherings, where NBA assistant coaches and scouts went, including the Portsmouth Invitational Tournament. If a player performed well in the 3-on-3 and 5-on-5 games, they became part of the group of 32 players to go to another invitational in Chicago or Orlando. Finally, most of the players attended the combine in Chicago, which, as one player described it, is a meat market of players, with trainers poking and prodding them.

After drafting Calbert Cheaney, the team still had two second-round choices. They batted successfully on one of their selections, as Gheorghe Muresan played center for three good years; however, their other second-round choice did not pan out. Unfortunately, the team did not select three strong players that remained on the board. Two point guards, Nick Van Exel and Chris Whitney, were available, as was small forward Byron Russell. The Bullets fit in the middle of the pack in this draft's success. Eleven teams made choices of players did not play in the league, and 10 more teams' selections played fewer than 75 NBA games.[7]

The first month of play in the 1993–1994 season went fairly well. The Bullets stood at .500, winning six games. The team initially placed its top draft pick in the starting lineup for the beginning of the year but soon brought on Don MacLean to improve their scoring output. Pervis Ellison continued his struggle to recover from injuries, and his missing presence in the middle proved fatal to the team's defense. Four of the team's most frequent starters did not have a reputation for defensive strengths, and the defense proved porous. Point guards drove the lane, having little fear of getting their shots blocked, with small forwards or shooting guards moving down the baseline without concern that someone would play help defense. The weaknesses showed as December began. The Bullets lost 10 games in a row, by an average of 11 points.

The team improved slightly, winning one of every three games. One of the Bullets' few strengths, Rex Chapman's scoring, disappeared when the guard landed wrong on Dennis Rodman's foot and was sidelined for several games. Then his replacement, Calbert Cheaney, sustained an injury. Despite all this, the team won two more games than the previous year. Wes Unseld retired from coaching, and John Nash hired Jim Lyman to lead the team. Lyman coached the Clippers with little success during the early 1980s. He also coached for four full seasons in Philadelphia, leading the team into the playoffs the first three years, although the 76ers never advanced past the semifinal round.

Fab Time

Jim Lyman joined with John Nash and others to make a series of moves. They decided to release Pervis Ellison from the team. In playing half the team's games, Ellison averaged about 25 minutes in the 47 games that he played in and shot the lowest percentage from the field since his rookie year. His rebounding and blocking of shots both dropped as well. The Bullets' brain trust did not think retaining him and the second-highest salary on the team added up. They met with every top college player, including those most likely to be available when the Bullets chose fifth in the 1994 draft. They also interviewed three of the top centers who would be available, as the team seemed particularly needy in that position. When the draft took place, the team selected power forward Juwan Howard and center Jim McIlvaine in the second round. Both choices proved good relative to the other players who were available. Perhaps only Brian Grant or Eddie Jones might have proved as useful a first-round selection.

Like many other teams in the NBA, the Bullets had to work out the team's annual salary structure while facing pressure from their new draft choices to be paid well. The new draft choices from the first round came prepared to bargain like few classes had before. With high-powered agents doing their negotiating, the players entered with both the expectations of a high salary and the leverage to win at the table. The leverage included a willingness to hold out until they got what they thought they deserved. Howard, represented by agent David Falk, expressed his wishes for a contract worth an average annual salary of close to $4 million. This was about the contract that the top pick in the draft received from the Milwaukee Bucks. That pick, Glenn Robinson, from Purdue University, sought a 13-year, $100 million contract. His contract negotiations became a subject to lampoon in the sports magazines, which envisioned a person applying for a job requesting that size of a contract without having any professional experience.

While Milwaukee's executives balked at that staggering amount, they did pay him $6.8 million per year for 10 years, the highest-ever rookie contract. Washington's John Nash and Abe Pollin also balked at Juwan Howard's demands. Their contract offer led to Howard's decision to not come to training camp. The Bullets' leaders noted that they faced a salary cap bind. The league salary cap for the 1994–1995 season amounted to about $16 million, and the Bullets already tabulated more than $15 million. Earlier in the summer, the team's salary burden rose because, in a trade with the Orlando Magic, the Bullets received guard Scott Skiles and his $2.1 million salary. Orlando sent Skiles to Washington and gave the Bullets a 1996 first-round draft pick in exchange for a 1996 second-round draft pick. The Magic needed the cap room to provide decent salary offers to free agents power forward Horace Grant and point guard Brian Shaw. The agent for Shaw called the cap situation the new NBA game, Salary Slot Pursuit.

The Brian Shaw deal offered insight into the view of the Bullets and their city in the minds of some in the league. The guard's agent tried to interest his client in Washington; however, the guard noted that Shaw wanted to play in Orlando because of winning, weather, and taxes and the fact that he liked Florida. He did not want to live in a cold-weather city and was particularly not confident that Washington would be able to win. Shaw remained adamant despite his agent informing him that Washington could offer more money; a starting position; and a great city for a single, young, black professional. The agent and client heard from both John Nash and John Gabriel, Orlando's player-personnel director. As the situation unfolded, Shaw informed his agent about his desire to play in Orlando. He said, "Get me there, winning is most important. I will make my money [later]."[8]

Days later, the Bullets' brass traded guard Michael Adams to the Charlotte Hornets for two second-round draft choices.[9] This freed up his $1.3 million salary, but David Falk rejected the cap as a problem. "I make my living negotiating through the salary cap rules. You don't pay a lottery pick like Juwan what's available, but you do whatever you have to do to sign him." Falk predicted that he did not expect a quick resolution to the negotiations.[10]

"I'm drained," general manager John Nash informed the media during an event the reporters dubbed a "fab day." Abe Pollin's team played the first seven games without its top draft choice. Now, Howard had signed an 11-year deal for $35.9 million. After the first two years, for which he would collect $3 million, Howard could decide to opt out of this contract and become a restricted free agent. The former member of Michigan University's "Fab Five" signed when another Fab Five member, center Chris Webber, became a Bullet as well. The team executed a trade that brought Webber from the Golden State Warriors to Washington in exchange for Tom Gugliotta and first-round draft picks for 1996, 1998, and 2000. The Warriors had signed Webber to a one-year deal with a one-year escape clause, and he wanted off the team. Intriguingly, on the day the Bullets signed a contract offering an escape clause, they acquired a player who exercised an escape clause that forced another team to trade him. Webber had a reputation as being undisciplined because he had butt heads with the Warriors' coach, Don Nelson, over his particular style, but he worked hard on his game and could be found to be a thoughtful person in one-on-one situations.[11] (figure 9.1)

The trading of a top draft pick was not unusual. Frequently, the trade arose due to friction with management or teammates and/or contractual disagreements. The Hornets felt compelled to trade center Alonzo Mourning after three years, and Dallas moved guard Jim Jackson; however, the provision of the escape clause made these circumstances somewhat different. During the off-season in 1993, the Portland Trailblazers signed free agent center Chris Dudley for $800,000 during the first of seven years. He would receive a 30% raise the following year or could elect to use his escape clause.

Fans and opposing players alike expected great things for the Bullets. "Those two young guys are going to be helluva players," said Celtics forward Dominique Wilkins.[12] The beat reporters announced that Washington's future was going to be nuclear bright. Howard and Webber needed a crash course in Washington's playbook, but every NBA team essentially had a set of 10 to 15 similar plays representing variations on those used at the National Collegiate Athletic Association level. Under Lyman, the team watched more video and spent more time breaking down opposing teams, which also sped up learning for the newcomers. Before the trade, the pundits had the Bullets near the bottom of the division based upon a defense that allowed opponents to shoot nearly 51% from the floor. With Webber, Bullets fans had their first basketball hero since the 1970s (figure 9.2).

Figure 9.1. Juwan Howard posts up.
Courtesy Steve Lipofsky, www.basketballphoto.com.

Figure 9.2. Juwan Howard and Chris Webber converse.
Courtesy Steve Lipofsky, www.basketballphoto.com.

With all of the news off the court, the trade did not stop the team's losing streak. Washington lost another four before winning one. After another loss and win, the team embarked on an eight-game losing streak. After a Christmastime win, they promptly lost 10 more. Injuries riddled the team, as many starters and some of the reserves endured some medical problems. The team defense proved as porous as ever, with team averaging more than 115 points during the stretch. Circumstances only became worse, as the team endured several more long losing streaks, resulting in a 21–61 record, the second lowest win total since Pollin first bought the team in 1963–1964. The team ranked fourth in the league in amount of time missed due to injuries, a total of 317 games missed by the roster of 14 players.

Since spending on free agent Bernard King, Abe Pollin and his basketball people invested little in the free agent market as an effort to improve the team's fortunes. Duirng the five seasons between 1990 and 1995, the Bullets signed and paid for five players that had at least a few seasons of NBA experience. This ranked tied with the league average of five signings during that same period. Chicago, Detroit, New Jersey, Orlando, Philadelphia, and Phoenix represented the most active teams, who all signed at least seven players.

Of these two point guards, two small forwards, and one power forward the Bullets signed, the team waived one of the small forwards near the start of one season. They received poor or adequate performances from the others. This was not surprising given that the Bullets spent less money on these free agents than the league average. Washington spent an average of $185,000 annually on the point guards, when the NBA averaged $482,000. Teams spent an average of $829,000 per year on small forwards and $923,000 per year on power forwards; the Bullets spent $575,000 and $400,000 for those positions. The biggest spenders featured the Phoenix Suns, who signed forwards A. C. Green and Danny Manning, and the Orlando Magic, who, as noted earlier, spent on Brian Shaw and Horace Grant.

Some of the free agents had grave concerns about whether they would have the opportunity to negotiate with teams. The league's Collective Bargaining Agreement negotiations went poorly. Owners imposed a lockout of the players after the completion of the 1995 finals. The move strained an already tenuous relationship, as the team owners, particularly the Chicago Bulls, had been found to be intentionally underreporting their revenue, resulting in the players earning less. The players brought the case to court and won a decision for almost $93 million dollars to go toward salaries and pension funding.

A small group of the union's leadership met secretly with the NBA hierarchy and reached a deal on a new Collective Bargaining Agreement, covering six years, early in the summer of 1995. The new agreement contained a luxury tax imposition on teams that exceeded the salary cap, a cap on rookie salaries, and provisions to make the escape clause more difficult to use, which aimed at managing salaries and limiting loopholes. The owners argued that average salaries had quintupled in the past decade, to almost $2 million, requiring that some strong action was necessary to reign in the cap system. Even with the salary cap increase from $16 million to $23 million, the exploitation of the system resulted in some teams already being over that limit. In fact, eight teams had already exceeded the new limit, and another 11 had salary obligations at more than $20 million. The Bullets ranked among the remaining eight teams in the league with a salary burden of a little more than $17 million.

When the news of the new agreement broke, players, including Michael Jordan and Patrick Ewing, sought to decertify the union in an effort to invalidate the contract. They thought that the new agreement contained provisions, like the luxury tax, that would impede veteran players' abilities to exercise the benefits of free agency. The player's union collected signatures in preparation to go before the National Labor Relations Board to hear what steps might be necessary for decertifying the union. The union imposed a deadline to push the NBA owners into providing concessions to the players on the agreement. The NBA hierarchy chose to drop the luxury tax and restore exceptions for veterans. Nonetheless, the players behind the decertification effort continued, and the decertification election occurred in September 1995. The players voted 226–134 against the decertification, and the player representatives voted 25–2 in favor of ratifying the agreement. The owners quickly voted 24–5 in favor of the agreement, and the owner-imposed lockout was lifted days later.[13]

The new agreement provided gains for both sides. The owners provided a lower percentage of revenues to players, but the sources of revenue expanded to include monies from luxury suites, international television, and arena signage. The rookie cap, with a graduated scale, now governed the first three years for every new player. Teams and veterans interested in free agents retained some of the benefits that came from various player exemptions to the cap.

The agreement prevented an intrusion of tribulation into the upcoming season. The labor strife, combined with the retirement of Michael Jordan, had already provided headaches to broadcasters, as ratings diminished for NBA games. The executives at NBC Sports had signed a new four-year contract beginning in 1994–1995 to broadcast the games for $750 million. TNT/TBS also inked another deal worth $352 million during the course of four years. The product needed to be delivered. In addition, the resolution enabled free agency and the college draft to resume. The Bullets held the number four pick in a draft that was considered good and deep but short on future superstars.[14]

The NBA expanded again for the 1995–1996 season. The two new teams, the Toronto Raptors and the Vancouver Grizzlies, represented a big return to Canada since the failure of the first Toronto franchise of the Basketball Association of America in 1947. The teams each paid $125 million to join the league, nearly $100 million more than the expansion teams five years earlier. The move into Canada represented the NBA's further attempt to internationalize its basketball. The internationalization occurred in stages, which included the trips to foreign countries by NBA champions during the 1970s, when the Bullets played in Israel and China. A second stage involved the drafting of more foreign players, of which the Bullets played an early part. A third aspect included the dizzying marketing of the game that occurred during the 1980s and continued through the Olympic Dream Team in 1992. The NBA revenues reached the $1 billion level, as arenas in the United States filled to about 92% of capacity. The time seemed opportune for the Canadian move and an eventual move into Mexico. Meanwhile, the expansion of television resulted in the league showing games in 140 countries (up from more than 50 in 1988) and a revenue source of greater than $100 million.[15]

Despite this growth, some teams lagged behind in fulfilling their revenue promise. Teams like the Bullets did not fill their arenas to the high degree, they did not have as many season ticket holders, and their broadcasting revenue did not maximize what the market might be able to bear; however, the president of the team, Susan O'Malley, had been working in the marketing area and helping the team to improve its market penetration. By starting a monthly newsletter and calls and player receptions, the team increased its season ticket renewal rates to 95%, up from only 62%. O'Malley's staff also helped generate additional radio revenue. The first year of having Chris Webber on the team generated an additional 1,200 orders for season-ticket plans in a single day, as having a star brought excitement back to the team.[16]

The existing NBA teams had to submit to the league a list of players whom they were protecting. The remaining group would become the pool of players from which the two Canadian teams would select their teams. While Toronto chose 14 players, Vancouver selected 13, including forward Larry Stewart from the Bullets. They eschewed Rex Chapman, whom the team had also left unprotected. With the glut that the Bullets had in that position, Stewart did not receive as much playing time as he had during his first two seasons with the team.

After the expansion draft, the league held its rookie draft. Despite the Bullets' needs at center and point guard and its glut at power forward, the team appeared to be interested in drafting another power forward. The team held the fourth pick in the 1995 draft and leaned toward Rasheed Wallace as their choice. General manager John Nash engaged in conversations with teams about trades; however, in exchange for point guard Rod Strickland, the Portland Trail Blazers wanted swingman Calbert Cheaney and not Rex Chapman. Washington sports columnists advocated for the Bullets to make a trade. They suggested Strickland, while noting that he tended to fight with coaches after two or three years on any team. Another player who appeared on their radar included B. J. Armstrong. No deal occurred. Basketball pundits noted that the draft featured one small forward with the biggest upside and the largest risk, teenager Kevin Garnett. The Bullets were less loaded in that position than power forward, but the team elected to take Rasheed Wallace. While Wallace and Webber were also capable of playing center, both preferred power forward, a position that Juwan Howard also played. While Nash felt that Wallace would complement Webber and Howard due to his passing ability, beat reporters wondered how Coach Lyman would keep everyone happy. The Bullets forsook the rarely done option that Minnesota took in drafting a player straight out of high school (Garnett) but was one of many teams to draft the 16 players who came out of college early, before their four full years. This proved to be the second draft in a row in which the numbers of underclassmen drafted jumped from single into double digits.

The growth in the numbers of underclassmen applying for the draft was not a surprise and could be expected to continue. The Bullets' Chris Webber and Juwan Howard both illustrated the amount of money that underclassmen could receive after being selected in the draft. Shaquille O'Neal, who entered the league one year earlier, obtained a high salary and illuminated how a player could be marketed. His team made O'Neal into the league's first prepackaged multimedia superstar, with a Terminator/Bambi image that included endorsements for Reebok's sneakers, Pepsi-Cola, Skybox sports memorabilia, a rap album, and a movie release. Even with the limits on rookie salaries, the underclassmen realized that they might as well join the NBA and start the three-year clock on their salary limitation clicking. The sooner they moved into the league, the sooner their chance for stardom and making the Forbes Super 40 list of top-earning athletes.[17]

Moving Downtown

It was twenty years before Abe Pollin became one of a few NBA owners to finance a new arena for his team. The Capital Centre had been a great deal for the magnet, as he created an environment for his professional sports teams to play in and made money hosting a large number of other events throughout the year. Yet, the arena's location dampened enthusiasm from many of its potential spectators, with its distance from downtown and the lack of public transportation service to the facility.

Following a trend established in Sacramento that others had been slow to adopt, Pollin negotiated with a corporation to buy the naming rights to his arena. Beginning in 1993, the Capital Centre became known as the USAir Arena. Philadelphia followed suit, with the CoreStates Spectrum, the following year. The arena lasted only four more seasons. Other teams had moved or had plans to move to contemporary arenas to maximize their profitability. America West Arena opened in 1992 and even awed the players. The vast majority of teams used local colleges as practice facilities. "We were all shocked and amazed the first time we walked into Phoenix's arena because they had practice facilities inside," Don MacLean noted.[18] The Spurs moved to the much larger Alamodome in 1993, and Seattle, Chicago, and Boston had plans to play in their new arenas by 1994 and 1995; however, Boston's citizens did not finance the Celtics' new home. The owners of the NBA's Bulls and the Blackhawks of the National Hockey League (NHL) paid for the United Center in Chicago. A public-private partnership paid for the $100 million renovation of Seattle's Key Arena. The teams wanted the luxury boxes, waiter service, and giant scoreboards to sell their seating for more money, with improved concessions to also increase revenues. Bernie Bickerstaff noted that as president of the Denver Nuggets, he had to work hard among the local politicians to win support for the team's new arena. Denver based their new arena off of the facility in Indianapolis, because it was simple but very nice and conducive to basketball.[19]

In 1993, Pollin complained about the USAir Arena during a visit to his friend Gordon Gund. Gund told Pollin that the city of Cleveland planned to finance a new arena for his Cleveland Cavaliers. Through an emissary, the Bullets' owner began negotiations with Washington, D.C., politicians, lawyers, business groups, and others to construct an arena in downtown Washington. Would the District of Columbia be able to do the same for him? Unlike Cleveland, Washington had no county or state money to help it fund its share. Meanwhile, after a review of eight potential sites, Pollin chose to build on a site along Seventh Street, near G Street, NW, a neighborhood known as Gallery Place/Chinatown. The D.C. Redevelopment Land Agency (RLA) owned the property, and its four board members would need to approve any deal. In the fall of 1994, Pollin and city officials negotiated a deal for public funding to construct an arena in Gallery Place, which had to be completed by August 1997, so that the team could begin playing the 1997–1998 season there.

The proposal to build a downtown arena interested many others. Black Entertainment Television founder Robert Johnson wanted in and proposed to Pollin that he include him in the land deal and ownership of the Bullets. Pollin politely declined. Johnson sought help from the city's power brokers, who were friends of both men, but they stated that they would not pressure Pollin into any deal. Johnson then announced that he would build an arena with private funds. He sought a guarantee that he could buy a piece of the Bullets in the future. While Johnson offered private as opposed to public funding, he had no guarantee that teams would play at his arena. Most of the media and power brokers advocated for the Pollin plan, but the decision lay with the RLA and reports indicated that they leaned toward awarding the rights to the land to Johnson.

The overspending of Washington's mayoral administrations from the 1980s through the early 1990s mired the District of Columbia in deficits. By late 1994, city leaders plead for a bailout from New York banks. Soon, Mayor Marion Barry petitioned Congress for a bailout. The money came in 1995, attached to the five-member District of Columbia Financial Responsibility and Management Assistance Authority, responsible for overseeing the city's expenditures. Certainly, the city could not build an arena. But lobbying efforts with regional House members made certain that the authority could not stop the building of the facility. Pollin offered to fund the construction of the arena at Gallery Place, and the city would pay for the necessary infrastructure. The RLA voted three to one for the Pollin plan.

As the deal moved forward, practical problems became evident. The original lot proved too small, resulting in the city needing to acquire land. Not only did that raise costs, but the change made the original plan to reroute G Street impossible. Instead, the street would have to be closed, violating the L'Enfant plan for the city and stirring opposition from civic groups, historic preservationists, planners, and activists. The opposition pushed the city to pay for a full environmental impact statement. Through skillful public and private negotiations, the statement ranked Gallery Place as the top location for the arena and led to the creation of an agreement that minimized the arena's impact on the historic character of the area. Not everyone thought highly of the process. The National Trust for Historic Preservation's regional director stated that the process had "blatantly frustrated meaningful public input and disregarded the need for concessions to address preservation concerns."[20]

In the fall of 1995, the ceremonial groundbreaking took place at Gallery Place. Pollin started building his 20,600-seat arena at a cost of $175 million. The city's part ranged up to about $130 million. The new telephone company, MCI, purchased the rights for the arena name. Now all Pollin needed was to bring successful teams there to play.[21]

Before anyone reported to training camp, the Bullets made the move of releasing guard Scott Skiles. Unfortunately, he did not prove to be the team's answer at point guard. The move enabled Washington to have an additional $2 million in salary to offer potential free agents. Unlike the situation with Juwan Howard two years before, the rookie salary scale now limited what first-year players could earn. Rasheed Wallace's draft position meant he could earn up to 120% of the average first-year pay of players drafted in the same position during the past seven years. Wallace signed with the team for nearly $1.5 million for his first year.

The experts pronounced that the "moribund" franchise had life. Several predicted that the Bullets were the third-best team in their division and appeared to have a good shot for making the playoffs. Reservations included the need for Chris Webber to stay healthy and for the team's new point guard, Mark Price, to recover from the injuries that had limited his play to half a season with Cleveland. The remaining key component required continued improvement from Juwan Howard.

The preseason addressed those questions. Chris Webber injured his shoulder, forcing him to miss exhibition and the start of the season. Mark Price injured his foot, resulting in his playing only seven games during the course of the season. The loss cost the Bullets the 1996 first-round draft choice, which they spent to acquire Price, but they needed to trade for another point guard. John Nash swung a deal for Denver's Robert Pack, which cost them backup guard Doug Overton and forward Don MacLean. Pack had only one year before be become eligible as a free agent. Nash also pulled off a deal resulting in Kevin Duckworth moving on to the Milwaukee Bucks in exchange for a backup center Bob McCann.

The Bullets started off the season playing close to .500 basketball. They remained near that mark through early February. Rasheed Wallace demonstrated his talent, but his emotional game led to many personal and technical fouls being called on him. Jim Lyman noted that, "Rasheed is an exceptional player with tremendous athletic talent."[22] Juwan Howard shouldered the scoring burden, running effective pick-and-rolls with the team's point guard,

Brent Price, and contributing strong rebounding and raising his assists; however, the clear improvement that the experts sought did not occur, as his field goal percentage remained the same as the previous year. Rebounds per game dropped and turnovers per game actually rose. Still, Howard represented a known face for a franchise that needed to build its fan base.

A road trip in early February led to a six-game losing streak. While the team swapped wins and losses for awhile afterward, near the end of March, a record of 32–38 placed them 20 games behind the first-place Orlando Magic in the Atlantic Division. Most of the other probable playoff teams in the Eastern Conference played in the Midwest Division, including Chicago, Indiana, Cleveland, Atlanta, and Detroit. The teams ahead of the Bullets in the Atlantic Division, the New York Knicks and the Miami Heat, featured defenses that suffocated their opponents' scoring, ranking as the fourth-and fifth-best teams in team defense. The Knicks sat nine and a half games ahead of the Bullets, and, with 12 games remaining, the Bullets needed a miracle to overtake them.

Miami held a three-and-a-half-game edge but had to host the Bullets on March 29. A win would put the Bullets within striking distance of the last playoff spot. The Bullets did not have Chris Webber, Mark Price, Rasheed Wallace, or Robert Pack available. The team had expected Pack to come back earlier, but he did not properly heal. The Heat jumped out to a 30–22 edge after the first quarter. Center Alonzo Mourning led everyone in scoring. The Heat defense held the Bullets to 19 second-quarter points, forging a double-digit halftime lead. The Bullets' centers could hardly slow Mourning down. Scoring 50 points, the Heat center shot more than 70% from the field in leading Miami to a 112–93 victory.

One week later, the teams matched up again at the USAir Arena. The Bullets came out on top behind amazing shooting from Ledell Eackles, Juwan Howard, Brent Price, and Tim Legler. The team only trailed Miami by one game in the standings. The Bullets won their next three games, for a seven-game winning streak. Miami matched them win for win. Four games remained. Miami won again for their fourth win in a row. The Bullets lost against the Orlando Magic. The next game, both teams lost, and the Bullets' opportunity to gain the eighth seed in the playoffs seemed lost as well. Miami went on to get swept in the first round of the playoffs by the eventual champion Chicago Bulls. A good portion of the team's success was due to Jim Lyman. According to Brent Price, "He was the best communicator and was able to explain about the game."[23]

The $100 Million Man

The upcoming off-season proved the most important in years. The free agency field included about 140 players. Several big names and many All-Stars offered their services to the highest and most enticing bidders. Teams had the chance to reshape their rosters and set their franchise's course for the near future. After five years of building the Bullets into a franchise on the verge of breaking into the playoff ranks, John Nash resigned at the end of the regular season. In a statement, Nash said, "For reasons that are personal, I have decided to resign from my position with the Washington Bullets, effective immediately."[24] Within a month, John Calipari of the New Jersey Nets described Nash as a "guy who understands the league and is not afraid to make suggestions and do things."[25] He hired him as the team's general manager.

This was not the best time to be making a change of executives with the chance to shape the team's future at hand, but Abe Pollin turned to Wes Unseld to take over as the team's general manager. Because of the trade to acquire Mark Price, the Bullets had only one second-round draft selection. The team's executives used the number 55 pick to select Ronnie Henderson, a shooting guard out of Louisiana State University. He never played a game in the NBA.

Washington shared with Orlando, Chicago, Miami, Indiana, and Detroit the plight of having a big name on their team opt out of his contract to join this free-agent crop. While Juwan Howard did not match the centers Shaquille O'Neal, Dikembe Mutombo, and Alonzo Mourning, he ranked with others who might leave their current teams, including shooting guard Allan Houston, point guard Kenny Anderson, and power forward Dale Davis. Many of the other teams might have wanted to hold on to their big name players, but most could not, although Michael Jordan stayed with the Chicago Bulls and Alonzo Mourning stayed with the Miami Heat.[26]

The Bullets seemed to have more players taking the option of free agency than many other teams. Besides Juwan Howard, other free agents included guards Brent Price and Robert Pack, and backup center Jim McIlvaine. Price had just come off of his best shooting year of the three with the Bullets. The Houston Rockets made him a seven-year offer, and the Bullets offered a two-year deal. John Lyman came to Price to see if he would stay. Said Price, "When I told Lyman, he said I can't blame you for taking it."[27] He signed with Houston for an average of $1.9 million a year and played two decent years with Houston before moving on to Vancouver. Pack signed with the New Jersey Nets for an average salary of $3 million a year and was later traded to Dallas. McIlvaine received an enormous offer of an average of $3.3 million a year from Seattle and played a couple of adequate years for them. "A lot of guys were offered deals that we couldn't refuse," Brent Price reflected.[28]

The biggest concern centered on how to handle the Juwan Howard negotiations. The power forward had been an important part of the publicity of the new Bullets. The sports media praised both his ability and personality. One person characterized him as playing like a veteran. Howard himself said all the right things. "I don't want to be one of those young guys who take the money and don't care about anything else," he said.[29] His friend Chris Webber received a contract for the previous season that offered him an average of $8 million a year. In early July, Howard made his request to earn about $10 million a year cleared through his agent, David Falk. The team did have a trio of guys playing the power forward position and had real needs for a point guard, center, and outside shooter. The Bullets' leaders made the determination not to offer Howard that much money, and Howard received an offer from the Miami Heat for that amount. The team renounced its rights to Howard.[30]

The reaction to the decision sat poorly with the Bullets' fans. In the interpretation of a few reporters, team management reacted to the fans' dissatisfaction and decided to trade Rasheed Wallace and Mitchell Butler for point guard Rod Strickland and the return of power forward Harvey Grant. Wallace had received both great praise for his play and criticism for being moody and lackluster. He had also been charged with an incident of domestic violence. But the first year player had amazing potential, and he would go on to have 14 successful years in the NBA. Strickland was known to get into fights with coaches after three years of being on a team. "That's some concern," Wes Unseld admitted. "We don't anticipate any problems." Strickland's production proved very good but then dropped to good in his last two seasons with the Bullets.[31]The Bullets did save money by not signing Juwan Howard. Wes Unseld and Abe Pollin used the money to sign small forward Tracy Murray at an average annual salary of $2.2 million and power forward Lorenzo Williams for about $1 million. Murray provided the team with a decent outside scoring threat and played well at his position for three of the four years with the team. Murray wanted to stay in Toronto, but the team did not have the cap space to be able to afford him. He negotiated with both the Lakers and Bullets, and Washington won out because they offered a seven-year deal, one more than Los Angeles. "Unseld was a good person to negotiate with, he's a straight shooter," Murray noted.[32] Williams served as a backup; however, the Bullets' executives could have done more, as they had more money with both of the Prices's salaries coming off the books. The team missed the opportunity to expend on a big name, such as Dikembe Mutombo, who played college basketball at Georgetown University in Washington, D.C., and would have filled a position that the Bullets' needed badly. Another choice might have been to sign a free agent, such as Kenny Anderson or Howard Eisley, to play point guard, rather than trade for Strickland.

The team received a huge surprise later that summer. The league reviewed the Heat's contract with Juwan Howard and determined that Miami had exceeded the salary cap. They voided the Howard contract and then allowed the power forward to renegotiate with other teams. The Bullets offered him a deal for $100 million during the course of seven years, and Howard returned to his original team. Since this put the Bullets over the salary cap, the league allowed them to keep all the players they had signed in exchange for losing their first-round draft choice in the next year's college draft. How the team executives and owner found him worth more than $10 million a year now, when they had not earlier, remained uncertain; however, the pundits proclaimed the team lucky and predicted a playoff squad. Some guys wondered about the amount, concerned that the team would lack the salary cap space to be able to sign a key player. Still, several experts placed the team as third best in the Atlantic Division, behind the Knicks and the Orlando Magic, without Shaquille O'Neal.[33]

The two newcomers from Portland started the first five games of the season. Juwan Howard played in the middle, instead of Gheorghe Muresan. When the 7-foot, 7-inch Romanian returned to action, Howard played the small forward role. Tracy Murray came off the bench. Before the season started, the small forward got submarined during an exhibition game against Portland and put his shooting hand down to break his fall. The team doctor told him he was ok. He got used to playing with the pain but experienced tough criticism for not making his shots. His reworked his shot and became more successful.

The team hovered around the .500 mark through the end of January. While the team could score points, they still ranked among the lower middle of the league as a defensive squad. The second West Coast trip of the year featured playoff-bound teams in Seattle, Los Angeles, and Utah, followed by the much weaker Denver Nuggets. The Bullets lost by a bucket to Seattle and then dropped their game against the Lakers by 30 points. The next evening, Utah took it to the Bullets and beat them by 22 points. Unseld flew out to Denver and met with Lyman to fire him. He referred to the two routs as "not acceptable." Unseld appointed an assistant coach as the interim head coach. The team lost that game by two points and returned home. The team owned its own airplane, but it broke down somewhat frequently, causing the team to have to use the ones owned by Charlotte or Atlanta. Unlike on Portland's Blazer 1, the team was not usually served balanced meals, which would have helped the guys stay trim and in playing shape, but rather tacos, burgers, and pizza.

Wes Unseld hired Bernie Bickerstaff to be the team's head coach (figure 9.3). The former assistant under Dick Motta noted that the players seemed out of shape and set about to rectify that situation. The newly regrouped team started slowly under their new coach, winning 10 and losing 10 games. At 32 wins and 35 losses, the team occupied fourth place in the Atlantic Division. The Orlando Magic held third place in the division and the seventh seed in the playoffs, with a 37–29 record. The Magic then won three in a row to solidify their playoff position. Meanwhile, the Cleveland Cavaliers led the race for the eighth and final playoff spot, three and a half games ahead of Washington and four games in front of the Indiana Pacers. In addition, the three assistant coaches for the team were all given responsibility for analyzing one-third of the teams in the league and returning to the team with a breakdown on the opponents and specific plays and guys.

While Washington had five of their next six games at USAir Arena, Indiana also had five of seven at home. Cleveland played five of their next 15 games on the road before hosting Washington in the last game of the season. The Bullets won a tough game against a good Portland Trail Blazers team. Former teammate Rasheed Wallace scored 25 points, and guard Isaiah Rider scored 28. Chris Webber led the team with 26 points and 12 rebounds, despite fouling out of the game. They followed this with three wins against weaker teams before heading out to play the Pacers.

Only one game separated the Bullets and Pacers when the teams met at Market Square Arena. The Bullets jumped out to a 10-point edge after one quarter. The team received balanced scoring from all its starters. Indiana's shooting guard, Reggie Miller, kept them in the game and, with Travis Best, led a turnaround in the second quarter. Washington expanded on its three-point halftime lead with a good run to close out the third quarter ahead by nine. The Pacers attempted a comeback but fell four points short. The win expanded the Bullets lead to two games over the Pacers, and Washington returned home to defeat Michael Jordan and the dominant Chicago Bulls. This sixth win in a row put the Bullets in a tie with Cleveland.

As the Bullets went 3–3 during the next six games, the Pacers could not make up ground and remained two games behind with three games left.

Figure 9.3. Rod Strickland surveys the court.
Courtesy Steve Lipofsky, www.basketballphoto.com.

Cleveland lost four of six and fell a game behind the Bullets. The team that could win its remaining three games would move on to the playoffs. Cleveland defeated Orlando and Detroit to boost its record to 42–39. The Bullets and Pacers faced off against one another in Washington. Both teams started slowly, scoring 23 and 19 points during the first quarter. Washington got scoring from reserve guard Jaren Jackson to boost its lead to six points by halftime. Reggie Miller had an off night shooting, and behind Rod Strickland (figure 9.4), Chris Webber, and Juwan Howard, Washington powered to a 16-point third-quarter bulge and won the game, 103–90.

The win knocked the Pacers out of contention. The Bullets faced a tough Orlando Magic team, which had fortunately already gained a spot in the playoffs. Orlando played tough and held a three-point halftime lead. Both Webber and Strickland had poor shooting nights, missing more than half of their shots. Howard chipped in 25 points, and Murray added 11, including two big three-pointers. Washington pleased the home crowd, seizing the lead for good in the third quarter.

Washington led Cleveland by one game as the two squared off at Gund Arena. The Cavaliers led the league in defense and looked to apply its pressure to take the remaining playoff spot. Things looked good for the home team, as their defense slowed the Bullets down and challenged their shots. Washington scored only 35 points, despite having three starters on the court for most of the half. Coming out of the locker room, the Bullets began to get offensive rebounds and reduced the turnovers. They whittled Cleveland's lead down to two points. Chris Webber led the team into the fourth quarter, and the Bullets sealed the win on a Juwan Howard jumper. With the spot on the line, Bernie Bickerstaff opted to play Juwan Howard and Rod Strickland for 45 of the 48 minutes, and Chris Webber played for 43 minutes.[34]

The Bullets fought hard to win the right to play the Chicago Bulls. "We played our behinds off and had a good time," Tracy Murray noted.[35] The top seed in the Eastern Conference had the great Michael Jordan and future Hall of Famers Scottie Pippen and Dennis Rodman, along with scorers Toni Kukoc and Ron Harper. The Bulls had won 69 games during the season, defeating Washington two of three times. The team went over video with each player. They went over opposing players' tendencies and analyzed the plays they ran for their guys.

The Bulls hosted game one at the United Center and gave their fans a little concern, starting off slowly. Rod Strickland, Juwan Howard, and Calbert Cheaney took the majority of the shots and kept the Bullets to within four points at halftime. With Toni Kukoc coming off an injury and Dennis Rodman slowed by a knee injury, Michael Jordan and Scottie Pippen carried

Figure 9.4. Coach Bernie Bickerstaff wears a wry smile.
Courtesy Steve Lipofsky, www.basketballphoto.com.

the load. In a third quarter, during which the teams combined for 30 points, the Bulls forced the Bullets into a ton of turnovers, while missing their own shots. A high-scoring, up-tempo final quarter ended with the Bulls taking the game by a 12-point margin. Jordan had a near triple-double of 29 points, eight rebounds, and eight assists.

Two nights later, in game two, the teams found their scoring abilities. The Bullets received balanced scoring from their starters and reserve forward Murray to take a halftime lead, 65–58. Jordan single-handedly kept the Bulls close and came out on fire in the last half. With occasional tallies from his teammates, he willed the Bulls into a 76–73 lead. But the Bullets made a few runs in response to the spurts by the Bulls. Halfway through the final quarter, Webber's third three-point shot of the game narrowed the Bulls advantage to 94–93. Jordan responded with a successful layup and then hit a 15-foot jump shot the next time down the court. He stole the ball and hit an arching shot over the extended hand of Juwan Howard to extend his team's lead to seven. "I have no problem carrying the team if I have to," Jordan said later.[36] "It was so frustrating," Webber said. "He would go by three defenders."[37] Jordan scored 55 points, making an astounding 63% of his shots. The Bullets received 26 points from Cheaney, 22 from Murray, and 21 from Webber and lost by five. Four Bullets starters played more than 40 minutes, and Webber fouled out for the second consecutive game.

Webber's foul trouble continued in the third game at USAir Arena. The game looked more like the first battle, a low-scoring affair. The Bulls struggled from the floor, but their ability to get offensive rebounds gave them second chances that offset Washington's more accurate field goal percentage. Both teams went into the locker room having tallied less than 50 points in the half. Pippen and Kukoc each provided points to balance the Chicago attack more so than in the earlier games. Washington relied on Strickland, Murray, Howard, and Webber and tied the score at 70 after three quarters. The Bullets executed well on both ends of the court to take a nine point lead with only four minutes left in the game. Jordan began to assert his game again but had barely eroded the lead when Webber fouled out of the game 30 seconds later. Jordan put his team in the lead before Howard sank two free throws with only 20 seconds left. Trailing by one, Jordan made a move against Murray and lost the ball. Pippen picked it up and slammed in the dunk that gave the Bulls the 96–95 victory. "You think you've done everything you can, then something happens," noted Howard.[38] Jordan did say that Washington was a team of the future. Murray returned home and visited the Lakers' team doctor, who pointed out that the forward had a big ligament torn in half on his shooting wrist.

The Bulls went on to win the NBA Championship over the Utah Jazz. Their repeat of taking the league championship might have been thrilling to watch, but it hardly surprised anyone. Much of the consternation that appeared about the NBA focused on what was perceived as the declining offensive abilities throughout the league. The NBA field goal percentage continued to decline, despite the league changing the rules to reduce the amount of contact that defenders can have with offensive players by limiting had checking more. The 45.5% accuracy for the completed season fell below the percentages from the early 1970s. Other groans and moans were related to the number of points typically scored in the game. Teams scored less than 80 points during the season more than twice as often as any season since the introduction of the 24-second shot clock.

Analysts and former players offered a variety of perspectives on the topic. Many went through mental lists of the "great" outside shooters and argued that shooters were either better during a particular era, or, that under the new league rules, shooters from the different era would be even better. Some observers tried to explain this phenomenon. The positive spin centered on bigger and better defense. Larger players, with greater athleticism and an increased focus on defense, made it harder for scorers to score. One less flattering opinion agreed with the greater athleticism but noted that the superior speed and quickness, as well as strength and jumping abilities of current athletes, did not translate into shooting ability. The second negative interpretation stated that these athletes depart college earlier, thus losing the chance to improve their shooting skills during those four years. Another view noted that since Dr. J opened up the door to dunking as an art, basketball players have focused on that and have had little interest in practicing the fundamentals, including shooting. Athletes and coaches received condemnation in the final interpretation, which argued that offenses have slowed to a crawl and that one or two players handle the ball during a possession instead of passing it to find the open shooter. The larger question for the NBA was whether the scoring and poor shooting was causing disinterest amongst fans and if it was affecting attendance and ratings.[39]

The Washington Wizards

Two years earlier, owner Abe Pollin indicated that he wanted to change the name of his basketball team. During the late 1980s and early 1990s, the city of Washington struggled with one of the highest homicide rates in the nation. Pollin thought that the team name of Bullets had acquired violent overtones. He had felt uncomfortable over the years, and the assassination of his longtime friend, Israeli prime minister Yitzhak Rabin, crystallized his decision to change the name. The team engaged the public in a naming contest, and selections were narrowed to the Dragons, Express, Stallions, Sea Dogs, or Wizards. The team officially became the Washington Wizards. A new logo was unveiled, and the team colors were changed from the traditional red, white, and blue to blue, black, and bronze, matching the colors of Pollin's NHL entry, the Washington Capitals, who also modified their team look.

Most team names changed because of team relocation, for example, the Baltimore Bullets becoming the Washington Bullets; however, the Bullets going to the Wizards represented only the seventh time a franchise in the league changed its team name among NBA teams. As noted in chapter 4, the Bullets came from the Chicago Packers and Zephyrs. In addition, the Syracuse Nationals changed to the Philadelphia 76ers; the Tri-Cities Blackhawks became the Milwaukee Hawks, the St. Louis Hawks, and then the Atlanta Hawks; the Rochester Royals (later the Cincinnati Royals) became the Kansas City Kings and then the Sacramento Kings; and the Buffalo Braves became the San Diego Clippers, and later Los Angeles Clippers. The Wizards would not be the last switch. The Seattle SuperSonics would become the Oklahoma City Thunder a decade later.

The practice occurred more often among American Basketball Association teams. Denver changed from the Rockets to the Nuggets, the San Antonio Spurs emerged from the Texas Chaparrals, and the New Jersey Americans moved through the New York Nets to become the New Jersey Nets. Other team changes included the Anaheim Amigos becoming the Los Angeles Stars and then the Utah Stars; the New Orleans Buccaneers becoming the Memphis Pros, the Tams and Sounds, and then the Baltimore Claws; the Pittsburgh Pipers becoming the Condors; the San Diego Conquistadors becoming the Sails; the Houston Mavericks becoming the Carolina Cougars and then the Spirits of St. Louis; the Minnesota Muskies becoming the Miami Floridians; and, of course, the Oakland Oaks became the Washington Capitals and then the Virginia Squires.

The 1997 NBA Draft held little promise for Washington. As mentioned earlier, the team had to forfeit its first-round selection to keep its free agent signings after the Juwan Howard situation. This was the second year in a row that the team did not have a first-round choice, limiting its ability to improve. Perhaps the team felt better after reading an analysis of the NBA draft in a sporting magazine. Teams base selections on intensive scouting, private workouts, psychiatric testing, and other checks, yet as the president of the Toronto Raptors, Isaiah Thomas, conceded, "You're still guessing."[40]

Of the 278 players drafted from 1992 to 1996, 184 were in the NBA, or 66%; however, the players did not necessarily remain with the team that drafted them. Only a little more than 20%, or 17 of the 80 top ten draftees over the same period, remained with their original team. League officials found the movement disconcerting, because they believed that a player remained more appealing to fans and was a greater marketing asset if he becomes identified with a specific franchise. Washington embodied many of these issues. Of the team's 10 picks during the course of these five years, seven were in the league. Half, or two of their top picks, remained with the team, and team officials experienced worry over losing a potential face of the franchise. They bemoaned the trading of Tom Gugliotta because he was a fan favorite and experienced fan wrath during the free agent negotiations with Juwan Howard.

The Wizards had two draft picks in the second round. They selected God Shammgod and Predrag Drobnjak. Shammgod played guard for two years at Providence College but lasted only 20 games with the team. Drobnjak, a center from Montenegro, elected to play professional basketball in Turkey for four years. The Wizards eventually traded him to Seattle in the summer of 2001. As disappointing as the draft seemed, Washington again placed in the middle of the pack. Ten selections never played a big-league game, and the 20 contests that Shammgod played outpaced four other selections.

Washington made a few middling acquisitions from the free-agent market. The most successful involved signing Terry Davis to a $272,500 contract. The forward and center played with Miami and Dallas, having two decent seasons out of seven. The Lakers, Hornets, and Magic made three of the high-price signings. Essentially, Washington went into the new season with the team that lost in the first-round of the playoffs; however, Juwan Howard had attended the first game of the NBA Finals at the United Center. He said, "I'm just here to watch and learn. I'm hoping some day our team will mature into a contender."[41] Since Bernie Bickerstaff helped the team increase its leadership and toughness, such improvement seemed quite probable. The coach expected that last year's seasoning would help the team blossom and bring the charged atmosphere to the MCI Center when they moved in late December. Prognosticators expected the improvement as well. The new arena contained a new practice facility and weight room, which provided the team with an innovative training environment for better conditioning.

This season of celebrations did not start well. Center Gheorghe Muresan stretched the tendon in his right ankle at the beginning of season. He went on to miss the entire 1997–1998 season. Bernie Bickerstaff included Lorenzo

Williams in the starting lineup, with Calbert Cheaney, Rod Strickland, Chris Webber, and Juwan Howard, and the team lost three of their first five games. Using Harvey Grant, and then Terry Davis, the team struggled through a six-game losing streak that put them at four wins and 10 defeats. At the final game at USAir Arena, the team honored the 11 finest players to wear a Bullets uniform. The group included Walt Bellamy, Earl Monroe, Wes Unseld, and Bobby Dandridge. Chicago overcame a 17-point deficit to win. The ceremony continued in downtown Washington with the opening of the MCI Center. President William J. Clinton, D.C. mayor Marion Barry, and NBA commissioner David Stern helped usher in the new era. "This is a day I will never, ever forget," Abe Pollin said.[42] His team went on to defeat Seattle.

Current events prompted sports reporters and columnists to wonder if the new arena was a testament to the league's growth or it's excess. Golden State Warrior Latrell Sprewell had recently threatened and then put his hands around the neck of coach P. J. Carlesimo. While not condoning the act, Wizard's guard Rod Strickland explained how he understood Sprewell's feelings. A fight in a hotel where the Wizards were staying between Strickland and Tracy Murray prompted the team to fine both men $250,000 but also spread more bad news. The NBA had been hypermarketing its superstars for nearly two decades and promoting a wholesome image. The league endured additional headaches from a special report on NBA players and their use of drugs, particularly marijuana. Arrests involving Allen Iverson, Isaiah Rider, and Marcus Camby illuminated the use of the drug, which some players and agents estimated to be used by nearly 70% of players. Some NBA players lead a fast lifestyle that included going out to clubs, drinking, and many opportunities for sexual activity.

A six-game winning streak enabled the Wizards to climb above the .500 mark for the first time all year, but the team did not turn the proverbial corner. They fell behind early in Houston and lost. They then went to their division rival, the New Jersey Nets, and blew the big lead they built in the first quarter, as Keith Van Horn torched them for 32 points. The Wizards' 16–16 record at the close of New Year's Eve left them five and a half games behind the Atlantic Division leaders, the Miami Heat. The New Year barely changed things for the team. Washington won three games in a row and then lost three in a row, and then won two and lost one, settling for a 5–5 record, when news broke about one of the Wizards' franchise players.

A policeman in Landover, Maryland, had pulled over a speeding car. On his way to practice at the MCI Center, Chris Webber was pulled over and appeared to be driving without a license and registration. An additional search revealed that the forward had marijuana in his possession. Charged with resisting arrest, assault, possession of marijuana, and other traffic-related violations, Webber played later that evening in the loss to Portland.

The team's other two stars had already encountered problems with the law. A month into the first season, after signing his new contract, Juwan Howard had a driving while under the influence violation, and Rod Strickland faced the same charges before the beginning of the 1997–1998 season. During the current season, Howard chose not to turn up for the filming of the team video and an autograph session. Strickland came late to practices and games and ate a poor diet, which raised issues about his longevity as a player. As many in the Washington area knew, Prince Georges County police had a problematic reputation with some of their citizens, particularly African Americans, whom they have been known to profile and give a difficult time to on occasion. The eventual exoneration of Webber for most of the charges illustrated this.[43]

The court did not offer a sanctuary for the players or a distraction from the problems for the fans that were coming in larger numbers. The new arena drew the largest crowd in franchise history, more than 800,000, 100,000 more than the previous highs. Spectators saw a team that continued winning a few, then losing a few, getting to a season-high of three games over .500 in early March and again in late March. Fans booed relentlessly, frequently targeting Webber after his run-in with police authorities.

After defeating the Nets, the Wizards gained possession of the final playoff spot. The eighth seed would again result in having to play the Bulls, on their way to a 62-win season. They trailed the New York Knicks for the seventh playoff spot by two games. The Wizards proceeded to lose four games in a row to forfeit their chance at the seventh spot. After rebounding to win two games, including beating the Orlando team also involved in the battle for the eighth seed, the Montgomery County Attorney's Office released news that a woman had filed sexual assault complaints against Juwan Howard and Chris Webber stemming from incidents that reportedly occurred during a party at Howard's house. Wizards' officials released public statements that recognized the seriousness of the charges and stated that they would await the court process. The players held these get-togethers at their homes to stay out of the clubs, where opportunists could try and take advantage of their celebrity and monetary situation. Unfortunately, the private home offered its own possibilities for taking advantage. Tracy Murray stated that these were difficult times and that his heart went out to the guys, who were some of the nicest men. A lot of players faced these circumstances, and they could make one paranoid.[44]

The Wizards went to Chicago and lost to the mighty Bulls. They returned home for games with the lowly Detroit Pistons and the strong Atlanta

Hawks. Unfortunately, Strickland tore a thigh muscle, putting him in street clothes for the final games of the season. Two games behind the Nets and tied with Orlando, the Wizards needed to win both home games. Detroit used a 14–0 run to take a 26–12 lead after the first quarter. Bickerstaff earned an ejection two minutes before halftime while arguing an offensive foul call, and Detroit raised its 23-point lead to 31 as they went to the visitor's locker room. The 102–83 victory earned the Wizards boos and catcalls from their fans and derailed their playoff hopes. From Coach Bickerstaff's perspective, "The team was hurt by a lot of guys who were paid but didn't play because of injuries."[45]

The expectations placed upon the team at the beginning of the year turned out misplaced. There was little that was spectacular about the team's performance during the season. Washington ranked 14th in field goal percentage, and opposing teams scored above the league average on them. They ranked slightly above average in rebounding and not committing turnovers but shot poorly at the free throw line. Their biggest discovery was the play of center Ben Wallace (figure 9.5), who they signed as a free agent. Tracy Murray improved his game as well, but both Chris Webber and Rod Strickland dropped slightly during the last season, and Juwan Howard's play fell more precipitously.[46]

The First to Go

The team's leadership could reportedly be heard saying that they had to separate these guys. The question was which one to get rid of. Certain teams in the league followed the practice of consulting their key players before making this decision. They could find out what it was like playing with the guys. Chris Webber could get the team a triple-double, but his play also made everyone better. With him, the team had playmakers at the post and at point. Juwan Howard could provide a 19 and 10 (points and rebounds), but his skills generated plays for himself more than for teammates. In actuality, the team could have chosen to trade one of their frontcourt men, or Calbert Cheaney or Rod Strickland, who was coming up for a contract negotiation. They decided to make a move before the legal issues with Webber and Howard had been resolved. They were resolved in the players' favor also. Wes Unseld traded Chris Webber to the Sacramento Kings for guard Mitch Richmond and center Otis Thorpe. Webber led the Wizards in points and rebounds and finished second on the team in assists and was high up in the rankings for field goal percentage. He was also one of the team's few three-point shooting threats.

Figure 9.5. Ben Wallace contests at the rim.
Courtesy Steve Lipofsky, www.basketballphoto.com.

Chris Webber went on to provide the Kings with four years of very high performance out of six seasons. Already in his mid-30s when he arrived in Washington, Mitch Richmond never reached his career-average level of performance. His best season came near to his averages in field goal percentage. Thirty-six-year-old Otis Thorpe played one season with the Wizards before signing a free-agent contract with the Miami Heat. While slipping on his rebounding averages, he shot at his career field goal percentage and gave the team a good season that still measured far short of what he did during his prime. Miami Heat coach Pat Riley observed that, "The Sacramento Kings got exactly what they wanted," noting that Miami was unable to provide an All-Star like Webber when they were trying to trade for Richmond.[47] The Wizards lost a great deal with this trade. Strickland noted at the time that, "They traded the wrong guy."[48] Bickerstaff, Murray, and others simply refer to the deal as "the trade" and cite it as the end of the team's chances to be great.[49]

For the third draft in a row, the Wizards did not have a selection in the first round. They chose two slots earlier than the year before, at number 43 in round two. Wes Unseld and staff selected a local player from Georgetown University, Jahidi White. The forward/center played five years with the team. One player drafted later by Dallas, point guard Greg Buckner, did have higher and more sustained peaks of value than White.

These would be among the last transactions occurring in the league. Since March, when the owners reopened the Collective Bargaining Agreement, they and the National Basketball Player's Association (NBPA) argued over the percentage of gross receipts that players should receive. Many owners claimed to either be losing money, or, as Abe Pollin put it, not getting the return that their investment in the team warranted. After the sides failed to reach an agreement, the owners locked the players out on June 22. The focus of their battle remained on the division of profits and never switched to improving the competitive balance in the league.

Abe Pollin played a key role as one of the members on the owner's committee. The group asserted that the 57% the players received as their share of the league profits amounted to too much. The players' union wondered how the teams could be losing money and requested to see the books. Only the Celtics and Spurs provided data that showed Boston doing fine and San Antonio losing a small amount. Indeed, certain teams, including the Wizards, Knicks, Bulls, 76ers, Pistons, and Trail Blazers, could shift revenue away from the team's treasury and move the money to the arena's account. These revenues included naming rights to the arena, premium seats, signage, catering, and theme activities. A *Forbes* magazine study of teams indicated that 10

NBA teams actually lost money, while 16 teams claimed to have lost money. During one moment in the negotiations, Michael Jordan suggested to Pollin that if he lost money with the Wizards, he should sell the team. Pollin got angry and needed Commissioner Stern to calm him down. "I'm not going to let Michael Jordan or anybody else tell me to sell my team," Pollin told an interviewer, retaining his angry tone weeks later.[50]

The owners made requests for several changes to the salary cap, including a ceiling on individual salaries. In addition, they sought the elimination of the Larry Bird exception and a rookie pay scale. While their requested changes in the agreement affected all players, each specific change only hurt the prospects of certain players. The overall ceiling would damage most of the players' salaries, but the Bird exception limit would only damage things for the superstars. The rookie changes obviously hurt the entry-level players. The players opposed the cap limits and elimination of the Bird exception. The owners then proposed a 50% tax on a team's spending greater than $2.6 million on a player's salary and a 100 to 150% tax on salaries above $10 million.

The players and their union made counterproposals with the assistance of their agents. By 1998, the league had 252 agents as registered representatives of various players, and they were far from the talent agents that used to negotiate contracts. These men and some women, brought law and economics skills, along with the strength of major corporations, to the players' side. The NPBA responded to the changes for the Bird exception with a proposal for a tax to start at a salary above $18 million, which would affect two teams, the Bulls, because of Michael Jordan, and the Knicks, due to Patrick Ewing. Their next proposal contained a lower tax rate than the owners wanted and recommended that the money be redistributed to those teams with the lowest revenue. Such a plan would increase the competitive balance of the sport. The owners rejected the proposal outright.

After never losing a game to labor difficulties in 52 years, the NBA cancelled the first two weeks of the season in mid-October. A week later, an arbitrator ruled that the owners did not have to pay players that had guaranteed contracts, hurting the players' cause. Meanwhile, the lockout did not damage the owners' wallets, because they continued to receive television revenue despite the absence of the games. The new contract with NBC reaped them $1.75 billion during a four-year span, while TNT/TBS earned the league another $890 million during the same period. The television and league executives' concerns over which players could be marketed to replace Michael Jordan obviously did not hurt the value of the league that significantly. Kobe Bryant, guard, and Shaquille O'Neal, center, both of the Los Angeles Lakers, appeared as two probabilities.

Hostilities increased between the sides as November and December passed. The sides did not come close to reaching an agreement. Just before Christmas, Commissioner Stern announced that the entire season would be eliminated if the two sides did not reach an agreement by January 7, 1999.

Schisms erupted among the different groups of players. Most of the players could not afford to go without pay checks. This was particularly true for the journeymen of the league, who counted on earning the minimum yearly salary. The NBPA membership pushed for its leadership to reach an agreement with the owners. On the final day before the season was to be eliminated, the two sides reached an agreement. The new Collective Bargaining Agreement capped players' salaries at between $9 million and $14 million, based upon years of service in the league. A pay scale based upon draft position scaled back the salary costs of new players. Even though the union achieved the retention of the Bird exception, new maximum annual pay raises put limits on it. The minimum salary rose to $287,500, resulting in a $15,000 raise.

The biggest change under the league's new Collective Bargaining Agreement involved the institution of a maximum salary. For the first time, teams would face a limit on what they could pay a single player. Michael Jordan had established a record salary of $35 million. The remaining members of the team made $25 million. The league's team owners thought the situation was untenable, so they pushed for this ceiling. The agreement contained an elaborate formula that based the salary limit upon the number of years of service a player had in the NBA. The lower limit started at $9 million, or 25% of the salary cap, and increased by approximately $20 million for a 10-year veteran in the sixth year of the agreement.[51]

Additional aspects to the new agreement included new "average" and "median" salary cap exemptions that enabled teams to sign one player per category regardless of their cap position. These changes capped the potential earnings in 1995 and 1996 of the players who would have made much more money as free agents under the former system. The agreement also limited the payouts of both those players due to receive balloon payments in the 1998–1999 season and the high salary draftees who did not remain in the NBA. The owners and union also changed the NBA drug policy. Beginning with the 1999–2000 season, players could be tested for the use of marijuana. In the spirit of equal treatment, coaches and other team personnel could also be tested. "I couldn't be happier," said Larry Brown, the 76ers' head coach. "I think it's great for the league, especially with the fact that all on-court personnel have to be a part of it." Point guard Eric Snow added, "Why not? If it's illegal, it's illegal. . . . There may be a lot of people [who] feel differently than I do. But that's how I see it."[52]

Agent David Falk, who played a significant role with the NBPA during the lockout, returned to his duties representing individual clients. The Wizards' guard Rod Strickland received an offer from the team of three years for $30 million. "I don't think he'll be back here," Falk told the Washington media. Falk explained that he would explore other options with four or five other teams interested in his client. Strickland would make the most money with Washington. To maximize his salary and play with one of the other teams, Strickland needed the Wizards' executives to decide to sign the guard and then trade him. A sign and trade deal was not at all unusual, but Wes Unseld and Abe Pollin would need to see how the deal would be advantageous to their team.[53]

Nearly 200 other players sat on the free-agent market. The Wizards eventually released Gheorghe Muresan, so they needed a center and could have bid on Vlade Divac, Isaac Austin, Chris Dudley, and perhaps a few others. Several intriguing small forwards existed, including Rick Fox and Clifford Robinson. According to the player ranking system that accompanied the preseason projections for every team, these two positions and the bench appeared quite weak for Washington, with Juwan Howard at power forward, the third lowest among the starters. The Wizards did not make a powerful new acquisition.

The lockout gave the league a black eye in terms of image and hurt its product. The team made a move to address these concerns, as they purchased a full-page ad in the *Washington Post* announcing their 10-point contract with their fans. The team owners stationed players outside the MCI Center to meet the crowd coming in to see an intersquad scrimmage and express their appreciation for the fans' support. As the crowd watched the game, many made their feelings clear with frequent chants of, "We want Rod!" The point guard star averaged almost 18 points and 11 assists a game during the previous season; however, he received a drunken driving conviction, missed team functions, and threw up on the bench before games because he gulped fast food down.

The Strickland–Wizard negotiations featured both sides providing the public with its broadsides against the other. Seemingly, the public cared more about on-court performance than off-court circumstances. Their inexperience did not allow them to see possible connections between the two. Unseld recognized these connections and sought to hold firm on only three guaranteed years and two more based on performance measurements; however, Pollin suggested that his general manager sweeten the deal, so the sides agreed to $30 million for three years. The fourth year included performance incentives but guaranteed another $5 million.

The Wizards engaged in a more public negotiation with Strickland than did most teams with their free-agent players, but they faced the same pressure to pay more and overspend on free agents that other teams in the league did. Contracts with a restricted free agent like Strickland at least had a ceiling. The salaries of unrestricted free agents, even with the revised salary cap system, still rose, as at least a few teams had sufficient money to overspend on an individual player's salary.

The experts viewed the Wizards as a playoff contender, but only with Strickland at point. Maybe Richmond would bring outside shooting that opened up the middle for Howard. Maybe Cheaney and Murray would go on hot streaks. The team had a weak center and a bench lacking depth. The veterans, like many around the league, lacked conditioning; however, only Bickerstaff put his team through three-a-days. Sore players and aching bodies seemed to be his major accomplishment. League officials squeezed 50 games into a shortened span of time, forcing youngsters to learn quickly and veterans to play without proper rest.

While every team felt the toughness of the condensed schedule, the Wizards had to adjust to a reshaping of the team on the court. Everyone had to adjust to having two new guys, including starter Mitch Richmond. Juwan Howard found that both his playing and feelings had changed without having his friend, Chris Webber, on the team. In addition, he had slipped from being the city's darling to the city's most hated. Coaches and teammates could not understand the quickness and intenseness of this switch. "Why did the fans get mad at him, he had the leverage, and so he made the money. Did they expect him to turn it down?" Bernie Bickerstaff asked.[54] Fans went overboard in their expression. One home game coming out of the tunnel, a player was hit in the head, as a fan threw a quarter intended to hit Howard. "It wasn't a great season," Rod Strickland noted.[55] Bickerstaff summed up the situation as more than basketball and partly going off-kilter in terms of cohesiveness of the organizational philosophy.

Before the start of the season in February, the team signed three little-known free agents. Two had marginal careers, and the third, Jeff McInnis, a young guard whom Denver drafted and released, required two more years of experience before he could blossom into a good player during three of his next four seasons. The Wizards started out playing .500 basketball but then endured two four-game losing streaks, as Wes Unseld fired Bernie Bickerstaff. Some said that the coach was too tense. Calbert Cheaney noted that, "In some cases, it did get a little tight."[56] Many players felt baffled by the coach's novel rotations, which included playing a starter for five minutes in the beginning and then leaving him on the bench for the remainder of the game.

The team tended to give games away in the fourth quarter. Bickerstaff sealed his fate when he commented that Miami was a better team than Washington. Unseld said, "The personnel we have should be in the playoffs."[57] Miami finished with the best record in the Eastern Conference during the regular season. Assistant coach Jim Brovelli took over the 13–19 team. The media projected that they would need to win 13 of their final 18 games to make the playoffs. Instead, Brovelli guided them to a 5–13 record.

The two coaches struggled in motivating the team. Regardless of Unseld's assessment, the team finished in next to last place in the Atlantic Division. They ranked 17th out of 29 teams in total offense and lower, 20th, in total defense. Cheaney finished among the bottom of small forwards and played so poorly that Howard was often moved from his natural power forward position to start at small forward. The team shot above average from two-point range but ranked next to the bottom in three-point shooting, and near the bottom in free throw shooting, steals, and blocks. Even the spectator turnout placed the team among the bottom grouping, despite the new arena.

The first major change in the off-season came among the ownership. Abe Pollin discovered that neither of his sons was interested in running his sports businesses. The Wizards' patriarch "did not want a repeat of the mess the Redskins went through with their [ownership] transition."[58] Pollin also wanted to make sure that the basketball team would stay in Washington. He made a deal to sell his hockey team and a minority interest in Washington Sports, which owns the Wizards; Ticketmaster; and the arena to a group headed by Ted Leonsis. An executive at American Online, Leonsis was a big sports buff who lived in the Washington, D.C., metropolitan area. The players who met him really liked him and thought that he was on top of things. Leonsis admitted that he planned to have little input in the running of the Wizards. He commented that, "We have our hands full with the hockey team."[59]

For the first time in a few years, the team held a first-round selection in the 1999 NBA Draft. While there were several good players selected ahead of Washington's number seven position, including Elton Brand and Lamar Odom, the Wizards chose University of Connecticut star Richard Hamilton to fill the outside shooter and small forward void. Some experts thought Hamilton too small to play the small forward position and projected him as a backup shooting guard. Guards Andre Miller and Jason Terry and forward Shawn Marion remained on the board and may have been valuable choices; however, the team already had the positions that they would play filled, at least for the current season. With their second-round selection, the Wizards picked center Calvin Booth. Unfortunately, he did not realize his lofty expectations. While there were few other intriguing picks on the board when Washington made its choice, the San Antonio Spurs, with a pick 22 positions later, found the draft's major sleeper, Manu Ginobili.

With several players opting for free agency, Wes Unseld faced a busy off-season. Calbert Cheaney declared free agency, and the general manager decided to let him find another team. He eventually signed a one-year deal with the Boston Celtics. For the second year in a row, the off-season spurred a contractual standoff with one of their starting guards. Mitch Richmond declared that he wanted to leave Washington. The Wizards tried to execute a sign-and-trade deal with Miami, Seattle, Golden State, or Sacramento, but none could fit his contract under their salary cap limit. As a result, Richmond signed a $40 million, four-year contract with the Wizards.

The new contract made the 36-year-old the highest-paid shooting guard in the league. Richmond earned $1 million more per year than Reggie Miller, Kobe Bryant, and Ray Allen. Miller shot much more accurately from the field than Richmond, with an effective field goal percentage of 52%, as opposed to 46%; had the same assist percentage; and made fewer turnovers. Bryant also bested Richmond with 48% in effective field goals, and he had a much higher rate of assists and rebounds. Allen shot at 51% and had a higher rate of assists and rebounds.

The general manager also signed a few free agents. Former Seattle SuperSonics forward Aaron Williams represented the splashiest signing. The Wizards offered him a one-year deal worth $1,100,000. Guard Reggie Jordan and guard/forward Gerard King signed for a tad more than the minimum salary. After their stints with the Wizards, neither would go on to play with another NBA team.[60]

The biggest move that Wes Unseld made during the year involved a trade for a big center. Unseld sought the Orlando Magic's Isaac "Ike" Austin, whom the Magic signed as a free agent a year before. The 30-year-old Austin had an adequate year with Orlando and only two good seasons out of seven in the league. Two years before, the Los Angeles Clippers had traded for the center and hoped he would strengthen them in the middle; however, his inconsistency in scoring and rebounding did not help stem the team's losses. Unseld made the deal, giving up the youngster Ben Wallace, the team's leading rebounder. The Magic also received guards Tim Legler and Jeff McInnis and forward Terry Davis. One of the Wizard beat reporters wrote that getting Ike Austin looked like a good move, referring to him as a legit center. Despite the four-for-one player nature, the Wizards gained about $300,000 in team salary, as Austin earned $4.8 million annually.

The Magic profited both on the court and in future salary from the deal. The team waived Davis and McInnis and let Legler go as a free agent. McInnis signed with the Los Angeles Clippers and went on to have four strong years playing with the Clippers and later the Cavaliers. Ben Wallace gave Orlando a strong season before being traded to the Detroit Pistons for forward Grant Hill. Unfortunately for Washington, Wallace became an All-Star center four years in a row, six monster years in total, including winning multiple Defensive Player of the Year Awards.

This revised team also had a new head coach. The Wizard's leadership hired the Detroit Pistons' assistant coach, Gar Heard. A power forward who played with five teams during the 1970s and early 1980s, Heard had a few good years and then became an assistant coach. During the 1992–1993 season, Heard inherited a Dallas Mavericks team that won two and lost 27 under head coach Richie Adubato and finished with a 9–44 record. Heard told fans that the Wizards had the talent but teams locked in on Rod, Mitch, and Juwan, and that shut down the offense. The Wizards would bring more motion into the offense under Heard's first, and only, season, and hoped that interior screens would free up players for shots.

The Wizards won their first game of the season. Juwan Howard scored 21 points and Rod Strickland had 10 assists, while strong bench play in the second quarter enabled the team to send the MCI Center crowd home happy. Then they lost seven in a row, including blowouts by the Nets and Pacers. After winning four of their next seven games, the Wizards opened up the month of December with a six-game losing streak. Ike Austin played his way to the bench. Heard inserted 1998's draft pick, Jahidi White, who provided a little offense and some decent defense. The team also gave its most recent draft choice, Richard Hamilton, the chance to gain some playing experience. The end of the month proved no better, as two tough losses to the Knicks and Cavaliers left the team with a 10–20 record.

After the first two months of the current season, the Wizards ranked among the league leaders in declining attendance. Overall, league attendance dropped 1.5%. Washington suffered a 16% decline, from more than 16,600 on average in 1998, to less than 14,000 in 1999–2000. Only Vancouver and Orlando dropped more, and the Nets and SuperSonics rounded out the top five.[61] While some blamed the lack of star power, others noted the feeling among fans of continuous losing. A third group pointed to the cost of going to a game. Twisting the NBA into the "National Bunco Association," columnist Rick Reilly noted that the cost of attending a game rose 11% from the previous year. A family of four paid $266 to see the average NBA game ($348 in 2010 dollars).[62]

The circumstances on the court had not changed. Even with the new coach and expensive players, the Wizards lost frequently. The fan base declined. The team drew significantly less than they needed to be financially successful. Behind the scenes, the ownership prepared for a major change in leadership, which they hoped would bring success on the court and fans to the stands.

Notes

1. "The NBA," *Sports Illustrated*, March 4, 1991, 11.

2. This and other details and quotes by Tom Hammonds were obtained during an interview with the author, March 1, 2012.

3. David Aldridge, "Exception Sought for Williams," *Washington Post*, January 3, 1992, D6; David Aldridge, "Bullets Seeks Answers in Season's 2nd Half," *Washington Post*, February 11, 1992, C4; Leonard Shapiro, "King and Williams: The What-If Factor,"*Washington Post*, March 2, 1992, C1.

4. This and other details and quotes by Don MacLean were obtained during an interview with the author, March 19, 2012.

5. David Aldridge, "Under Losses' Weight Struggle to Keep Hope Afloat," *Washington Post*, April 10, 1993, D1.

6. This and other details and quotes by Brent Price were obtained during an interview with the author, February 25, 2012.

7. This and other details and quotes by Brent Price were obtained during an interview with the author, February 25, 2012.

8. "Diary of a Deal," *Sports Illustrated*, November 7, 1994, 90.

9. "Former Bullet Ellison Joins Celtics," *Washington Post*, August 2, 1994, E1.

10. Mark Asher, "Bullets Anticipate Restructuring to Sign Howard," *Washington Post*, August 20, 1994, C1.

11. Richard Justice, "Bullets' Fab Day Nets Webber, Howard," *Washington Post*, November 18, 1994, C1; Larry Platt, *Keeping It Real: A Turbulent Season at the Crossroads with the NBA* (New York: Avon Books, 1999), 63–65.

12. David Aldridge, "Bullets Finally See the Light," *Washington Post*, November 20, 1994, D13.

13. "A Three-Way Jump Ball in the NBA," *Business Week*, September 4, 1995, 58; Robert Bradley, "Labor Pains Nothing New to the NBA," Association for Professional Basketball Research, www.apbr.org/labor.html (retrieved October 9, 2009).

14. Mario R. Sarmento, "The NBA on Network Television: A Historical Analysis," Thesis, University of Florida, 1998, 79–80, appendix B.

15. Edward Cone, "Playing the Global Game," *Forbes*, January 23, 1989, 90; "Slam Dunk," *Forbes*, March 13, 1995, 164; Carl Desens, "The NBA's Fast Break Overseas," *Business Week*, December 5, 1994, 94.

16. Michael Wilbon, "After Bullets Article," *Washington Post*, November 27, 1994, D1.

17. Randall Lane, "Prepackaged Celebrity," *Forbes*, December 20, 1994, 86; James Ketelsen, "Olajuwater," *Forbes*, March 27, 1995, 18.

18. MacLean interview, March 19, 2012.

19. MacLean interview, March 19, 2012; Bernie Bickerstaff, interview by author, March 17, 2012.

20. Peter Perl, "Full-Court Press," *Washington Post*, April 21, 1996, 27.

21. "MCI Arena Deal," *Washington Post*, April 21, 1996, 10.

22. Samuel Davis, "Rasheed Wallace Grows, On and Off the Court," *Philadelphia Tribune*, November 7, 1995, 8_c.

23. Brent Price interview, February 25, 2012.

24. Jerry Bembry, "Nash Quits as GM of Bullets," *Baltimore Sun*, May 1, 1996 http://articles.baltimoresun.com/1996-05-01/sports/1996122017_1_nash-bullets-omalley (retrieved October 16, 2010).

25. Raad Cawthon, "Bristow to Interview for Sixers GM Job," *Philadelphia Inquirer*, May 1, 1996.

26. Jack McCallum, "Going, Going, Gone," *Sports Illustrated*, May 20, 1996, 52.

27. Brent Price interview, February 25, 2012.

28. Brent Price interview, February 25, 2012.

29. Clifton Brown, "Howard: 2 Deals, 2 Teams, $200 Million," *New York Times*, August 6, 1996, C1.

30. Clifton Brown. "After Smokes Settles, Questions Surface," *New York Times*, August 12, 1996, C4.

31. Jerry Bembry, "Bullets Get Strickland," *Baltimore Sun*, July 16, 1996. http://articles.baltimoresun.com/1996-07-16/sports/1996198087_1_rod-strickland-bullets-brent-price (retrieved August 18, 2011).

32. This and other details and quotes by Tracy Murray were obtained during an interview with the author, March 12, 2012.

33. Clifton Brown, "Howard Will Remain a Bullet, After All," *New York Times*, August 11, 1996, S5.

34. "Bullets Fire Losing Coach Lyman," *Chicago Tribune*, February 5, 1997. http://articles.chicagotribune.com/1997-02-05/news/9702060067_1_jim-lynam-buzz-braman-general-manager-wes-unseld (retrieved August 18, 2011).

35. Murray interview, March 12, 2012.

36. Ira Berkow, "Jordan Amazes Even Bulls with 55-Point Spectacular," *New York Times*, April 28, 1997, C1.

37. Berkow, "Jordan Amazes Even Bulls with 55-Point Spectacular," C1.

38. Selena Roberts, "Bulls Prevail, But Bullets Go Out Fighting," *New York Times*, May 1, 1997, B22.

39. Phil Taylor, "Clang, Clang, Clang Goes the Ball," *Sports Illustrated*, December 16, 1996, 64.

40. Jackie MacMullen, "Why Bother?" *Sports Illustrated*, June 23, 1997, 50.

41. Jackie MacMullen, "No. 3 Washington Wizards," *Sports Illustrated*, November 10, 1997, 108.

42. Ruben Castaneda, "Wizards Play Final Game on Old Court," *Washington Post*, November 30, 1997, B1.
43. Platt, *Keeping It Real*, 116–17.
44. Platt, *Keeping It Real*, 240–42; Murray interview, March 12, 2012.
45. Bickerstaff interview, March 17, 2012.
46. "1996–97 Washington Bullets Roster and Statistics," Basketball-Reference.com, www.basketball-reference.com/teams/WSB/1997.html (retrieved September 16, 2010).
47. Ira Winderman, "Richmond Trade No Shock to Riley," *Miami Herald*, May 20, 1998, http://articles.sun-sentinel.com/1998-05-20/news/9805190330_1_pat-riley-eric-reid-david-halberstam (retrieved August 15, 2011).
48. Platt, *Keeping It Real*, 272.
49. Bickerstaff interview, March 17, 2012; Murray interview, March 12, 2012.
50. Richard Sandomir, "The N.B.A.'s Senior Owner Speaks Out, and Bluntly," *New York Times*, November 12, 1998, D1.
51. Larry Coon, "Larry Coon's NBA Salary Cap FAQ, 2011 Collective Bargaining Agreement," https://webfiles.uci.edu/lcoon/cbafaq/salarycap.htm (retrieved May 9, 2011).
52. Stephen A. Smith, "NBA's New Drug Policy Being Implemented," *Philadelphia Inquirer*, October 9, 1999.
53. Chris Sheridan, "NBA Lockout Officially Settled," *New Pittsburgh Courier*, February 6, 1999, 7.
54. Bickerstaff interview, March 17, 2012.
55. Michael Lee, "NBA's 50-Game Season," http://www.washingtonpost.com/sports/wizards/nbas-50-game-season-everything-was-just-so-discombobulated/2011/12/03/gIQAdEUCQO_story.html (retrieved January 16, 2012).
56. Joseph White, "Wizards Fire Bickerstaff," *New Pittsburgh Courier*, April 24, 1999, 6.
57. White, "Wizards Fire Bickerstaff," 6.
58. "Pollin Sells Capitals, Part of Wizards," *Seattle Times*), May 12, 1999. http://community.seattletimes.nwsource.com/archive/?date=19990512&slug=2960198 (retrieved July 19, 2011).
59. "Pollin Sells Capitals, Part of Wizards."
60. "Plus: Pro Basketball," *New York Times*, August 19, 1999, 44; "1999 NBA Draft," Basketball-Reference.com, www.basketball-reference.com/draft/NBA_1999.html (retrieved September 26, 2010).
61. Mike Wise, "Empty Seats Are a Concern for the NBA," *New York Times*, December 19, 1999, SP7.
62. Rick Reilly, "National Bunco Association," *Sports Illustrated*, November 22, 1999, 117.

CHAPTER TEN

~

Abe Pollin, Ted Leonsis, Michael Jordan, and the Washington Wizards

The Wizards two owners started the New Year in quiet negotiations with a basketball legend. Michael Jordan retired from the Chicago Bulls in January 1999. He tried to buy into the Charlotte Hornets basketball team and run its operations, but the deal collapsed. The Wizards' leadership took advantage of the opportunity and began conversations with Jordan about coming to Washington to run the Wizards. They believed that he would bring the energy and skills from the court to the executive office. The final weeks of negotiations in January 2000 focused on the size of the ownership stake offered to Jordan and its cost. The former player also needed to clear associations with his agent, David Falk, to satisfy the league officials that no potential conflict of interest would exist.[1]

A New Sheriff in Town

Wes Unseld retained the general manager position as Michael Jordan took over as head of basketball operations. Jordan oversaw the trading, signing, and drafting of players and the running of the entire front-office operations of the team. A large crowd assembled for the announcement of Jordan's position, including Mayor Anthony Williams, who stated, "He will show our children what it takes to be an executive. He will electrify the city."[2] Jordan downplayed the difficulty of the transition from the court to the executive suite. He said, "But this is an easy transition for me. Basketball is my life. I know it inside and out."[3]

Publicly, the National Basketball Association (NBA) expressed its pleasure over having the superstar back in the basketball community. League officials stated that it was a terrific idea. Active general managers generally thought Jordan would be successful. Donnie Walsh of the Indiana Pacers stated, "He knows the players, he knows what it takes to win."[4] Privately, Red Auerbach was not as certain. He asked, "Is he really going to want to do the work you gotta do to rebuild the team? Is he gonna put in the hours, do the scouting, make the phone calls and the tough calls?"[5] A sportswriter also observed that Jordan would not be like Jerry West or Kevin McHale were as general managers and go see college basketball games. He noted that Jordan walked into a difficult situation because of the number of overpaid, underachieving players whose expensive, long-term contracts made them hard to trade.[6]

The new leader offered his assessment of the Wizards' situation, saying, "It's an underachieving team. Everybody is being paid some hefty checks, and I'll be evaluating everybody."[7] Jordan insisted that he would go to practices to view players from that perspective as well. One of the first things he arranged involved firing the coach, Gar Heard. Jordan actually asked Wes Unseld to do the duty while he went to Atlanta to enjoy the pre-Super Bowl festivities. Heard's hard-edged, demanding style did not thrill his veterans, and the team as a whole did not respond to his direction. "It's been tough around here," Rod Strickland said. "The atmosphere hasn't been good."[8] Two of Heard's assistant coaches were also fired, while one assistant remained with the team.

After attempting to hire one coach, a current assistant coach for the Golden State Warriors, and shying away, the Wizards' leadership sought an interim coach. Jordan hired Darrell Walker. The hiring had similarities to hires the Bullets had made in the past. Like Gene Shue and Kevin Loughery, Darrell Walker was a former guard who played with the team he would be taking over. And in his final season as a player, he served as a backup guard on the 1992–1993 Chicago Bulls championship team. The second head coach of the expansion Toronto Raptors, Walker had a rough season and a half before being replaced by one of his own assistants.

The media framed Michael Jordan's job as trading away the underachievers. As the trading deadline for the league neared, rumors and gossip spread. The 24-hour sports news cycle of the ESPN network increased the amount of sports news programming on local and regional sports networks, and the information available on the Internet spurred attention to any activities by teams, real or imagined. Juwan Howard, along with Cleveland's Shawn Kemp, were both linked to deals with the Los Angeles Lakers, only to discover that any possible deal emerged from Internet/talk show discussions and not from discussions among the teams. The number of teams in the league feeling disgruntled with particular players or having a disgruntled player on the roster seemed abnormally high, numbering more than one-third, probably accounting for the high amount of talk and interest in trades. Jordan could not find a trading partner.

The NBA instituted several significant rule changes for the upcoming season. The pace of the game was increased, as the length of timeouts was reduced from 100 to 60 seconds, and, if the offense won a jump ball, they now got only 14 seconds rather than 24 seconds to shoot. Other rule changes reduced the physical nature of the game, including prohibiting defenders from using their bodies to reroute or hold-up an offensive player and banning clutching or grabbing to impede the progress of the screener. Many observed that the league constantly tweaked the rules of the game, trying to create what it imagined to be the product that fans would find most entertaining.[9]

The new Wizards team had long since abandoned the physical nature of the 1980s Bullets, so they were not greatly hindered by the changes. The team improved marginally on the court. Darrell Walker removed rookie Richard Hamilton from the starting lineup. The team rolled off a seven-game losing streak. They returned to the MCI Center with a 15–38 record, and the coach inserted Gerard King in the lineup for Michael Smith. The team traded wins and losses throughout most of the final months of the season and ended up with a 29–53 record. The offense and defense ranked 19th out of 29 teams. They shot the ball from the field at a better rate than in the recent past, particularly from three-point range, but the rebounding, assists, and steals all ranked significantly less than the league average. As had been the case in previous years, teams scored frequently on the Wizards, and the team's defense did not help itself in rebounds, steals, or blocks.

For years, the Wizards ran with a smaller front office than most of the teams in the NBA. Michael Jordan set about making the changes to improve the team's executive staff. He promoted the team's interim coach, Darrell Walker, to director of player personnel. He hired Rod Higgins as the assistant general manager. A lawyer and marketing expert from Nike, Fred Whitfield became the Wizards' assistant for basketball operations and assistant general counsel. This new structure put people in place to make the regular decisions that the team required and provided the head of basketball operations with the ability to narrow his work focus.[10] Would the new personnel take into account some of the possibilities that the expansion of computer technology and the Internet had wrought? Websites like Basketball-Reference.com and 82games.com presented reams of data, not only about the typical statistics, like field goal percentage and rebounds per game, they featured more obscure and significant factors, such as a plus/minus rating about points scored by teams or scored against them when a certain player was on the floor. Some teams had already incorporated some of this knowledge into their review, particularly the Dallas Mavericks and Seattle SuperSonics.

The new structure enabled the team to create the player development staff that other teams already realized that the NBA required. As more and more players came directly from high school basketball or played one or two years of college basketball before entering the NBA, players did not receive training in the game the way they used to through playing four full years in college. The new players joining NBA teams lacked specific skills and experience that drills and game situations in college used to teach. As a result, the teams hired former players to serve as coaches who offered one-on-one instruction to the rookies. These coaches taught the NBA newbies skills, ran drills, and incorporated the drills into the practices to get the rookies to a higher level of understanding of the plays and of the style of game played in the NBA. As the league opted to add rule changes, the revisions to the game would also need to be taught to the entire team.

Jordan needed to address the draft and free agency before the start of the 2000–2001 season. The first Chris Webber trade left the Wizards without a first-round selection. This was certainly where the player personnel staff would earn its money. They spent the majority of their time sorting through the less obvious candidates for the draft, and this required seeing the players perform in person. The observations included watching such reactions as whether a player pouted if he did not like something or if he paid attention to the coach going over the mechanics on his shot. The staff member would then fill out a form after witnessing the performance and then meet with other scouts and staff the week before the draft to reach a consensus.

The team held the sixth pick in round two and selected forward Mike Smith. He played only 17 games with the team and then one year of development league basketball, and he never returned to the NBA. Several compelling players remained on the board. Miami chose guard Eddie House, Houston picked forward Eduardo Najera, Milwaukee selected guard Michael Redd, and Detroit took forward Brian Cardinal. The Wizards did not have any free agents on their roster that they needed to keep and lacked the salary cap room to sign any additional ones.

With Darrell Walker moving into the front office, the Wizards needed to find a new coach. Michael Jordan reportedly had an interest in hiring a successful college coach, and he zeroed in on Mike Jarvis of St. Johns University. Rob Ades, Jarvis's lawyer, stated that Jarvis wanted the job, but not just at any cost. Jarvis sought five years at $3 million a year because the Atlanta

Hawks had just hired the coach at Illinois for that amount. The pair agreed that four years at a guaranteed $2 million would make it worthwhile for Jarvis to make the move. Jordan stunned Ades with an offer of two years at $1 million each. The highest Jordan reached was three years for $1.8 million, and Jarvis turned him down. "With only three years guaranteed, it's too easy to fire a guy after one year, let him take the blame," Ades observed.[11]

Jordan remained fixed on finding a college coach and working on the team's discipline and fundamentals, but college coaches moving to the NBA had not been very successful. Rick Pitino, P. J. Carlesimo, John Calipari, and Jerry Tarkanian had all struggled once they moved up. By mid-June, Jordan had hired Leonard Hamilton, the head coach of the University of Miami, to a five-year, $10 million contract, the contract he would not give to Jarvis.

As the off-season came to a close, Jordan completed the first trade of his career. He sent disgruntled center Ike Austin to the Vancouver Grizzlies for shooting guard Dennis Scott, center Obinna Ekezie, guard Felipe Lopez, and forward Cherokee Parks. Scott retired instead of coming east to play for Washington. A month later, small forward Tracy Murray went into the office, where across the desk were two top 50 of all-time players, and told them that he wanted to be traded. Murray felt he could not go through the inconsistency that came with another head coach, the fifth in his four years on the team. Looking back now, he deems his move a mistake. The team shipped the small forward to the Denver Nuggets for forward Popeye Jones and a second-round draft choice in 2002. Murray had been one of the Wizards' scorers and had a few good seasons with the team. Power forward Jones was a notable scrapper on the boards and a hustler on the court. Jones broke his index finger on his left hand and played in only half of the team's games. Another effort went toward improving the team's traveling circumstances.

By the beginning of the twenty-first century, a league style of travel had developed, and Miami set the standard. Don MacLean recalled that the "Heat were over the top; best plane in league and only stayed at the Four Seasons and . . . they had great arena facilities."[12] Other teams, particularly those on the West Coast, developed sleep regimens and other methods to improve their players' health and the team's performance. Flights would leave after a game, whether in the day or evening, rather than early the next morning, to get to the next city as soon as possible, providing the players with a better opportunity to rest. The teams hired sleep experts to help with this process. Teams kept players' body clocks on the same time that they would be on at home. Practices that would start at 11 a.m. on the West Coast would begin at 2 p.m. on the East Coast. Getting to the game involved two buses, one for the team and one for the traveling media. A separate truck with all the baggage and training equipment trailed behind.

The Wizards found themselves with a 4–11 record just after Thanksgiving. Jordan shipped two of the players he received for Ike Austin (Cherokee Parks and Obinna Ekezie) to the Los Angeles Clippers for their forward, Tyrone Nesby. Nesby had a few poor years, and the Wizards hoped he could regain his form from his rookie season. The revolving door of players on the roster continued all season. The Wizards ended up with 21 players on the roster, an amazingly high number. Nesby became one of several projects that Jordan had in trying to shape a Wizard into a mini-Jordan. Courtney Alexander would become another.

Unfortunately, quantity did not equate to quality. After getting blown out at home against an Atlanta team that had lost its last 22 games on the road, the Wizards lost eight more, but this would not be the only nine-game losing streak on the season. The second one, in mid-January, left the team with a 7–34 record. Leonard Hamilton tried six different lineups, and they usually included Rod Strickland; however, the point guard injured his shoulder and then clashed with team leaders over his work habits. This was the concern that Wes Unseld had expressed during contract negotiations. When Strickland received a drunken driving charge, the team looked to see if they could fulfill the player's wish to be traded. Without a viable option, the team and player negotiated a deal to cut his guaranteed $5 million payment for the final year on his contract down to $2.5 million, and the Wizards waived him.

Chris Whitney replaced Rod Strickland in the lineup, and Richard Hamilton became another regular. Jordan dealt another of the team's long-term troublesome contracts. He shipped Juwan Howard to the Dallas Mavericks, along with center Calvin Booth, for forwards Christian Laettner and Loy Vaught, guards Courtney Alexander and Hubert Davis, center Etan Thomas, and $3 million. Vaught had two years left on a $5 million a year contract and went on to play only 14 games with the Wizards, despite the team having to pay him both years. While everyone thought Howard might benefit from the change of scenery, they saw the removal of his $18.75 million contract as a big gain for the Wizards and thought that the team picked up promising players in Alexander and Thomas. Against all hopes, the player swap did not lead to quick magic, and the Wizards endured several more losing streaks. They ended the season with a 19–63 record.

Hamilton and Jordan met at the close of the season. The coach then submitted his resignation. "I think it's in the best interests of everybody that I allow their progress to move on with me going in another direction," Hamilton said, as he had been thinking about quitting for some time. While many felt surprised or shocked, college basketball commentator Dick Vitale thought that college coaches were used to having total control and that one of their greatest strengths involved exciting players.[13] The NBA negated those strengths, as it is impossible for the 82-game schedule to be played with that kind of intensity. Within days, the team hired former player and coach Doug Collins, who had coached Jordan for three seasons with the Chicago Bulls. Jordan asked Collins to come to Washington and help him by taking over the team. "It was easy, once he said that." Collins noted.[14] The basketball world knew that many found Collins to be anal and overbearing, and he reportedly drove players away from the Pistons when he coached the team.[15]

Coming Out of Retirement

The hiring of Doug Collins spurred speculation that Michael Jordan might come out of retirement. Jordan tried to deny any interest in playing again, but the rumors persisted. Meanwhile, Jordan and his team faced their first college draft with a first-round selection. The team won the lottery and received the first pick of the 2001 draft. The Wizards became the first team ever to select a high school player as the top draft pick overall, when Jordan selected forward Kwame Brown. Two years later, Cleveland would do the same when they chose LeBron James. With the success of such players as Kevin Garnett, Kobe Bryant, and Tracy McGrady coming out of high school, the fears that the player might not be mature enough to handle professional basketball had subsided. The Chicago Bulls made two high school players their selections in the first round of the 2001 draft. Recently, there had been other high school players who had not performed well in the NBA, including Jonathan Bender, Indiana's top pick in 1999, Leon Smith, San Antonio's top pick in the same draft, and Portland's Chris Anstey in 1997. While considering collegiate and European players, draft choices included suppositions regarding how their play against different competition will translate in the NBA, but this process proved more difficult when evaluating high school players.

The numbers of underclassmen coming out of college or not going to college at all and entering the NBA had climbed steadily throughout the 1990s. Three of the first four choices were high school players. Among the first-round selections, there were nearly as many one-and-done (one year of college) players (three) as there were four-year attendees (four).The number of underclassmen among the total drafted climbed to 30, from 23 in 1997. Being a NBA player had become a profession in its own right, with the potential to provide a career and requisite income. Most of the men who reached the level of basketball ability that they would be considered in the draft engaged in little consideration of any other career path, and so they did not need the four years of college to attempt to matriculate in another occupational area. As noted in last chapter, it also did not seem to make sense to learn your basketball trade in college for four years.

The National Collegiate Athletic Association (NCAA) did not fail to take notice of the trend. Men's basketball was an income generator on college campuses, and the organizations and individual universities sensed the need to induce players to stay in college. Many people can name their favorite example of the illegal activities carried out to keep athletes in university programs that schools knew or did not know about, but they lie outside the scope of this book. The NCAA also tried to promote its own attempt to keep players in school. The organization's leadership met and returned with a proposal to provide the elite athletes with a one-time bank loan worth $20,000. The problems with the offer were obvious. Aside from the idea that the money was a loan, it was not very much money. Arizona basketball player Richard Jefferson said, "Heck no," to the question as to whether that loan would entice him to return to play his senior year. The NCAA would have to come up with a lot more than that.[16]

The off-season proved busy for the Wizards' executives. They traded Predrag Drobnjak, the team's second-round draft selection in 1997, to Seattle for forward Bobby Simmons. Jordan and company traded their 2005 first-round draft pick and forward Laron Profit for center Brendan Haywood. The Cleveland Cavaliers selected Haywood with their first pick of the 2001 draft and then shipped him to the Orlando Magic. Mitch Richmond received the final year of his salary but signed on with the Los Angeles Lakers for the 2001–2002 season, his last in the NBA. Jordan also inked two free agents. Jordan signed point guard Tyronn Lue for two years at $1.75 million. The backup, who got some time playing with the Los Angeles Lakers, would be the first point guard off the bench with his new team. Jordan also signed himself to play for $1 million per season. "I am returning as a player to the game I love," Jordan told the media. Abe Pollin assessed the excitement surrounding his team and added, "The greatest player in the history of the game is joining my team, and for that I am extremely honored and pleased."[17]

The news overwhelmed the movement of the Vancouver Grizzlies franchise to Memphis, Tennessee. The league maintained stability for 15 years, but the British Columbian outpost could not succeed. Handicapped by NBA decisions to restrict the ability of the team to land a top draft pick, the Grizzlies proved terrible on the court. The original owner, Arthur Griffiths, also owned the National Hockey League Vancouver Canucks but sold both after cost overruns in building a new arena. The new owner vowed to keep the basketball team in Vancouver, but then he sold to Michael Heisley, who also promised to keep the team in the city; however, after making claims of suffering millions in losses, the new owner found a new location in Memphis.[18]

Michael Jordan had worked hard to return to playing condition. After overcoming a pair of broken ribs, he joined the Wizards' rookies and free agents in a mini-camp in July. The announcement of his return had to be delayed due to the events of September 11, 2001, with the destruction of the World Trade Center in Manhattan, damage to the Pentagon in Virginia, and the loss of thousands of lives. Since rules prohibited players from owning a portion of teams, Jordan needed to sell his holdings in the team to Ted Leonsis. Sales of season tickets and game tickets greatly increased, as everyone wanted to see the legend play again.

Fans had the chance to enjoy number 23 driving his 38-year-old body through the NBA grind. With the goal of getting the team back to the playoffs, Jordan worked hard at stirring the competitive instincts of his teammates during workouts and practices. He started as the team's shooting guard. But the Wizards' lost eight in a row to fall to 2–9. Coming into the locker room and yelling at the team, "We stink," did little to endear him or build a sense of trust. Neither did taking more than a few shots expecting to regain his old form, which proved impossible, as his legs had lost their spring. The situation led to Richard Hamilton offering the observation to the media that, "There are other guys in this locker room that can play too."[19]

During the second month of the season, a road trip through Texas ignited the lineup of Michael Jordan, Richard Hamilton, Christian Laettner, Jahidi White, and Chris Whitney to win five in a row. Despite losing Laettner to injury, the team won four more to move above .500. The nine-game winning streak had everyone pleased.

The team appeared to be making a concerted run. They snagged the eighth and final spot, and Jordan focused on imparting basketball wisdom to his teammates. Coach Collins stated that Popeye Jones, Brendan Haywood, and Jahidi White gave the Wizards an inside foundation for the post–Michael era. Then the team endured four losses, including two disappointing ones in mid-January. They hovered around .500 until a five-game winning streak in early February boosted the team to 26 wins and 21 losses. The team trailed Boston in the Atlantic Division race for second place by two games. Jordan averaged 25 points a game during the streak, with additional scoring from Chris Whitney, Richard Hamilton, and Popeye Jones. Jones and some of the team's youngsters, including Jahidi White, Tyrone Nesby, and Brendan Haywood, provided the team with rebounding.

Washington had not been the focus of much of the NBA marketing throughout the 1980s and early 1990s. The signing of Juwan Howard and the trade for Chris Webber in the middle 1990s gave the team youth and appeal. The team saw a rise in the national sports coverage it received and the appearance on national television, but the blip of being a playoff team proved short-lived, as the team disintegrated. The return of Michael Jordan to the court vaulted the team to national attention. ESPN carried the team six times and drew higher than its average ratings (1.27 to 1.2). TNT aired the Wizards seven times and garnered a 1.22 rating over its usual 1.2. Jordan's comeback placed the Wizards in the limelight, and people wanted to see things unfold. As the Boston Celtics' Antoine Walker argued, opponents noticed that the best part of Jordan's return for the Wizards was that the team got the maximum games you can play on TNT and NBC, and they played in front of sold-out crowds every night.[20]

The team went out to the West Coast and lost two of three and went on to lose seven more in a row. During that span, Washington also lost Jordan. He could no longer endure the pain emanating from his knees, which resulted from a torn lateral meniscus cartilage, and he went into surgery. While the Wizards played a few of the best teams in the NBA, they lost a home-and-home series to a weak Miami team and one to the struggling Bulls. Two wins raised their record to 29–30, but they promptly went on the road and lost five in a row to fall below .500 for good. Despite the tailspin, the Wizards remained in playoff contention. The Milwaukee Bucks had the fourth seed, with a 36–27 record, but they went on to experience a few losing streaks that took them out of contention. The Magic and Knicks had 34–30 records, the Pacers were 32–32, the Hornets were 31–33, and the Raptors had a 30–34 record. The Wizards 29–35 record left them in 10th position with 18 games remaining on the schedule.

The remaining six games of their long road trip resulted in three wins and two losses. The final game pitted the team against the Toronto Raptors. The Wizards had a game advantage on Toronto and trailed the teams with the last playoff spots, which included Indiana, Charlotte, and Orlando, by two, three, and four games, respectively. Jordan played in only a few of the previous road games, as he injured his knee and was coming off the bench against Toronto. The Raptors took an eight-point lead going into halftime. The Wizards played tough defense in the third quarter and cut the home team's lead down to two points. Both teams shot well in the final period. Laettner, Nesby, and Hamilton shot well, and Whitney and Jordan contributed 13 and 14 points, respectively, but the Wizards lost by one. The team responded well to the tough loss and won their first two home games. The remaining two home games were against two very good teams, the Dallas Mavericks and Los Angeles Lakers. Both defeated the Wizards handily and all but ended any hopes of the Washington team making the playoffs.

The day before the 2002 draft, Jordan pulled a trade. He shipped guard Courtney Alexander to the Charlotte Hornets for their first-round draft pick. The Wizards had two first-round and two second-round picks. The draft appeared not to be that deep. The Wizards chose the Indiana University forward Jared Jeffries and a local standout, shooting guard Juan Dixon, from the University of Maryland. Some professionals thought Jeffries had the chance to become a key player, and Dixon represented a role player. There were two highly desirable players remaining on the board, even after the Dixon selection: forward Tayshaun Prince and guard John Salmons. The two second-round selections hardly played in the league. Rod Grizzard did not, while Juan Carlos Navarro played one year with the Memphis Grizzlies. Two players available for selection continued to play in the league as of 2011: forwards Matt Barnes and Darius Songaila.

Jordan sought to reshape the team into a winner now rather than in the future, as he planned to play only one more year. He negotiated contracts with three free agents and signed point guard Larry Hughes to a three-year contract worth about $5 million annually. "We've been . . . trying to secure Larry for two years. . . . We feel real comfortable that he is going to bring some more versatility to our basketball team," Wes Unseld said at the Hughes signing. Hughes stated, "It's a tremendous opportunity to come into an organization whose goal is focused on winning."[21] Washington bested other big suitors, including Philadelphia, Minnesota, and Miami. The four-year veteran had played fair to decent ball with Golden State.

Then Jordan signed small forward Byron Russell to a one-year, $1.5 million contract, creating the room to trade Richard Hamilton. Russell went on to have a so-so year with the team and moved on to have better years with the Lakers and Nuggets. Finally, Jordan inked veteran power forward Charles Oakley. The 39-year-old played 42 games for the veteran's minimum with the Wizards and played only seven more NBA games afterward.

Other big moves involved two trades. The first involved swapping a future All-Star shooting guard, Richard Hamilton, for a current All-Star, Jerry Stackhouse. The Detroit Pistons included Brian Cardinal and Ratko Varda, while Washington included Bobby Simmons and guard Hubert Davis. Stackhouse had taken fewer shots than was his usual practice, which helped Detroit win their first Central Division crown in more than a decade. Hamilton moved well without the ball, a seeming advantage in a place where Jordan controlled the ball. He had been one of the Wizards' consistent players, and

Jordan noted in an interview that he wanted Hamilton to raise his intensity on the defensive end but expressed pleasure with Hamilton's play and expected even more in the future. Hamilton had chafed playing alongside Jordan, but apparently Jordan did not want to wait for Hamilton's development to continue, so he traded him for a more established player. A month later, Jordan shipped point guard Chris Whitney to Denver for guard George McCloud. The team dumped McCloud but paid him more than $2.5 million that season. Denver waived Whitney later in the season.[22]

What did the experts think about the Wizards' chances of being a winning team? The plan was for Jordan to be the team's sixth man off the bench. This reduced the number of minutes he played and would hopefully make him more effective when he got on the court. One set of columnists thought that Jordan had built a playoff squad, particularly because of the weakness throughout the Eastern Conference. Yet, one thought that Jordan eyed a last attempt to win a NBA Championship. An eye of a scout noted that Jordan would play better as a sixth man against second-team or winded first-line players. He thought the team would be satisfactory at power forward, was weaker at small forward, and had question marks at center and point.[23]

Another franchise struggled in their current location, necessitating the second franchise move in the same number of years. Charlotte had several successful teams on the court; however, the owner, George Schinn, pushed for particular personnel moves that hurt the franchise from the fans' perspective. After finishing in the lower ranks of the league in attendance for a few years, Schinn received permission to move his team to New Orleans for the start of the 2002–2003 season.[24]

If the team managed to make the playoffs, they would experience a change. The NBA switched the format of the first round of the playoffs. The old best-of-five format expired with the 2001–2002 season. For the 2002–2003 season, all first-round playoff matches became best-of-seven games. The top seed in each of the first-round contests with the five-game format hosted the first two and the last game if necessary. In the new format, the team that is seeded higher would host the first two and the fifth and seventh games, when necessary. Many perceived that this change benefitted the higher seeds, as it reduced the likelihood of an upset. A team that swept might also wait up to two weeks to play its next series if the opponent in the next round played a full series in its first round. Players accepted a greater payoff from the playoff money pool and would get a reduced training camp period, while owners received more revenue from all of their sources.

Jerry Stackhouse wondered whether Michael Jordan would remain on the bench as the sixth man. He might smell the popcorn and want to get in, the guard thought. The Wizards played well, particularly on defense, and had a 6–4 record through two weeks. They went on the first extended road trip of the year and lost three ugly games. After losing both games of a home-and-home with Indiana, they fell at home to the improved 76ers. Jordan wanted to return to the starting lineup, and he and Doug Collins made the decision. It took a five-game winning streak in early January for the team to return to .500, but they spent most of the next month one to two games below. A three-game losing streak in March, followed by four in April, sealed the team as a below-average squad.

While cruising in at 37–45, as they had the previous year, the friction in the squad increased. Jordan and Stackhouse had arguments. Stackhouse stated, "He's part owner of the team. Having him on the team hasn't been a detriment in any way, but having him looking over your shoulder . . ."[25] Jordan ripped the team on national television in a loss to the New York Knicks for not matching his desire. Collins complained about how some of the players disrespected him. Collins and Jordan seemed to berate Kwame Brown into a shell, as the player continued to perform beneath their expectations. In the final home game, the squad looked disgruntled and gave another unimpressive performance.

Friction and confrontation did not only happen on the court. The Wizards' front office had divisions as well. As one might expect, new and old regimes did not necessarily get along. Jordan and team president, Susan O'Malley, grew increasingly at odds. Sides would leak stories that conflicted and made the other look bad. Egos, power struggles, differing team cultures, and losing tend to generate this kind of disruption. The sports media increasingly covered these conflict and "gotcha stories" and added more insight and expanded coverage as game coverage appeared in other kinds of sources. The relationships between players and the media grew increasingly poor. Players and teams found additional ways of promoting themselves, so they tended to provide less direct contact to reporters.[26]

Good-bye, Mr. Jordan

Michael Jordan thought that he had Abe Pollin and Ted Leonsis's assurance that he would return to the executive suite after retiring from playing. Leonsis and Jordan dined together the night before the planned meeting with Pollin. There was no discussion in the meeting. Pollin stated that Jordan would not be welcomed back. In the midst of the half hour, Pollin offered Jordan a $10 million severance payment, but Jordan declined. Jordan left and asserted that he had been reassured that he would return as the team's president.

Pollin replied, "The only thing I said to Michael Jordan is that I would be fair, and I have lived up to that in every conceivable way."[27]

The dismissal of the best basketball player in NBA history from the team proved a public relations fiasco. Fans who had come to see Jordan play and run the franchise would understandably side with him in the dispute. Talk radio and some others in broadcasting flamed Pollin for his choice or his handling of the situation.

The major media took the opportunity to review Michael Jordan's legacy in the NBA. The primary question became, Should Jordan have been fired? Reporters and columnists noted that Jordan had been frequently absent from Washington, D.C., during his tenure as president and that he had assembled many on the current roster. They also discussed the tensions that existed within the organization. Still, a few thought that Jordan ought to have had one more year, particularly since he had an up-close view of the team and players. Most thought that Abe Pollin could have handled the situation more adroitly. As Robert Johnson, Abe Pollin's adversary over the arena who now owned the expansion Charlotte Bobcats, said, "Abe could've handled this with a little more class."[28]

The secondary focus became figuring out why Jordan failed. While Michael Jordan, Abe Pollin, and others associated with the NBA hierarchy would not accept the premise, most of the columnists viewed the team's inability to win as a sign of failure. Doug Collins thought that many of the other players lacked Jordan's tough-minded way. The coach thought that the players shrunk from his criticism rather than using it to spur improvement. Former Knicks great Walt Frazier stated, "These guys don't have the tenacity he does. The players are different today; they have a different mind-set."[29] Wizards point guard Tyronn Lue observed that, "I think we let him down. But we also let ourselves down."[30] But one columnist thought that Jordan should have stayed in the suite and launched a simple, resolute plan for improvement of the team rather than an extended bow.[31]

The team could only win so many games given the statistical performances of its players. At point guard and small forward, the Wizards' starters finished well down in the rankings of the players at those positions. Their center placed in the middle of the pack, as did their power forward. Stackhouse improved by a third over Hamilton's performance from the previous year. Yet, he and Jordan each ranked slightly above middle of the pack for shooting guards. Regardless of the team's performance, Jordan's choice to play helped the team financially. The year before Jordan joined the front office, the Wizards ranked 22nd out of 29 teams in attendance. It climbed to 18th place when Jordan moved into the executive suite. The attendance increased by 200,000 during his first year back on the court. The 839,000 spectators placed the team third in the league. Despite losing nearly 10,000 the next year, the Wizards ranked second in attendance, trailing only the Detroit Pistons.[32]

Within a month of Jordan's departure, one of his selections got fired. The Wizards' leadership dismissed Doug Collins, who had two years remaining on his coaching contract. "With seven head coaching positions available in the league . . . I felt that it was only fair that Doug be given a chance to pursue other interests," a statement from Abe Pollin asserted. In another statement, Pollin promised fans who were "not satisfied with the direction of [the] basketball franchise after [the] summer" that he would "refund [their] season-ticket deposit in full."[33]

Wes Unseld stepped into the leadership void on a temporary basis. As he prepared for the upcoming 2003 draft, the Wizards' leadership hired a new coach. They sought high-profile coaches, including Larry Brown and Jeff Van Gundy; however, both elected to lead other teams. The leadership hired Eddie Jordan. Jordan had spent the last few seasons as an assistant coach with the Eastern Conference champion New Jersey Nets. "I'm coming home to Washington. . . . We have a lot of young talent on this roster, and I look forward to working with these guys and developing this team into a contender," Jordan said.[34] A week later, the team used their first pick in the draft to take forward Jarvis Hayes. With their second-round pick, they took another local favorite who played on a championship team with Juan Dixon at the University of Maryland, point guard Steve Blake. Other intriguing names on the board included power forward Nick Collison, who played seven decent to good years in the NBA; shooting guard Luke Ridnour, who produced five decent to good years; and small forward David West, who logged many very good years in the league. Guard Mo Williams and forward Kyle Korver remained available to draft when the team selected in the second round.

Next, the team needed to hire a person to assume Michael Jordan's old position. Abe Pollin and his executives hired a new president of basketball operations in late June 2003. They chose the general manager of the Milwaukee Bucks, Ernie Grunfeld. Grunfeld had also been successful with the New York Knicks during the early 1990s. Grunfeld made a bold move in the free agent market by signing point guard Gilbert Arenas to a six-year, $63 million contract after selecting the Wizards over his current team, the Golden State Warriors. After five years, Arenas could elect to use an early termination clause and become a free agent. The new leader also signed two guards, Chris Whitney and Mitchell Butler, to single-year deals that averaged around $1 million each. As the season began, Grunfeld traded Jahidi White to the Phoenix Suns for another point guard, Brevin Knight.[35]

The beginning of the season seemed similar to the others. The team started slowly, enduring four losing streaks of four games or more. Before January, the team sat at 8–21, saved from the basement of the Atlantic Division by Orlando. Gilbert Arenas played hurt, as did others. The limited offense and strong defensive club that Doug Collins had run lost much of its defensive strength but scored more points. Both Jerry Stackhouse and Christian Laettner saw their minutes reduced significantly.

The team never did get untracked. They finished with a 25–57 record, placing them above Orlando and Chicago in the Eastern Conference. The team rebounded and stole the ball well; however, the Wizards shot below the league average percentage on both two- and three-point shots, as well as free throws. Attendance dropped to the lower third of the NBA without Jordan on the court. Like the other teams, the Wizards had to make a choice regarding which players would be left unprotected in the upcoming Charlotte Bobcats expansion draft. The Bobcats selected 19 players and took forward Lonny Baxter from the Wizards. Baxter was the third Wizard to have played on the University of Maryland's NCAA championship team. The Bobcats released him as part of establishing their roster.

Charlotte received their second league franchise. The original Hornets received approval from the Board of Governors to move to New Orleans for the start of the 2002–2003 season. The new team paid an entry fee of $300 million, which the existing 29 teams split. Nine years earlier, the entry fee had been less than half that amount. Despite concerns through the years about whom the league would market to the mainstream after the departure of Michael Jordan, the NBA remained lucrative. The television deal with ESPN and ABC, and also TNT, starting with the 2002–2003 season, amounted to $765 million a year, up from the $615 million they brought in from TNT and NBC in 1998. NBC bid less because of a slipping in the ratings and an inability to match ESPN's dual revenue streams of advertisers and subscribers to cable. Even more intriguingly, TNT and the NBA solidified a deal for an all-sports channel. "We're going to launch the channel," said commissioner David Stern. "We're in it." The former NBA.com TV moved on to become a channel carried by a variety of cable and satellite companies as part of a sports package purchase. The increasing number of sports specialty channels and more sports news shows broadcast everywhere brought more focus on the league, from great plays to personal pratfalls.[36]

Ernie Grunfeld and his team prepared for the upcoming college draft. Again, Washington awaited the results from the lottery balls. They drew the fifth pick, a slight drop, since they had the third-worst record in the league. On draft day, the Wizards chose guard Devin Harris and then shipped him,

Christian Laettner, and Jerry Stackhouse to Dallas for forward Antawn Jamison. While Laettner had only one season left, Stackhouse had several and Harris played several good years with the Mavericks and later with the Nets. Washington picked third in the second round and chose Peter John Ramos, a center from Puerto Rico. The year generated more than the usual number of unsuccessful selections in the second round. Thirteen choices did not play in a NBA game, and 11 more played less than 100 games. Washington sat in the midst of the group of 11. In the previous year, the numbers for second rounders were more the average: eleven never played, and eight played less than 100 games, the same as in 2001 and 2000. The most successful players from the second round were both selected later, namely guard Chris Duhon and forward Trevor Ariza.

A number of the middle to late first-round draftees engaged in a new, more elaborate process before coming to the team's mini-camps and facing evaluation: They still hired agents, but now those agents requested that they go to experts to receive preparation to be ready for mini-camps. Former NBA players, like one-time Bullet Don MacLean, ran programs that began as soon as the college season ended. These draft hopefuls went to California, and the program enabled them to either highlight their strengths or improve their weaknesses, or both. This training allowed players to look more impressive in a team's eyes, but it could also enable the draftee to impress to the extent that he moved up in the rankings and become an earlier selection. With the rookie pay scales in place, draftees had higher earning potential than ever before.

New Playoff Success

Under direction from the Commissioner's Office and with the expansion into Charlotte, the NBA took the opportunity to realign each conference. The switch made each into three divisions rather than two that were in existence prior to the 2004–2005 season. The Atlantic and Central divisions in the Eastern Conference became the Atlantic, Central, and Southeast divisions. Washington, Orlando, and Miami moved from the Atlantic Division, Atlanta from the Central Division, and expansion Charlotte comprised the new Southeast Division. Each team played its other division members four times, each conference team three or four times, and one home and one away game against all the teams in the other conference. A team could benefit from playing more games in a softer division, while another could be hurt by being with a stronger grouping of teams. Washington moved, along with two teams with similar records, an expansion team, and the Heat, who were two games above .500 during the 2003–2004 season.

Before the start of the season, the Wizards engaged in free agent shopping. They signed guard Anthony Peeler to a single-year, $1,600,000 deal. He played 40 games. Ernie Grunfeld announced the signing of power forward Michael Ruffin. Said Grunfeld, "He is a good defender, has strong rebounding skills, and gives us depth and experience at the forward position."[37] Ruffin received a one-year contract for $745,000. The team appreciated his toughness and signed him for two more years at about $1.7 million annually. He produced one additional fair year. Forward Samaki Walker signed for $995,000, and the team released him near the close of the season.

The vast majority of NBA teams ventured into the free agent market during the off-season. Most of this group invested in second- or third-level players, as did the Wizards. These teams, which included Cleveland, Denver, Miami, Minnesota, and New Jersey, acquired guys on one-year contracts ranging from $1 million to $2 million. Still, a significant number invested in the highest caliber of players. Phoenix signed guard Steve Nash, Utah inked forward Carlos Boozer, Dallas signed power forward Alan Henderson, and Detroit took Antonio McDyess off the market, while the Los Angeles Lakers did the same with center Vlade Divac and Golden State did likewise with guard Derek Fisher.

The league made additional rule changes designed to open the game up for more offense. They featured the curtailing of hand-checking, the clarifying of blocking fouls, and the calling of defensive three seconds. During the past 40 years, the number of offensive possessions had significantly declined. In chapter four, we note that during the early 1960s, teams generated about 152 ball possessions in an average game. By 1979–1980, the average team shot about 91 times a game, which, factoring in turnovers, results in roughly more than 100 possessions per game. In 2002–2003, shot attempts dropped to about 81, for a total of more than 91 possessions. The coaches slowed the game down with defense, which led to a decline in total points. The schemes and variations on plays, as well as the increased knowledge of each player's strengths and weaknesses, also led to decreased shooting and possessions. Others have noted that poor three-point shooting and an emphasis on getting back on defense rather than hanging around and battling for an offensive rebound have also contributed to lower point totals and lower field goal percentages throughout the league. For this year, the season league average percentage would edge up to slightly less than 45%, from a low of less than 44% the year before.

The Wizards came out of the training camp in good stead. Although it took a few games to settle in, coach Eddie Jordan found a solid starting lineup of Gilbert Arenas, Larry Hughes, Antawn Jamison, Brendan Haywood, and Jared Jeffries in the second week. The quintet enjoyed winning streaks of three, four, and seven games and had the team out to a 22–13 record. The Wizards set a pattern that lasted all season. They won their home games, and they beat the weaker teams in the NBA.

The team's success, particularly at the MCI Center, helped change the landscape of downtown Washington, D.C. Once one of the city's vibrant shopping corridors, Seventh Street, NW, suffered from urban flight to the suburbs and the riots of the 1960s. The decay and abandoned stores and streets lacked a draw to bring the people back. An arts district on the lower portion of the street generated some interest and renovation. With the development of the MCI Center, the arrival of related businesses started the drive to create a lively shopping and entertainment district. Upscale chains, restaurants, and a movie theater soon followed, creating a buzzing atmosphere and inspiring an increased amount of residential construction.[38]

The team played well through January. Holding a 26–17 record placed them second in the Southeast Division, two games ahead of Orlando and five games behind Miami. The Wizards held the fourth seed in the playoffs. February started with a four-game losing streak, but the team went on to win four games at the MCI Center. The month ended with the team dropping five of their last six games and a holding 31–24 record. The Wizards remained entrenched in second place in their division, as the only other team with a winning record, Miami, held a firm grasp on first place. The top three seeds in the playoffs were the first-place teams in each division, and where the Wizards' record would place them among the remaining five spots remained to be seen.

During March, the team played 15 games. They won nine, for a 40–30 record. The Chicago Bulls, with rookie scoring sensation Ben Gordon and young centers Eddy Curry and Tyson Chandler, ended the month on an eight-game winning streak to finish one game behind the Wizards for the fourth seed and home field advantage in the playoffs. The Indiana Pacers trailed by three games. The Allen Iverson–led Philadelphia 76ers remained slightly behind the Pacers. Despite playing to an 8–3, record the 76ers could only seize the seventh seed, just ahead of the New Jersey Nets. Indiana beat Washington twice during the team's first five games in April, evening the teams' records. The Wizards dropped their next game, as did Indiana. Meanwhile Chicago won again, widening their hold on the fourth seed to three games. The Wizards snapped their losing streak, and then handily defeated the Bulls at home. As Washington went on to win two more, they solidified their hold on the fifth seed and their first playoff appearance since 1997.

Washington had the talent on the floor to win; however, the success occurred because of strong coaching, which involved the process of planning for their games against specific opponents. Like all teams, the assistant coaches, who number as high as four or five, review video for information about their team and also about their opposition. Players received insight into their own actions related to specific plays and patterns, but they also reviewed in detail what to expect from their opponents. Each game began with an initial game plan, designed by an assistant coach, that focused on defense against two major plays, the pick-and-roll and the post-ups. Each team made choices about their plan and then decided upon adjustments at quarters and especially at halftime. Now Washington had the chance to add a wrinkle. They could bring something new to their game that their playoff opponent might not expect.

In the first year of this new playoff format, Miami, as the team with the best record in the Eastern Conference, played the eighth seed, New Jersey. Detroit played the seventh-seeded 76ers; Boston, as number three, played number six Indiana; and Chicago hosted Washington. The two teams won their home games against one another during the season, setting up the Bulls with the advantage in the series because four out of the best-of-seven would be played in Chicago.

The series held to the form of the regular season. After winning game one, 103–94, behind the shooting of rookies Ben Gordon and Andres Nocioni, the United Center crowd enjoyed second-year guard Kirk Hinrich keeping the Wizards at bay, with 21 points in the fourth quarter. Washington trailed by 20 points but whittled it down to six behind Gilbert Arenas's outburst of 39 points. Chicago won by 10, 113–103.Washington gave an intense defensive effort early on and then "got too far ahead of ourselves," in the view of coach Eddie Jordan, and the Bulls came back to seize the big lead.[39]

At the MCI Center over the weekend, the Wizards came back behind the acrobatic drives and long three-pointers of Gilbert Arenas. The guard scored 32 points, which sparked his team to a 117–99 triumph, their first in the series. The fans went crazy as Arenas took off his jersey at the final buzzer and found a fan he deemed worthy to have it.

The crowd continued its excitement for the fourth game, chanting MVP when Arenas had the ball and exalting with shooting guard Juan Dixon, who scored 35 points. The Bulls started shooting poorly and trailed 80–60 after three quarters. They rode Kirk Hinrich and Jannero Pargo to narrow the lead to six but could not get any closer. The Wizards evened the series with the 106–99 victory.

The Wizards had unhappy players to contend with as well. Jordan's first-round draft selection, Kwame Brown, had assumed a role as a bench player with the team; however, after sulking over his dwindling playing time, Brown missed game four, saying he was sick. The Wizards' management suspended him the next day. They forbade Brown from traveling or practicing with the team when they left for Chicago.

After being rattled on the road, Chicago returned home. The environmental change did not seem to have the expected influence. Washington jumped out to a 63–49 lead at halftime. Larry Hughes and Antawn Jamison, the team's other big scorers during the regular season, got untracked. Jared Jeffries and Brendan Haywood made nearly all the shots they took. Chicago barely took a nick out of the lead during the third quarter, and then Ben Gordon, Kirk Hinrich, and Tyson Chandler directed a big push in the last quarter to score 37 points and tie the game. Gilbert Arenas's jump shot as time expired gave the Wizards the 112–110 victory.

At the MCI Center, Chicago jumped out to the lead in game six. They led by 10 points during the third quarter and held a 91–87 advantage with less than three minutes remaining. Hinrich stole the ball from Hughes and drove in for a layup, but Arenas hustled back to block the shot. Washington scored on its next possessions, including a steal and a dunk by Jeffries, and held the Bulls blank. When Chicago missed its attempt to tie with six seconds left, the Wizards celebrated a 94–91 win. Fans ran onto the court, and Arenas tossed another jersey into the stands. Arenas told the media that, "All I kept saying was that I wasn't going back to Chicago."[40]

The Wizards moved on to the conference semifinals against the strong Miami Heat team at their American Airlines Arena. In game one, Shaquille O'Neal, the Heat's center, played hindered by a thigh bruise. Despite getting only five points from star guard Dwyane Wade, Miami held a two-point lead on the Wizards at halftime. The second half featured a hot-shooting Wade and contributions from other team members. Miami expanded the lead to seven and then broke the game open with a 20–5 run during the third quarter, winning 105–86.The loss carried additional complications for Washington, as Antawn Jamison came up with a balky right knee. "He's hurting a little," Eddie Jordan explained. "He's on the training table. We're giving him some treatment now."[41]

Antawn Jamison returned for game two. Miami jumped out to a 10-point lead, as Washington again had a low-scoring quarter. The Wizards chipped away at the deficit before halftime, with Jamison leading the charge on his way to a team-high 32 points, despite playing with an injured knee. Washington struggled to get closer than five, as all the Heat's starters reached double figures, and Miami won 108–102. Forward Etan Thomas reinjured an abdominal strain that he had sustained in the beginning of the season, increasing speculation that Kwame Brown might be reinstated; however, the

Wizards' management quashed the rumor with a definitive, "No, there's not [a chance for him to return]."[42]

Home court and a short bench did not change the results. Washington returned to a raucous MCI Center crowd for game three. For the first time the entire series, they held the lead after one quarter. With the help of Juan Dixon's shooting, Washington went into the locker room on top, 51–49. In the third quarter, Dwyane Wade took over, scoring numerous points on his way to a game high 31. Meanwhile, the Heat defense clamped down on Washington, limiting the Wizards to 19 points. The big three struggled, as Gilbert Arenas, Larry Hughes, and Antawn Jamison missed several shots. A valiant attempt to rally fell way short, and the team fell into a three games to none hole, 102–97.

The Miami point guard finished the Wizards off with a 42-point performance in game four. Arenas focused on driving to the basket and managed 25 points, but he shot only 37% from the field. He fouled out and removed his jersey before leaving the court, drawing a technical foul, which some viewed as an embarrassment. Washington did not quit and took a 95-94 lead on a Jamison three-pointer. Eddie Jones put the Heat ahead on a three-pointer, and then Alonzo Mourning blocked Larry Hughes's layup to preserve the victory, 99–95.

Regardless of the quick exit from the semifinals, Washington had a successful year. The playoffs brought the team to more peoples' attention. They had a star in Gilbert Arenas, whose personality pleased fans, gave the team a reason to be shown on NBA telecasts, and helped peddle team merchandise. While Washington did not rank among the top 10 teams in the league in sales of jerseys during a four-year period, the sales of Arenas jerseys placed him 20th among players. This type of sales and marketing resulted from the hierarchy promoting a sellable image of the players. One of the league's biggest draws, Kobe Bryant, had faced charges of sexual assault one year earlier, and legal proceedings ended a year later. Bryant's jersey sales plummeted from a top position to number 72, and eventually to number 90. This slide illuminated one major reason why the league so jealously guarded its stars' personas.[43]

The first year of the Charlotte Bobcats presented insight into both the team's and the league's financial situation. After an 18–64 year, the team drew roughly 14,400 fans, to place 29 out of 30. Corporate sponsorship did not jump onboard quickly. Owner Robert Johnson's regional sports television network failed. Time Warner carried C-SET as a premium digital service instead of on basic cable, reducing its reach to less than half of the total market. The cable situation was set to change for the coming season, and the team's outreach into the community had the potential of bringing in corporate and other support. According to Forbes, Charlotte ranked 17th in value among the teams in the NBA, at $300 million.

As one would expect, the teams in the most populated cities in the country had the most value. The Knicks led at $543 million, followed closely by the Lakers at $529 million. Houston, Chicago, Dallas, and Detroit were in the lower $400 million range, with Phoenix slightly behind. Six franchises had a value around $350 million (Miami, Cleveland, Boston, Philadelphia, San Antonio, and Sacramento). Indiana, Washington, and Minnesota fell in the lower $300 million, just ahead of Charlotte. New York's value also rose because of the advantage of owning its own broadcasting station. Abe Pollin sold his team's television rights to Comcast Sports Network, and, combined with other income, the team had $106 million in annual revenues, 14th highest in the league. Washington also had a $14.3 million operating income, which was the ninth highest in the NBA.[44]

Dueling with the Cavaliers

Washington faced the upcoming draft without a first-round pick due to the acquisition of Brendan Haywood. According to experts, the selection process had become more challenging and speculative due to high school starts, early entrants from college, and international players. "You're talking about a lot of guys who are not ready but have a lot of potential," Ernie Grunfeld observed.[45] Only six All-Stars have emerged from the 143 players selected in the first round between 2000 and 2004, and only 47 were full-time starters.

With their later second-round selection, the Wizards chose forward Andray Blatche, another high school player. Blatche ranked among the 32 players selected who had not completed four years of college basketball. Four-year collegiate Ryan Gomes, another forward, could have been an intriguing choice. Washington might have imagined Blatche as a replacement for Kwame Brown. They immediately shipped Brown off to the Lakers, along with Laron Profit, for forward Caron Butler and guard Chucky Atkins. Butler went on to bring the team offense at the small forward position. As the season started, Abe Pollin signed Butler to a five-year contract extension worth $50 million. Jared Jeffries ranked among the lowest in production at the position. The team also lost both University of Maryland products, Steve Blake and Juan Dixon, through free agency, hurting the team's depth.

Meanwhile, the team faced decisions regarding the guard position. Starting point guard Larry Hughes left when Cleveland offered him a five-year, $60 million contract. Six teams had been involved in the chase, including

Washington, which offered $54 million and then raised its six-year offer to $60 million. By the time the offer rose to $72 million, the guard and his agent told Ernie Grunfeld that it was too late. Hughes had given Washington good production, ranking in the top 10 in overall stats at the position. The Wizards' general manager signed free agent guard Antonio Daniels for $5 million a year. "We have a lot of outstanding players on this team, including All-Stars Gilbert Arenas and Antawn Jamison. . . . Our goals remain the same, which is to be a perennial playoff contender," Grunfeld announced.[46]

Grunfeld and other executives hoped that Washington could continue to take advantage of the rule changes that led to a reenergizing of the offensive part of the game. The 2004–2005 team represented one of six squads that averaged more than 100 points a game. Of those six teams, all qualified for the playoffs. The Wizards' problem resided on the defensive side of the ball, where they were one of 11 teams giving up more than 100 points a game. Four in this grouping qualified for the playoffs, and only the Phoenix Suns lasted longer than Washington. As the training camps began to open, Blatche took a shot in a drive-by shooting in Alexandria, Virginia. News broke that the bullet missed vital organs and that he would be out of the hospital in a few days.

The experts observed the team's off-season changes and placed them eighth best in the Eastern Conference. The team added veterans on the bench and shooting on the perimeter. The biggest plus would be the continued maturing of Gilbert Arenas and the expectation that Caron Butler, Chucky Atkins, and Antonio Daniels would be able to make up, if not surpass, the loss of Larry Hughes's scoring. But the team lacked defense, and none of the starters had a powerful defensive focus. Meanwhile, other teams, including the Nets and Cavaliers, had markedly improved their squads, making the road to a top playoff spot that much more difficult for Washington.

Some of the perfected squads jumped out quickly on the court. Detroit had a 27–4 record by New Year's Eve. Miami's 18–13 mark at the same point again put them on top in the Southeast Division. The Wizards started out with wins in five of six games and then went on the road and lost five in a row. They finished the calendar year with a 12–16 mark, which had them in third place in the division, a half a game behind the Orlando Magic. The defense lagged behind, but the lack of effective shooting hurt the team as badly.

Despite not reaching the .500 mark until early February, the Wizards sat in second place, as Orlando stumbled, while New Orleans and Charlotte had never gotten started. The team waived Atkins, who went on to play much better in Memphis' style of offense. Miami held the top slot in the Southeast Division, while Detroit and New Jersey led their respective divisions to round out the top three seeds. Cleveland had a 28–19 record, Indiana held at 23–22, and Milwaukee stood at 24–23, half a game ahead of Washington, positioned as the seventh seed. During the next month, Washington went on short winning and losing streaks, falling five of the six times that their opponent scored more than 100 points. Their record stood at 30–30. They had leapt over the Bucks but trailed Cleveland and Indiana.

Nine wins in 14 games placed the team four games over .500. At 39–35, they passed Indiana but trailed Cleveland by six games for the fourth seed and home court advantage. The defense failed them, ceding more than 100 points in losing to weak Atlanta and three playoff teams. Now they needed wins in the last games of the season to hold on to the fifth seed. Arenas scored 43 points to lead the team to a 116–103 win over Milwaukee. They beat Detroit with a strong overall team effort that enabled the team to finish one game ahead of Indiana and Chicago to take the fifth seed. The Wizards scored the third most points in the league, while shooting at a percentage below the league average for both two and three points. The team accomplished the feat with a monster year rebounding offensive shots, again ranking third best. One major difficulty with the team's poor shooting, especially from three-point range, was that the Wizards could not be as effective spreading out the defense of the opposing team, or igniting their own offense and exciting their home crowd or dulling the crowd on the road with the three-point dagger. Each of these factors helped make it easier to win in the playoffs against the better caliber of teams.

All the top seeds went into the playoffs as the predicted winners. While the Wizards won three of four playing the Cavaliers, experts pointed to their low-ranking defense as a glaring weakness. They also had to contend with the person who many argued was the best player in the league, LeBron James. The 21-year-old small forward, playing in his first postseason NBA game, missed his first shots but came on to score 13 and dish out four assists to lead his team to a 31–20 first-quarter advantage. With the crowd chanting "M-V-P! M-V-P!" when he had the ball, James led Cleveland to a double-digit lead deep into the third quarter. Arenas, Butler, and Jamison scored a combined 48 points, 20 below their season average. The Wizards missed a ton of three-pointers and many free throws and lost the game, 97–86. "What hurt me the most was my team not playing the way we are supposed to play," Coach Jordan stated following the game.[47]

Eddie Jordan drew up a series of different one-on-one defenses, which his team executed well during game two. Washington trailed by 15 early on. Center Brendan Haywood saw LeBron James coming into the paint and fouled him hard, putting him into a headlock. James went without a field goal for 13 minutes. Washington engineered an 18–0 run at the end of the first quarter. Gilbert Arenas led his team with 30 points, and Antawn Jamison scored 11 in the fourth quarter alone to lead Washington to a five point win, 89–84.

Back home for game three, Washington had a late lead, but LeBron James dribbled past guard Antonio Daniels, took a hop step, made a pump fake, and scored on a layup with 5.7 seconds remaining, sealing the win by a score of 97–96. Cleveland looked like it was going win both games at the MCI Center, when they rode Ronald "Flip" Murray and LeBron James's scoring to an 11-point halftime lead. The Wizards regrouped and tied the game at the close of the third period. Using only seven men, Washington then coasted to a 10-point win, 106–96, with four men in double figures in points.

Back at Cleveland's Quicken Loans Arena, the two teams engaged in a titanic battle. Both shot the ball extremely well, and they went into halftime 52–51, Cleveland. James had to sit down after collecting his fourth foul midway through the third quarter. Flip Murray and Larry Hughes picked up the slack and enabled Cleveland to build a four-point advantage. Despite getting scoring from their big three, Washington trailed by seven points with a little more than a minute left to play. Antonio Daniels made a three-pointer that sparked Washington to cut the lead to 107–105, with 10 seconds to play. Daniels deflected James's pass and pushed the ball up to Butler for a layup that tied the game. James's jumper banged off the rim at the buzzer, sending the game into overtime. The big three and Antonio Daniels countered Eric Snow and James in overtime to give Washington a one-point edge with less than four seconds left. James zipped past two defenders and rose in front of the rim and, in a shot off his fingertips, gave his team a 121–120 victory.

The next game proved to be just as gripping. The home team again led by one at halftime. The visitors again got contributions from Flip Murray and Donyell Marshall to hang close. Washington received 22 points from Antonio Daniels and 17 from Brendan Haywood and held a seven-point edge with just under five minutes remaining. Cleveland clawed back to take the lead and left the Wizards with the need for a long bomb from Gilbert Arenas to send the game into overtime. Neither team shot well in the overtime, and Washington had the chance to increase their lead, but Arenas missed at the free throw line. Cleveland came down the court and set up a short jumper by Damon Jones that gave them a one-point lead with about five seconds left. Caron Butler missed a three-pointer that gave Cleveland the series, 114–113. Arenas spent the next few days lifting weights and shooting jumpers, as the sting of losing three close games remained with him.

Team management reviewed the 2006 draft with an eye for finding both offensive and defensive help. "There is no clear-cut number one, but more like groupings, starting with the top five or six. . . . You'd be able to get a solid player down through the 20s," Ernie Grunfeld noted happily, as Washington held the 18th selection.[48] With it, they chose Oleksiy Pecherov, a 20-year-old Ukrainian center. He proved to be one of eight men picked out of the 30 that went on to play less than 200 NBA games. The strong remaining players on the board proved to be guards, who could have added bench strength to the Wizards. Grunfeld selected Vladimir Veremeenko in the second round. He did not play in the NBA, one of eight chosen in the round. Fourteen others played fewer than 100 games. Of the eight players in this weak draft who played more than 100 games, only Leon Powe and Ryan Hollins remained available to choose when Washington picked.

Now the team looked to fill a few areas of need through the free-agent market. After his strong year, the team resigned Antonio Daniels for $5.4 million. They signed forward Darius Songaila for three years at nearly $4 million annually. The three-year pro had one good and two decently productive years playing for Sacramento and Chicago. He appeared to be someone on the rise, yet the experts did not discuss his presence on the team when evaluating the Wizards' chances for the season. The Wizards also inked the Magic's starting shooting guard, DeShawn Stevenson, for three years at about $2 million per year. The experts noted that he was much better coming off the bench and would provide more value in that role than in the starting lineup. Other players, like Roger Mason, had been out of the league playing in Greece and Israel and were brought on the team for about $700,000 a year. The team sat near the salary cap of $53 million, with Jamison claiming $15 million, and Arenas another $11 million. The team lost forward Jared Jeffries, who signed as a free agent with the New York Knicks.

Arenas sought to establish himself as a defensive maven, something that the team desperately needed; however, they needed it on the inside as well. Things started out a little rocky, as the Wizards endured losing streaks of three and four games in November. Eddie Jordan swapped Etan Thomas with Brendan Haywood in the starting lineup, and the team went 12–4 in December. Even without Jamison for a run of games, the team played almost as well in January. At 27–18, Washington sat atop the Southeast Division, seven games ahead of the defending NBA champion Miami Heat.

Orlando positioned itself in second place, with a 24–22 record. Toronto and New Jersey battled for supremacy in the Atlantic, while three teams (Detroit, Cleveland, and Chicago) struggled for the hold on the Central Division. Before the start of the season, the NBA Board of Governors altered the playoff seeding system. Instead of each of the division champions receiving the seeds, one, two, and three, the champions and another team in the conference with the best record were seeded one through four based upon their won-loss record. This guaranteed that the division champions would be no lower than the fourth seed and also ensured that a conference's two best teams (by record) were ranked as the top two.

Washington continued to pour on the offense. Nearly scoring at a rate of 115 points per game, the Wizards went on two three-game win streaks. Arenas had the tendency to explode for 30 or 40, sometimes 60, points, and he had popularized the number zero, saying "[The jersey] is for anybody who feels unappreciated or feels like somebody is telling them that they are worth nothing."[49] Caron Butler contributed a steady 15 to 20 points per game. His style of slashing and perimeter jump-shooting ability suited Eddie Jordan's "Princeton" offense. Still, without Antawn Jamison due to a knee injury, the Wizards lost seven games in February. Even when Jamison returned, they floundered and dropped eight in March, because the offense had trouble getting untracked or their defense proved too porous. After a tough overtime loss to Toronto, they stood at 38–33. Miami defeated Minnesota to take first place in the division. Orlando dropped to third position and had to improve quickly to fight for a spot in the playoffs. In the Central Division, Detroit held first place, Cleveland kept pace, with a 44–29 record, and Chicago nipped at their heels with its 43–31 record.

Six of the losses over these winter months came on Washington's home court, the newly christened Verizon Center. Verizon purchased MCI and thus the naming rights as well. The arena approached its 10th anniversary as a great success. It enlivened Washington's downtown and held the ninth position among global venues, having attracted 2.5 million fans to more than 220 events yearly. Abe Pollin argued that its role in the renaissance of downtown warranted a $50 million contribution from the city toward the upgrade of the arena's 110 luxury suites and the replacement of its outdated scoreboard. The Washington Wizards' owners found themselves in the middle of a trend. Other NBA teams had asked or planned to seek public financial support for arena improvements. Cleveland renovated Quicken Loans Arena in 2005. The Boston Celtics made luxury box additions and other alterations the following year. They sought more revenue for the team from concessions sales and luxury box rentals. The Milwaukee Bucks enjoyed the improvements made to the Bradley Center by the center's owners and then sought a lease providing the team more revenue to allow it to continue competing against larger-market NBA teams.[50]

Washington had the sixth seed in the playoffs as the league moved into April. With 11 games to play, the Wizards had a decent chance of catching Chicago for the fifth position and overtaking Miami to become one of the top four seeds. Etan Thomas started instead of Brendan Haywood on the road in Milwaukee, where a 121-point outburst gave Washington the victory, but the win proved costly. Caron Butler broke his hand attempting to block a shot. Butler, who posted career highs in several categories, appeared to be lost for the remainder of the season. Jarvis Hayes would have to fill in. Then, in the first of back-to-back games against the Charlotte Bobcats, Gerald Wallace fell into Gilbert Arenas's leg and the star required an MRI to determine a fracture. Without their big scorers, the team lost seven out of nine and squeezed into the playoffs as the seventh seed and drew the Cleveland Cavaliers.

The second-seeded Cavaliers returned with basically the same team that previously dispatched Washington, but a year stronger. In game one, they defeated Washington by 15, 97–82, as Jamison and Hayes were the only Wizards in double figures in scoring. James twisted his ankle but returned for game two and managed 27 points, eight rebounds, and seven assists. Cleveland took a big lead.

After shooting a low percentage in game one, Antawn Jamison made half of his 24 attempts in game two. He received help throughout the lineup, and Jarvis Hayes's three-pointer with 18 seconds left cut the deficit down to three points. Washington fouled former Wizard guard Larry Hughes, who calmly made his free throws to seal the victory, 109–102.

At the Verizon Center, the Cavaliers brought inside and outside scoring to bear. LeBron James shot 50% from the floor, including three of five from downtown, and center Zydrunas Ilgauskas scored on 10 of his 13 shots, as Cleveland sprinted out to a huge halftime lead. Antawn Jamison, Antonio Daniels, and Jarvis Hayes brought their team back to within two points at the close of the third, but a fourth-quarter burst from the Cavaliers provided the 98–92 margin of victory. Cleveland also won game four, 97–90, and made it to the finals, where they lost to the San Antonio Spurs.

Before the start of the 2007 draft, Washington's executives heard that Arenas had opted out of his six-year, $65 million contract. "Gilbert has said that his intention is to remain with the organization, and we are committed to having him spend his entire career as a Washington Wizard," said Grunfeld in a statement issued to the media.[51] What would it cost Washington to resign the recently injured but hugely popular star player? Jamison was slated to make $16 million, and Butler added another $8 million. Thomas,

Daniels, Haywood, and Songaila added another $20 million to the total. The remaining four players left over from the 2006–2007 team earned $6 million. The team had a range of $11 million to $16 million remaining, including the contracts of Arenas and two draft selections. Hayes signed a free-agent contract with the Detroit Pistons.

Washington had a 16th pick in the first round, in the middle of the pack. They selected Nick Young from the University of Southern California, a shooter who played guard and could be moved to small forward. Power forward Jared Dudley, forward Wilson Chandler, and guard Arron Afflalo represented intriguing choices left on the board. In the second round, the Wizards picked forward Dominic McGuire. Their selection represented one of eight players chosen who played more than 100 games in the NBA. Unfortunately, he did not play most of them with the Wizards. Of the eight men, only Marc Gasol, picked right after McGuire, has played with one team in his career.

The year brought about the first rumblings in some time about teams struggling financially. Eight of the NBA's smaller market teams, ranging from Milwaukee to Sacramento, made an argument that they needed financial support to stay in operation. The league's revenues continued to grow, but mostly through local television rights, and they benefitted teams in Los Angeles, New York, Chicago, and Boston. The small-market owners sought greater revenue sharing. While the National Football League teams shared the vast majority of the league's income, Major League Baseball had instituted a luxury tax in the mid-2000s, with the New York Yankees putting in the vast majority of the money. Did that income save teams from financial ruin? Did the income help the teams spend to become more competitive? An argument could be made for the former.

Despite different teams winning the World Series during the 2000s, the tax had little to do with the success of these different teams. The NBA established a degree of revenue sharing beginning with the 2001–2002 season, when teams earned a rebate from the league if their payroll finished the season below the salary cap level. Only Charlotte and Utah accomplished that feat. The Wizards did not earn the rebate, and, as a team in a larger population market with a decent television rights deal, Washington ranked in the middle of the league's teams in financial strength.[52]

As the team came to training camp, Ernie Grunfeld traded guard Juan Carlos Navarro to Memphis for a 2010 first-round draft choice and signed Gilbert Arenas to a new six-year, $111 million contract. Antawn Jamison estimated that 80% of camp workouts focused on defense. He commented that, "In the past we'd do [play defensive schemes] for five to 10 games, then we'd slack off for 10 to 15 games."[53] A scout wondered aloud about the team and the coaches' lack of defense in their makeup. He added that that loss of Etan Thomas to a heart condition would hurt their interior defending. Strikingly, he thought that Arenas's persona might be the team's downfall as Arenas became bigger than the team, as was the case with Allen Iverson in Philadelphia.

The starting lineup of Gilbert Arenas, Caron Butler, Brendan Haywood, Antawn Jamison, and DeShawn Stevenson lost its first five games. As Arenas and Jamison improved their shooting percentages, the team took three games. Butler and Jamison had arranged a players only meeting and discovered that too many players didn't know their roles and felt confused on the court. But Arenas's play came to a quick end. He experienced swelling and soreness in the knee he had surgically repaired, which led to a test that showed a cartilage tear. Antonio Daniels rejoined the starting lineup, and the Wizards went 7–5. Eddie Jordan slipped in other guards, including rookie Nick Young and veteran Roger Mason, and the team did a little worse. Daniels got the other players involved, with Haywood averaging double digits in points for the first time in his seven-year career.

Nearing the end of January, the team's 24–19 record placed the Wizards second in their division, a few games behind the Orlando Magic, but comfortably ahead of third-place Atlanta. The Southeast had the only close divisional race. In the Atlantic, Boston's trio of Paul Pierce, Ray Allen, and Kevin Garnett led the team to a final record of 66–16, placing them as the top seed in the playoffs. The Detroit Pistons won 59 games to take the Central Division and the second seed. Defending conference champion Cleveland had a half game edge over Washington and Toronto for the fourth spot.

After beating Toronto at home, the Wizards went to Toronto and got shellacked. The next two home games featured the Utah Jazz and the Los Angeles Lakers. Both of these strong Western Conference teams defeated Washington, holding the team to well below its scoring average. As the team faced more stiff competition from the best in the West, Andray Blatche stepped in to replace an ailing Caron Butler, and the losing continued. After eight straight losses, Washington beat the Los Angeles Clippers but then dropped two more. As LeBron James and the Cavaliers came to the Verizon Center, the Wizards remained a game under .500. James dropped 25 points, and Sasha Pavlovic chipped in 24. Butler returned to the starting lineup and led the team in scoring, with 19 points. With the remaining starters and two key reserves scoring in double figures, the home team won a 101–99 thriller.

Cleveland remained virtually tied with Toronto, four games ahead of Washington for the fourth seed. Orlando held a 10-game advantage atop the division. With 18 games left, the odds of winning the division seemed low;

however, a long winning streak could help the Wizards pass Toronto and Cleveland and get home court advantage in the first round of the playoffs. The Wizards cut the lead in half but went on the road to face the Lakers and Jazz.

The Lakers held an 11-point halftime lead, but Washington stormed out of the locker room and tied the game by the end of the third quarter. The teams traded baskets and ended up tied at 111 at the buzzer. Both teams used 10 players during the contest. Feeling the Phoenix Suns chasing them for first place in the Pacific Division, the Lakers played Kobe Bryant and Lamar Odom for more than 46 minutes each. The home team won, 126–120.

The next night in Utah, the Wizards played the type of game that can sometimes result from a draining travel schedule. Washington scored only 87 points and lost by 42. At home, two nights later, a fourth-quarter collapse led to a bad loss to the Milwaukee Bucks. Winning five of their last seven enabled the Wizards to take the fifth seed.

Playing without Gilbert Arenas for nearly the entire season, Washington relied on a team effort to make the playoffs. Several players experienced career years during the 2007–2008 season. Center Brendan Haywood set new personal records for minutes played and field goal and free throw attempts. He also topped out in assists and turnovers. His production would be his highest up to the present (2012). DeShawn Stevenson shot his career high in field goal percentage (46%) and three-point shooting percentage (40%), setting his standard for production up to the 2012 season. Forwards Caron Butler and Antawn Jamison each played one of their top seasons, while guard Roger Mason Jr. had the second-best season of his career. Out of the 15 players at their position in the Eastern Conference, Haywood's season placed him in the top three of centers; Jamison ranked fourth-best among power forwards; Butler placed in the lower middle among small forwards; Stevenson placed in the lower portion among shooting guards, and Daniels finished in the middle of the pack of point guards.[54]

For the third consecutive year, Cleveland and Washington tangled in the first round of the NBA Playoffs. Cleveland finished two games better in the standings, but the teams split their four contests. Both teams won their home games. Experts were split on who they expected to win, but they also noted that Arenas had been without knee swelling for the past two months and might be able play quite a few minutes in this series. Arenas and Stevenson added that James was "overrated."[55]

Cleveland jumped out to a lead, but Washington held close behind Brendan Haywood's scoring and Antawn Jamison's rebounding. Gilbert Arenas checked into the game with five minutes remaining to a resounding chorus of boos. After a bad miss, he canned two three-pointers, and Washington finished the quarter up by five. After starting the second with a good run, LeBron James got untracked, and Cleveland went on a run to narrow the Wizards' lead to 42–38. Zydrunas Ilgauskas added 14 points and seven rebounds to enable the game to be tied at 46. In the third quarter, the Wizards continued strong shooting from the floor, while Cleveland kept getting to the free throw line. Despite more turnovers, Washington held on to a four-point lead. In the fourth, Ilgauskas and James put the Cavaliers ahead by five, but Washington engineered a 7–0 run to take the lead. James drove past three defenders to score. As the game progressed, Washington's shooters went cold. Neither Antawn Jamison, Gilbert Arenas, of Caron Butler could make a shot. James drove to the hoop again, and the game slipped out of reach, 93–86.

In game two, Cleveland came out with the intensity needed to protect their home court. They controlled the tempo and, as the Wizards missed their shots, Cleveland grabbed a 27–22 lead in the first quarter. Washington answered back in the beginning of the second. Darius Songaila made a shot and two nice assists to give his team the lead. After trading a few buckets, the Wizards continued to play a lot of one-on-one, dribbling a few times and then launching a shot, which often missed. The Cavaliers went on a 16–2 run that gave them a 13-point halftime lead. "We wanted to come out in the second half and chip away at the lead," said guard Antonio Daniels. Instead, when Cleveland made a few baskets, Washington did more one-on-one. "We didn't use each other to get back into the game," observed Daniels.[56] Brendan Haywood pushed LeBron James as the star vaulted in to the air during a layup. James crash-landed safely; the referee ejected Haywood from the game, and Cleveland used the extra motivation to win by a 116–86 margin.

The Wizards happily returned home. "We've got two at home, and we have to win those two. . . . The series doesn't start until the visiting team wins," Arenas stated, as he found out at the last minute that he would be starting.[57] Washington hit the boards higher and harder, helping the team in what amounted to be a turnover-ridden quarter. A late second bucket and the foul gave James a three-point play that pulled his team to within three, 21–17. Blatche defended Ilgauskas well and started fast breaks with quick rebounds, enabling the Wizards to lead by 11. Cleveland edged its way back into the game. Arenas limped into the locker room with three minutes remaining in the half. Washington ignited an 11–2 run and led by 16 to the roar of the Verizon Center faithful. Washington continued to double team James to force the ball out of his hands in the beginning of the second half. As Mason and Jamison led the scoring, the romp was on. Washington won resoundingly, 108–72.

After two days off due to the number of playoff games and interests of the broadcast media, the Wizards came out firing and led 28–24 in the first quarter. Cleveland started the second quarter banging hard to grab offensive rebounds. The second chances led to a 20–2 run that enabled Cleveland to take a 10-point lead. James hit a three-pointer to push the lead to 15. Washington replied by making its shots and pulling off three steals that cut the lead down to two. The Wizards went cold, as did the Cavaliers, but Washington's ability to pull down offensive rebounds led to a 5–0 run to close the quarter. Haywood, Jamison, and Butler kept shooting at a high enough clip to keep the Wizards hanging around, trailing by six with less than three minutes remaining. Butler made another jumper, and Arenas drew a foul and made his free throws. James missed, and Arenas sailed down the court and banked in the tying layup. Twenty-eight seconds remained. Guard Delonte West got open in the corner and launched a three-point shot, giving the Cavaliers the victory, 100–97. "The season comes down to one game," Jamison said. "As long as I'm the captain, we are always going to believe we are going to win."[58]

Back in Cleveland for game five, Antonio Daniels returned to the starting lineup, as Gilbert Arenas was unable to play. Bringing a clampdown defense and a hot hand by Caron Butler, Washington took a 23–16 advantage. The lead dwindled by halftime, as Zydrunas Ilgauskas scored 10 points, with six coming from putbacks of missed Cavalier shots. DeShawn Stevenson scored nine to help the Wizards get back to a two-point advantage. A dreadful string of 13 consecutive misfires only put the Wizards in a six-point hole, and a 16–6 run at the end of the third led to a four-point fourth quarter lead. After trading a few baskets, Cleveland engineered a 6–0 run that enabled them to lead by five points with less than two minutes remaining. The teams swapped misses before Caron Butler led the team on a great comeback, capping it with a layup over LeBron James with four seconds remaining to give Washington an 88–87 win, pushing the series to game six.

Washington again started the game with a good shooting touch and jumped out to a 31–27 lead. Antawn Jamison scored 11 points, and the starters shot 54%. "Then [Cleveland] started making shots with their bench. They picked up the intensity about seven minutes before the half," Eddie Jordan noted.[59] The Cavaliers used a 21–2 run to build a double-digit lead. While LeBron James had a triple-double (points, assists, and rebounds all in double digits), Wally Szczerbiak and Daniel Gibson also played exceptionally well. When the Cavaliers celebrated the series win with their 105–88 triumph, the Wizards' fans gave their team a standing ovation. "We believed in each other all year," Antonio Daniels added. "I'm very proud of this team and the coaching staff."[60]

With season's end, the team's executives faced many choices. First, they prepared for the 2008 draft. Picking number 18, they selected JaVale McGee, a seven-footer who had played center at the University of Nevada for two years. As one of the best players remaining on the board and the team needing help at center, McGee proved a good selection. The team also required help at shooting guard to provide a long-distance shooting threat, and possibly at point guard, depending upon Arenas's health, which had not been good during the previous two seasons. The second round of the draft proved weak. Out of the 30 players selected, 10 never played in the NBA, and 11 played less than 100 games. Washington immediately sold its second-round selection, forward Bill Walker, to the Boston Celtics.

The Wizards faced decisions on the free-agent front. Both Arenas and Jamison became free agents. The market appeared thin, so teams coveted these players. Should the team resign the 32-year-old Jamison, and, if so, for how long? While he had improved his perimeter game, he had lost most of his post game, another Washington weakness. What about the much younger Arenas, who had his third surgery in two years on his left knee?

The team executives constructed the team so that it could win now. Fans and some experts believed that the team would resign both men, essentially switching the value of their contracts (Arenas receiving the money that Jamison got in his last contract and vice versa). Washington resigned Jamison for $11 million annually during a course of four years. Both Memphis and Philadelphia reportedly made similar offers. Arenas renegotiated for $111 million spread over six seasons. Adding Butler's $10 million resulted in the three men taking $37 million of the $58 million salary the team could spend. Additional, smaller free-agent moves included resigning Juan Dixon for less than $1 million and inking a contract with a point guard, Daniel "Dee" Brown, who had previously played a year for the Utah Jazz before being let go, for about $200,000.

Pundits argued that by keeping their big three together, the Wizards' leaders ensured that the team would remain in playoff contention for at least a decade. Others viewed Washington as a lower seed in the conference playoffs. Additional voices later arose questioning committing to a trio that never led the team to a 50-win season and only made it past the first round of the playoffs once in four tries. Scouts saw the team as running the offense more efficiently the previous season, without Arenas, whose tendency to take early shots and focus on making plays for himself enabled defenses to collapse on him. Years earlier, analysis done of the success of teams through purchasing free agents had revealed information with implications for the Wizards. Teams might have a majority of their budgets taken up by two or three stars, but real success came when a team found the most proficient "bargain-basement" players to match up with the stars.[61]

Brendan Haywood, coming off his top season, injured his wrist in the preseason. Etan Thomas, back from his heart issues, took Haywood's spot in the starting lineup for the first set of games. Eddie Jordan made a switch to rookie JaVale McGee after the team started the season with a 1–7 record. Dee Brown stepped in as the starting point guard for the veteran Antonio Daniels. Washington lost three more games. Management fired coach Eddie Jordan. The team's director of player development, Ed Tapscott, took over the reins. Under the new leadership, the team started 3–5. The front office arranged a three-team trade. Washington sent Antonio Daniels to the New Orleans Hornets and their 2010 first-round draft selection to the Memphis Grizzlies. The Wizards received 21-year-old point guard Javaris Crittenton from Memphis and 33-year-old guard Mike James from New Orleans. Scouts assessed the former as a sizable, pretty good defender, who was neither a natural shooter nor a point guard. The latter had a career year shooting for Toronto in 2005–2006. The team also waived Dee Brown.[62]

Mike James and Andray Blatche joined the starting lineup for JaVale McGee and Juan Dixon, and the team continued its way to an eight-game losing streak. At 4–23, Washington fell to the bottom of the Southeast Division. The lineup continued to change, with different youngsters getting a chance to play while the team had the opportunity to assess its strengths and weaknesses. The final 19–63 record equaled the 2000–2001 campaign.

The Passing of Mr. Pollin

The front office sought to lock up a veteran coach with a winning past to helm their squad. Rumors included Avery Johnson, who won at Dallas before being fired after a first-round playoff loss in 2007–2008, and Flip Saunders, who reached the playoffs multiple times in Minnesota and Detroit. Saunders took over. Fans waited for the new season, viewing the last one as unusual due to Gilbert Arenas playing in only two games and Brendan Haywood solely taking part in the final six. Chairman Abe Pollin shared this perception, saying, "I know our fans share in my anticipation of what we can accomplish with new leadership, a healthy roster, and a renewed commitment to excellence."[63]

Ernie Grunfeld focused on trades right before the upcoming 2009 draft. The Minnesota Timberwolves had also suffered a rough season. Having used 10 forwards during the season and five guards, they traded forward Mike Miller, known as a good outside shooter, for his nearly $10 million annually, and point guard Randy Foye ($3.5 million a year), to Washington. The Wizards yielded three big men, centers Etan Thomas and Oleksiy Pecherov and forward Darius Songaila, and their 2009 first-round draft pick. The front office then signed free agent forward Fabricio Oberto for more than $2 million. The Argentinean played four seasons with San Antonio before being traded to Milwaukee and Detroit, who waived him during the summer. General manager Grunfeld went all in with this move, expecting that the team would rebound significantly from the 19-win season and needing a little more veteran strength.

As with 2008, the college draft for Washington started with the second round. They selected shooting guard Jermaine Taylor from the University of Central Florida. In 2008, the Celtics bought the Wizards' pick. This time, the Houston Rockets bought him. Taylor fell short of the 100-game threshold, as did six of the remaining 29. Thirteen more never played in the NBA, accounting for two-thirds of the second-round selections. San Antonio's choice, DeJuan Blair, and Chase Budinger, with Houston, appeared as the most successful of this group.

The Wizards training camp had 16 players, including seven guards. Crittenton arrived with an ankle injury, which had happened during a Pro-Am basketball game in Atlanta, where he lived during the off-season. The starting lineup for the first group of games included the return of Gilbert Arenas and Brendan Haywood, along with Caron Butler, Mike Miller, and Fabricio Oberto. They started 2–5, and Andray Blatche joined the starting lineup in time for the last two games of the six-game losing streak. Antawn Jamison replaced Fabricio Oberto, and the team won one and lost two, for a 3–9 record. Before the start of the November 24 game at home against Philadelphia, the Wizards organization and city learned that chairman Abe Pollin had died. The businessman, real estate developer, philanthropist, and sports owner was dearly missed by friends, family, the organizations, and fans. One of the few remaining owners from the old-school, Pollin's sports teams were treated like a family business, and his strong personality and deep loyalties shaped their operation. Tributes came from everywhere, including from President Barack Obama, and, of course, Wes Unseld, who said, "I just lost a real good friend. I think it is more than any of you will ever understand."[64]

The game began with a tribute: a moment of silence before the national anthem. The team won an emotional game, 108–107, when a last-second shot rimmed out. "Maybe Abe's spirit knocked that out," 76ers coach Eddie Jordan said.[65] The Wizards put up a tribute page on the team's website. In addition, the family and organization held a public memorial service at the Verizon Center early the next month.

Washington won two games to start the new month. Unfortunately, a six-game losing streak followed. On the bright side, the team lost no game by more than three points. They sometimes fell behind and made a valiant, but short, comeback. Other times, the opposing team won with a burst in the last quarter. A win at Golden State finally snapped the streak.

After losing at Phoenix, the team returned home to face Philadelphia on December 24. Few people knew of an explosive locker room incident that happened that night. The team won and then beat Milwaukee in Wisconsin for a 10–17 record. Javaris Crittenton left the team, reportedly to have his ankle examined in Indianapolis. The team issued an odd announcement on Christmas Day. Gilbert Arenas admitted to bringing guns into the locker room and had turned them over to team security. Arenas claimed that he wanted them out of his house so that they would be away from his children. The team then traveled to Minnesota for a December 26 game. Washington lost that game and the final road game before returning to the Verizon Center for one game before and one game after the New Year's holiday.

As the team went on to lose their next game, on January 2, reports were leaked of a December 21 confrontation in the locker room between two of the team's guards. Crittenton reportedly grew angry with Arenas for not making good on a gambling debt. According to a league source close to the Wizards, Crittenton shouted at Arenas, "I'm not your punk!" Arenas apparently had handguns in the locker room. He drew one on Crittenton, who then pulled one out to aim at Arenas. No one fired, but observers were quite concerned until the situation was defused. A team statement noted that they were taking the situation and the ongoing investigation very seriously. The executive director of the National Basketball Player's Association (NBPA), Billy Hunter, said, "I've never heard of players pulling guns on each other in a locker room."[66]

While Arenas denied that he had pointed a gun at a teammate, the city of Washington had such strict gun laws that Arenas faced legal problems with merely possessing the firearms. Crittenton faced similar problems. He told the team that he did not have a gun in the locker room. Both the sports and mainstream media offered a variety of stories and speculation about the incident.

Meanwhile, the Wizards lost the game that Saturday to the San Antonio Spurs. They went up to Philadelphia for an evening game on January 5. As Arenas came out during introductions, ever the joker, he joined his teammates in a circle and mocked shooting them with a finger gun. Arenas received an indefinite suspension from the Commissioner's Office pending the investigation into the locker room incident, as did Crittenton, and his teammates accepted fines from the team for the Philadelphia incident.[67]

The team won six games and lost 10 in January and then dropped three of four before the All-Star break. Ernie Grunfeld worked hard to reshape the team. He shipped Caron Butler, Brendan Haywood, and DeShawn Stevenson to Dallas in exchange for forwards Drew Gooden, Josh Howard, and James Singleton, plus guard Quinton Ross. A few days later, Drew Gooden went to the Los Angeles Clippers, while Antawn Jamison went to the Cleveland Cavaliers. The Wizards received forward Al Thornton from the Clippers and center Zydrunas Ilgauskas from Cleveland, along with a 2010 first-round draft pick. The team waived Ilgauskas later in the month after he did not play a game with the team. This series of moves made Washington younger and freed up a lot of salary for the future, but the team suffered from the decision made earlier in the year to cede a draft pick for Randy Foye and Mike Miller.

After going 4–3 to close out February, the team began a home-and-home series against the Milwaukee Bucks on March 3. Washington did not win from then until March 31, a string of 16 games. The Wizards ended the season with a 26–56 record. The best part of the season was that many of the steps that needed to be taken had occurred and rebuilding could begin.

The Washington Wizards Today

Under Ted Leonsis, the Wizards have begun a rebuilding process, both in terms of the staff and players. Senior directors head up individual departments for camps and clinics, communications, and community relations. Directors handle game operations, new media and analytics, and basketball communications. Under the president of basketball operations sit vice presidents of player personnel and basketball operations. The head athletic trainer serves as the lead of two assistant trainers, as well as a conditioning person. These days, the team staff features five assistant coaches and a separate person to handle video coordination. In addition, there are directors of college scouting and player personnel who have their own staffs.

The effort that began before the All-Star Game continued through the 2009–2010 season. While the team organization rarely used the word *rebuilding* under the ownership of Abe Pollin, management used the term to describe their efforts during the course of the next two years. Indeed, every team in any sport has had to undergo a rebuilding process at some point in their organization's history. The players on the good and great teams age and lose effectiveness. The youngsters coming in to join squads require time to acquire the proper skills and experience. Sometimes the veterans age quickly or unexpectedly, and the youngsters never quite attain their expected level of proficiency.

During the period in the NBA covered in this book, every team fell to the bottom and needed to reconstruct itself on some level at some point. It helps the effort when you are able to add a superstar at the same time that you create a stable nucleus of a team, as the Lakers did in trading for Kareem Abdul-Jabbar after winning only 30 games in 1974–1975, or as did Boston in drafting Larry Bird and going from 29 wins to 61. Sometimes, the buildup occurs over a few seasons. Houston drafted Ralph Sampson and doubled its win output and then drafted Hakeem Olajuwon and added another 19 wins.

The rebuilding process does not occur in a vacuum. One major factor centers on the salary limit. A team can only spend so much on its talent. The annual cost and length of contracts are two major, but not the only, factors involved. A team can only reshape its roster working within its own caps and the salary caps of its potential trading partners. Personnel decisions also have to take into account fans and the entertainment and marketing impact they can have. The NBA is in the entertainment business, and teams need to continue to draw fans and expand their fan base and merchandising viability. The metropolitan-area market in which a team plays must also be considered. The size of an area plays a role in shaping its fan base and potential interest in the team. The urban area also contains amenities and other elements that will factor into the decisions of many players as to whether they want to sign with one team or join another. The appeal of a team to players is also shaped by the reputation of the team, both its history and how it treats its players. The players on the current roster are also a factor, as the decision of LeBron James and Chris Bosh to join Dwyane Wade in Miami illuminated.

As fans of teams learn, the rebuilding process requires many steps. The first foundation of the new build for Washington occurred when the Wizards won the draft lottery in 2010. With the first pick, they selected point guard John Wall, who had played one year at the University of Kentucky. Under terms of the NBA rookie salary scale and as the top selection, the Wizards signed Wall to three years for $16.5 million, with a team option of $7.5 million and more than $9 million as a qualifying offer during the 2014–2015 season. This draft featured more than 50 underclassmen who signed up to participate and potentially be among those selected to play in the league.[68]

Wheeling and dealing characterized the remaining days of the month of June. The team traded their second pick in the first round to Minnesota for a young forward and a young center. A draft choice from an earlier year went to Chicago for veteran guard Kirk Hinrich and another young forward. The guard picked up in the December trade with Dallas went to the New Jersey Nets for their big forward, Yi Jianlian, and cash.

A third part of the process involves being open and examining a range of players to see who the team will keep. Along with many youngsters, six free agents signed with the team and attended training camp. Two free agents did not last the month. Another two were waived before the halfway point. The team retained the youngsters to see who could play in the league.

Meanwhile, Gilbert Arenas returned from his suspension for the start of the 2010–2011 season. His field goal percentage, while rebounding slightly from the low the previous year, ranked among the lowest of his career. In early December, Ernie Grunfeld sent Arenas to Orlando for forward Rashard Lewis and a swap of monster contracts. Lewis would receive nearly $22 million a year until the close of the 2012–2013 season and bring more perimeter shooting to the squad, along with a steady veteran presence. The next trade to bring in more youth occurred two months later. The Atlanta Hawks traded for Hilton Armstrong and Kirk Hinrich. They gave Washington veteran guards Mike Bibby and Maurice Evans, young wing player Jordan Crawford, and a 2011 first-round draft choice. As they did with Zydrunas Ilgauskas the prior year, they waived Bibby and he caught on with a team, making a playoff run. The Wizards also waived Al Thornton, who signed on as a free agent with Golden State.

After using 24 players the previous year, the Wizards had 23 men play for them during the season. The process gave the coaches and player development scouts the opportunity to assess the abilities of the players. The trades also provided another foundation piece or pieces, as Washington selected two players in the first round of the 2011 draft for the second year in a row. The lottery luck did not hold up for the second year. Despite having the fourth-worst record in the league, Washington received the sixth pick in the draft. With it, they chose Jan Vesely, a forward from the Czech Republic who was 21 years of age. Under the scale terms, Vesely signed for $6.5 million during the course of two years, and then the team holds two club option years for an average of about $4.1 million. The 18th pick enabled the team to take another forward, Chris Singleton. The 22-year-old played three years of collegiate basketball at Florida State University. He is another player that the Wizards have locked up for a good amount of time, inexpensively, with a two-year deal worth $3.18 million and two more club option years for $1.7 and $2.7 million, respectively.

Hired to bring increased wins to a veteran team, coach Flip Saunders began his second year of working with a young team. His 2011 squad lost three more games than the prior year, while playing a little better offense and significantly worse defense. Rookies including John Wall, Jordan Crawford, Trevor Booker, Kevin Seraphin, and Hamady N'Diaye played minutes in games and during practices to gain valuable experience.

At the close of the season, the owners locked out the players. This battle seemed similar to the circumstances behind the 1998–1999 lockout discussed in the previous chapter. The struggle centered on the percentages of revenue allocated to players and owners. The league's teams claimed to be unable to turn a profit and sought a reduction in the amount of the player's share in the revenue. The NBPA disputed the owners' claims and rejected an offer to split revenue 50/50.[69]

As the talks continued throughout the summer, the Commissioner's Office announced the cancellation of the exhibition season. Soon, the first month of had games passed. The NBPA considered a decertification of their union as a move to enable them to pursue an antitrust lawsuit against the NBA. Commissioner David Stern warned the union against the move. The players brought suits against the league in California and Minnesota and then consolidated their effort in the latter's court. Despite the attempts of a federal mediator, the talks dragged on for 161 days, with the cancellation of games, sparking some players to commit to contracts with basketball teams in other countries. The players received 51.2% of revenue for 2011–2012, with a 49% to 51% range available for subsequent years. The owners gained the ability to use a one-time amnesty exemption to waive one player and remove him from the team's salary cap.[70]

While the owners and players struggled to reach an agreement, occasional stories emerged about the divisions among the team owners. A committee headed by the Boston Celtics' owner, Wyc Grousbeck, devised a revenue sharing plan. "The goal of the plan . . . [was] to work with the new Collective Bargaining Agreement to enable our league to be more competitive and more financially sound," Grousbeck said.[71] The complex formula involved all teams contributing up to half of their revenue, minus particular expenses, such as arena operating costs. After all, teams received a payout of the league's average payroll, and the lower revenue teams would receive an additional payout from the revenue pool that made up the difference between the team's revenue total and the average team payroll amount. To fully profit, a lower-revenue team would be required to generate at least 70% of the leaguewide average in total team revenue. Large-market teams were required to generate 130% of that same leaguewide average. Expectations were that as many as half of the teams in the league will receive payments and that seven of these teams—Milwaukee, Memphis, Charlotte, Sacramento, Atlanta, Indiana, and Minnesota—would require larger sums. New Orleans would have required the most funding, but their ownership vacated, and the league now runs the franchise.[72]

While Washington was not a team suffering financially, the team had recently dropped from the upper middle of the pack to the lower middle in valuations. There were significant areas for growth in revenue per fan and in television ratings for the team. During the 2010 season, the team had generated revenue per fan of $20. This ranked Washington above Chicago and Philadelphia in this category, but the team finished in the bottom third of the league. The team ranked worse in average Nielsen rating for their regular-season game, finishing 24 out of 30.[73]

The Wizards made a variety of personnel decisions before the start of the 2011–2012, 66-game season. They allowed Josh Howard to sign a free agent deal with the Utah Jazz and released rookie guard Mustafa Shakur and rookie forward Larry Owners. They also released Yi Jianlian. They resigned Nick Young for $3.7 million.

The Wizards started poorly in 2011–2012, losing their first eight games. One win and a four-game losing streak, followed by a second win and a three-game losing streak, spelled the end for Flip Saunders. Pundits, as well as Saunders, felt particular frustration with some of the team's players who had been around the league for a while. Nick Young, JaVale McGee, and Andray Blatche have been accused of not studying the game enough and spending time on frivolous activities instead.

The team's leadership made more moves at the trade deadline for the strike-shortened season. They traded Nick Young to the Los Angeles Clippers for forward Brian Cook and a second-round draft pick. Pundits viewed the trade as the loss of a talented player who proved inefficient in his play and not worth the headache for the Wizards. The Wizards also traded centers JaVale McGee and Ronny Turiaf to the Denver Nuggets for center Nene. The hopeful view was that Nene would bring toughness and a winning culture to the Wizards.[74]

Ernie Grunfeld accomplished most of what media observers sought with these moves, although many interpreted them more as efforts to clean out a dysfunctional culture than attempts to create a brighter future. The calls for Grunfeld's departure continued on the basis that people who lead franchises were evaluated on decision making, and this would be the team's fourth consecutive year of such poor play that they will be a lottery team during the forthcoming draft.[75]

Notes

1. Mitchell Krugel, *One Last Shot: The Story of Michael Jordan's Comeback* (New York: T. Dunne Books, 2002), 60–65.

2. Richard Sandomir, "Jordan Sheds Uniform for Suit as a Wizards Owner," *New York Times*, January 20, 2000, D1.

3. "A Hurdle in Jordan-Wizards deal," *Los Angeles Sentinel*, January 20, 2000, B3.

4. Jack Chevalier, "Jordan Takes on Major Task," *Philadelphia Tribune*, January 21, 2000, 1C.

5. Red Auerbach, with John Feinstein, *Let Me Tell You A Story: A Lifetime in the Game* (Boston: Little, Brown and Company, 2004), 207–9.

6. Sam Smith, "Michael, You're Smart but No Wizard," *Chicago Tribune*, January 16, 2000, http://articles.chicagotribune.com/2000-01-16/sports/0001160194_1_nba-executive-salary-cap-washington-wizards. (retrieved June 19, 2011).

7. Chevalier, "Jordan Takes on Major Task."

8. "D.C. Shakedown," http://sportsillustrated.cnn.com/basketball/nba/news/2000/01/29/heard_fired_ap/, January 21, 2000.

9. "NBA Rules History," NBA.com, www.nba.com/analysis/rules_history.html (retrieved February 2, 2010); this and other details and quotes by Greg Ballard were obtained during an interview with the author, April 23, 2012.

10. "Jordan Shakes Up Wizards Front Office," *Philadelphia Tribune*, May 19, 2000, 2A.

11. Red Auerbach, and John Feinstein, *Let Me Tell You A Story: A Lifetime in the Game* (Boston: Little, Brown and Company, 2004); Joseph White, "Wizards Finally Land Hamilton,"*Atlanta Daily World*, June 18, 2000, 10.

12. This and other details and quotes by Don MacLean were obtained during an interview with the author, March 19, 2012.

13. Joseph White, "Leonard Hamilton Resigns as Wizards Coach," LubbockOnline, April 19, 2001, www.lubbockonline.com/stories/041901/upd_075-1411.shtml (retrieved June 19, 2011).

14. "Coaching Carousel," *Seattle Times*, April 20, 2001, http://community.seattletimes.nwsource.com/archive/?date=20010420&slug=nba20 (retrieved June 19, 2011).

15. Larry Platt, *Keeping It Real: A Turbulent Season at the Crossroads with the NBA* (New York: Avon Books, 1999), 136.

16. Seth Davis, "A Loan at the Top," *Sports Illustrated*, April 30, 2001, 12.

17. Joseph White, "Jordan Returns to Play for Wizards," *Philadelphia Tribune*, September 28, 2001, 5B.

18. "Memphis Sounds Franchise Index," Basketball-Reference.com, www.basketball-reference.com/teams/MMS/ (retrieved August 21, 2011).

19. Mitchell Krugel, *One Last Shot: The Story of Michael Jordan's Comeback* (New York: T. Dunne Books, 2002), 107.

20. Krugel, *One Last Shot*, 144, 179–201, 245; Roscoe Nance, "Jordan Can't Spread the Magic to Other Wizards," *USA Today*, April 15, 2003, D1.

21. "Wizards Sign Hughes to Multiyear Deal," *Sports Illustrated*, July 18, 2002.

22. Krugel, *One Last Shot*, 179–201.

23. Chris Ballard, "Enemy Lines: An Opposing Team's Scout Sizes Up the Wizards," *Sports Illustrated*, October 28, 2002.

24. Ron Green Jr., "Shinn: I Messed Up in Charlotte," *Charlotte Observer*, November 11, 2008, www.charlotteobserver.com/2008/11/02/294986/shinn-i-messed-up-in-charlotte.html (retrieved October 19, 2011).

25. Roscoe Nance, "Jordan Can't Spread the Magic to Other Wizards," *USA Today*, April 15, 2003, D1.

26. Erik Brady, "Wizards Show Jordan the Door," *USA Today*, May 7, 2003, D1.

27. Ian O'Connor, "Keeping Score Column," *USA Today*, May 7, 2003, D1.

28. O'Connor, "Keeping Score Column," D1.

29. Jon Saraceno, "Jordan's Big Finish Falls Flat," *USA Today*, April 15, 2003, D1.

30. "Jordan's Big Finish Falls Flat," *USA Today*, April 15, 2003, D1.

31. Jon Saraceno, "Jordan's Big Finish Falls Flat," *USA Today*, April 15, 2003, C1.

32. "2002–2003 NBA Season Summary," Basketball-Reference.com, www.basketball-reference.com/leagues/NBA_2003.html (retrieved September 26, 2010).

33. "Wizards Fire Collins as Coach," *New York Times*, May 31, 2003. http://www.nytimes.com/2003/05/31/sports/nba-roundup-wizards-fire-collins-as-coach.html (retrieved October 22, 2011).

34. "A New Jordan in Town," *Sports Illustrated*, June 19, 2003. http://sportsillustrated.cnn.com/basketball/news/2003/06/19/wizards_jordan_ap/ (retrieved October 22, 2011).

35. "Executives: Ernie Grunfeld," Basketball-Reference.com, www.basketball-reference.com/executives/grunfer01x.html (retrieved September 26, 2010).

36. Rudy Martzke, "NBA Finalizes TV Deals: Good-bye NBC," *USA Today*, January 22, 2002.

37. "Wizards Sign Michael Ruffin," *Washington Post*, August 3, 2004.

38. Terry Pristin, "Washington Makes Downtown a Destination Again," *New York Times*, September 1, 2004, C8.

39. Liz Robbins, "Back with a Vengeance," *New York Times*, April 25, 2005, D6.

40. Dave Curtis, "Many Hands Seize Moment for Wizards," *New York Times*, May 7, 2005, D1.

41. Charles Nobles, "Heat Proves It Can Prevail with Its Stars Flickering," *New York Times*, May 9, 2005, D1.

42. Dave Curtis, "Down 2–0, Wizards Get More Bad News," *New York Times*, May 12, 2005, D8.

43. Dave Curtis, "Heat and Wade Use 3rd Quarter to Finish off the Wizards," *New York Times*, May 15, 2005. H1.

44. Kurt Badenhausen, "Full-Court Press," *Forbes*, vol. 177 (January 9, 2006), 128–29.

45. Christian Ewell, "Wizards Lose Hughes to Cavs," *Baltimore Sun*, July 9, 2005, D1; Howard Beck, "Four Years Later, N.B.A. Sees the Points," *New York Times*, May 13, 2005, D1.

46. Ian Thomsen, "How Larry Got to Cleveland," *Sports Illustrated*, August 15, 2005.

47. "With James, Cavaliers Win Easily," *New York Times*, April 23, 2006, H6.

48. Liz Robbins, "Consensus Is That This Draft Has No Clear No. 1," *New York Times*, June 27, 2006, D6.

49. Lee Jenkins, "The Value of Zero Is Rising," *New York Times*, March 15, 2007, D1.

50. Mark Kass, "Bucks Want Longer Lease," *Business Journal*, May 15, 2008; Nikita Stewart and Thomas Heath, "Pollin Asks D.C. to Pay for Verizon Center Renovations," *Washington Post*, January 27, 2007, *Boston Herald*, August 19, 2006.

51. "Wizards' Arenas Seeks to Opt Out," *New York Times*, June 11, 2007, D8.

52. "The Business of Basketball," *Forbes*, December 6, 2007, http://www.forbes.com/2007/12/06/business-basketball-nba-biz-07nba-cz_kb_mo_cs_1206nbaintro.html (retrieved October 9, 2011).

53. Marty Burns, "7 Washington Wizards," *Sports Illustrated*, October 29, 2007.

54. 2007–08 Washington Wizards Roster and Statistics," Basketball-Reference.com, www.basketball-reference.com/teams/WAS/2008.html (retrieved September 26, 2010).

55. "Stevenson: LeBron Is Overrated," http://hoopeduponline.com/2008/03/14/stevenson-lebron-is-overrated/ (retrieved March 3, 2010).

56. Andrew Rosen, "Wizards Fall Behind Early, Never Recover," April 21, 2008, http://www.nba.com/wizards/news/wizcavsgame2recap_080421.html (retrieved March 6, 2010).

57. Rosen, "Wizards Fall Behind Early, Never Recover."

58. Andrew Rosen, "Wizards Fall Behind Early, Never Recover," April 27, 2008, http://www.nba.com/wizards/news/wizcavsgame4recap_080427.html (retrieved March 6, 2010).

59. Andrew Rosen, "Short-Handed Wizards Fall to Cavs," May 2, 2008, http://www.nba.com/wizards/news/wizcavs_080502.html (retrieved March 6, 2010).

60. Rosen, "Short-Handed Wizards Fall to Cavs," May 2, 2008 http://www.nba.com/wizards/news/wizcavs_080502.html (retrieved March 6, 2010).

61. Vishnu Parasuraman, "What Do You Do about a Problem Like the Wizards," Grandland.com, February 15, 2012, www.grantland.com/story/_/id/7575336/ernie-grunfeld-john-wall-rashard-lewis-how-fix-washington-wizards (retrieved September 26, 2010).

62. "Wizards Fire Coach Eddie Jordan," *CBC Sports*, November 24, 2008, http://www.cbc.ca/sports/basketball/story/2008/11/24/wizards-Jordan.html. (retrieved September 9, 2011); Ivan Carter, "Jordan Fired, Tapscott to Take Over," *Washington Post*, November 24, 2008, http://voices.washingtonpost.com/wizardsinsider/2008/11/jordan_fired.html (retrieved September 9, 2011).

63. "Washington Wizards Hire Flip Saunders as New Head Coach," InsideHoops, April 22, 2009, www.insidehoops.com/blog/?p=4222 (retrieved September 11, 2010).

64. "Abe Pollin Dies at Age 85," ESPN.com, November 25, 2009, http://sports.espn.go.com/nba/news/story?id=4686480 (retrieved October 22, 2010).

65. "Abe Pollin Built More Than Wizards," AolNews.com, November 25, 2009, www.aolnews.com/2009/11/25/abe-pollin-built-more-than-wizards/ (retrieved September 26, 2010).

66. Peter Vecsey, and David K. Li, "Wizards' Gilbert Arenas and Javaris Crittenton Pull Pistols on Each Other," *New York Post*, January 2, 2010.

67. "Gilbert Arenas's Fake Gun-Play Might Cost Wizards Teammates," That NBA, January 8, 2010, www.thatnbalotterypick.com/2010/01/gilbert-arenas-fake-gun-play-might-cost.html (retrieved December 9, 2010).

68. Phil Taylor, "One and Done to Death," *Sports Illustrated*, April 26, 2010,

69. "NBA Lockout: Union Disbanding Seriously Jeopardizes the 2011–2012 Season," *Los Angeles Times*, November 11, 2011; James Johnson, "Good-bye 2011–2012 Season, Lockout Deal Rejected as Players Look to Decertify Union," *Inquisitr*, November 14, 2011, www.inquisitr.com/159640/goodbye-2011-2012-nba-season-lock-out-deal-rejected-as-players-look-to-decertify-union/ (retrieved December 11, 2011).

70. Howard Beck, "NBA Reaches a Tentative Deal to Save the Season," *New York Times*, November 26, 2011. http://www.nytimes.com/2011/11/27/sports/basketball/nba-and-basketball-players-reach-deal-to-end-lockout.html?pagewanted=all (retrieved January 8, 2012).

71. John Lombardo, "Inside NBA's Revenue Sharing," *Sports Business Journal*, Janaury 23, 2012, 1.

72. "NBA Board of Governors Ratify 10-Year CBA," NBA.com, December 8, 2011, www.nba.com/2011/news/12/08/labor-deal-reached/index.html (retrieved February 26, 2012).

73. Kurt Badenhausen, and Mike Ozanian, "NBA Team Values: The Business of Basketball," *Forbes*, January 25, 2102, www.forbes.com/nba-valuations (retrieved February 26, 2012).

74. Chad Ford, "Trade Deadline Evaluations, Part 1," ESPN.com, March 16, 2012, http://insider.espn.go.com/nba/story?id=7695406&_slug_=nba-trade-deadline-evaluations-every-team-part-one (retrieved March 17, 2012).

75. Jason Reid, "Grunfeld Should Clean Out His Desk," *Washington Post*, March 21, 2012, D1.

CHAPTER ELEVEN

~

Conclusion: The Teams, the Fans, and Current State of Basketball in D.C.

In five leagues and for 90 years, professional basketball in North America has undergone an amazing transformation. Washington, D.C., has been involved throughout the history of the sport. The city placed teams in every league. Those teams have often represented Washington well. Many squads made the playoffs or at least finished in the upper tier of the league, winning more often than losing. Nonetheless, the city's franchises have frequently experienced the limitations wrought by an undercapitalized ownership or an ownership unable or unwilling to lose a large amount of money on the team.

Washington, D.C.'s, first team emerged out of a local league and the barnstorming tradition. They represented a local company, the Palace Laundry chain, owned by George Preston Marshall. Marshall played a significant role in shaping the operation and rules of this first national basketball league. The Palace Five finished in second or third place for the half seasons during the league's first two years; however, Marshall's decisions with regard to personnel and a large barnstorming schedule probably harmed the team's performance in the league.

The owner's decisions during the third season proved deleterious to his squad. Marshall promoted trades that proved too one-sided against team or directly hurt the team because the new player did not sign with the Palace club. His salary battles with several important players led to a significant drop in the talent left on the team. As the team's record worsened, the number of fans attending the games and the evening dance that often followed declined. Ever the publicist and promoter, Marshall made himself into the injured party and took advantage of a unique situation to sell his team midseason.

Marshall remained unique among professional basketball team owners in Washington, D.C., and other places in unloading his franchise so brazenly. Unfortunately, the next owner followed his path with a problematic personnel decision that undercut the success of the team on the court. Mike Uline ran one of the city's largest ice manufacturers and turned part of his building into an arena. He joined with other large-city arena owners to start a new national league in the immediate post–World War II era. Unlike Marshall, Uline turned the basketball operations of his Washington Capitols over to a local basketball man, Red Auerbach. His team succeeded on the courts far more than Marshall's squad. Yet, the owner toyed with replacing his coach and general manager. During the third season, the Capitols reached the finals, but Uline balked at giving Auerbach a long-term contract. The decision to let his insightful coach and executive leave precipitated the team's progressively steep decline on the floor and in the stands, which ultimately prompted the team's withdrawal from the league within two seasons.

A decade later, a business man who purchased Uline Arena joined a new basketball league and started to compete against the National Basketball Association (NBA). Quickly sensing his undercapitalization, owner Harry Lynn sought partners and formed the Washington Tapers. Like most of the teams involved in this venture, the Tapers barely drew any size crowd. They started a trend for the league's franchises of moving in a vain hope of finding a fan base, when they relocated to Long Island, New York.

What Washington lost in the beginning of the 1960s, the city gained at the close of the decade. Washington lawyer Earl Foreman purchased the champion Oakland Oaks of the American Basketball Association (ABA) and moved them to D.C. Foreman had a playoff team but spent much of the year attempting to facilitate the merger of his Washington Capitols and the rest of the ABA into the NBA. The location of the Washington Capitols proved the major sticking point in the negotiations, so Foreman moved the team to Virginia, where his undercapitalization did not allow him to wait out the court cases that were holding up the merger.

Back in 1964, Foreman and two partners purchased an expansion Chicago team in the NBA and moved it to Baltimore. The Bullets made the playoffs in consecutive seasons, but the owners' inability to maintain a long-term coach and general manager hampered the team. A lack of attendance and a financial squeeze for the owners ended this ownership structure at the end of the 1960s. Under the remaining owner, Abe Pollin, the Bullets moved to the suburbs of Washington, D.C., and proved the team of the decade in the 1970s, but limited financial commitments and other decisions led to the team squeaking into the playoffs in the early and mid-1980s, and then dropping to a poor franchise through the mid-1990s. A series of personnel decisions constructed a playoff team with great promise, but other decisions made in the aftermath of one playoff season quickly removed the base for the foundation and the team crashed. Pollin hired a new executive for basketball operations, and his work wrought a team slightly above .500 during the season that lost early in the playoffs four consecutive years before a crash and burn that mandated a rebuilding operation.

This biography of the various Washington, D.C., teams illustrates the amazing degree of changes that have occurred in the world of professional basketball. What initially started as a game that offered dancing afterward to entice patrons developed into a multibillion-dollar worldwide conglomerate that spurred the development of subsidiary businesses. In conjunction with this growth, the players, the game, and game operations have changed as drastically.

The majority of the game's players used to and still do come from ethnic, urban, working-class backgrounds. During the early years of the NBA, most were college graduates after playing four years in school, and the league initially restricted itself to only caucasian players in the American Basketball League during the 1920s. This barrier came down in 1950, and, throughout the next 20 years, the switch to a majority of players being African American occurred. During the 1970s, the change in the requirement that players needed to wait four years after high school before becoming draft eligible led to a slow decline in the number of college graduate players. By the mid-1990s, the first wave of players coming straight from high school entered the league, and, in this new century, many have established a one-and-done track of getting one year of college or European professional ball experience before going into the NBA Draft. Since the mid-1980s, an increasing number of players have come from countries all around the globe.

Demographics were but one of the changes. The perspective of playing the game and the potential of making it into a career changed dramatically as well. The guys playing the game in the 1920s might have started playing the game as kids, perhaps in the local YMCA and YMHA. They moved from team to team and engaged in barnstorming and other exhibition activities to piece together an existence as a professional player. By the mid 1940s through the mid-1960s, players started as children playing in school and local city gyms, or, if they lived in rural areas, shooting baskets in the backyard and on high school teams. They received better salaries than their predecessors, but the vast majority needed to work second jobs during the off-season.

Several noted that if they did not or could not work the second job, it was necessary for them to obtain food stamps or unemployment compensation to support their families. Some viewed the game as a good time for three or so years before they settled down to the real world of regular work. Demonstrations of player solidarity in unions helped win concessions on health and pension issues for current players.

Throughout the late 1960s and 1970s, players emerged from the playgrounds, where they learned the trade by playing with neighborhood characters and occasionally within grassroots leagues. Most guys retired by 30 years of age, if they lasted that long. The existence of a competing league gave players the increased leverage to negotiate for higher salaries and more guaranteed years on their contracts. The merger of the leagues won the players free agency and control of their professional careers. In the 1980s, leagues for elementary school-aged children emerged. As the best of these youngsters played on traveling teams, this represented the origins of what would morph into the Amateur Athletic Union leagues.

Salaries of players continue to rise, with veteran exemptions put into place to offset some of the salary cap limitations. Minimum salaries on salary scales have increased the pay for all players. During the last two decades, continuous strife over each of the new Collective Bargaining Agreements has emerged. The players have continued to battle to hold on to what they deem as a fair share of the revenue split that serves as the cornerstone behind the agreements.

The circumstances for teams in the league have improved as dramatically as they have for players. Starting in the 1920s as a subsidiary business for a larger service or industrial company, the basketball teams through the 1950s ran out of a small office in a storefront that had a few employees who performed multiple jobs. General managers still had their hands in all operations through the 1970s, but the 1980s led to the beginnings of the separation of the basketball and business operations. Players still came in to the front offices to get their mail and interacted with the administrative assistants for a feeling of one big team. The business operations moved to a separate location downtown, with executives running separate divisions with their own sizable staffs.

The occasional scout and team coaches reportedly knew most of the top talent in the early days of the NBA Draft through watching college games, particularly the National Invitational Tournament and National Collegiate Athletic Association Tournament. They expanded their search into smaller college tournaments and regional tournaments, particularly the Portsmouth Invitational. Increasingly, the rankings of college players became more sophisticated, and invitational tournaments became places to watch potential draftees play against one another to fine tune player evaluations. By the mid-1980s, the NBA developed a Chicago Combine, which at first offered teams another view of a player in action. It has primarily become a location for trainers to poke and prod players to measure their athleticism and observe concerns about previous injuries and health.

The locations where the teams played changed greatly. In the 1920s, many teams played in dance halls. This improved to armories or small arenas, which they shared with professional hockey teams. The places had cramped locker rooms and few amenities for fans. By the late 1960s and early 1970s, arenas appeared in the suburbs of cities, offering larger and more elaborate concession stands and electronic scoreboards. Teams still practiced at local colleges. Today, there are huge downtown complexes, with arenas, practice courts, weight room facilities, and training rooms sectioned off for players and team personnel only. Large corporate boxes line one tier across the entire seating area. Near the floor, more plush and expensive seating has priced out the average fan.

On the court, by the late 1960s, teams had a scout and an assistant coach who were sometimes the same person. Ten years later, some teams had multiple assistant coaches and regional scouts. These staffs continued to grow and added strength and conditioning coaches, video tape coordinators, and such specialists as sleep experts. In the early days, traveling accommodations included cramming players four to a car to get to the arena just in time for tip-off. From the 1960s through the 1980s, the trainer served as road secretary and handled many of the traveling arrangements, which usually involved commercial airlines and bus rentals. Some teams adopted charter travel, and, by the middle to late 1990s, teams owned their own planes and took two buses plus a truck for luggage.

There has been an incredible range of rule changes. The game always had a rough edge, from the early days of stalling and continuous passing until players got high-percentage shots, through the initial installation of the 24-second shot clock and development of the jump shot. The early NBA players frowned upon dunking the ball, and, through the 1960s, teams played a high-paced game, with each side having more than 150 possessions. Ever more elaborate defensive schemes, changing the size of the paint area, and the use of zone defenses led to an increasingly complicated game, with a 40% decline in the number of possessions per team.

These changes have shaped the NBA industry. As arenas become obsolete, teams will move again, presumably pricing more individuals out of being able to attend. Personnel will expand, and salaries will continue to grow, while efforts of free-agent players to unite and go to a single franchise may become more likely. Playing rules will be modified, as players adapt to the current game and shape the style of play to draw an increased interest from spectators. The league has now become a multibillion-dollar industry, able to support numerous ancillary businesses. Yet, the biggest leap occurred with the Collective Bargaining Agreement of 2011–2012. The owners attempted to address the financial imbalance among the 30 teams. The NBA's version of revenue sharing intended to keep existing teams solvent and competitive. With full implementation a few years away, any determination of success on either of these fronts awaits the passage of even more time.[1]

The Washington Wizards sat in the middle of the financial circumstances. The franchise did not appear poised to be a receiver of funds from the pool of revenues but would presumably contribute a small amount, if any, after the payout to all teams based on average NBA player salaries. The potential of the Washington Metropolitan Area market struck me as the most intriguing element. The area represented the eighth-largest television market in the country, a large source of revenue from local television broadcast of games. Yet, the low ratings of the games currently limited the ability to collect higher revenue for the broadcasts. The area has nine of the top 20 richest counties in the United States. Undoubtedly, this presented to the team an amazing market left to tap.[2]

The team obviously needed to expand its fan base. Experts in psychology have observed that children typically develop the ability to identify a favorite team by the time they reach eight or nine years of age. This emerges when children develop their operational level of thinking. Such factors as family loyalties, local ties, and fan interest of peers all shape the fan interests of youngsters. Many retain this connection with the team throughout their lifetime if they remain interested in the sport. The history of the Bullets and Wizards illuminates the particular disadvantages the franchise has faced in creating a fan base. Like any expansion team, they emerged in the sport after many fans had already developed their rooting interests and loyalties to existing teams. They lost a portion of the fan base that developed through connection to a local city by moving twice early in their history. Certainly some fans retained their rooting interest in the Bullets when they moved from Baltimore, but many dropped their allegiance, because the two cities had different populations and a degree of dislike for one another.

Historically, the limited fan base that the Bullets/Wizards generated has been attributed to two aspects of Washington's population. Many residents are originally from other locations and have preestablished allegiances to other franchises. The second, although related, claim involves the city being populated with transients, lacking an interest or desire to develop a rooting interest for the Washington team. The unanswered question for those people who share this view was this: Why had the Washington Redskins of the National Football League developed a large and devoted fan base? The Washington Metropolitan Area has witnessed significant population growth during the era in which the Bullets and Wizards have been the area's basketball team. In 1970, the area was home to more than 3.1 million people. This number climbed to 3.4 million by 1980. A huge jump to 4.1 million occurred during the next decade. A gain of 600,000 raised the area's population to nearly 4.8 million by 2000. A decade later, the population rose to 5.5 million people. While some of this group retained their old basketball loyalties, others changed to support the local team or adopted the Washington squad as a second team. These people also had children who grew up in the area and supported the local team.[3]

With this increase in more than 2 million people to the area, it would seem that the Bullets/Wizards fan base would have grown significantly. What happened to the fans? The area of fan psychology has started to document what fans are and what motivates them. Being a fan of a team provides a sense of belonging, a sense of community. A fan's linkage to a team serves as an extension of the self and a specific identity. This identification also extends to certain players, most especially the team's star or superstar players.[4] As the NBA focused on the marketing of stars since the 1980s, this type of identification has only increased, for example, with the "Be like Mike" phenomenon. Fans gain an outlet for escape from the daily world and also experience a range of emotions, particularly euphoria, dejection, and stress. Those fans who are loosely connected to a team interact with their teams through basking in reflected glory (BIRGing) and cutting off reflective failures (CORFing). As the terms suggest, the fan enjoys credit during the periods when the team succeeds and denies any connection when the team fails.[5]

Anecdotal evidence suggests some plausible answers to the basketball team's limited numbers among traditional, fantasy, and casual fan bases. A few former fans during the team's championship years claimed to have lost interest in the pro game (the NBA). Their reasons for dropping the game and spending more time watching collegiate basketball include changes to the style of play, the game becoming less of a team effort and much more about individual accomplishments, and a lack of player loyalty. Among the next-younger generation of fans, people in the thirties, their changes in team loyalty or disinterest in the Washington Wizards came with explanations that they never saw the team on national television or that they were not familiar with the players on the team. A few people among a younger group of basketball fans claim not to have a team loyalty, but, instead, they root for particular players. They follow the player or players regardless of team affiliation and would not support a team if they did not have the player or players on the squad.

As noted, the interests of traditional fans in teams often feature identification with the team's star players. The Baltimore Bullets had two stars. Unfortunately, the team lost the most dynamic figure of the pair (Earl Monroe). Once the more workmanlike Wes Unseld and Elvin Hayes left the scene in the early 1980s, the team lacked star power for several years. The Bullets' limited star power coincided with the league's new marketing approach to promote its stars. Figures like Dr. J, Magic Johnson, Larry Bird, and Michael Jordan appeared in televised games, promotions, and commercials, and they captured the interests of new fans through the power of identification. Washington's basketball team had a star three times during the 15 seasons since the mid-1990s. The sales of tickets, publicity, and television coverage all increased. The team reached the playoffs on five occasions, advancing to the next round once. Each team-star relationship ended badly, undermining the gains from the fan identification. The executives traded Chris Webber, they ended their partnership with Michael Jordan, and they traded Gilbert Arenas after his firearms incident.

Today, a different type of fan, the fantasy fan, may also seek out a team with the top players. The identification process working through a fantasy league structure places the fan in the position of owner and manager to the player. This viewpoint has been explored more deeply in recent sitcoms, like *The League*, and referred to in scenes in various movies about sports. The fantasy phenomenon prompts fans to root for the statistical production of players who are on their fantasy team, regardless of the professional team that they play on. They root for the success of their fantasy team, rather than the success of a particular basketball team in the NBA; however, if a NBA team lacked a star or, particularly, a superstar, fantasy fans may not have a member from that team on their fantasy team. Thus, these fans would rarely pay attention to that NBA team. The Wizards are often one of those teams that fantasy fans ignore because of their lack of a star or superstar to buy for a fantasy team.

Casual fans pay rare attention to the sport. They jump on bandwagons when the team in their area wins, or they pay attention if a team's player becomes a celebrity who crosses into different interest areas, such as music, movies, or fashion. Washington teams have never had a superstar, like Magic Johnson, Larry Bird, Michael Jordan in his prime, Shaquille O'Neal, Kobe Bryant, Dwyane Wade, or LeBron James, who mastered most aspects of the game or always worked on improving them. The teams have lacked that player who can lead his team to a championship and has that electric personality that the team and league can market to become a multimedia celebrity and reach the consciousness of the person with little interest in the sport.

Washington's limited success on the court has played a role in limiting the demonstration of fan support and the accumulation of more marginal fans. The esteem that fans receive from a successful team was rarely bestowed by the Bullets/Wizards, leaving their fans less likely to buy and wear team merchandise. The team's limited success in games has provided casual fans with little opportunity to engage in the basking of reflected glory. Meanwhile, it enhances their changes of cutting off reflected failures.

The Washington Wizards' brain trust is aware that they need to solidify and expand their current fan base. They know that they need a superstar, consistency from management, and continuous success on the court. They selected John Wall in the draft, made him the face of the franchise, and built him up as a star—a potential superstar. This has had its drawbacks, as his game has lacked certain requisite skills, and the team around him proved incapable of making the leap to the next level of play. As the 2011–2012 season closed, the team made moves that indicate that they recognize these inequalities and know that there is much more to do before they can really expect a leap in the fan base and a change in the fan base's perspective on the team.

Notes

1. Kurt Badenhausen, and Mike Ozanian, "NBA Team Values: The Business of Basketball," *Forbes*, January 25, 2102, www.forbes.com/nba-valuations (retrieved February 26, 2012).

2. Radley Balko, "Washington's Wealth Boom," Reason.com, January 14, 2009, http://reason.com/archives/2009/01/14/washingtons-wealth-boom (retrieved March 20, 2012).

3. Jeffrey D. James, "Becoming a Sports Fan and Understanding Cognitive Development and Socialization in the Development of Fan Loyalty," doctoral dissertation retrieved from the OhioLINK ETD Center, www.city-data.com/forum/city-vs-city/1197522-population-metropolitan-area-msa-populations-1970-a.html#post17798454 (retrieved March 27, 2012).

4. Shirley Wang, "The Science Behind Fanatic Behavior," *APS Observer*, May 2006, www.psychologicalscience.org/observer/getArticle.cfm?id=1986 (retrieved March 11, 2012).

5. Susan Krauss Whitbourne, "The Psychology of Sports Fans," *Psychology Today*, December 30, 2011, www.psychologytoday.com/blog/fulfillment-any-age/201112/the-psychology-sports-fans (retrieved March 19, 2012).

~

Bibliography

"1953–54 NBA Season Summary." Basketball-Reference.com, www.basketball-reference.com/leagues/NBA_1954.html (retrieved February 14, 2011).

"1959–60 NBA Season Summary." Basketball-Reference.com, www.basketball-reference.com/leagues/NBA_1960.html (retrieved February 14, 2011).

"1960–61 Boston Celtics Roster and Statistics." Basketball-Reference.com, www.basketball-reference.com/teams/BOS/1961.html (retrieved February 14, 2011).

"1963–64 Baltimore Bullets Roster and Statistics." Basketball-Reference.com, www.basketball-reference.com/teams/BAL/1964.html (retrieved October 10, 2010).

"1967–68 Baltimore Bullets Roster and Statistics." Basketball-Reference.com, www.basketball-reference.com/teams/BAL/1968.html (retrieved October 10, 2010).

"1968–69 Baltimore Bullets Roster and Statistics." Basketball-Reference.com, www.basketball-reference.com/teams/BAL/1969.html (retrieved May 7, 2010).

"1969–70 Washington Capitols Roster and Statistics," Basketball-Reference.com, www.basketball-reference.com/teams/WSA/1970.html (retrieved October 10, 2010).

"1984 NBA Draft." Basketball-Reference.com, www.basketball-reference.com/draft/NBA_1984.html (retrieved February 14, 2011).

"1988 NBA Draft." Basketball-Reference.com, www.basketball-reference.com/draft/NBA_1988.html (retrieved February 14, 2012).

"1988–89 Washington Bullets Roster and Statistics." Basketball-Reference.com, www.basketball-reference.com/teams/WSB/1989.html (retrieved February 14, 2012).

"1996–97 Washington Bullets Roster and Statistics." Basketball-Reference.com, www.basketball-reference.com/teams/WSB/1997.html (retrieved September 16, 2010).

"1999 NBA Draft." Basketball-Reference.com, www.basketball-reference.com/draft/NBA_1999.html (retrieved September 26, 2010).
"2002–2003 NBA Season Summary." Basketball-Reference.com, www.basketball-reference.com/leagues/NBA_2003.html (retrieved September 26, 2010).
"2007–08 Washington Wizards Roster and Statistics." Basketball-Reference.com, www.basketball-reference.com/teams/WAS/2008.html (retrieved September 26, 2010).
"A Round-up of Sports Information of the Week." *Sports Illustrated*, May 17, 1965, 110.
"ABA Boss Says Caps Aren't about to Leave." *Washington Star*, January 24, 1970, A-13.
"ABA Head Makes Peace Bid to NBA; Caps One Stumbling Block." *Washington Post*, January 9, 1970, D1
"Abe Pollin Built More Than Wizards." AolNews.com, November 25, 2009, www.aolnews.com/2009/11/25/abe-pollin-built-more-than-wizards/ (retrieved September 26, 2010).
"Abe Pollin Dies at Age 85." ESPN.com, November 25, 2009, http://sports.espn.go.com/nba/news/story?id=4686480 (retrieved October 22, 2010).
Addie, Bob. "Basketball Begins." *Washington Post*, October 27, 1961, C3;
———."The Ball Bounces." *Washington Post*, August 22, 1969, D1.
Aldridge, David. "Bullets Could Face Hard Choice in Lottery: Size or Versatility," *Washington Post*, April 25, 1989, C5
———. "Clunk! No. 9 Bullets Aren't Lottery Kings," *Washington Post*, May 22, 1989, C1.
———. "Pollin, Ferry, Unseld: Talent at the Top," *Washington Post*, January 30, 1989, C1;
Alfieri, Gus. *Lapchik: The Life of a Legendary Player and Coach in the Glory Days of Basketball*. Guilford, CT: Lyons Press, 2006.
American Institute of Steel Construction. *Modern Steel Construction*, XV (Fourth Quarter 1975), 3–9.
Architectural Record, 1940–1980.
Associated Press. "Stags Swap Gilmur for Caps' Hermsen." *Christian Science Monitor*, October 5, 1949, 18.
———. "Capitols Only .500 Club." *Christian Science Monitor*, December 7, 1949, 18.
Asher, Mark. "30 Home Games of Caps Head for Coliseum." *Washington Post*, August 22, 1969, D1.
———. "ABA Proposes Four Plans for Merger." *Washington Post*, March 11, 1970, D1.
———. "Balance Shifting in NBA," *Washington Post*, October 15, 1974, D1.
———. "Barry Scores 45 Caps Dump Denver." April 20, 1970, D-1.
———.Bid Made to Move Oaks Out of Oakland," *Washington Post*, August 19, 1969, B1.
———. "Bid to Bring Oakland Oaks Here Hits Scheduling Snag." *Washington Post*, August 20, 1969, D1.

———. "Capital Centre's Bookings Reach 175 for 81/2 months,"
———. "Foreman Brings ABA Kings Here." *Washington Post*, August 21, 1969, B1.
———. "Hayes Paints Rosy Future." *Washington Post*, August 4, 1972, D4.
———. "Israel Trip Caps Dream Year." *Washington Post*, September 3, 1978, D4
———. New Owners Keep Bullets in Baltimore." *Washington Times Herald*, November 24, 1964, D2.
———. "Pollin Bids for NHL." *Washington Post*, March 14, 1972, D3
———. "This Man and His Red, White and Blue Basketball Have Plently to Laugh about." *Washington Post*, November 22, 1970, 265.
———. "Petty Jealousies Cause Caps' Fall." *Washington Post*, April 30, 1970, F1.
———. "Regular Season Hurting NBA." *Washington Post*, April 2, 1972, F2.
Atkin, Ross. "Warriors' Sweep of Finals: Fantasyland Comes to NBA." *Christian Science Monitor*, May 28, 1975, 22.
Attner, Paul. "76ers Tie It, 110-104, Rouse Bullet Anger." *Washington Post*, May 4, 1978, D1.
———. "Bullets Outlast Hawks." *Washington Post*, April 13, 1978, D1.
———. "Bullets Outlast Hawks." *Washington Post*, April 30, 1979, D1.
———. "Bullets Stumble 116-105." *Washington Post*, April 26, 1978, D3.
———. "Cheap Seats from Furlow Anger Bullets." *Washington Post*, April 28, 1979, D1
———. "Free Agent Talks Center of Dispute," *Washington Post*, July 16, 1977, C1.
———. "Hawks Proving They Have Heart." *Washington Post*, April 26, 1979, D1
———. "Motta Accuses Bullets of 'Barnyard Basketball.'" *Washington Post*, April 17, 1978, D4.
———. "Motta Patterns an Open Secret." *Washington Post*, May 18, 1978, D1.
———. "Motta Simmers at His Team's Cool." *Washington Post*, May 8, 1979, D1.
———. "SuperSonics Capture NBA Title 97–93." *Washington Post*, June 2, 1979, D1.
Auerbach, Red, and John Feinstein. *Let Me Tell You A Story: A Lifetime in the Game*. Boston: Little, Brown and Company, 2004.
Axthelm, Pete. "Why Pro Basketball Is Sick." *Newsweek*, November 22, 1976, 87.
Badenhausen, Kurt. "Full-Court Press." *Forbes*, vol. 177 (January 9, 2006), 128–29.
Badenhausen, Kurt, and Mike Ozanian, "NBA Team Values: The Business of Basketball." *Forbes*, January 25, 2102, www.forbes.com/nba-valuations (retrieved February 26, 2012).
Bains, Bill. "Caps' Superstitions," *Washington Star*, March 27, 1949, B-2.
Balko, Radley. "Washington's Wealth Boom." Reason.com, January 14, 2009, http://reason.com/archives/2009/01/14/washingtons-wealth-boom (retrieved March 20, 2012).
Ballard, Chris. "Enemy Lines: An Opposing Team's Scout Sizes Up the Wizards." *Sports Illustrated*, October 28, 2002.
Ballard, Greg. Interview by author. Telephone, April 23, 2012.
Baltimore Afro-American, 1946–1988.
Baltimore Sun, March 1, 1925–December 31, 2010.

Basketball Association of America. "League Minutes 1946–1949." Association for Professional Basketball Research, www.apbr.org/baaminutes.html (retrieved February 4, 2010).

Basketball Reference, 1946–2010.

Batchelor, Bob, ed. *Basketball in America: From the Playgrounds to Jordan's Game and Beyond*. New York: Haworth Press, 2005.

Beck, Howard. "NBA Reaches a Tentative Deal to Save the Season." *New York Times*, November 26, 2011.

Bembry, Jerry. "Nash Quits as GM of Bullets," *Baltimore Sun*, May 1, 1996 http://articles.baltimoresun.com/1996-05-01/sports/1996122017_1_nash-bullets-omalley (retrieved October 16, 2010).

Bianchi, Al. Interview by author. Telephone, February 28, 2012.

Bickerstaff, Bernie. Interview by author. Telephone, March 17, 2012.

Bleier, Howard. "Taper Five Moves to Long Island: Pro Club to Operate at Commack Arena." *New York Times*, January 1, 1962, 18

———. "Troubles Beset Debut of Tapers." *New York Times*, January 17, 1962, 54.

Boston Globe, 1925–1992.

"Boston Makes All the Right Moves." *Los Angeles Times*, May 13, 1974, C1.

Boyd and Ball Consulting. "A Historical Study of Near Northeast Washington, D.C." H Street Community Development Corporation, July 15, 2001, section V.

Bradley, Bill. *Life on the Run*. New Brunswick, NJ: Transaction Publishers, 2000.

Bradley, Robert D. *The Compendium of Professional Basketball*. Tempe, AZ: Xaler Press, 2010.

———. "History of the American Basketball League," Association for Professional Basketball Research, www.apbr.org/ablhist.html (retrieved May 12, 2011).

———. "Labor Pains Nothing New to the NBA." Association for Professional Basketball Research, www.apbr.org/labor.html (retrieved October 9, 2009).

———. "Major Legal Cases in Pro Basketball History." Association for Professional Basketball Research, www.apbr.org/forum/viewtopic.php?t=3505&start=25 (retrieved February 14, 2011).

Bradley, Robert D., John Hogrogian, John Grasso, and Steve Brainerd. "American Basketball League," Association for Professional Basketball Research, www.apbr.org/abl2552.html (retrieved September 11, 2009).

Brady, Dave. "Pleased Bullets' Officials Plan More TV Exposure." *Washington Post*, March 26, 1965, D4

———. "Ripley Fired, Caps, Now Tapers, Get New Money, Coaches, Players." *Washington Post*, September 22, 1961, C1.

Brady, Erik. "Wizards Show Jordan the Door." *USA Today*, May 7, 2003.

Bronstein, Lloyd C. *Sports Law: Antitrust Suit Fails to Knock off NBA's Salary Cap*. 6 Loy. L.A. Ent. L. Rev. 231 (1986).

Brown, Clifton. "After Smokes Settles, Questions Surface," *New York Times*, August 12, 1996, C4.

"Bullets Get Mel Counts for Howell." *Washington Post*, September 2, 1966, E4.

"Bullets Go after Playoff First." *Washington Post*, March 31, 1970, D2.
"Bullets Rout Celtics." *New York Times*, May 1, 1975, 64.
"Bullets Sign Unseld, Claim Contract Tops Hayes' $440,000 at San Diego." *Washington Post*, April 19, 1968, D4
"Bullets' Stock Sale Near Final Stages," *Chicago Daily Defender*, July 18, 1968, 41;
"Bullets Trade 3 for Five Pistons." *Washington Post*, June 10, 1964, D4.
"Bullets Trade Walt Bellamy," *Chicago Daily Defender*, November 1965, 8.
Burns, Marty. "7 Washington Wizards." *Sports Illustrated*, October 29, 2007.
"The Business of Basketball." *Forbes*, December 6, 2007, http://www.forbes.com/2007/12/06/business-basketball-nba-biz-07nba-cz_kb_mo_cs_1206nbaintro.html (retrieved October 9, 2011).
Business Week, 1963–2010.
"Capital Five Nips Chicago," *Baltimore Sun*, November 3, 1961, S16.
"Capitols Only .500 Club," *Christian Science Monitor*, December 7, 1949, 18.
"Capitols Sign Markowitz, Willie Jones." *Washington Post*, May 11, 1961, A18
"Caps Draft Two Sepia Cage Stars into NBA." *Pittsburgh Courier*, April 29, 1950, 23.
"Caps' Prexy Mum about Club's Future." *Washington Star*, February 16, 1970, C3.
"Caps Reject Tri-City's Bid to Buy Team and Merge It." *Washington Post*, December 14, 1950, B8.
"Caps Sign Auerbach Again; Riley Leads Lions Once More." *Washington Post*, May 16, 1948, C4.
"Caps Try to Replace Auerbach; Carnevale Turns Down Offer." *Washington Post*, March 11, 1948, B5
Carry, Peter. "A Circus with One Tilted Ring." *Sports Illustrated*, April 15, 1974, 24.
———. "Having a Ball with the ABA." *Sports Illustrated*, March 18, 1974.
———. "Playing the Comedy Circuit." *Sports Illustrated*, November 8, 1971, 62
Carter, Ivan. "Jordan Fired, Tapscott to Take Over." *Washington Post*, November 24, 2008, http://voices.washingtonpost.com/wizardsinsider/2008/11/jordan_fired.html (retrieved September 9, 2011).
Castaneda, Ruben. "Wizards Play Final Game on Old Court." *Washington Post*, November 30, 1997, B1.
CBS SportsLine.com, 2005–2010.
"Central." *Sports Illustrated*, October 26, 1970, 39.
"Celtics Ponder Strategy." *Los Angeles Times*, April 26, 1974, B16
"Celtics Win 101-90." *New York Times*, May 4, 1975, 227.
Chafe, William. *The Unfinished Journey: America since World War II*. New York: Oxford University Press, 2010.
Chester Times, March 1, 1925–1946.
Chevalier, Jack. "Jordan Takes on Major Task," *Philadelphia Tribune*, January 21, 2000, 1C.
Chicago Daily Defender, 1909–1975.
Christian Science Monitor, 1908–1998.

Claiborne, William. "Bullets Pilgrims in Jerusalem," *Washington Post*, September 7, 1978, G1.
———. "Fat Lady Sings." *Washington Post*, September 8, 1978, E1.
"Coaching Carousel," *Seattle Times*, April 20, 2001, http://community.seattletimes.nwsource.com/archive/?date=20010420&slug=nba20 (retrieved June 19, 2011).
Cole, Lewis. *A Loose Game*. Indianapolis, IN: Bobbs-Merrill, 1978.
Colliers, 1948.
Commerce Clearing House. *Selective Service Act of 1948*, Public Law 80-759, 62 (1948).
Committee on the Judiciary. *Report Authorizing the Merger of Two or More Professional Basketball Leagues, and for Other Purposes*, U.S. Senate, 92nd Congress, Rep. No. 92-1151 (1972).
Congressional Record, March 1, 1925–December 31, 2010.
Coon, Larry. "Larry Coon's NBA Salary Cap FAQ, 2011 Collective Bargaining Agreement." https://webfiles.uci.edu/lcoon/cbafaq/salarycap.htm (retrieved May 9, 2011).
Cotton, Anthony. "Bullets Follow Jeff Malone to Overtime Win," *Washington Post*, May 3, 1988, E1.
———. "Pollin Stays Upbeat on Bullets," *Washington Post*, December 8, 1987, E1.
———. "Uncertainties Breed Anxieties for Bullets," *Washington Post*, October 27, 1987, E1.
Cromie, Robert. "Pro Basketball League Adds Two Cities," *Chicago Daily Tribune*, May 11, 1960, C4.
Daily Courier (Connellsville, PA), November 1, 1960–1970.
Daily Leader Times, March 1, 1925–1948.
Daily Mail, March 1, 1925–1948.
Daily Messenger (Canandaigua, NY), November 1, 1960–1970.
Davies, Richard O. *America's Obsession: Sports and Society Since 1945*. Fort Worth, TX: Harcourt Brace College Publishers, 1994.
Davis, Charles. Interview by author. Telephone, March 14, 2012.
Davis, Seth. "A Loan at the Top." *Sports Illustrated*, April 30, 2001.
Deford, Frank. "The Last Hurrah in Hyannis." *Sports Illustrated*, June 28, 1976.
Denlinger, Kenneth. "Basketball Disputed." *Washington Post*, May 3, 1972, D1.
———. "Did Bullets Win or Celtics Lose?" *Washington Post*, April 28, 1975, D1.
———. "Superstar Reportedly Joining Caps."*Washington Post*, September 2, 1969, D3.
———. "Wright Exit Spells Doom for Bullets." *Washington Post*, April 30, 1977, D1.
Desens, Carl. "The NBA's Fast Break Overseas." *Business Week*, December 5, 1994, 94.
Detroit News, 1925–2000.
Deveney, Sean. "Missing the Points." *Sporting News*, vol. 226 (December 30, 2002), 38–39.
District of Columbia Board of Commissioners. *Report of the Government of the District of Columbia*. Washington, DC: U.S. Government Printing Office, 1945.

District of Columbia Building Permits, 1890–2000.

DuPree, David . "Barry Unstoppable in 109-101 Romp." *Washington Post*, May 24, 1975, D1.

———. "Bing Gives Bullets Inside Track to Title." *Washington Post*, August 29, 1975, D1.

———. "Bing Upset at Motta' Clean Bill." *Washington Post*, May 13, 1977, C1.

———. "Bullets Break Down Celtics." *Washington Post*, April 28, 1975, D1.

———. "Bullets Deal Dick Gibbs to Braves." *Washington Post*, July 31, 1975, C1.

———. "Bullets Get Henderson in Trade for Robinson." *Washington Post*, January 21, 1977, D1.

———. "Bullets Qualify for Hardship." *Washington Post*, May 29, 1975, D1

———. "Bullets Seen Nearing Deal on Guard," *Washington Post*, November 5, 1976, D1.

———. "Grevey Says Not Playing Frustrating." *Washington Post*, January 19, 1977, D1.

———. "Inconsistent Bullets Face Rockets Today." *Washington Post*, May 1, 1977, 33

———. "Rockets Draw Hot Hand." *Washington Post*, May 1, 1977, D1.

———. "Rockets Even Series at 2-2." *Washington Post*, April 27, 1977, E1.

Durr, Kenneth D. *Behind the Backlash: White Working-Class Politics in Baltimore, 1940–1980*. Chapel Hill: University of North Carolina Press, 2007.

Ebony, 1968–1999.

Elderkin, Phil. "Surprise! Knicks Emerge as Quality Product." *Christian Science Monitor*, December 11, 1974, 9.

Eskenazi, Gerald. "Cable TV Begins to Make Big Changes in Professional Sports." *New York Times*, April 19, 1981, S1.

ESPN.com, 2003–2010.

Evening Independent, March 1, 1925–1948.

Ewell, Christian. "Wizards Lose Hughes to Cavs." *Baltimore Sun*, July 9, 2005.

"Executives: Ernie Grunfeld." Basketball-Reference.com, www.basketball-reference.com/executives/grunfer01x.html (retrieved September 26, 2010).

Fabrikant, Geraldine. "For Cable Networks, the Road Gets a Little Steeper." *New York Times*, February 26, 1989.

Ferry, Bob. Interview by author. Telephone, March 17, 2012.

"First West, Then the Rest." *Sports Illustrated*, October 16, 1972, 54.

"For the Record." *Sports Illustrated*, April 19, 1971, 101.

Forbes, 1965–2009.

Ford, Chad. "Trade Deadline Evaluations, Part 1." ESPN.com, March 16, 2012, http://insider.espn.go.com/nba/story?id=7695406&_slug_=nba-trade-deadline-evaluations-every-team-part-one (retrieved March 17, 2012).

Foreman, Earl. Interview by author. Telephone, May 4, 2011.

Frazier, Walt, with Neil Offen. *Walt Frazier: One Magic Season and a Basketball Life*. New York: Time Books, 1988.

Fredrick Post, March 1, 1925–1948.

Gardner, Ev. "Foul 'Em and Beat 'Em Is the Anti-Caps Formula." *Washington Daily News*, January 29, 1949.

"Gene Conley Jumps NBA Signs with Washington," *Hartford Courant*, October 13, 1961, 21.

Gentlemen's Quarterly, 2000–2008.

"Gilbert Arenas's Fake Gun-Play Might Cost Wizards Teammates." That NBA, January 8, 2010, www.thatnbalotterypick.com/2010/01/gilbert-arenas-fake-gun-play-might-cost.html (retrieved December 9, 2010).

Gildea, William. "Bullets Figure to Hire K.C. Jones as Coach." *Washington Post*, June 14, 1973, D1.

———. "'Tired' Johnson Wants to Be Traded by Bullets." *Washington Post*, March 30, 1965, C3.

"Golbert, Brotman Appointed by Senators, Caps." *Washington Post*, July 13, 1961, B6.

Goldpar, Sam. "76ers to Renew Drive Today against Bullets." *New York Times*, April 30, 1978, S8.

———. "Sonics Tie Series." *New York Times*, May 25, 1979, A19.

Goldstein, Alan. "Bullet Post Still Open," *Baltimore Sun*, April 10, 1966, A-7

———. "Bullet Sale May Be Near." *Baltimore Sun*, October 16, 1964, 22;

———. "Bullet Search for 'Giant' Set to Begin New Chapter," *Baltimore Sun*, June 1, 1970, C4.

———. "Bullets Sign LeRoy Ellis to Three-Year contract," *Baltimore Sun*, August 17, 1968, B1.

———. "Bullets Take No-Frills Flight in NBA Playoffs," *Baltimore Sun*, April 25, 1982, 45.

———. "Heft Looks, But Can't Find Any Takers for Bullets." *Baltimore Sun*, June 30, 1968, A6.

———. "Houston Syndicate Bidding for Bullets." *Baltimore Sun*, June 2, 1968, SP4.

———. "Offers Made for Bullets," *Baltimore Sun*, May 12, 1968, A1

———. "Upstart ABA Claims 'Who Needs NBA' Crows Jim Gardner," *Baltimore Sun*, March 18, 1970, C4.

Gould, Todd. *Pioneers of the Hardwood: Indiana and the Birth of Professional Basketball*. Bloomington: Indiana University Press, 1998.

Green Jr., Ron. "Shinn: I Messed Up in Charlotte." *Charlotte Observer*, November 11, 2008, www.charlotteobserver.com/2008/11/02/294986/shinn-i-messed-up-in-charlotte.html (retrieved October 19, 2011).

Guback, Steve. "Armory Schedule Biggest Obstacle." *Washington Star*, September 13, 1969

Ham, Eldon L. *The Playmasters: From Sellouts to Lockouts: An Unauthorized History of the NBA*. Chicago: Contemporary Books, 2000.

Hammonds, Tom. Interview by author. Telephone, March 1, 2012.

Hardnett, Charles. Interview by author. Telephone, February 24, 2012.

Harge, Ira. Interview by author. Telephone, February 22, 2012.

"Harlem Globetrotters Celebrate 75 Years Anniversary Gala in Chicago." *Jet*, vol. 99 (January 20, 2001), 46–49.

Harrison, Don. "A League of Their Own." *Virginia Living*, vol. 6 (April 2008), 153–59.

Hartford Courant, March 1, 1925–1986.

"Hawks Whip Bullets." *Washington Post*, March 28, 1966, D1

Hayes, Elvin, and Bill Gilbert. *They Call Me "The Big E."* Englewood Cliffs, NJ: Prentice Hall, 1978.

Haywood, Spencer, with Scott Ostler. *Spencer Haywood: The Rise, the Fall, the Recovery*. New York: Amistad, 1992.

Heft, Herb "Foster Says Four Others Also in Red." *Washington Post*, December 15, 1950, B9.

Howell, Bailey. Interview by author. Telephone, February 23, 2012.

Hubbard, Jan, ed. *The Official NBA Encyclopedia*. New York: Doubleday, 2000.

Isaacs, Neil D. *Vintage NBA: The Pioneer Era, 1946–1956*. Indianapolis, IN: Masters Press, 1996.

Jabali, Warren. Interview by author. Telephone, February 22, 2012.

"Jack Sullivan, Area Star, Signs with Caps." *Washington Post*, June 13, 1961, A18;

James, Jeffrey D. "Becoming a Sports Fan and Understanding Cognitive Development and Socialization in the Development of Fan Loyalty." Doctoral dissertation retrieved from the OhioLINK ETD Center, www.city-data.com/forum/city-vs-city/1197522-population-metropolitan-area-msa-populations-1970-a.html#post17798454 (retrieved March 27, 2012).

Jet Magazine, 1971–2008.

Johnson, Arthur T. "Congress and Professional Sports, 1951–1978." *Annals of the American Academy of Political and Social Science*, vol. 445 (September 1979): 102–15.

Johnson, James. "Good-bye 2011–2012 Season, Lockout Deal Rejected as Players Look to Decertify Union.," *Inquisitr*, November 14, 2011, www.inquisitr.com/159640/goodbye-2011-2012-nba-season-lockout-deal-rejected-as-players-look-to-decertify-union/ (retrieved December 11, 2011).

Jones, K.C. with Jack Warner: *Rebound: Autobiography of K.C. Jones and an Inside Look at the Champion Boston Celtics*. Boston: Quinlan Press, 1986.

Jozsa Frank P., and John J. Guthrie. *Relocation Teams and Expanding Leagues in Professional Sports: How the Major Leagues Respond to Market Conditions*. Westport, CT: Greenwood, 1999.

Justice, Richard. "Pollin Says He Will Not Sell Bullets," *Washington Post*, January 25, 1989, D1.

Kaiser, Roger. Interview by author. Telephone, February 16, 2012.

"Kaiser Talk of League as Tapers Come Home." *Washington Post*, December 15, 1961, D4.

Kane, Martin. "Scorecard," *Sports Illustrated*, March 29, 1971, 11.

Kass, Mark. "Bucks Want Longer Lease." *Business Journal*, May 15, 2008.

Kennedy, Ray. "Clevelanders Win Cage Title." *Washington Post*, April 10, 1926, 15.

———. "Kennedy Picks Brooklyn to Win." *Washington Post*, April 7, 1926, 15.

Ketelsen, James. "Olajuwater." *Forbes*, March 27, 1995, 18.

Kiersh, Edward. "The Two Faces of Abe: Both Sides of Washington's Legendary Sports Impresario." *Regardie's Magazine*, 10 (March 1990), 66, www.accessmylibrary.com/article-1G1-8986101/two-faces-abe-both.html (retrieved September 12, 2011).

Kingsport Times, March 1, 1925–1948.

Koppett, Leonard. *24 Seconds to Shoot: The Birth and Improbable Rise of the NBA*. New York: Total Sports, 1999.

———. "Bullets Eliminate Knicks 93-91." *New York Times*, April 20, 1971, 55.

Koppett, Leonard, Bob Bellotti, Bob Ryan, Ken Shouler, and Stan Smith. *Total Basketball: The Ultimate Basketball Encyclopedia*. New York: Sportclassic Books, 2003.

Kram, Mark. "Lost Bullets in Disasterville." *Sports Illustrated*, November 8, 1965, 26.

Kropp, Tom. Interview by author. Telephone, March 6, 2012.

Krugel, Mitchell. *One Last Shot: The Story of Michael Jordan's Comeback*. New York: T. Dunne Books, 2002.

Kupchak, Mitch. Interview by author. Telephone, April 25, 2012.

Kurda, Bob. *How Washington and New York Gave Birth to Black Basketball and Changed America's Game Forever*. Charlottesville: University of Virginia Press, 2006.

Lancaster Daily Eagle, March 1, 1925–1948.

Lane, Randall. "Prepackaged Celebrity." *Forbes*, December 20, 1994, 86.

Leftwich, George. Interview by author. Telephone April 22, 2012.

Leigh, Fred. "Capital Sportlight." *Baltimore Afro-American*, February 7, 1948, 17.

Leonard, Bob "Slick." Interview by author. Telephone, February 24, 2012.

Lloyd, Earl, and Sean Kirst. *Moonfixer: The Basketball Journey of Earl Lloyd*. Syracuse, NY: Syracuse University Press, 2010.

Long Beach Independent, November 1, 1960–1970.

Lorge, Barry. "Star Back But Celts Still Lose." *Washington Post*, January 15, 1977, E1

Los Angeles Sentinel, 1934–2005.

Los Angeles Times, March 1, 1925–December 31, 2000.

Lucas, John, with Joseph Moriarity. *Winning a Day at a Time*. Center City, MN: Hazelden, 1994.

"MCI Arena Deal," *Washington Post*, April 21, 1996, 10.Mack, Casey. "The Architect: The Legendary Howard Garfinkel Reflects on His Legacy in Youth Basketball." Five-Star Basketball.com, http://fivestarbasketball.com/originals/04-01-2011-the-architect-howard-garfinkel-1 (retrieved March 9, 2012).

MacLean, Don. Interview by author. Telephone, March 19, 2012.

MacMullen, Jackie. "No. 3 Washington Wizards." *Sports Illustrated*, November 10, 1997.

———. "Why Bother?" *Sports Illustrated*, June 23, 1997.

Maisel, Bob. "The Morning After," *Baltimore Sun*, November 24, 1964, S21.

———. "The Morning After." *Baltimore Sun*, January 6, 1967, C1.

Mallozzi, Vincent M. *Doc: The Rise and Rise of Julius Erving*. New York: John Wiley & Sons, 2010.

Mansfield News, March 1, 1925–1948.

Martzke, Rudy. "NBA Finalizes TV Deals: Good-bye NBC." *USA Today*, January 22, 2002.

Maxey, Wendell. "The Suns 1987 Drug Scandal." Hoopsworld.com, reposted on apbr.com, www.apbr.org/forum/viewtopic.php?t=2487 (retrieved September 11, 2010).

McAdam, Douglas. *Political Process and the Development of Black Insurgency, 1930–1970*. Chicago: University of Chicago Press, 1999.

McCallum, Jack. "Getting Fooled by Drugs," *Sports Illustrated*, January 26, 1987.

———. "Going, Going, Gone." *Sports Illustrated*, May 20, 1996.

———. "What about the Rest?" *Sports Illustrated*, November 7, 1988.

"Memphis Sounds Franchise Index." Basketball-Reference.com, www.basketball-reference.com/teams/MMS/ (retrieved August 21, 2011).

McCombs, Philip, A. "The Offer Prince George's Couldn't Refuse." *Washington Post*, August 20, 1972, B1.

"McKinney to Coach Washington Capitols." *Baltimore Sun*, March 10, 1950, 19.

"Merge Talks Called in Basketball." *Washington Post*, April 13, 1976, D1.

"Merger Seen No Closer." *New York Times*, August 15, 1973, 30.

Mexta Daily News, March 1, 1925– .

Meyer, Eugene L. " His Approval of NW Arena Held Dim Despite NHL Grant." *Washington Post*, June 10, 1972, B1.

Miami Herald, March 1, 1925– .

"Million-Dollar War," *Newsweek*, April 6, 1970, 63–64.

"Mr. Pollin Picks Largo." *Washington Post*, August 3, 1972, A22.

Mittleman, Jerry. "Has NBA Shooting Really Gone South?" InsideHoops, www.insidehoops.com/shooting-121503.shtml (retrieved January 13, 2010).

Montville, Leigh. *Manute: The Center of Two Worlds*. New York: Simon & Schuster, 1993.

Murray, Tracy. Interview by author. Telephone, March 12, 2012.

"NBA Arenas." NBA Hoops Online, http://nbahoopsonline.com/History/Leagues/NBA/Arenas.html (retrieved May 13, 2010).

"NBA Board of Governors Ratify 10-Year CBA." NBA.com, December 8, 2011, www.nba.com/2011/news/12/08/labor-deal-reached/index.html (retrieved February 26, 2012).

"NBA Lockout: Union Disbanding Seriously Jeopardizes the 2011–2012 Season," *Los Angeles Times*, November 11, 2011.

"NBA Meeting Weighs Expansion." *Washington Star*, January 19, 1970, C-1

"NBA Quits Merger Talk after ABA Breech of Faith." *Washington Post*, August 26, 1969, D1

"NBA Rules History." NBA.com, www.nba.com/analysis/rules_history.html (retrieved February 2, 2010).

Neal-Lunsford, Jeff. "Sport in the Land of Television: The Use of Sport in Network Prime-Time Schedules, 1946–1950." *Journal of Sport History*, vol. 19, no. 1 (Spring 1992), 65–76.

Nelson, Murray. "The Original Celtics and the 1926–27 American Basketball League." *Journal of Popular Culture*, vol. 30 (Fall 1996), 87–100.

New Pittsburgh Courier, 1911–2002.

New York Amsterdam News, 1922–1993.

New York Post.

New York Times, March 1, 1925–December 31, 2008.

Newsweek, 1965–2009.

"No Tears at This Farewell," *Baltimore Afro-American*, December 13, 1947, 15.

"Noon Today Is Deadline for NBA Row." *Washington Post*, March 14, 1967, D1.

O'Connor, Ian. "Keeping Score Column." *USA Today*, May 7, 2003.

Oelwein Daily Register, March 1, 1925–1948.

Ohl, Don. Interview by author. Telephone, February 26, 2012.

Oscar Robertson v. National Basketball Association, 556 F.2d 682 (2d Cir. 1977), U.S. Court of Appeals for the Second District.

"The Pack Closes in on Boston." *Sports Illustrated*, October 26, 1964, 50.

Palermo, Sam. "More ABA-NBA: The Fans Speak Out." *Basketball Digest*, http://en.wikipedia.org/wiki/ABA%E2%80%93NBA_merger.

Parasuraman, Vishnu. "What Do You Do about a Problem Like the Wizards." Grantland.com, February 15, 2012, www.grantland.com/story/_/id/7575336/ernie-grunfeld-john-wall-rashard-lewis-how-fix-washington-wizards (retrieved September 26, 2010).

"Paul Seymour Quits; Bullets, Celtics One Game Away from Elimination." *Washington Post*, March 29, 1966, C2.

Peacock, Shane. "Pro Basketball's False Start." *Beaver*, vol. 76, no. 5 (October/November 1996), 33–38.

Peterson, Robert W. *Cages to Jump Shots: Pro Basketball's Early Years*. New York: Oxford University Press, 1990.

"Petition to Stop Ken Sears from Playing Denied." *Washington Star*, October 28, 1961, B1.

Phegley, Roger. Interview by author. Telephone, February 27, 2012.

Philadelphia Inquirer

Philadelphia Tribune, March 1, 1925–2001.

"Pizza Hut Basketball Classic." *Harvard Crimson*, January 9, 1973, www.thecrimson.com/article/1973/1/9/pizza-hut-basketball-classic-pthe-balloting/ (retrieved October 10, 2011).

Platt, Larry. *Keeping It Real: A Turbulent Season at the Crossroads with the NBA*. New York: Avon Books, 1999.

"Players Hoping to Block Merger." *Washington Star*, January 19, 1970, C-1

Pluto, Terry. *Loose Balls: The Short, Wild Life of the American Basketball Association*. New York: Simon & Schuster, 1990.

Portsmouth Daily Times, March 1, 1925–1950.

Portsmouth Invitational Tournament. "General Information," www.portsmouthinvitational.com/info.php (retrieved October 8, 2011).

Povich, Shirley. "This Morning," *Washington Post*, April 30, 1950, C1
———. "This Morning," *Washington Post*, September 5, 1969, D1.
Price, Brent. Interview by author. Telephone, February 25, 2012.
Putnam, Pat, and Jane Gross. "The NBA Said No Way." *Sports Illustrated*, October 28, 1974, 68.
Putnam, Pat. "A Beaut of a Brawl." *Sports Illustrated*, April 28, 1975, 14.
———. "In the NBA It's Muscle." *Sports Illustrated*, April 14, 1975, 32
———. "When Low Down, Go Down Lower." *Sports Illustrated*, May 12, 1975, 28
Records of U.S. District and Other Courts in the District of Columbia 1921–1993, National Archives and Records Administration.
The Register, March 1, 1925–1948.
Reid, Jason. "Grunfeld Should Clean out His Desk." *Washington Post*, March 21, 2012, D1.
Reilly, Rick. "National Bunco Association." *Sports Illustrated*, November 29, 1999.
"Results." *Washington Post*, March 29, 1970, 37
"Rockets Overtake Caps for 1-0 lead." *Washington Post*, April 18, 1970, F-3.
"Rockets Rout Caps and Capture Series." *New York Times*, April 29, 1970, 68
Rogers, Thomas. "Embattled Knicks Are Strong Again," *New York Times*, April 1, 1970, 71.
———. "The Pearl Happy to Let Mate Carry Load in Bullets' Victory." *New York Times*, April 6, 1970, 69.
Rosen, Charley. *The First Tip-Off: The Incredible Story of the Birth of the NBA*. New York: McGraw-Hill, 2008.
"Roundup of week April 21–27." *Sports Illustrated*, May 5, 1975, 78
"Roundup of week May 5–11." *Sports Illustrated*, May 19, 1975, 87.
"Roundup of week May 12–18." *Sports Illustrated*, May 26, 1975, 99.
"Roundup of week May 19–25." *Sports Illustrated*, June 2, 1975
Salzberg, Charles. *From Set Shot to Slam Dunk: The Glory Days of Basketball in the Words of Those Who Played It*. New York: E. P. Dutton, 1987.
Sandborn Maps. Washington, DC, 1900–2010.
Sandomir, Richard. "Jordan Sheds Uniform for Suit as a Wizards Owner," *New York Times*, January 20, 2000, D1.
Saperstein, Abe. Harlem Globetrotters Papers, 1928–1991. Austin, TX: Dolph Briscoe Center for American History, University of Texas at Austin.
Sarmento, Mario R. "The NBA on Network Television: A Historical Analysis." Thesis, University of Florida, 1998.
"Scouting Reports." *Sports Illustrated*, October 24, 1966, 40.
Scrapbooks: BAA November 1946–March 1947, at Naismith Basketball Hall of Fame Library.
Siegel, Morris. "Foreman Hopeful Roundballing Caps Don't Foul Out." *Washington Star*, December 21, 1969, S-8.
———. "Mahnken May Go as Player Deals Are Hinted," *Washington Post*, March 27, 1948, 10.

——. "Auerbach May Quit as Caps' Coach," *Washington Post*, April 24, 1949, C1.
Shapiro, Leonard. "Knicks Prepare for Showdown." *Washington Post*, April 13, 1972, G8.
——. "Playoffs Let Bullets Cash in." *Washington Post*, May 13, 1975, D1.
Shue, Gene. Interview by author. Telephone, March 5, 2012.
"Silverdome History." NBA Hoops Online, www.silverdomeevents.com/about-us/history.html (retrieved July 14, 2010).
Simmons, Bill. *The Book of Basketball: The NBA According to the Sports Guy*. New York: Ballantine Books, 2009.
Smith, Sam. "Michael, You're Smart but No Wizard." *Chicago Tribune*, January 16, 2000.
Smith, Seymour S. "Arena Again Costs Quintet," *Baltimore Sun*, April 28, 1960, S25.
——. "Pollin in Sole Charge of Bullets," *Baltimore Sun*, July 24, 1968, C5.
——. "Westley Unseld of Louiville Signs Rich Contract With Bullets," *Baltimore Sun*, April 19, 1968, C1.
Smith, Stephen A. "NBA's New Drug Policy Being Implemented." *Philadelphia Inquirer*, October 9, 1999.
Solomon, George. "Title-Minded Bullets Select KC Jones." *Washington Post*, June 19, 1973, D1.
——. "Tremendously Successful Capital Centre Still Has Bugs." *Washington Post*, July 7, 1974, C1.
Sport, 1947–2000.
Sporting News, January 1, 1990– .
Sports Illustrated, 1956–2010.
Staudohar, Paul D., and James A. Mangan. *The Business of Professional Sports*. Urbana: University of Illinois Press, 1991.
"Stevenson: LeBron Is Overrated," http://hoopeduponline.com/2008/03/14/stevenson-lebron-is-overrated/ (retrieved March 3, 2010).
Stewart, Nikita, and Thomas Heath. "Pollin Asks D.C. to Pay for Verizon Center Renovations." *Washington Post*, January 27, 2007.
Strine, Gerald. "Knicks Great; DeBusschere Superb." *Washington Post*, April 6, 1973, D2
Taylor, Phil. "Clang, Clang, Clang Goes the Ball." *Sports Illustrated*, December 16, 1996.
——. "One and Done to Death." *Sports Illustrated*, April 26, 2010.
Taylor, Roland "Fatty." Interview by author. Telephone, March 4, 2012.
"The Bullets Are Biting." *Time*, March 10, 1975, 73.
"The collapse at Capital Centre." *Washington Post*, May 28, 1975, A18.
Thomas, Ron. *They Cleared the Lane: The NBA's Black Pioneers*. Lincoln: University of Nebraska Press. 2002.
Thomsen, Ian. "How Larry Got to Cleveland." *Sports Illustrated*, August 15, 2005.
"Three Contests Start NBA Playoffs," *Baltimore Sun*, March 25, 1970, C1.
"A Three-Way Jump Ball in the NBA." *Business Week*, September 4, 1995, 58.

Trachtenberg, Jeffrey A. "Playing the Global Game." *Forbes*, January 23, 1989, 90.
Traughber, Bill. "Commodore History Corner: Q&A with Charles Davis," February 28, 2008, www.vucommodores.com/sports/m-baskbl/spec-rel/022708aae.html (retrieved November 11, 2011).
"Two Problems Face NBA Pro Court League." *Christian Science Monitor*, January 9, 1951, 10.
U.S. Census Bureau. *U.S. Decennial Census, 1970*. Washington, DC: U.S. Government Printing Office, 1970.
———. *U.S. Decennial Census, 1950 Census of Population: Volume II: Characteristics of the People, Part 9: Washington, DC*. Washington, DC: U.S. Government Printing Office, 1950.
———. *U.S. Decennial Census, 1940*. Washington, DC: U.S. Government Printing Office, 1940.
"Uline Tells Armstrong off on DC Arena Bias," *New York Amsterdam News*, February 8, 1947, 11.
USA Today, 1981–2010.
Vecsey, Peter, and David K. Li. "Wizards' Gilbert Arenas and Javaris Crittenton Pull Pistols on Each Other." *New York Post*, January 2, 2010.
Vertical Files, Washingtoniana Room, D.C. Public Library.
Virginia Living, 2008.
"Virginia Squires," www.remembertheaba.com/TeamMaterial/VirginiaMaterial/OaksCapsSquiresYearly.html (retrieved October 31, 2010).
Walker, Darrell. "The Collecting of African American Art VIII: Elliot Perry and Darrell Walker in Conversation with Michael D. Harris." Discussion held at the National Gallery of Art, Washington, DC, February 26, 2012.
Walsh, Jack. "Red Says Secret of Caps' Success No Secret; It's 4 Teams—'Rough, Smooth, Fast, Big.'" *Washington Post*, November 27, 1948, 14.
———. "Basketball Loop Merge, Caps Stay In: Pro Basketball Merges into 18-Team Loop." *Washington Post*, August 4, 1949, 15.
———. "Club Won't Fold Despite Being in Red, Foster Says." *Washington Post*, February 14, 1950, 12.
———. "Lynn Says New League Banking on TV Deal." *Washington Post*, April 23, 1960, D7.
———. "Sports Arena Sold by Ulines." *Washington Post*, December 18, 1959, C1.
———. "Washington Awarded Pro Basketball Team." *Washington Post*, April 22, 1960, C5.
Wang, Shirley. "The Science behind Fanatic Behavior." *APS Observer*, May 2006, www.psychologicalscience.org/observer/getArticle.cfm?id=1986 (retrieved March 11, 2012).
Washington Post, January 1, 1905–2012.
Washington Star, January 1, 1905–1981.
"Washington Subdues Syracuse Five, 87-85,"*Baltimore Sun*, December 29, 1949, 15.
"Washington Wizards Hire Flip Saunders as New Head Coach." InsideHoops, April 22, 2009, www.insidehoops.com/blog/?p=4222 (retrieved September 11, 2010).

Weinstein, David. *The Forgotten Network: DuMont and the Birth of American Television*. Philadelphia: Temple University Press, 2004.

———. *Live from the Nation's Capital: A History of Television in Washington, D.C., 1946–1958*. Ann Arbor, MI: UMI, 1997.

Whitbourne, Susan Krauss. "The Psychology of Sports Fans." *Psychology Today*, December 30, 2011, www.psychologytoday.com/blog/fulfillment-any-age/201112/the-psychology-sports-fans (retrieved March 19, 2012).

White, Joseph. "Leonard Hamilton Resigns as Wizards Coach." LubbockOnline, April 19, 2001, www.lubbockonline.com/stories/041901/upd_075-1411.shtml (retrieved June 19, 2011).

Wilbon, Michael. "After Bullets Article," *Washington Post*, November 27, 1994, D1.

"Wizards Sign Michael Ruffin," *Washington Post*, August 3, 2004, D1.

Wolf, Catherine. "Roundup." *Sports Illustrated*, May 11, 1987.

Wong, Glenn M., and Chris Deubert. "National Basketball Association General Managers: An Analysis of the Responsibilities, Qualifications, and Characteristics." *Villanova Sports and Entertainment Law Journal*, vol. 18 (2011), 213–66.

"WTTG Plans Carrying 12 Bullets Games' on TV." *Washington Post*, May 17, 1966, D3.

Young, A. S. Doc. "Good Morning Sports," 1965.

Yorke, Tom. "ABA Eying Caps for Norfolk Area." *Washington Star*, March 8, 1970, C-2.

———. "Caps' Average Attendance of 2,012 Shakes Foreman." *Washington Star*, December 23, 1969, C-1.

———. "Caps Schedule in 16 Cities with 30 Games Listed Here." *Washington Star*, October 14, 1969, C-4.

———. "Caps Will Outdraw Half of NBA-Foreman." *Washington Star*, October 15, 1969, C-3.

———. "City Seen as Pro Cage Battleground." *Washington Star*, January 22, 1970, C-1.

———. "Merger Units Hear Foreman." *Washington Star*, March 10, 1970, A-19.

Zimmerman, Paul. "Sportscripts: AFL Yelps over Cannon Premature," *Los Angeles Times*, April 29, 1960, C1.

———. "Sportscripts: New Loop Spirs Action by NBA," *Los Angeles Times*, April 23, 1960, A1.

~

Index

~

About the Authors

Brett L. Abrams is an archivist of electronic records. He is a cultural and urban historian whose previous books include *Capital Sporting Grounds: A History of Stadium and Ballpark Construction in Washington, D.C.* (2009) and *Hollywood Bohemians: Transgressive Sexuality and the Selling of the Movieland Dream* (2008).

Raphael Mazzone is an archivist, specializing in electronic records and audiovisual material.